M000293879

Trading
Price
Action
TRENDS

Founded in 1807, John Wiley & Sons is the oldest independent publishing company in the United States. With offices in North America, Europe, Australia, and Asia, Wiley is globally committed to developing and marketing print and electronic products and services for our customers' professional and personal knowledge and understanding.

The Wiley Trading series features books by traders who have survived the market's ever changing temperament and have prospered—some by reinventing systems, others by getting back to basics. Whether a novice trader, professional, or somewhere in-between, these books will provide the advice and strategies needed to prosper today and well into the future.

For a list of available titles, please visit our Web site at www.WileyFinance.com.

Trading
Price
Action
TRENDS

TECHNICAL ANALYSIS OF PRICE CHARTS
BAR BY BAR FOR THE SERIOUS TRADER

AL BROOKS

WILEY

John Wiley & Sons, Inc.

The first edition of this book, titled *Reading Price Charts Bar by Bar: The Technical Analysis of Price Action for the Serious Trader*, was published in 2009.

Published by John Wiley & Sons, Inc., Hoboken, New Jersey.
Published simultaneously in Canada.

All charts were created with TradeStation. © TradeStation Technologies, Inc. All rights reserved.

For general information on our other products and services or for technical support, please contact our Customer Care Department within the United States at (800) 762-2974, outside the United States at (317) 572-3993 or fax (317) 572-4002.

Wiley also publishes its books in a variety of electronic formats. Some content that appears in print may not be available in electronic books. For more information about Wiley products, visit our web site at www.wiley.com.

Library of Congress Cataloging-in-Publication Data:

Brooks, Al, 1952–
  Trading price action trends : technical analysis of price charts bar by bar for the serious trader / Al Brooks.
    p. cm. – (The Wiley trading series)
  "The first edition of this book titled, Reading price charts bar by bar : the technical analysis of price action for the serious trader, was published in 2009"–T.p. verso.
  Includes index.
  ISBN 978-1-118-06651-5 (cloth); ISBN 978-1-118-16623-9 (ebk);
  ISBN 978-1-118-16624-6 (ebk); ISBN 978-1-118-16625-3 (ebk)
  1. Stocks–Prices–Charts, diagrams, etc.   I. Brooks, Al, 1952– Reading price charts bar by bar.
II. Title.
  HG4638.B765   2012
  332.63′2042–dc23

                                                                                              2011029297

Printed in the United States of America

SKY10033912_032322

I would like to dedicate this book to my wonderfully kind daughter, Tess Brooks, who sees life as filled with opportunities and seeks them out around the world without hesitation. She is a bold, original thinker and a doer, and fills her life with the dreams that the rest of us have but are too afraid to pursue.

Contents

Acknowledgments

My primary goal is to present a series of comprehensive books on price action that addresses the greatest concern among readers, which was how difficult my earlier book, *Reading Price Charts Bar by Bar*, was to read. I am deeply appreciative of all of the constructive comments that readers have provided and those from the participants in my daily live webinars. Many of these comments were incredibly insightful, and I have incorporated them in this current edition. I am also thankful to all of the traders who have been in my live trading room, because they have given me the opportunity to say things repeatedly until I could clearly articulate what I am seeing and doing. They have also asked many questions that have helped me find the words to communicate more effectively, and I have put those words into these books.

I would like to give a special thank-you to Victor Brancale, who spent long hours proofreading the manuscripts and providing hundreds of very helpful edits and suggestions, and to Robert Gjerde, who built and administers my website and has given me candid feedback on the chat room and the website. Finally, I want to thank Ginger Szala, the Group Editorial Director of *Futures* magazine, for giving me ongoing opportunities to publish articles and speak in webinars, and for regularly giving me very helpful advice on how to become more involved with the trading community.

List of Terms Used in This Book

All of these terms are defined in a practical way to be helpful to traders and not necessarily in the theoretical way often described by technicians.

always in   If you have to be in the market at all times, either long or short, this is whatever your current position is (always in long or always in short). If at any time you are forced to decide between initiating a long or a short trade and are confident in your choice, then the market is in always-in mode at that moment. Almost all of these trades require a spike in the direction of the trend before traders will have confidence.

barbwire   A trading range of three or more bars that largely overlap and one or more is a doji. It is a type of tight trading range with prominent tails and often relatively large bars.

bar pullback   In an upswing, a bar pullback is a bar with a low below the low of the prior bar. In a downswing, it is a bar with a high above that of the prior bar.

bear reversal   A change in trend from up to down (a bear trend).

blown account   An account that your losses have reduced below the minimum margin requirements set by your broker, and you will not be allowed to place a trade unless you deposit more money.

breakout   The high or low of the current bar extends beyond some prior price of significance such as a swing high or low, the high or low of any prior bar, a trend line, or a trend channel.

breakout bar (or bar breakout)   A bar that creates a breakout. It is usually a strong trend bar.

breakout mode   A setup where a breakout in either direction should have follow-through.

breakout pullback   A small pullback of one to about five bars that occurs within a few bars after a breakout. Since you see it as a pullback, you are expecting the breakout to resume and the pullback is a setup for that resumption. If instead you thought that the breakout would fail, you would not use the term *pullback* and instead would see the pullback as a failed breakout. For example, if there was a five-bar breakout above a bear trend line but you believed that the bear trend would continue, you would be considering shorting this bear flag and not looking to buy a pullback immediately after it broke out to the downside.

breakout test   A breakout pullback that comes close to the original entry price to test a breakeven stop. It may overshoot it or undershoot it by a few ticks. It can occur within a bar or two of entry or after an extended move or even 20 or more bars later.

bull reversal   A change in trend from a downtrend to an uptrend (a bull trend).

buying pressure   Strong bulls are asserting themselves and their buying is creating bull trend bars, bars with tails at the bottoms, and two-bar bull reversals. The effect is cumulative and usually is eventually followed by higher prices.

candle   A chart representation of price action in which the body is the area between the open and the close. If the close is above the open, it is a bull candle and is shown as white. If it is below, it is a bear candle and is black. The lines above and below are called tails (some technicians call them wicks or shadows).

chart type   A line, bar, candle, volume, tick, or other type of chart.

climax   A move that has gone too far too fast and has now reversed direction to either a trading range or an opposite trend. Most climaxes end with trend channel overshoots and reversals, but most of those reversals result in trading ranges and not an opposite trend.

countertrend   A trade or setup that is in the opposite direction from the current trend (the current always-in direction). This is a losing strategy for most traders since the risk is usually at least as large as the reward and the probability is rarely high enough to make the trader's equation favorable.

countertrend scalp   A trade taken in the belief that there is more to go in the trend but that a small pullback is due; you enter countertrend to capture a small profit as that small pullback is forming. This is usually a mistake and should be avoided.

day trade   A trade where the intent is to exit on the day of entry.

directional probability   The probability that the market will move either up or down any number of ticks before it reaches a certain number of ticks in the opposite direction. If you are looking at an equidistant move up and down, it hovers around 50 percent most of the time, which means that there is a 50–50 chance that the market will move up by X ticks before it moves down X ticks, and a 50–50 chance that it will move down X ticks before it moves up X ticks.

doji   A candle with a small body or no body at all. On a 5 minute chart, the body would be only one or two ticks; but on a daily chart, the body might be 10 or more ticks and still appear almost nonexistent. Neither the bulls nor the bears control the bar. All bars are either trend bars or nontrend bars, and those nontrend bars are called dojis.

double bottom   A chart formation in which the low of the current bar is about the same as the low of a prior swing low. That prior low can be just one bar earlier or 20 or more bars earlier. It does not have to be at the low of the day, and it commonly forms in bull flags (a double bottom bull flag).

double bottom bull flag   A pause or bull flag in a bull trend that has two spikes down to around the same price and then reverses back into a bull trend.

double bottom pullback   A buy setup composed of a double bottom followed by a deep pullback that forms a higher low.

double top   A chart formation in which the high of the current bar is about the same as the high of a prior swing high. That prior high can be just one bar earlier or 20 or more bars earlier. It does not have to be at the high of the day, and it commonly forms in bear flags (a double top bear flag).

double top bear flag   A pause or bear flag in a bear trend that has two spikes up to around the same price and then reverses back into a bear trend.

double top pullback   A sell setup composed of a double top followed by a deep pullback that forms a lower high.

early longs   Traders who buy as a bull signal bar is forming rather than waiting for it to close and then entering on a buy stop at one tick above its high.

early shorts   Traders who sell as a bear signal bar is forming rather than waiting for it to close and then entering on a sell stop at one tick below its low.

edge   A setup with a positive trader's equation. The trader has a mathematical advantage if he trades the setup. Edges are always small and fleeting because they need someone on the other side, and the market is filled with smart traders who won't allow an edge to be big and persistent.

EMA   See *exponential moving average (EMA)*.

entry bar   The bar during which a trade is entered.

exponential moving average (EMA)   The charts in these books use a 20-bar exponential moving average, but any moving average can be useful.

fade   To place a trade in the opposite direction of the trend (for example, selling a bull breakout that you expect to fail and reverse downward).

failed failure   A failure that fails, resuming in the direction of the original breakout, and therefore a breakout pullback. Since it is a second signal, it is more reliable. For example, if there is a breakout above a trading range and the bar after the breakout is a bear reversal bar, if the market trades below that bar, the breakout has failed. If the market then trades above the high of a prior bar within the next few bars, the failed breakout has failed and now the breakout is resuming. This means that the failed breakout became a small bull flag and just a pullback from the breakout.

failure (a failed move)   A move where the protective stop is hit before a scalper's profit is secured or before the trader's objective is reached, usually leading to a move in the opposite direction as trapped traders are forced to exit at a loss. Currently, a scalper's target in the Emini of four ticks usually requires a six-tick move, and a target in the QQQQ of 10 ticks usually requires a move of 12 cents.

false   Failed, failure.

five-tick failure   A trade in the Emini that reaches five ticks beyond the signal bar and then reverses. For example, a breakout of a bull flag runs five ticks, and once the bar closes, the next bar has a low that is lower. Most limit orders to take a one-point profit would fail to get filled since a move usually has to go one tick beyond the order before it is filled. It is often a setup for a trade in the opposite direction.

flat   Refers to a trader who is not currently holding any positions.

follow-through   After the initial move, like a breakout, it is one or more bars that extend the move. Traders like to see follow-through on the next bar and on the several bars after that, hoping for a trend where they stand to make more profit.

follow-through bar   A bar that creates follow-through after the entry bar; it is usually the next bar but sometimes forms a couple of bars later.

fractal   Every pattern is a fractal of a pattern on a higher time frame chart. This means that every pattern is a micro pattern on a higher time frame and every micro pattern is a standard pattern on a smaller time frame.

gap   A space between any two price bars on the chart. An opening gap is a common occurrence and is present if the open of the first bar of today is beyond the high or low of the prior bar (the last bar of yesterday) or of the entire day. A moving average gap is present when the low of a bar is above a flat or falling moving average, or the high of a bar is below a flat or rising moving average. Traditional gaps (breakout, measuring, and exhaustion) on daily charts have intraday equivalents in the form of various trend bars.

gap bar   See *moving average gap bar*.

gap reversal   A formation in which the current bar extends one tick beyond the prior bar back into the gap. For example, if there is a gap up open and the second bar of the day trades one tick below the low of the first bar, this is a gap reversal.

HFT See *high-frequency trading (HFT)*.

higher high A swing high that is higher than a previous swing high.

higher low A swing low that is higher than a previous swing low.

higher time frame (HTF) A chart covering the same amount of time as the current chart, but having fewer bars. For example, compared to the day session 5 minute Emini chart on an average day, examples of higher time frame charts include a 15 minute chart, a tick chart with 25,000 ticks per bar, and a volume chart with 100,000 contracts per bar (each of these charts usually has fewer than 30 bars on an average day, compared to the 81 bars on the 5 minute chart).

high-frequency trading (HFT) Also known as algorithmic trading or black box trading, it is a type of program trading where firms place millions of orders a day in thousands of stocks to scalp profits as small as a penny, and the trading is based on statistical analysis rather than fundamentals.

high/low 1 or 2 Either a high 1 or 2 or a low 1 or 2.

high 1, 2, 3, or 4 A high 1 is a bar with a high above the prior bar in a bull flag or near the bottom of a trading range. If there is then a bar with a lower high (it can occur one or several bars later), the next bar in this correction whose high is above the prior bar's high is a high 2. Third and fourth occurrences are a high 3 and 4. A high 3 is a wedge bull flag variant.

HTF See *higher time frame (HTF)*.

ii Consecutive inside bars, where the second is inside the first. At the end of a leg, it is a breakout mode setup and can become a flag or a reversal setup. A less reliable version is a "bodies-only ii," where you ignore the tails. Here, the second body is inside the first body, which is inside the body before it.

iii Three inside bars in a row, and a somewhat more reliable pattern than an ii.

inside bar A bar with a high that is at or below the high of the prior bar and a low that is at or above the low of the prior bar.

institution Also called the smart money, it can be a pension fund, hedge fund, insurance company, bank, broker, large individual trader, or any other entity that trades enough volume to impact the market. Market movement is the cumulative effect of many institutions placing trades, and a single institution alone usually cannot move a major market for very long. Traditional institutions place trades based on fundamentals, and they used to be the sole determinant of the market's direction. However, HFT firms now have a significant influence on the day's movement since their trading currently generates most of the day's volume. HFT firms are a special type of institutional firm and their trading is based on statistics and not fundamentals. Traditional institutions determine the direction and target, but mathematicians determine the path that the market takes to get there.

ioi   Inside-outside-inside—three consecutive bars where the second bar is an outside bar, and the third bar is an inside bar. It is often a breakout mode setup where a trader looks to buy above the inside bar or sell below it.

ledge   A bull ledge is a small trading range with a bottom created by two or more bars with identical lows; a bear ledge is a small trading range with a top created by two or more bars with identical highs.

leg   A small trend that breaks a trend line of any size; the term is used only where there are at least two legs on the chart. It is any smaller trend that is part of a larger trend and it can be a pullback (a countertrend move), a swing in a trend or in a sideways market, or a with-trend move in a trend that occurs between any two pullbacks within the trend.

likely   At least 60 percent certain.

long   A person who buys a position in a market or the actual position itself.

lot   The smallest position size that can be traded in a market. It is a share when referring to stocks and a contract when referring to Eminis or other futures.

lower high   A swing high that is lower than a previous swing high.

lower low   A swing low that is lower than a previous swing low.

low 1, 2, 3, or 4   A low 1 is a bar with a low below the prior bar in a bear flag or near the top of a trading range. If there is then a bar with a higher low (it can occur one or several bars later), the next bar in this correction whose low is below the prior bar's low is a low 2. Third and fourth occurrences are a low 3 and 4. A low 3 is a wedge bear flag variant.

major trend line   Any trend line that contains most of the price action on the screen and is typically drawn using bars that are at least 10 bars apart.

major trend reversal   A reversal from a bull to a bear trend or from a bear trend to a bull trend. The setup must include a test of the old trend extreme after a break of the trend line.

meltdown   A sell-off in a bear spike or a tight bear channel without significant pullbacks and that extends further than the fundamentals would dictate.

melt-up   A rally in a bull spike or a tight bull channel without significant pullbacks and that extends further than the fundamentals would dictate.

micro   Any traditional pattern can form over one to about five bars and still be valid, although easily overlooked. When it forms, it is a micro version of the pattern. Every micro pattern is a traditional pattern on a smaller time frame chart, and every traditional pattern is a micro pattern on a higher time frame chart.

micro channel   A very tight channel where most of the bars have their highs and lows touching the trend line and, often, also the trend channel line. It is the most extreme form of a tight channel, and it has no pullbacks or only one or two small pullbacks.

micro double bottom   Consecutive or nearly consecutive bars with lows that are near the same price.

micro double top   Consecutive or nearly consecutive bars with highs that are near the same price.

micro measuring gap   When the bar before and the bar after a strong trend bar do not overlap, this is a sign of strength and often leads to a measured move. For example, if there is a strong bull trend bar and the low of the bar after it is at or above the high of the bar before it, the midpoint between that low and that high is the micro measuring gap.

micro trend channel line   A trend channel line drawn across the highs or lows of three to five consecutive bars.

micro trend line breakout   A trend line on any time frame that is drawn across from two to about 10 bars where most of the bars touch or are close to the trend line, and then one of the bars has a false breakout through the trend line. This false breakout sets up a with-trend entry. If it fails within a bar or two, then there is usually a countertrend trade.

money stop   A stop based on a fixed dollar amount or number of points, like two points in the Eminis or a dollar in a stock.

moving average   The charts in this book use a 20-bar exponential moving average, but any moving average can be useful.

moving average gap bar (gap bar)   A bar that does not touch the moving average. The space between the bar and the moving average is the gap. The first pullback in a strong trend that results in a moving average gap bar is usually followed by a test of the trend's extreme. For example, when there is a strong bull trend and there is a pullback that finally has a bar with a high below the moving average, this is often a buy setup for a test of the high of the trend.

nesting   Sometimes a pattern has a smaller version of a comparable pattern "nested" within it. For example, it is common for the right shoulder of a head and shoulders top to be either a small head and shoulders top or a double top.

news   Useless information generated by the media for the sole purpose of selling advertising and making money for the media company. It is unrelated to trading, is impossible to evaluate, and should always be ignored.

oio   Outside-inside-outside, an outside bar followed by an inside bar, followed by an outside bar.

oo   Outside-outside, an outside bar followed by a larger outside bar.

opening reversal   A reversal in the first hour or so of the day.

outside bar   A bar with a high that is above or at the high of the prior bar and a low that is below the low of the prior bar, or a bar with a low that is below or at the low of the prior bar and a high that is above the high of the prior bar.

outside down bar   An outside bar with a close below its open.

outside up bar   An outside bar with a close above its open.

overshoot   The market surpasses a prior price of significance like a swing point or a trend line.

pause bar   A bar that does not extend the trend. In a bull trend, a pause bar has a high that is at or below the prior bar, or a small bar with a high that is only a tick or so higher than the previous bar when the previous bar is a strong bull trend bar. It is a type of pullback.

pip   A tick in the foreign exchange (forex) market. However, some data vendors provide quotes with an extra decimal place, which should be ignored.

pressing their longs   In a bull trend, bulls add to their longs as in a bull spike and as the market breaks out to a new high, because they expect another leg up to about a measured move.

pressing their shorts   In a bear trend, bears add to their shorts in a bear spike and as the market breaks out to a new low, because they expect another leg down to about a measured move.

price action   Any change in price on any chart type or time frame.

probability   The chance of success. For example, if a trader looks back at the most recent 100 times a certain setup led to a trade and finds that it led to a profitable trade 60 times, then that would indicate that the setup has about a 60 percent probability of success. There are many variables that can never be fully tested, so probabilities are only approximations and at times can be very misleading.

probably   At least 60 percent certain.

pullback   A temporary pause or countertrend move that is part of a trend, swing, or leg and does not retrace beyond the start of the trend, swing, or leg. It is a small trading range where traders expect the trend to resume soon. For example, a bear pullback is a sideways to upward move in a bear trend, swing, or leg that will be followed by at least a test of the prior low. It can be as small as a one-tick move above the high of the prior bar or it can even be a pause, like an inside bar.

pullback bar   A bar that reverses the prior bar by at least one tick. In an uptrend, it is a bar with a low below that of the prior bar.

reasonable   A setup with a favorable trader's equation.

reversal   A change to an opposite type of behavior. Most technicians use the term to mean a change from a bull trend to a bear trend or from a bear trend to a bull trend. However, trading range behavior is opposite to trending behavior, so when a trend becomes a trading range, this is also a reversal. When a trading range becomes a trend, it is a reversal but is usually called a breakout.

reversal bar   A trend bar in the opposite direction of the trend. When a bear leg is reversing up, a bull reversal bar is a bull trend bar, and the classic description includes a tail at the bottom and a close above the open and near the top. A bear reversal bar is a bear trend bar in a bull leg, and the traditional description includes a tail at the top and a close below the open and near the bottom.

reward   The number of ticks that a trader expects to make from a trade. For example, if the trader exits with a limit order at a profit target, it is the number of ticks between the entry price and the profit target.

risk   The number of ticks from a trader's entry price to a protective stop. It is the minimum that the trader will lose if a trade goes against him (slippage and other factors can make the actual risk greater than the theoretical risk).

risk off   When traders think that the stock market will fall, they become risk averse, sell out of volatile stocks and currencies, and transition into safe-haven investments, like Johnson & Johnson (JNJ), Altria Group (MO), Procter & Gamble (PG), the U.S. dollar, and the Swiss franc.

risk on   When traders think that the stock market is strong, they are willing to take more risks and invest in stocks that tend to rise faster than the overall market, and invest in more volatile currencies, like the Australian dollar or the Swedish krona.

risky   When the trader's equation is unclear or barely favorable for a trade. It can also mean that the probability of success for a trade is 50 percent or less, regardless of the risk and potential reward.

scalp   A trade that is exited with a small profit, usually before there are any pullbacks. In the Emini, when the average range is about 10 to 15 points, a scalp trade is usually any trade where the goal is less than four points. For the SPY or stocks, it might be 10 to 30 cents. For more expensive stocks, it can be $1 to $2. Since the profit is often smaller than the risk, a trader has to win at least 70 percent of the time, which is an unrealistic goal for most traders. Traders should take trades only where the potential reward is at least as great as the risk unless they are extremely skilled.

scalper   A trader who primarily scalps for small profits, usually using a tight stop.

scalper's profit   A typical amount of profit that a scalper would be targeting.

scratch   A trade that is close to breakeven with either a small profit or a loss.

second entry   The second time within a few bars of the first entry where there is an entry bar based on the same logic as the first entry. For example, if a breakout above a wedge bull flag fails and pulls back to a double bottom bull flag, this pullback sets up a second buy signal for the wedge bull flag.

second moving average gap bar setup   If there is a first moving average gap bar and a reversal toward the moving average does not reach the moving average, and instead the move away from the moving average continues, it is the next reversal in the direction of the moving average.

second signal   The second time within a few bars of the first signal where there is a setup based on the same logic as the first signal.

selling pressure   Strong bears are asserting themselves and their selling is creating bear trend bars, bars with tails at the tops, and two-bar bear reversals. The effect is cumulative and usually is eventually followed by lower prices.

setup   A pattern of one or more bars used by traders as the basis to place entry orders. If an entry order is filled, the last bar of the setup becomes the signal bar. Most setups are just a single bar.

shaved body   A candle with no tail at one or both ends. A shaved top has no tail at the top and a shaved bottom has no tail at the bottom.

short   As a verb, to sell a stock or futures contract to initiate a new position (not to exit a prior purchase). As a noun, a person who sells something short, or the actual position itself.

shrinking stairs   A stairs pattern where the most recent breakout is smaller than the previous one. It is a series of three or more trending highs in a bull trend or lows in a bear trend where each breakout to a new extreme is by fewer ticks than the prior breakout, indicating waning momentum. It can be a three-push pattern, but it does not have to resemble a wedge and can be any series of broad swings in a trend.

signal bar   The bar immediately before the bar in which an entry order is filled (the entry bar). It is the final bar of a setup.

smaller time frame (STF)   A chart covering the same amount of time as the current chart, but having more bars. For example, compared to the day session 5 minute Emini chart on an average day, examples of smaller time frame charts include a 1 minute chart, a tick chart with 500 ticks per bar, and a volume chart with 1,000 contracts per bar (each of these charts usually has more than 200 bars on an average day, compared to the 81 bars on the 5 minute chart).

smart traders   Consistently profitable traders who are usually trading large positions and are generally on the right side of the market.

spike and channel   A breakout into a trend in which the follow-through is in the form of a channel where the momentum is less and there is two-sided trading taking place.

stair   A push to a new extreme in a trending trading range trend or a broad channel trend where there is a series of three or more trending swings that resembles a sloping trading range and is roughly contained in a channel. After the breakout, there is a breakout pullback that retraces at least slightly into the prior trading range, which is not a requirement of other trending trading ranges. Two-way trading is taking place but one side is in slightly more control, accounting for the slope.

STF   See *smaller time frame (STF)*.

strong bulls and bears   Institutional traders and their cumulative buying and selling determine the direction of the market.

success   Refers to traders achieving their objective. Their profit target was reached before their protective stop was hit.

swing   A smaller trend that breaks a trend line of any size; the term is used only when there are at least two on the chart. They can occur within a larger trend or in a sideways market.

swing high   A bar that looks like a spike up on the chart and extends up beyond the neighboring bars. Its high is at or above that of the bar before it and that of the bar after it.

swing high/low   Either a swing high or a swing low.

swing low   A bar that looks like a spike down on the chart and extends down beyond the neighboring bars. Its low is at or below that of the bar before it and that of the bar after it.

swing point   Either a swing high or a swing low.

swing trade   For a day trader using a short-term intraday chart like the 5 minute, it is any trade that lasts longer than a scalp and that the trader will hold through one or more pullbacks. For a trader using higher time frame charts, it is a trade that lasts for hours to several days. Typically, at least part of the trade is held without a profit target, since the trader is hoping for an extended move. The potential reward is usually at least as large as the risk. Small swing trades are called scalps by many traders. In the Emini, when the average range is about 10 to 15 points, a swing trade is usually any trade where the goal is four or more points.

test   When the market approaches a prior price of significance and can overshoot or undershoot the target. The term *failed test* is used to mean opposite things by different traders. Most traders believe that if the market then reverses, the test was successful, and if it does not and the move continues beyond the test area, the test failed and a breakout has occurred.

three pushes   Three swing highs where each swing high is usually higher or three swing lows where each swing low is usually lower. It trades the same as a wedge and should be considered a variant. When it is part of a flag, the move can be mostly horizontal and each push does not have to extend beyond the prior one. For example, in a wedge bull flag or any other type of triangle, the second push down can be at, above, or below the first, and the third push down can be at, above, or below either the second or the first, or both.

tick   The smallest unit of price movement. For most stocks, it is one penny; for 10-Year U.S. Treasury Note Futures, it is 1/64th of a point; and for Eminis, it is 0.25 points. On tick charts and on time and sales tables, a tick is every trade that takes place no matter the size and even if there is no price change. If you look at a time and sales table, every trade is counted as one tick when TradeStation charting software creates a tick chart.

tight channel   A channel where the trend line and trend channel line are close together, and the pullbacks are small and last for only one to three bars.

tight trading range   A trading range of two or more bars with lots of overlap in the bars and in which most reversals are too small to trade profitably with stop entries. The bulls and bears are in balance.

time frame   The length of time contained in one bar on the chart (a 5 minute time frame is made of bars that close every five minutes). It can also refer to bars not based on time, such as those based on volume or the number of ticks traded.

tradable   A setup that you believe has a reasonable chance of leading to at least a scalper's profit.

trader's equation   To take a trade, you must believe that the probability of success times the potential reward is greater than the probability of failure times the risk. You set the reward and risk because the potential reward is the distance to your profit target and the risk is the distance to your stop. The difficulty in solving the equation is assigning a value to the probability, which can never be known with certainty. As a guideline, if you are uncertain, assume that you have a 50 percent chance of winning or losing, and if you are confident, assume that you have a 60 percent chance of winning and a 40 percent chance of losing.

trading range   The minimum requirement is a single bar with a range that is largely overlapped by the bar before it. It is sideways movement and neither the bull nor the bears are in control, although one side is often stronger. It is often a pullback in a trend where the pullback has lasted long enough to lose most of its certainty. In other words, traders have become uncertain about the direction of the breakout in the short term, and the market will have repeated breakout attempts up and down that will fail. It will usually ultimately break out in the direction of the trend, and is a pullback on a higher time frame chart.

trailing a stop   As the trade becomes increasingly profitable, traders will often move, or trail, the protective stop to protect more of their open profit. For example, if they are long in a bull trend, every time the market moves to a new high, they might raise the protective stop to just below the most recent higher low.

trap   An entry that immediately reverses to the opposite direction before a scalper's profit target is reached, trapping traders in their new position and ultimately forcing them to cover at a loss. It can also scare traders out of a good trade.

trapped in a trade   A trader with an open loss on a trade that did not result in a scalper's profit, and if there is a pullback beyond the entry or signal bars, the trader will likely exit with a loss.

trapped out of a trade   A pullback that scares a trader into exiting a trade, but then the pullback fails. The move quickly resumes in the direction of the trade, making it difficult emotionally for the trader to get back in at the worse price that is now available. The trader will have to chase the market.

trend   A series of price changes that are either mostly up (a bull trend) or down (a bear trend). There are three loosely defined smaller versions: swings, legs, and pullbacks. A chart will show only one or two major trends. If there are more, one of the other terms is more appropriate.

trend bar   A bar with a body, which means that the close was above or below the open, indicating that there is at least a minor price movement.

trend channel line   A line in the direction of the trend but drawn on the opposite side of the bars compared to a trend line. A bull trend channel line is above the highs and rising to the right, and a bear trend channel line is below the lows and falling to the right.

trend channel line overshoot   One or more bars penetrating a trend channel line.

trend channel line undershoot   A bar approaches a trend channel line but the market reverses away from the line without reaching or penetrating it.

trend from the open   A trend that begins at the first or one of the first bars of the day and extends for many bars without a pullback, and the start of the trend remains as one of the extremes of the day for much if not all of the day.

trending closes   Three or more bars where the closes are trending. In a bull trend, each close is above the prior close, and in a bear trend, each close is lower. If the pattern extends for many bars, there can be one or two bars where the closes are not trending.

trending highs or lows   The same as trending closes except based on the highs or lows of the bars.

trending swings   Three or more swings where the swing highs and lows are both higher than the prior swing highs and lows (trending bull swings), or both lower (trending bear swings).

trending trading ranges   Two or more trading ranges separated by a breakout.

trend line   A line drawn in the direction of the trend; it is sloped up and is below the bars in a bull trend, and it is sloped down and is above the bars in a bear trend. Most often, it is constructed from either swing highs or swing lows but can be based on linear regression or just a best fit (eyeballing).

trend reversal   A trend change from up to down or down to up, or from a trend to a trading range.

20 moving average gap bars   Twenty or more consecutive bars that have not touched the moving average. Once the market finally touches the moving average, it usually creates a setup for a test of the trend's extreme.

undershoot   The market approaches but does not reach a prior price of significance like a swing point or a trend line.

unlikely   At most 40 percent certain.

unreasonable   A setup with an unfavorable trader's equation.

usually   At least 60 percent certain.

vacuum   A buy vacuum occurs when the strong bears believe that the price will soon be higher so they wait to short until it reaches some magnet above the market. The result is that there is a vacuum that sucks the market quickly up to the magnet in the form of one or more bull trend bars. Once there, the strong bears sell aggressively and turn the market down. A sell vacuum occurs when the strong bulls believe that the market will soon be lower so they wait to buy until it falls to some magnet below the market. The result is that there is a vacuum that sucks the market down quickly to the magnet in the form of one or more bear trend bars. Once there, strong bulls buy aggressively and turn the market back up.

wedge   Traditionally, a three-push move with each push extending further and the trend line and trend channel line at least minimally convergent, creating a rising or descending triangle with a wedge shape. For a trader, the wedge shape increases the chances of a successful trade, but any three-push pattern trades like a wedge and can be considered one. A wedge can be a reversal pattern or a pullback in a trend (a bull or bear flag).

wedge flag   A wedge-shaped or three-push pullback in a trend, such as a high 3 in a bull trend (a type of bull flag) or a low 3 in a bear trend (a type of bear flag). Since it is a with-trend setup, enter on the first signal.

wedge reversal   A wedge that is reversing a bull trend into a bear trend or a bear trend into a bull trend. Since it is countertrend, unless it is very strong, it is better to take a second signal. For example, if there is a bear trend and then a descending wedge, wait for a breakout above this potential wedge bottom and then try to buy a pullback to a higher low.

with trend   Refers to a trade or a setup that is in the direction of the prevailing trend. In general, the direction of the most recent 5 minute chart signal should be assumed to be the trend's direction. Also, if most of the past 10 or 20 bars are above the moving average, trend setups and trades are likely on the buy side.

Trading
Price
Action
TRENDS

Introduction

There is a reason why there is no other comprehensive book about price action written by a trader. It takes thousands of hours, and the financial reward is meager compared to that from trading. However, with my three girls now away in grad school, I have a void to fill and this has been a very satisfying project. I originally planned on updating the first edition of *Reading Price Charts Bar by Bar* (John Wiley & Sons, 2009), but as I got into it, I decided instead to go into great detail about how I view and trade the markets. I am metaphorically teaching you how to play the violin. Everything you need to know to make a living at it is in these books, but it is up to you to spend the countless hours learning your trade. After a year of answering thousands of questions from traders on my website at www.brookspriceaction.com, I think that I have found ways to express my ideas much more clearly, and these books should be easier to read than that one. The earlier book focused on reading price action, and this series of books is instead centered on how to use price action to trade the markets. Since the book grew to more than four times as many words as the first book, John Wiley & Sons decided to divide it into three separate books. This first book covers price action basics and trends. The second book is on trading ranges, order management, and the mathematics of trading, and the final book is about trend reversals, day trading, daily charts, options, and the best setups for all time frames. Many of the charts are also in *Reading Price Charts Bar by Bar*, but most have been updated and the discussion about the charts has also been largely rewritten. Only about 5 percent of the 120,000 words from that book are present in the 570,000 words in this new series, so readers will find little duplication.

My goals in writing this series of three books are to describe my understanding of why the carefully selected trades offer great risk/reward ratios, and to present ways to profit from the setups. I am presenting material that I hope will be interesting to professional traders and students in business school, but I also hope that even traders starting out will find some useful ideas. Everyone looks at price charts but usually just briefly and with a specific or limited goal. However, every chart has an incredible amount of information that can be used to make profitable trades, but much of it can be used effectively only if traders spend time to carefully understand what each bar on the chart is telling them about what institutional money is doing.

Ninety percent or more of all trading in large markets is done by institutions, which means that the market is simply a collection of institutions. Almost all are profitable over time, and the few that are not soon go out of business. Since institutions are profitable and they are the market, every trade that you take has a profitable trader (a part of the collection of institutions) taking the other side of your trade. No trade can take place without one institution willing to take one side and another willing to take the other. The small-volume trades made by individuals can only take place if an institution is willing to take the same trade. If you want to buy at a certain price, the market will not get to that price unless one or more institutions also want to buy at that price. You cannot sell at any price unless one or more institutions are willing to sell there, because the market can only go to a price where there are institutions willing to buy and others willing to sell. If the Emini is at 1,264 and you are long with a protective sell stop at 1,262, your stop cannot get hit unless there is an institution who is also willing to sell at 1,262. This is true for virtually all trades.

If you trade 200 Emini contracts, then you are trading institutional volume and are effectively an institution, and you will sometimes be able to move the market a tick or two. Most individual traders, however, have no ability to move the market, no matter how stupidly they are willing to trade. The market will not run your stops. The market might test the price where your protective stop is, but it has nothing to do with your stop. It will only test that price if one or more institutions believe that it is financially sound to sell there and other institutions believe that it is profitable to buy there. At every tick, there are institutions buying and other institutions selling, and all have proven systems that will make money by placing those trades. You should always be trading in the direction of the majority of institutional dollars because they control where the market is heading.

At the end of the day when you look at a printout of the day's chart, how can you tell what the institutions did during the day? The answer is simple: whenever the market went up, the bulk of institutional money was buying, and whenever the market went down, more money went into selling. Just look at any segment of the chart where the market went up or down and study every bar, and you will soon notice many repeatable patterns. With time, you will begin to see those patterns unfold in real time, and that will give you confidence to place your trades. Some of the price action is subtle, so be open to every possibility. For example, sometimes when the market is working higher, a bar will trade below the low of the prior bar, yet the trend continues higher. You have to assume that the big money was buying at and below the low of that prior bar, and that is also what many experienced traders were doing. They bought exactly where weak traders let themselves get stopped out with a loss or where other weak traders shorted, believing that the market was beginning to sell off. Once you get comfortable with the idea that strong trends often have pullbacks and big money is buying them rather than selling them, you will be in a position to make some great trades that you previously thought were exactly the wrong thing to do. Don't think too hard about it. If the market is going up, institutions are buying constantly, even at times when you think that you should stop yourself out of your long with a loss. Your job is to follow their behavior and not use too much logic to deny what is happening right in front of you. It does not matter if it seems counterintuitive. All that matters is that the market is going up and therefore institutions are predominantly buying and so should you.

Institutions are generally considered to be smart money, meaning that they are smart enough to make a living by trading and they trade a large volume every day. Television still uses the term *institution* to refer to traditional institutions like mutual funds, banks, brokerage houses, insurance companies, pension funds, and hedge funds; these companies used to account for most of the volume, and they mostly trade on fundamentals. Their trading controls the direction of the market on daily and weekly charts and a lot of the big intraday swings. Until a decade or so ago, most of the trade decisions were made and most trading was done by very smart traders, but it is now increasingly being done by computers. They have programs that can instantly analyze economic data and immediately place trades based on that analysis, without a person ever being involved in the trade. In addition, other firms trade huge volumes by using computer programs that place trades based on the statistical analysis of price action. Computer-generated trading now accounts for as much as 70 percent of the day's volume.

Computers are very good at making decisions, and playing chess and winning at *Jeopardy!* are more difficult than trading stocks. Gary Kasparov for years made the best chess decisions in the world, yet a computer made better decisions in 1997 and beat him. Ken Jennings was heralded as the greatest *Jeopardy!* player of all time, yet a computer destroyed him in 2011. It is only a matter of time before computers are widely accepted as the best decision makers for institutional trading.

Since programs use objective mathematical analysis, there should be a tendency for support and resistance areas to become more clearly defined. For example, measured move projections should become more precise as more of the volume is traded based on precise mathematical logic. Also, there might be a tendency toward more protracted tight channels as programs buy small pullbacks on the daily chart. However, if enough programs exit longs or go short at the same key levels, sell-offs might become larger and faster. Will the changes be dramatic? Probably not, since the same general forces were operating when everything was done manually, but nonetheless there should be some move toward mathematical perfection as more of the emotion is removed from trading. As these other firms contribute more and more to the movement of the market and as traditional institutions increasingly use computers to analyze and place their trades, the term *institution* is becoming vague. It is better for an individual trader to think of an institution as any of the different entities that trade enough volume to be a significant contributor to the price action.

Since these buy and sell programs generate most of the volume, they are the most important contributor to the appearance of every chart and they create most of the trading opportunities for individual investors. Yes, it's nice to know that Cisco Systems (CSCO) had a strong earnings report and is moving up, and if you are an investor who wants to hold stock for many months, then do what the traditional institutions are doing and buy CSCO. However, if you are a day trader, ignore the news and look at the chart, because the programs will create patterns that are purely statistically based and have nothing to do with fundamentals, yet offer great trading opportunities. The traditional institutions placing trades based on fundamentals determine the direction and the approximate target of a stock over the next several months, but, increasingly, firms using statistical analysis to make day trades and other short-term trades determine the path to that target and the ultimate high or low of the move. Even on a macro level, fundamentals are only approximate at best. Look at the crashes in 1987 and 2009. Both had violent sell-offs and rallies, yet the fundamentals did not change violently in the same short period of time. In both cases, the market got sucked slightly below the monthly trend line and reversed sharply up from it. The market fell because of perceived fundamentals, but the extent of the fall was determined by the charts.

There are some large patterns that repeat over and over on all time frames and in all markets, like trends, trading ranges, climaxes, and channels. There are also lots of smaller tradable patterns that are based on just the most recent few bars. These books are a comprehensive guide to help traders understand everything they see on a chart, giving them more opportunities to make profitable trades and to avoid losers.

The most important message that I can deliver is to focus on the absolute best trades, avoid the absolute worst setups, use a profit objective (reward) that is at least as large as your protective stop (risk), and work on increasing the number of shares that you are trading. I freely recognize that every one of my reasons behind each setup is just my opinion, and my reasoning about why a trade works might be completely wrong. However, that is irrelevant. What is important is that reading price action is a very effective way to trade, and I have thought a lot about why certain things happen the way they do. I am comfortable with my explanations and they give me confidence when I place a trade; however, they are irrelevant to my placing trades, so it is not important to me that they are right. Just as I can reverse my opinion about the direction of the market in an instant, I can also reverse my opinion about why a particular pattern works if I come across a reason that is more logical or if I discover a flaw in my logic. I am providing the opinions because they appear to make sense, they might help readers become more comfortable trading certain setups, and they might be intellectually stimulating, but they are not needed for any price action trades.

The books are very detailed and difficult to read and are directed toward serious traders who want to learn as much as they can about reading price charts. However, the concepts are useful to traders at all levels. The books cover many of the standard techniques described by Robert D. Edwards and John Magee (*Technical Analysis of Stock Trends*, AMACOM, 9th ed., 2007) and others, but focus more on individual bars to demonstrate how the information they provide can significantly enhance the risk/reward ratio of trading. Most books point out three or four trades on a chart, which implies that everything else on the chart is incomprehensible, meaningless, or risky. I believe that there is something to be learned from every tick that takes place during the day and that there are far more great trades on every chart than just the few obvious ones; but to see them, you have to understand price action and you cannot dismiss any bars as unimportant. I learned from performing thousands of operations through a microscope that some of the most important things can be very small.

I read charts bar by bar and look for any information that each bar is telling me. They are all important. At the end of every bar, most traders ask themselves, "What just took place?" With most bars, they conclude that there is nothing worth trading at the moment so it is just not worth the effort to try to understand. Instead, they choose to wait for some clearer and usually larger pattern. It is as if they believe that the bar did not exist, or they dismiss it as just institutional program activity that is not tradable by an individual trader. They do not feel like they are part of the market at these times, but these times constitute the vast majority of the day. Yet, if they look at the volume, all of those bars that they are ignoring have as much volume as the bars they are using for the bases for their trades. Clearly, a lot of trading is taking place, but they don't understand how that can be and essentially pretend that it does not exist. But that is denying reality. There is always trading taking place, and as a trader, you owe it to yourself to understand why it's taking place and to figure out a way to make money off of it. Learning what the market is telling you is very time-consuming and difficult, but it gives you the foundation that you need to be a successful trader.

Unlike most books on candle charts where the majority of readers feel compelled to memorize patterns, these three books of mine provide a rationale for why particular patterns are reliable setups for traders. Some of the terms used have specific meaning to market technicians but different meanings to traders, and I am writing this entirely from a trader's perspective. I am certain that many traders already understand everything in these books, but likely wouldn't describe price action in the same way that I do. There are no secrets among successful traders; they all know common setups, and many have their own names for each one. All of them are buying and selling pretty much at the same time, catching the same swings, and they all have their own reasons for getting into a trade. Many trade price action intuitively without ever feeling a need to articulate why a certain setup works. I hope that they enjoy reading my understanding of and perspective on price action and that this gives them some insights that will improve their already successful trading.

The goal for most traders is to maximize trading profits through a style that is compatible with their personalities. Without that compatibility, I believe that it is virtually impossible to trade profitably for the long term. Many traders wonder how long it will take them to be successful and are willing to lose money for some period of time, even a few years. However, it took me over 10 years to be able to trade successfully. Each of us has many considerations and distractions, so the time will vary, but a trader has to work though most obstacles before becoming consistently profitable. I had several major problems that had to be corrected, including raising three wonderful daughters who always filled my mind with thoughts of them and what I needed to be doing as their father. That was solved as they got older and more independent. Then it took me a long time to accept many personality traits as real and unchangeable (or at least I concluded that I was unwilling to change them). And finally there was the issue of confidence. I have always been confident to the point of arrogance in so many things that those who know me would be surprised that this was difficult for me. However, deep inside I believed that I really would never come up with a consistently profitable approach that I would enjoy employing for many years. Instead, I bought many systems, wrote and tested countless indicators and systems, read many books and magazines, went to seminars, hired tutors, and joined chat rooms. I talked with people who presented themselves as successful traders, but I never saw their account statements and suspect that most could teach but few, if any, could trade. Usually in trading, those who know don't talk and those who talk don't know.

This was all extremely helpful because it showed all of the things that I needed to avoid before becoming successful. Any nontrader who looks at a chart will invariably conclude that trading has to be extremely easy, and that is part of the appeal. At the end of the day, anyone can look at any chart and see very clear entry and exit points. However, it is much more difficult to do it in real time. There is a natural tendency to want to buy the exact low and never have the trade come back. If it does, a novice will take the loss to avoid a bigger loss, resulting in a series of losing trades that will ultimately bust the trader's account. Using wide stops solves that to some extent, but invariably traders will soon hit a few big losses that will put them into the red and make them too scared to continue using that approach.

Should you be concerned that making the information in these books available will create lots of great price action traders, all doing the same thing at the same time, thereby removing the late entrants needed to drive the market to your price target? No, because the institutions control the market and they already have the smartest traders in the world and those traders already know everything in these books, at least intuitively. At every moment, there is an extremely smart institutional bull taking the opposite side of the trade being placed by an extremely smart institutional bear. Since the most important players already know price action, having more players know it will not tip the balance one way or the other. I therefore have no concern that what I am writing will stop price action from working. Because of that balance, any edge that anyone has is always going to be extremely small, and any small mistake will result in a loss, no matter how well a person reads a chart. Although it is very difficult to make money as a trader without understanding price action, that knowledge alone is not enough. It takes a long time to learn how to trade *after* a trader learns to read charts, and trading is just as difficult as chart reading. I wrote these books to help people learn to read charts better and to trade better, and if you can do both well, you deserve to be able to take money from the accounts of others and put it into yours.

The reason why the patterns that we all see do unfold as they do is because that is the appearance that occurs in an efficient market with countless traders placing orders for thousands of different reasons, but with the controlling volume being traded based on sound logic. That is just what it looks like, and it has been that way forever. The same patterns unfold in all time frames in all markets around the world, and it would simply be impossible for all of it to be manipulated instantaneously on so many different levels. Price action is a manifestation of human behavior and therefore actually has a genetic basis. Until we evolve, it will likely remain largely unchanged, just as it has been unchanged for the 80 years of charts that I have reviewed. Program trading might have changed the appearance slightly, although I can find no evidence to support that theory. If anything, it would make the charts smoother because it is unemotional and it has greatly increased the volume. Now that most of the volume is being traded automatically by computers and the volume is so huge, irrational and emotional behavior is an insignificant component of the markets and the charts are a purer expression of human tendencies.

Since price action comes from our DNA, it will not change until we evolve. When you look at the two charts in Figure I.1, your first reaction is that they are just a couple of ordinary charts, but look at the dates at the bottom. These weekly Dow Jones Industrial Average charts from the Depression era and from World War II have the same patterns that we see today on all charts, despite most of today's volume being traded by computers.

If everyone suddenly became a price action scalper, the smaller patterns might change a little for a while, but over time, the efficient market will win out and the votes by all traders will get distilled into standard price action patterns because that is the inescapable result of countless people behaving logically. Also, the reality is that it is very difficult to trade well, and although basing trades on price action is a sound approach, it is still very difficult to do successfully in real time.

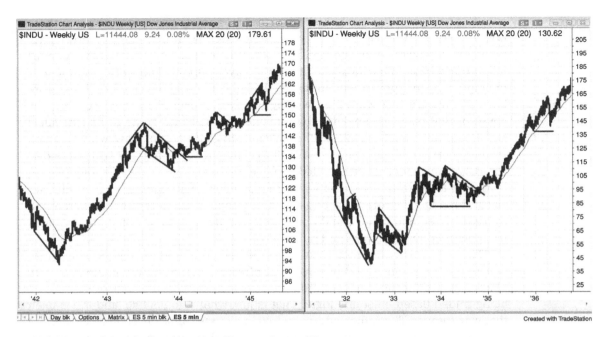

FIGURE I.1 Price Action Has Not Changed over Time

There just won't be enough traders doing it well enough, all at the same time, to have any significant influence over time on the patterns. Just look at Edwards and Magee. The best traders in the world have been using those ideas for decades and they continue to work, again for the same reason—charts look the way they do because that is the unchangeable fingerprint of an efficient market filled with a huge number of smart people using a huge number of approaches and time frames, all trying to make the most money that they can. For example, Tiger Woods is not hiding anything that he does in golf, and anyone is free to copy him. However, very few people can play golf well enough to make a living at it. The same is true of trading. A trader can know just about everything there is to know and still lose money because applying all that knowledge in a way that consistently makes money is very difficult to do.

Why do so many business schools continue to recommend Edwards and Magee when their book is essentially simplistic, largely using trend lines, breakouts, and pullbacks as the basis for trading? It is because it works and it always has and it always will. Now that just about all traders have computers with access to intraday data, many of those techniques can be adapted to day trading. Also, candle charts give additional information about who is controlling the market, which results in a more timely entry with smaller risk. Edwards and Magee's focus is on the overall trend. I use those same basic techniques but pay much closer attention to the individual bars on the chart to improve the risk/reward ratio, and I devote considerable attention to intraday charts.

It seemed obvious to me that if one could simply read the charts well enough to be able to enter at the exact times when the move would take off and not come back, then that trader would have a huge advantage. The trader would have a high winning percentage, and the few losses would be small. I decided that this would be my starting point, and what I discovered was that nothing had to be added. In fact, any additions are distractions that result in lower profitability. This sounds so obvious and easy that it is difficult for most people to believe.

I am a day trader who relies entirely on price action on the intraday Emini S&P 500 Futures charts, and I believe that reading price action well is an invaluable skill for all traders. Beginners often instead have a deep-seated belief that something more is required, that maybe some complex mathematical formula that very few use would give them just the edge that they need. Goldman Sachs is so rich and sophisticated that its traders must have a supercomputer and high-powered software that gives them an advantage that ensures that all the individual traders are doomed to failure. They start looking at all kinds of indicators and playing with the inputs to customize the indicators to make them just right. Every indicator works some of the time, but for me, they obfuscate instead of elucidate. In fact, without even looking at a chart, you can place a buy order and have a 50 percent chance of being right!

I am not dismissing indicators and systems out of ignorance of their subtleties. I have spent over 10,000 hours writing and testing indicators and systems over the years, and that probably is far more experience than most have. This extensive experience with indicators and systems was an essential part of my becoming a successful trader. Indicators work well for many traders, but the best success comes once a trader finds an approach that is compatible with his or her personality. My single biggest problem with indicators and systems was that I never fully trusted them. At every setup, I saw exceptions that needed to be tested. I always wanted every last penny out of the market and was never satisfied with a return from a system if I could incorporate a new twist that would make it better. You can optimize constantly, but, since the market is always changing from strong trends to tight trading ranges and then back again and your optimizations are based on what has recently happened, they will soon fail as the market transitions into a new phase. I am simply too controlling, compulsive, restless, observant, and untrusting to make money in the long term off indicators or automated systems, but I am at the extreme in many ways and most people don't have these same issues.

Many traders, especially beginners, are drawn to indicators (or any other higher power, guru, TV pundit, or newsletter that they want to believe will protect them and show their love and approval of them as human beings by giving them lots of money), hoping that an indicator will show them when to enter a trade. What they don't realize is that the vast majority of indicators are based on simple price action, and when I am placing trades, I simply cannot think fast enough to process what several indicators might be telling me. If there is a bull trend, a pullback, and then a rally to a new high, but the rally has lots of overlapping bars, many bear bodies, a couple of small pullbacks, and prominent tails on the tops of the bars, any experienced trader would see that it is a weak test of the trend high and that this should not be happening if the bull trend was still strong. The market is almost certainly transitioning into a trading range and possibly into a bear trend. Traders don't need an oscillator to tell them this. Also, oscillators tend to make traders look for reversals and focus less on price charts. These can be effective tools on most days when the market has two or three reversals lasting an hour or more. The problem comes when the market is trending strongly. If you focus too much on your indicators, you will see that they are forming divergences all day long and you might find yourself repeatedly entering countertrend and losing money. By the time you come to accept that the market is trending, you will not have enough time left in the day to recoup your losses. Instead, if you were simply looking at a bar or candle chart, you would see that the market is clearly trending and you would not be tempted by indicators to look for trend reversals. The most common successful reversals first break a trend line with strong momentum and then pull back to test the extreme, and if traders focus too much on divergences, they will often overlook this fundamental fact. Placing a trade because of a divergence in the absence of a prior countertrend momentum surge that breaks a trend line is a losing strategy. Wait for the trend line break and then see if the test of the old extreme reverses or if the old trend resumes. You do not need an indicator to tell you that a strong reversal here is a high-probability trade, at least for a scalp, and there will almost certainly be a divergence, so why complicate your thinking by adding the indicator to your calculus?

Some pundits recommend a combination of time frames, indicators, wave counting, and Fibonacci retracements and extensions, but when it comes time to place the trade, they will do it only if there is a good price action setup. Also, when they see a good price action setup, they start looking for indicators that show divergences, different time frames for moving average tests, wave counts, or Fibonacci setups to confirm what is in front of them. In reality, they are price action traders who are trading exclusively off price action on only one chart but don't feel comfortable admitting it. They are complicating their trading to the point that they certainly are missing many, many trades because their overanalysis takes too much time for them to place their orders and they are forced to wait for the next setup. The logic just isn't there for making the simple so complicated. Obviously, adding any information can lead to better decision making and many people might be able to process lots of inputs when deciding whether to place a trade. Ignoring data because of a simplistic ideology alone is foolish. The goal is to make money, and traders should do everything they can to maximize their profits. I simply cannot process multiple indicators and time frames well in the time needed to place my orders accurately, and I find that carefully reading a single chart is far more profitable for me. Also, if I rely on indicators, I find that I get lazy in my price action reading and often miss the obvious. Price action is far more important than any other information, and if you sacrifice some of what it is telling you to gain information from something else, you are likely making a bad decision.

One of the most frustrating things for traders when they are starting out is that everything is so subjective. They want to find a clear set of rules that guarantee a profit, and they hate how a pattern works on one day but fails on another. Markets are very efficient because you have countless very smart people playing a zero-sum game. For a trader to make money, he has to be consistently better than about half of the other traders out there. Since most of the competitors are profitable institutions, a trader has to be very good. Whenever an edge exists, it is quickly discovered and it disappears. Remember, someone has to be taking the opposite side of your trade. It won't take them long to figure out your magical system, and once they do, they will stop giving you money. Part of the appeal of trading is that it is a zero-sum game with very small edges, and it is intellectually satisfying and financially rewarding to be able to spot and capitalize on these small, fleeting opportunities. It can be done, but it is very hard work and it requires relentless discipline. Discipline simply means doing what you do not want to do. We are all intellectually curious and we have a natural tendency to try new or different things, but the very best traders resist the temptation. You have to stick to your rules and avoid emotion, and you have to patiently wait to take only the best trades. This all appears easy to do when you look at a printed chart at the end of the day, but it is very difficult in real time as you wait bar by bar, and sometimes hour by hour. Once a great setup appears, if you are distracted or lulled into complacency, you will miss it and you will then be forced to wait even longer. But if you can develop the patience and the discipline to follow a sound system, the profit potential is huge.

There are countless ways to make money trading stocks and Eminis, but all require movement (well, except for shorting options). If you learn to read the charts, you will catch a great number of these profitable trades every day without ever knowing why some institution started the trend and without ever knowing what any indicator is showing. You don't need these institutions' software or analysts because they will show you what they are doing. All you have to do is piggyback onto their trades and you will make a profit. Price action will tell you what they are doing and allow you an early entry with a tight stop.

I have found that I consistently make far more money by minimizing what I have to consider when placing a trade. All I need is a single chart on my laptop computer with no indicators except a 20-bar exponential moving average (EMA), which does not require too much analysis and clarifies many good setups each day. Some traders might also look at volume because an unusually large volume spike sometimes comes near the end of a bear trend, and the next new swing low or two often provide profitable long scalps. Volume spikes also sometimes occur on daily charts when a sell-off is overdone. However, it is not reliable enough to warrant my attention.

Many traders consider price action only when trading divergences and trend pullbacks. In fact, most traders using indicators won't take a trade unless there is a strong signal bar, and many would enter on a strong signal bar if the context was right, even if there was no divergence. They like to see a strong close on a large reversal bar, but in reality this is a fairly rare occurrence. The most useful tools for understanding price action are trend lines and trend channel lines, prior highs and lows, breakouts and failed breakouts, the sizes of bodies and tails on candles, and relationships between the current bar to the prior several bars. In particular, how the open, high, low, and close of the current bar compare to the action of the prior several bars tells a lot about what will happen next. Charts provide far more information about who is in control of the market than most traders realize. Almost every bar offers important clues as to where the market is going, and a trader who dismisses any activity as noise is passing up many profitable trades each day. Most of the observations in these books are directly related to placing trades, but a few have to do with simple curious price action tendencies without sufficient dependability to be the basis for a trade.

I personally rely mainly on candle charts for my Emini, futures, and stock trading, but most signals are also visible on any type of chart and many are even evident on simple line charts. I focus primarily on 5 minute candle charts to illustrate basic principles but also discuss daily and weekly charts as well. Since I also trade stocks, forex, Treasury note futures, and options, I discuss how price action can be used as the basis for this type of trading.

As a trader, I see everything in shades of gray and am constantly thinking in terms of probabilities. If a pattern is setting up and is not perfect but is reasonably similar to a reliable setup, it will likely behave similarly as well. Close is usually close enough. If something resembles a textbook setup, the trade will likely unfold in a way that is similar to the trade from the textbook setup. This is the art of trading and it takes years to become good at trading in the gray zone. Everyone wants concrete, clear rules or indicators, and chat rooms, newsletters, hotlines, or tutors that will tell them when exactly to get in to minimize risk and maximize profit, but none of it works in the long run. You have to take responsibility for your decisions, but you first have to learn how to make them and that means that you have to get used to operating in the gray fog. Nothing is ever as clear as black and white, and I have been doing this long enough to appreciate that anything, no matter how unlikely, can and will happen. It's like quantum physics. Every conceivable event has a probability, and so do events that you have yet to consider. It is not emotional, and the reasons why something happens are irrelevant. Watching to see if the Federal Reserve cuts rates today is a waste of time because there is both a bullish and bearish interpretation of anything that the Fed does. What is key is to see what the market does, not what the Fed does.

If you think about it, trading is a zero-sum game and it is impossible to have a zero-sum game where rules consistently work. If they worked, everyone would use them and then there would be no one on the other side of the trade. Therefore, the trade could not exist. Guidelines are very helpful but reliable rules cannot exist, and this is usually very troubling to a trader starting out who wants to believe that trading is a game that can be very profitable if only you can come up with just the right set of rules. All rules work some of the time, and usually just often enough to fool you into believing that you just need to tweak them a little to get them to work all of the time. You are trying to create a trading god who will protect you, but you are fooling yourself and looking for an easy solution to a game where only hard solutions work. You are competing against the smartest people in the world, and if you are smart enough to come up with a foolproof rule set, so are they, and then everyone is faced with the zero-sum game dilemma. You cannot make money trading unless you are flexible, because you need to go where the market is going, and the market is extremely flexible. It can bend in every direction and for much longer than most would ever imagine. It can also reverse repeatedly every few bars for a long, long time. Finally, it can and will do everything in between. Never get upset by this, and just accept it as reality and admire it as part of the beauty of the game.

The market gravitates toward uncertainty. During most of the day, every market has a directional probability of 50–50 of an equidistant move up or down. By that I mean that if you don't even look at a chart and you buy any stock and then place a one cancels the other (OCO) order to exit on a profit-taking limit order X cents above your entry or on a protective stop at X cents below your entry, you have about a 50 percent chance of being right. Likewise, if you sell any stock at any point in the day without looking at a chart and then place a profit-taking limit order X cents lower and a protective stop X cents higher, you have about a 50 percent chance of winning and about a 50 percent chance of losing. There is the obvious exception of X being too large relative the price of the stock. You can't have X be $60 in a $50 stock, because you would have a 0 percent chance of losing $60. You also can't have X be $49, because the odds of losing $49 would also be minuscule. But if you pick a value for X that is within reasonable reach on your time frame, this is generally true. When the market is 50–50, it is uncertain and you cannot rationally have an opinion about its direction. This is the hallmark of a trading range, so whenever you are uncertain, assume that the market is in a trading range. There are brief times on a chart when the directional probability is higher. During a strong trend, it might be 60 or even 70 percent, but that cannot last long because it will gravitate toward uncertainty and a 50–50 market where both the bulls and bears feel there is value. When there is a trend and some level of directional certainty, the market will also gravitate toward areas of support and resistance, which are usually some type of measured move away, and those areas are invariably where uncertainty returns and a trading range develops, at least briefly.

Never watch the news during the trading day. If you want to know what a news event means, the chart in front of you will tell you. Reporters believe that the news is the most important thing in the world, and that everything that happens has to be caused by their biggest news story of the day. Since reporters are in the news business, news must be the center of the universe and the cause of everything that happens in the financial markets. When the stock market sold off in mid-March 2011, they attributed it to the earthquake in Japan. It did not matter to them that the market began to sell off three weeks earlier, after a buy climax. I told the members of my chat room in late February that the odds were good that the market was going to have a significant correction when I saw 15 consecutive bull trend bars on the daily chart after a protracted bull run. This was an unusually strong buy climax, and an important statement by the market. I had no idea that an earthquake was going to happen in a few weeks, and did not need to know that, anyway. The chart was telling me what traders were doing; they were getting ready to exit their longs and initiate shorts.

Television experts are also useless. Invariably when the market makes a huge move, the reporter will find some confident, convincing expert who predicted it and interview him or her, leading the viewers to believe that this pundit has an uncanny ability to predict the market, despite the untold reality that this same pundit has been wrong in his last 10 predictions. The pundit then makes some future prediction and naïve viewers will attach significance to it and let it affect their trading. What the viewers may not realize is that some pundits are bullish 100 percent of the time and others are bearish 100 percent of the time, and still others just swing for the fences all the time and make outrageous predictions. The reporter just rushes to the one who is consistent with the day's news, which is totally useless to traders and in fact it is destructive because it can influence their trading and make them question and deviate from their own methods. No one is ever consistently right more than 60 percent of the time on these major predictions, and just because pundits are convincing does not make them reliable. There are equally smart and convincing people who believe the opposite but are not being heard. This is the same as watching a trial and listening to only the defense side of the argument. Hearing only one side is always convincing and always misleading, and rarely better than 50 percent reliable.

Institutional bulls and bears are placing trades all the time, and that is why there is constant uncertainty about the direction of the market. Even in the absence of breaking news, the business channels air interviews all day long and each reporter gets to pick one pundit for her report. What you have to realize is that she has a 50–50 chance of picking the right one in terms of the market's direction over the next hour or so. If you decide to rely on the pundit to make a trading decision and he says that the market will sell off after midday and instead it just keeps going up, are you going to look to short? Should you believe this very convincing head trader at one of Wall Street's top firms? He obviously is making over a million dollars a year and they would not pay him that much unless he was able to correctly and consistently predict the market's direction. In fact, he probably can and he is probably a good stock picker, but he almost certainly is not a day trader. It is foolish to believe that just because he can make 15 percent annually managing money he can correctly predict the market's direction over the next hour or two. Do the math. If he had that ability, he would be making 1 percent two or three times a day and maybe 1,000 percent a year. Since he is not, you know that he does not have that ability. His time frame is months and yours is minutes. Since he is unable to make money by day trading, why would you ever want to make a trade based on someone who is a proven failure as a day trader? He has shown you that he cannot make money by day trading by the simple fact that he is not a successful day trader. That immediately tells you that if he day trades, he loses money because if he was successful at it, that is what he would choose to do and he would make far more than he is currently making. Even if you are holding trades for months at a time in an attempt to duplicate the results of his fund, it is still foolish to take his advice, because he might change his mind next week and you would never know it. Managing a trade once you are in is just as important as placing the trade. If you are following the pundit and hope to make 15 percent a year like he does, you need to follow his management, but you have no ability to do so and you will lose over time employing this strategy. Yes, you will make an occasional great trade, but you can simply do that by randomly buying any stock. The key is whether the approach makes money over 100 trades, not over the first one or two. Follow the advice that you give your kids: don't fool yourself into believing that what you see on television is real, no matter how polished and convincing it appears to be.

As I said, there will be pundits who will see the news as bullish and others who will see it as bearish, and the reporter gets to pick one for her report. Are you going to let a reporter make trading decisions for you? That's insane! If that reporter could trade, she would be a trader and make hundreds of times more money than she is making as a reporter. Why would you ever allow her to influence your decision making? You might do so only out of a lack of confidence in your ability, or perhaps you are searching for a father figure who will love and protect you. If you are prone to be influenced by a reporter's decision, you should not take the trade. The pundit she chooses is not your father, and he will not protect you or your money. Even if the reporter picks a pundit who is correct on the direction, that pundit will not stay with you to manage your trade, and you will likely be stopped out with a loss on a pullback.

Financial news stations do not exist to provide public service. They are in business to make money, and that means they need as large an audience as possible to maximize their advertising income. Yes, they want to be accurate in their reporting, but their primary objective is to make money. They are fully aware that they can maximize their audience size only if they are pleasing to watch. That means that they have to have interesting guests, including some who will make outrageous predictions, others who are professorial and reassuring, and some who are just physically attractive; most of them have to have some entertainment value. Although some guests are great traders, they cannot help you. For example, if they interview one of the world's most successful bond traders, he will usually only speak in general terms about the trend over the next several months, and he will do so only weeks after he has already placed his trades. If you are a day trader, this does not help you, because every bull or bear market on the monthly chart has just about as many up moves on the intraday chart as down moves, and there will be long and short trades every day. His time frame is very different from yours, and his trading has nothing to do with what you are doing. They will also often interview a chartist from a major Wall Street firm, who, while his credentials are good, will be basing his opinion on a weekly chart, but the viewers are looking to take profits within a few days. To the chartist, that bull trend that he is recommending buying will still be intact, even if the market falls 10 percent over the next couple of months. The viewers, however, will take their losses long before that, and will never benefit from the new high that comes three months later. Unless the chartist is addressing your specific goals and time frame, whatever he says is useless. When television interviews a day trader instead, he will talk about the trades that he already took, and the information is too late to help you make money. By the time he is on television, the market might already be going in the opposite direction. If he is talking while still in his day trade, he will continue to manage his trade long after his two-minute interview is over, and he will not manage it while on the air. Even if you enter the trade that he is in, he will not be there when you invariably will have to make an important decision about getting out as the market turns against you, or as the market goes in your direction and you are thinking about taking profits. Watching television for trading advice under any circumstances, even after a very important report, is a sure way to lose money and you should never do it.

Only look at the chart and it will tell you what you need to know. The chart is what will give you money or take money from you, so it is the only thing that you should ever consider when trading. If you are on the floor, you can't even trust what your best friend is doing. He might be offering a lot of orange juice calls but secretly having a broker looking to buy 10 times as many below the market. Your friend is just trying to create a panic to drive the market down so he can load up through a surrogate at a much better price.

Friends and colleagues freely offer opinions for you to ignore. Occasionally traders will tell me that they have a great setup and want to discuss it with me. I invariably get them angry with me when I tell them that I am not interested. They immediately perceive me as selfish, stubborn, and close-minded, and when it comes to trading, I am all of that and probably much more. The skills that make you money are generally seen as flaws to the layperson. Why do I no longer read books or articles about trading, or talk to other traders about their ideas? As I said, the chart tells me all that I need to know and any other information is a distraction. Several people have been offended by my attitude, but I think in part it comes from me turning down what they are presenting as something helpful to me when in reality they are making an offering, hoping that I will reciprocate with some tutoring. They become frustrated and angry when I tell them that I don't want to hear about anyone else's trading techniques. I tell them that I haven't even mastered my own and probably never will, but I am confident that I will make far more money perfecting what I already know than trying to incorporate non-price-action approaches into my trading. I ask them if James Galway offered a beautiful flute to Yo-Yo Ma and insisted that Ma start learning to play the flute because Galway makes so much money by playing his flute, should Ma accept the offer? Clearly not. Ma should continue to play the cello and by doing so he will make far more money than if he also started playing the flute. I am no Galway or Ma, but the concept is the same. Price action is the only instrument that I want to play, and I strongly believe that I will make far more money by mastering it than by incorporating ideas from other successful traders.

The charts, not the experts on television, will tell you exactly how the institutions are interpreting the news.

Yesterday, Costco's earnings were up 32 percent on the quarter and above analysts' expectations (see Figure I.2). COST gapped up on the open, tested the gap on the first bar, and then ran up over a dollar in 20 minutes. It then drifted down to test yesterday's close. It had two rallies that broke bear trend lines, and both failed. This created a double top (bars 2 and 3) bear flag or triple top (bars 1, 2, and 3), and the market then plunged $3, below the prior day's low. If you were unaware of the report, you would have shorted at the failed bear trend line breaks at bars 2 and 3 and you would have sold more below bar 4, which was a pullback that followed the breakout below yesterday's low. You would have reversed to long on the bar 5 big reversal bar, which was the second attempt to reverse the breakout below yesterday's low and a climactic reversal of the breakout of the bottom of the steep bear trend channel line.

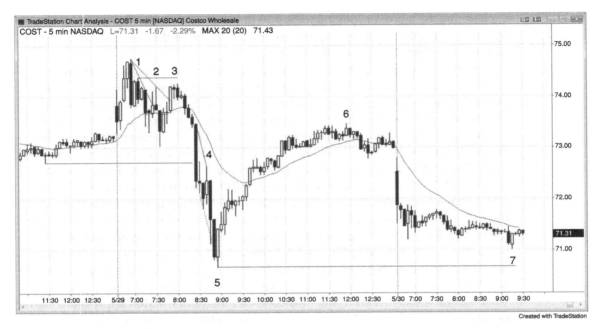

FIGURE I.2 Ignore the News

Alternatively, you could have bought the open because of the bullish report, and then worried about why the stock was collapsing instead of soaring the way the TV analysts predicted, and you likely would have sold out your long on the second plunge down to bar 5 with a $2 loss.

Any trend that covers a lot of points in very few bars, meaning that there is some combination of large bars and bars that overlap each other only minimally, will eventually have a pullback. These trends have such strong momentum that the odds favor resumption of the trend after the pullback and then a test of the trend's extreme. Usually the extreme will be exceeded, as long as the pullback does not turn into a new trend in the opposite direction and extend beyond the start of the original trend. In general, the odds that a pullback will get back to the prior trend's extreme fall substantially if the pullback retraces 75 percent or more. For a pullback in a bear trend, at that point, a trader is better off thinking of the pullback as a new bull trend rather than a pullback in an old bear trend. Bar 6 was about a 70 percent pullback and then the market tested the climactic bear low on the open of the next day.

Just because the market gaps up on a news item does not mean that it will continue up, despite how bullish the news is.

As shown in Figure I.3, before the open of bar 1 on both Yahoo! (YHOO) charts (daily on the left, weekly on the right), the news reported that Microsoft was

FIGURE I.3 Markets Can Fall on Bullish News

looking to take over Yahoo! at $31 a share, and the market gapped up almost to that price. Many traders assumed that it had to be a done deal because Microsoft is one of the best companies in the world and if it wanted to buy Yahoo!, it certainly could make it happen. Not only that—Microsoft has so much cash that it would likely be willing to sweeten the deal if needed. Well, the CEO of Yahoo! said that his company was worth more like $40 a share, but Microsoft never countered. The deal slowly evaporated, along with Yahoo!'s price. In October, Yahoo! was 20 percent below the price where it was before the deal was announced and 50 percent lower than on the day of the announcement, and it continues to fall. So much for strong fundamentals and a takeover offer from a serious suitor. To a price action trader, a huge up move in a bear market is probably just a bear flag, unless the move is followed by a series of higher lows and higher highs. It could be followed by a bull flag and then more of a rally, but until the bull trend is confirmed, you must be aware that the larger weekly trend is more important.

The only thing that is as it seems is the chart. If you cannot figure out what it is telling you, do not trade. Wait for clarity. It will always come. But once it is there, you must place the trade and assume the risk and follow your plan. Do not dial down to a 1 minute chart and tighten your stop, because you will lose. The problem with the 1 minute chart is that it tempts you by offering lots of entries with smaller bars and therefore smaller risk. However, you will not be able to take them all and you will instead cherry-pick, which will lead to the death of your account because you will invariably pick too many bad cherries. When you enter on a 5 minute chart, your trade is based on your analysis of the 5 minute chart without any idea of what the 1 minute chart looks like. You must therefore rely on your five-minute stops and targets, and just accept the reality that the 1 minute chart will move against you and hit a one-minute stop frequently. If you watch the 1 minute chart, you will not be devoting your full attention to the 5 minute chart and a good trader will take your money from your account and put it into his account. If you want to compete, you must minimize all distractions and all inputs other than what is on the chart in front of you, and trust that if you do you will make a lot of money. It will seem unreal but it is very real. Never question it. Just keep things simple and follow your simple rules. It is extremely difficult to consistently do something simple, but in my opinion, it is the best way to trade. Ultimately, as a trader understands price action better and better, trading becomes much less stressful and actually pretty boring, but much more profitable.

Although I never gamble (because the combination of odds, risk, and reward are against me, and I never want to bet against math), there are some similarities with gambling, especially in the minds of those who don't trade. Gambling is a game of chance, but I prefer to restrict the definition to situations where the odds are slightly against you and you will lose over time. Why this restriction? Because without it, every investment is a gamble since there is always an element of luck and a risk of total loss, even if you buy investment real estate, buy a home, start a business, buy a blue-chip stock, or even buy Treasury bonds (the government might choose to devalue the dollar to reduce the real size of our debt, and in so doing, the purchasing power of the dollars that you will get back from those bonds would be much less than when you originally bought the bonds).

Some traders use simple game theory and increase the size of a trade after one or more losing trades (this is called a martingale approach to trading). Blackjack card counters are very similar to trading range traders. The card counters are trying to determine when the math has gone too far in one direction. In particular, they want to know when the remaining cards in the deck are likely overweighed with face cards. When the count indicates that this is likely, they place a trade (bet) based on the probability that a disproportionate number of face cards will be coming up, increasing the odds of winning. Trading range traders are looking for times when they think the market has gone too far in one direction and then they place a trade in the opposite direction (a fade).

I tried playing poker online a few times without using real money to find similarities to and differences from trading. I discovered early on that there was a deal breaker for me: I was constantly anxious because of the inherent unfairness due to luck, and I never want luck to be a large component of the odds for my success. This is a huge difference and makes me see gambling and trading as fundamentally different, despite public perception. In trading, everyone is dealt the same cards so the game is always fair and, over time, you get rewarded or penalized entirely due to your skill as a trader. Obviously, sometimes you can trade correctly and lose, and this can happen several times in a row due to the probability curve of all possible outcomes. There is a real but microscopic chance that you can trade well and lose 10 or even 100 times or more in a row; but I cannot remember the last time I saw as many as four good signals fail in a row, so this is a chance that I am willing to take. If you trade well, over time you should make money because it is a zero-sum game (except for commissions, which should be small if you choose an appropriate broker). If you are better than most of the other traders, you will win their money.

There are two types of gambling that are different from pure games of chance, and both are similar to trading. In both sports betting and poker, gamblers are trying to take money from other gamblers rather than from the house, and therefore they can create odds in their favor if they are significantly better than their competitors. However, the "commissions" that they pay can be far greater than those that a trader pays, especially with sports betting, where the vig is usually 10 percent, and that is why incredibly successful sports gamblers like Billy Walters are so rare: they have to be at least 10 percent better than the competition just to break even. Successful poker players are more common, as can be seen on all of the poker shows on TV. However, even the best poker players do not make anything comparable to what the best traders make, because the practical limits to their trading size are much smaller.

I personally find trading not to be stressful, because the luck factor is so tiny that it is not worth considering. However, there is one thing that trading and playing poker share, and that is the value of patience. In poker, you stand to make far more money if you patiently wait to bet on only the very best hands, and traders make more when they have the patience to wait for the very best setups. For me, this protracted downtime is much easier in trading because I can see all of the other "cards" during the slow times, and it is intellectually stimulating to look for subtle price action phenomena.

There is an important adage in gambling that is true in all endeavors, and that is that you should not bet until you have a good hand. In trading, that is true as well. Wait for a good setup before placing a trade. If you trade without discipline and without a sound method, then you are relying on luck and hope for your profits, and your trading is unquestionably a form of gambling.

One unfortunate comparison is from nontraders who assume that all day traders, and all market traders for that matter, are addicted gamblers and therefore have a mental illness. I suspect that many are addicted, in the sense that they are doing it more for excitement than for profit. They are willing to make low-probability bets and lose large sums of money because of the huge rush they feel when they occasionally win. However, most successful traders are essentially investors, just like an investor who buys commercial real estate or a small business. The only real differences from any other type of investing are that the time frame is shorter and the leverage is greater.

Unfortunately, it is common for beginners to occasionally gamble, and it invariably costs them money. Every successful trader trades on the basis of rules. Whenever traders deviate from those rules for any reason, they are trading on hope rather than logic and are then gambling. Beginning traders often find themselves gambling right after having a couple of losses. They are eager to be made whole again and are willing to take some chances to make that happen. They will take trades that they normally would not take, because they are eager to get back the money they just lost. Since they are now taking a trade that they believe is a low-probability trade and they are taking it because of anxiety and sadness over their losses, they are now gambling and not trading. After they lose on their gamble, they feel even worse. Not only are they even further down on the day, but they feel especially sad because they are faced with the reality that they did not have the discipline to stick to their system when they know that discipline is one of the critical ingredients to success.

Interestingly, neurofinance researchers have found that brain scan images of traders about to make a trade are indistinguishable from those of drug addicts about to take a hit. They found a snowball effect and an increased desire to continue, regardless of the outcome of their behavior. Unfortunately, when faced with losses, traders assume more risk rather than less, often leading to the death of their accounts. Without knowing the neuroscience, Warren Buffett clearly understood the problem, as seen in his statement, "Once you have ordinary intelligence, what you need is the temperament to control the urges that get other people into trouble in investing." The great traders control their emotions and constantly follow their rules.

One final point about gambling: There is a natural tendency to assume that nothing can last forever and that every behavior regresses toward a mean. If the market has three or four losing trades, surely the odds favor the next one being a winner. It's just like flipping a coin, isn't it? Unfortunately, that is not how markets behave. When a market is trending, most attempts to reverse fail. When it is in a trading range, most attempts to break out fail. This is the opposite of coin flips, where the odds are always 50–50. In trading, the odds are more like 70 percent or better that what just happened will continue to happen again and again. Because of the coin flip logic, most traders at some point begin to consider game theory.

Martingale techniques work well in theory but not in practice because of the conflict between math and emotion. That is the martingale paradox. If you double (or even triple) your position size and reverse at each loss, you will theoretically make money. Although four losers in a row is uncommon on the 5 minute Emini chart if you choose your trades carefully, they will happen, and so will a dozen or more, even though I can't remember ever seeing that. In any case, if you are comfortable trading 10 contracts, but start with just one and plan to double up and reverse with each loss, four consecutive losers would require 16 contracts on your next trade and eight consecutive losers would require 256 contracts! It is unlikely that you would place a trade that is larger than your comfort zone following four or more losers. Anyone willing to trade one contract initially would never be willing to trade 16 or 256 contracts, and anyone willing to trade 256 contracts would never be willing to initiate this strategy with just one. This is the inherent, insurmountable, mathematical problem with this approach.

Since trading is fun and competitive, it is natural for people to compare it to games, and because wagering is involved, gambling is usually the first thing that comes to mind. However, a far more apt analogy is to chess. In chess, you can see exactly what your opponent is doing, unlike in card games where you don't know your opponent's cards. Also, in poker, the cards that you are dealt are yours purely by chance, but in chess, the location of your pieces is entirely due to your decisions. In chess nothing is hidden and it is simply your skill compared to that of your opponent that determines the outcome. Your ability to read what is in front of you and determine what will likely follow is a great asset both to a chess player and to a trader.

Laypeople are also concerned about the possibility of crashes, and because of that risk, they again associate trading with gambling. Crashes are very rare events on daily charts. These nontraders are afraid of their inability to function effectively during extremely emotional events. Although the term *crash* is generally reserved for daily charts and applied to bear markets of about 20 percent or more happening in a short time frame, like in 1927 and 1987, it is more useful to think of it as just another chart pattern because that removes the emotion and helps traders follow their rules. If you remove the time and price axes from a chart and focus simply on the price action, there are market movements that occur frequently on intraday charts that are indistinguishable from the patterns in a classic crash. If you can get past the emotion, you can make money off crashes, because with all charts, they display tradable price action.

Figure I.4 (from TradeStation) shows how markets can crash in any time frame. The one on the left is a daily chart of GE during the 1987 crash, the middle is a 5 minute chart of COST after a very strong earnings report, and the one on the right is a 1 minute Emini chart. Although the term *crash* is used almost exclusively to refer to a 20 percent or more sell-off over a short time on a daily chart and was widely used only twice in the past hundred years, a price action trader looks for shape, and the same crash pattern is common on intraday charts. Since crashes are so common intraday, there is no need to apply the term, because from a trading perspective they are just a bear swing with tradable price action.

Created with TradeStation

FIGURE I.4 Crashes Are Common

Incidentally, the concept that the same patterns appear on all time frames means that the principles of fractal mathematics might be useful in designing trading systems. In other words, every pattern subdivides into standard price action patterns in smaller time frame charts, and trading decisions based on price action analysis therefore work in all time frames.

HOW TO READ THESE BOOKS

I tried to group the material in the three books in a sequence that should be helpful to traders.

Book 1: *Trading Price Action Trends: Technical Analysis of Price Charts Bar by Bar for the Serious Trader*
- *The basics of price action and candles.* The market is either trending or in a trading range. That is true of every time frame down to even an individual bar, which can be a trend bar or a nontrend bar (doji).
- *Trend lines and trend channel lines.* These are basic tools that can be used to highlight the existence of trends and trading ranges.
- *Trends.* These are the most conspicuous and profitable components of every chart.

Book 2: *Trading Price Action Trading Ranges: Technical Analysis of Price Charts Bar by Bar for the Serious Trader*

- *Breakouts.* These are transitions from trading ranges into trends.
- *Gaps.* Breakouts often create several types of intraday gaps that can be helpful to traders, but these gaps are evident only if you use a broad definition.
- *Magnets, support, and resistance.* Once the market breaks out and begins its move, it is often drawn to certain prices, and these magnets often set up reversals.
- *Pullbacks.* These are transitions from trends to temporary trading ranges.
- *Trading ranges.* These are areas of largely sideways price activity, but each leg is a small trend and an entire trading range is usually a pullback in a trend on a higher time frame chart.
- *Order and trade management.* Traders need as many tools as possible and need to understand scalping, swing trading, and scaling into and out of trades, as well as how to enter and exit on stops and limit orders.
- *The mathematics of trading.* There is a mathematical basis for all trading, and when you see why things are unfolding the way they do, trading becomes much less stressful.

Book 3: *Trading Price Action Reversals: Technical Analysis of Price Charts Bar by Bar for the Serious Trader*

- *Trend reversals.* These offer the best risk/reward ratios of any type of trade, but since most fail, traders need to be selective.
- *Day trading.* Now that readers understand price action, they can use it to trade. The chapters on day trading, trading the first hour, and detailed examples show how.
- *Daily, weekly, and monthly charts.* These charts have very reliable price action setups.
- *Options.* Price action can be used effectively in option trading.
- *Best trades.* Some price action setups are especially good, and beginners should focus on these.
- *Guidelines.* There are many important concepts that can help keep traders focused.

If you come across an unfamiliar term, you should be able to find its definition in the List of Terms at the beginning of the book.

Some books show charts that use the time zone of the location of the market, but now that trading is electronic and global, that is no longer relevant. Since I trade in California, the charts are in Pacific standard time (PST). All of the charts were created with TradeStation. Since every chart has dozens of noteworthy price action events that have not yet been covered, I describe many of them immediately after the primary discussion under "Deeper Discussion of This Chart." Even though you might find this incomprehensible when you first read it, you will understand it on a second reading of the books. The more variations of standard patterns that you see, the better you will be able to spot them as they are developing in real time. I also usually point out the major one or two trades on the chart. If you prefer, you can ignore that supplemental discussion on your first read and then look at the charts again after completing the books when the deeper discussion would be understandable. Since many of the setups are excellent examples of important concepts, even though not yet covered, many readers will appreciate having the discussion if they go through the books again.

At the time of publication, I am posting a daily end-of-day analysis of the Emini and providing real-time chart reading during the trading day at www.brookspriceaction.com.

All of the charts in the three books will be in a larger format on John Wiley & Sons' site at www.wiley.com/go/tradingtrends. (See the "About the Website" page at the back of the book.) You will be able to zoom in to see the details, download the charts, or print them. Having a printout of a chart when the description is several pages long will make it easier to follow the commentary.

SIGNS OF STRENGTH: TRENDS, BREAKOUTS, REVERSAL BARS, AND REVERSALS

Here are some characteristics that are commonly found in strong trends:

- There is a big gap opening on the day.
- There are trending highs and lows (swings).
- Most of the bars are trend bars in the direction of the trend.
- There is very little overlap of the bodies of consecutive bars. For example, in a bull spike, many bars have lows that are at or just one tick below the closes of the prior bar. Some bars have lows that are at and not below the close of the prior bar, so traders trying to buy on a limit order at the close of the prior bar do not get their orders filled and they have to buy higher.
- There are bars with no tails or small tails in either direction, indicating urgency. For example, in a bull trend, if a bull trend bar opens on its low tick and trends up, traders were eager to buy it as soon as the prior bar closed. If it closes on or near its high tick, traders continued their strong buying in anticipation of new buyers entering right after the bar closes. They were willing to buy going into the close because they were afraid that if they waited for the bar to close, they might have to buy a tick or two higher.

- Occasionally, there are gaps between the bodies (for example, the open of a bar might be above the close of the prior bar in a bull trend).
- A breakout gap appears in the form of a strong trend bar at the start of the trend.
- Measuring gaps occur where the breakout test does not overlap the breakout point. For example, the pullback from a bull breakout does not drop below the high of the bar where the breakout occurred.
- Micro measuring gaps appear where there is a strong trend bar and a gap between the bar before it and the bar after it. For example, if the low of the bar after a strong bull trend bar in a bull trend is at or above the high of the bar before the trend bar, this is a gap and a breakout test and a sign of strength.
- No big climaxes appear.
- Not many large bars appear (not even large trend bars). Often, the largest trend bars are countertrend, trapping traders into looking for countertrend trades and missing with-trend trades. The countertrend setups almost always look better than the with-trend setups.
- No significant trend channel line overshoots occur, and the minor ones result in only sideways corrections.
- There are sideways corrections after trend line breaks.
- Failed wedges and other failed reversals occur.
- There is a sequence of 20 moving average gap bars (20 or more consecutive bars that do not touch the moving average, discussed in book 2).
- Few if any profitable countertrend trades are found.
- There are small, infrequent, and mostly sideways pullbacks. For example, if the Emini's average range is 12 points, the pullbacks will all likely be less than three or four points, and the market will often go for five or more bars without a pullback.
- There is a sense of urgency. You find yourself waiting through countless bars for a good with-trend pullback and one never comes, yet the market slowly continues to trend.
- The pullbacks have strong setups. For example, the high 1 and high 2 pullbacks in a bull trend have strong bull reversal bars for signal bars.
- In the strongest trends, the pullbacks usually have weak signal bars, making many traders not take them, and forcing traders to chase the market. For example, in a bear trend the signal bars for a low 2 short are often small bull bars in two or three bar bull spikes, and some of the entry bars are outside down bars. It has trending "anything": closes, highs, lows, or bodies.
- Repeated two-legged pullbacks are setting up with trend entries.
- No two consecutive trend bar closes occur on the opposite side of the moving average.

- The trend goes very far and breaks several resistance levels, like the moving average, prior swing highs, and trend lines, and each by many ticks.
- Reversal attempts in the form of spikes against the trend have no follow-through, fail, and become flags in the direction of the trend.

The more of the following characteristics that a bull breakout has, the more likely the breakout will be strong:

- The breakout bar has a large bull trend body and small tails or no tails. The larger the bar, the more likely the breakout will succeed.
- If the volume of the large breakout bar is 10 to 20 times the average volume of recent bars, the chance of follow-through buying and a possible measured move increases.
- The spike goes very far, lasts several bars, and breaks several resistance levels, like the moving average, prior swing highs, and trend lines, and each by many ticks.
- As the first bar of the breakout bar is forming, it spends most of its time near its high and the pullbacks are small (less than a quarter of the height of the growing bar).
- There is a sense of urgency. You feel like you have to buy but you want a pullback, yet it never comes.
- The next two or three bars also have bull bodies that are at least the average size of the recent bull and bear bodies. Even if the bodies are relatively small and the tails are prominent, if the follow-through bar (the bar after the initial breakout bar) is large, the odds of the trend continuing are greater.
- The spike grows to five to 10 bars without pulling back for more than a bar or so.
- One or more bars in the spike have a low that is at or just one tick below the close of the prior bar.
- One or more bars in the spike have an open that is above the close of the prior bar.
- One or more bars in the spike have a close on the bar's high or just one tick below its high.
- The low of the bar after a bull trend bar is at or above the high of the bar before the bull trend bar, creating a micro gap, which is a sign of strength. These gaps sometimes become measuring gaps. Although it is not significant to trading, according to Elliott Wave Theory they probably represent the space between a smaller time frame Elliott Wave 1 high and a Wave 4 pullback, which can touch but not overlap.

- The overall context makes a breakout likely, like the resumption of a trend after a pullback, or a higher low or lower low test of the bear low after a strong break above the bear trend line.
- The market has had several strong bull trend days recently.
- There is growing buying pressure in the trading range, represented by many large bull trend bars, and the bull trend bars are clearly more prominent than the bear trend bars in the range.
- The first pullback occurs only after three or more bars of breaking out.
- The first pullback lasts only one or two bars, and it follows a bar that is not a strong bear reversal bar.
- The first pullback does not reach the breakout point and does not hit a breakeven stop (the entry price).
- The breakout reverses many recent closes and highs. For example, when there is a bear channel and a large bull bar forms, this breakout bar has a high and close that are above the highs and closes of five or even 20 or more bars. A large number of bars reversed by the close of the bull bar is a stronger sign than a similar number of bars reversed by the high.

The more of the following characteristics that a bear breakout has, the more likely the breakout will be strong:

- The breakout bar has a large bear trend body and small tails or no tails. The larger the bar, the more likely the breakout will succeed.
- If the volume of the large breakout bar is 10 to 20 times the average volume of recent bars, the chance of follow-through selling and a possible measured move down increases.
- The spike goes very far, lasts several bars, and breaks several support levels like the moving average, prior swing lows, and trend lines, and each by many ticks.
- As the first bar of the breakout bar is forming, it spends most of its time near its low and the pullbacks are small (less than a quarter of the height of the growing bar).
- There is a sense of urgency. You feel like you have to sell but you want a pull-back, yet it never comes.
- The next two or three bars also have bear bodies that are at least the average size of the recent bull and bear bodies. Even if the bodies are relatively small and the tails are prominent, if the follow-through bar (the bar after the initial breakout bar) is large, the odds of the trend continuing are greater.
- The spike grows to five to 10 bars without pulling back for more than a bar or so.

- As a bear breakout goes below a prior significant swing low, the move below the low goes far enough for a scalper to make a profit if he entered on a stop at one tick below that swing low.
- One or more bars in the spike has a high that is at or just one tick above the close of the prior bar.
- One or more bars in the spike has an open that is below the close of the prior bar.
- One or more bars in the spike has a close on its low or just one tick above its low.
- The high of the bar after a bear trend bar is at or below the low of the bar before the bear trend bar, creating a micro gap, which is a sign of strength. These gaps sometimes become measuring gaps. Although it is not significant to trading, they probably represent the space between a smaller time frame Elliott wave 1 low and a wave 4 pullback, which can touch but not overlap.
- The overall context makes a breakout likely, like the resumption of a trend after a pullback, or a lower high or higher high test of the bull high after a strong break below the bull trend line.
- The market has had several strong bear trend days recently.
- There was growing selling pressure in the trading range, represented by many large bear trend bars, and the bear trend bars were clearly more prominent than the bull trend bars in the range.
- The first pullback occurs only after three or more bars of breaking out.
- The first pullback lasts only one or two bars and it follows a bar that is not a strong bull reversal bar.
- The first pullback does not reach the breakout point and does not hit a breakeven stop (the entry price).
- The breakout reverses many recent closes and lows. For example, when there is a bull channel and a large bear bar forms, this breakout bar has a low and close that are below the lows and closes of five or even 20 or more bars. A large number of bars reversed by the close of the bear bar is a stronger sign than a similar number of bars reversed by its low.

The best-known signal bar is the reversal bar and the minimum that a bull reversal bar should have is either a close above its open (a bull body) or a close above its midpoint. The best bull reversal bars have more than one of the following:

- An open near or below the close of the prior bar and a close above the open and above the prior bar's close.
- A lower tail that is about one-third to one-half the height of the bar and a small or nonexistent upper tail.
- Not much overlap with the prior bar or bars.

- The bar after the signal bar is not a doji inside bar and instead is a strong entry bar (a bull trend bar with a relatively large body and small tails).
- A close that reverses (closes above) the closes and highs of more than one bar.

The minimum that a bear reversal bar should have is either a close below its open (a bear body) or a close below its midpoint. The best bear reversal bars have:

- An open near or above the close of the prior bar and a close well below the prior bar's close.
- An upper tail that is about one-third to one-half the height of the bar and a small or nonexistent lower tail.
- Not much overlap with the prior bar or bars.
- The bar after the signal bar is not a doji inside bar and instead is a strong entry bar (a bear trend bar with a relatively large body and small tails).
- A close that reverses (closes below) the closes and extremes of more than one bar.

Here are a number of characteristics that are common in strong bull reversals:

- There is a strong bull reversal bar with a large bull trend body and small tails or no tails.
- The next two or three bars also have bull bodies that are at least the average size of the recent bull and bear bodies.
- The spike grows to five to 10 bars without pulling back for more than a bar or so, and it reverses many bars, swing highs, and bear flags of the prior bear trend.
- One or more bars in the spike have a low that is at or just one tick below the close of the prior bar.
- One or more bars in the spike have an open that is above the close of the prior bar.
- One or more bars in the spike have a close on the high of the bar or just one tick below its high.
- The overall context makes a reversal likely, like a higher low or lower low test of the bear low after a strong break above the bear trend line.
- The first pullback occurs only after three or more bars.
- The first pullback lasts only one or two bars, and it follows a bar that is not a strong bear reversal bar.
- The first pullback does not hit a breakeven stop (the entry price).
- The spike goes very far and breaks several resistance levels like the moving average, prior swing highs, and trend lines, and each by many ticks.

- As the first bar of the reversal is forming, it spends most of its time near its high and the pullbacks are less than a quarter of the height of the growing bar.
- There is a sense of urgency. You feel like you have to buy but you want a pullback, yet it never comes.
- The signal is the second attempt to reverse within the past few bars (a second signal).
- The reversal began as a reversal from an overshoot of a trend channel line from the old trend.
- It is reversing a significant swing high or low (e.g., it breaks below a strong prior swing low and reverses up).
- The high 1 and high 2 pullbacks have strong bull reversal bars for signal bars.
- It has trending "anything": closes, highs, lows, or bodies.
- The pullbacks are small and sideways.
- There were prior breaks of earlier bear trend lines (this isn't the first sign of bullish strength).
- The pullback to test the bear low lacks momentum, as evidenced by its having many overlapping bars with many being bull trend bars.
- The pullback that tests the bear low fails at the moving average or the old bear trend line.
- The breakout reverses many recent closes and highs. For example, when there is a bear channel and a large bull bar forms, this breakout bar has a high and close that are above the highs and closes of five or even 20 or more bars. A large number of bars reversed by the close of the bull bar is a stronger sign than a similar number of bars reversed by only its high.

Here are a number of characteristics that are common in strong bear reversals:

- A strong bear reversal bar with a large bear trend body and small tails or no tails.
- The next two or three bars also have bear bodies that are at least the average size of the recent bull and bear bodies.
- The spike grows to five to 10 bars without pulling back for more than a bar or so, and it reverses many bars, swing lows, and bull flags of the prior bull trend.
- One or more bars in the spike has a high that is at or just one tick above the close of the prior bar.
- One or more bars in the spike has an open that is below the close of the prior bar.
- One or more bars in the spike has a close on its low or just one tick above its low.
- The overall context makes a reversal likely, like a lower high or higher high test of the bull high after a strong break below the bull trend line.

- The first pullback occurs only after three or more bars.
- The first pullback lasts only one or two bars and it follows a bar that is not a strong bull reversal bar.
- The first pullback does not hit a breakeven stop (the entry price).
- The spike goes very far and breaks several support levels like the moving average, prior swing lows, and trend lines, and each by many ticks.
- As the first bar of the reversal is forming, it spends most of its time near its low and the pullbacks are less than a quarter of the height of the growing bar.
- There is a sense of urgency. You feel like you have to sell, but you want a pullback, yet it never comes.
- The signal is the second attempt to reverse within the past few bars (a second signal).
- The reversal began as a reversal from an overshoot of a trend channel line from the old trend.
- It is reversing at a significant swing high or low area (e.g., breaks above a strong prior swing high and reverses down).
- The low 1 and low 2 pullbacks have strong bear reversal bars for signal bars.
- It has trending "anything": closes, highs, lows, or bodies.
- The pullbacks are small and sideways.
- There were prior breaks of earlier bull trend lines (this isn't the first sign of bearish strength).
- The pullback to test the bull high lacks momentum, as evidenced by it having many overlapping bars with many being bear trend bars.
- The pullback that tests the bull high fails at the moving average or the old bull trend line.
- The breakout reverses many recent closes and lows. For example, when there is a bull channel and a large bear bar forms, this breakout bar has a low and close that are below the lows and closes of five or even 20 or more bars. A large number of bars reversed by the close of the bear bar is a stronger sign than a similar number of bars reversed by only its low.

BAR COUNTING BASICS: HIGH 1, HIGH 2, LOW 1, LOW 2

A reliable sign that a pullback in a bull trend or in a trading range has ended is when the current bar's high extends at least one tick above the high of the prior bar. This leads to a useful concept of counting the number of times that this occurs, which is called bar counting. In a sideways or downward move in a bull trend or a trading range, the first bar whose high is above the high of the prior bar is a high 1, and this ends the first leg of the sideways or down move, although this leg may become a small leg in a larger pullback. If the market does not turn into a bull swing and instead continues sideways or down, label the next occurrence of a bar with a high above the high of the prior bar as a high 2, ending the second leg.

A high 2 in a bull trend and a low 2 in a bear trend are often referred to as ABC corrections where the first leg is the A, the change in direction that forms the high 1 or low 1 entry is the B, and the final leg of the pullback is the C. The breakout from the C is a high 2 entry bar in a bull ABC correction and a low 2 entry bar in a bear ABC correction.

If the bull pullback ends after a third leg, the buy setup is a high 3 and is usually a type of wedge bull flag. When a bear rally ends in a third leg, it is a low 3 sell setup and usually a wedge bear flag.

Some bull pullbacks can grow further and form a high 4. When a high 4 forms, it sometimes begins with a high 2 and this high 2 fails to go very far. It is instead followed by another two legs down and a second high 2, and the entire move is simply a high 2 in a higher time frame. At other times, the high 4 is a small spike and channel bear trend where the first or second push down is a bear spike and the next pushes down are in a bear channel. If the high 4 fails to resume the trend and the market falls below its low, it is likely that the market is no longer forming a pullback in a bull trend and instead is in a bear swing. Wait for more price action to unfold before placing a trade.

When a bear trend or a sideways market is correcting sideways or up, the first bar with a low below the low of the prior bar is a low 1, ending the first leg of the correction, which can be as brief as that single bar. Subsequent occurrences are called the low 2, low 3, and low 4 entries. If the low 4 fails (a bar extends above the high of the low 4 signal bar after the low 4 short is triggered), the price action indicates that the bears have lost control and either the market will become two-sided, with bulls and bears alternating control, or the bulls will gain control. In any case, the bears can best demonstrate that they have regained control by breaking a bull trend line with strong momentum.

PART I

Price Action

The most useful definition of price action for a trader is also the simplest: it is any change in price on any type of chart or time frame. The smallest unit of change is the tick, which has a different value for each market. Incidentally, a tick has two meanings. It is the smallest unit of change in price that a market can make, which for most stocks is a penny. It is also every trade that takes place during the day, so each entry on a time and sales table is a tick, even if it is at the same price as the prior trade. Every time the price changes, that change is an example of price action. There is no universally accepted definition of price action, and since you always need to try to be aware of even the seemingly least significant piece of information that the market is offering, you must have a very broad definition. You cannot dismiss anything, because very often something that initially appears minor leads to a great trade.

The definition alone does not tell you anything about placing a trade, because every bar is a potential signal both for a short and for a long trade. There are traders out there who will be looking to short the next tick because they believe that the market won't go one tick higher and others who will buy it believing that the market will likely not go one tick lower. They might be looking at the same chart and one trader sees a bullish pattern and the other thinks there is a bearish pattern that is stronger. They might be relying on fundamental data or any of a thousand other reasons for their opinions. One side will be right and the other will be wrong. If the buyers are wrong and the market goes one tick lower and then another and then another, they will begin to entertain the prospect that their belief is wrong. At some point, they will have to sell their positions at a loss, making them new sellers and no longer buyers, and this will drive the market down further. Sellers will continue to enter the market either as new shorts or as longs forced to liquidate until some point when more buyers start coming in. These buyers will be a combination of new buyers, profit-taking shorts, and new shorts who now have a loss and will have to buy to cover their positions. The market will continue up until the process reverses once again.

For traders, the fundamental issue that confronts them repeatedly throughout the day is the decision about whether the market is trending or not trending. Even if they are looking at a single bar, they are deciding if the market is trending or not trending during that bar. Is that bar a trend bar, opening near one end and closing near the other, or is it a trading range bar with a small body and one or two large tails? If they are looking at a collection of bars, they are trying to decide if the market is trending or it is in a trading range. For example, if it is trending up, they will look to buy high or low, even on a breakout of the top of the move, whereas if it is in a trading range, they are only looking to buy at the bottom of the range and they want to sell instead of buy at the top of the range. If it is in any traditional pattern like a triangle or a head and shoulders top or bottom, it is in a trading range. Calling it one of those terms is not helpful because all that matters is whether the market is trending, and not whether they can spot some common pattern and give it a label. Their goal is to make money, and the single most important piece of information that they can discern is whether the market is trending. If it is trending, they assume that the trend will continue and they will look to enter in the direction of the trend (*with trend*). If it is not trending, they will look to enter in the opposite direction of the most recent move (*fade* or *countertrend*). A trend can be as short as a single bar (on a smaller time frame, there can be a strong trend contained within that bar) or, on a 5 minute chart, it can last a day or more. How do they make this decision? They do so by reading the price action on the chart in front of them.

It is important to understand that most of the time there is a 50 percent chance that the next tick will be up and a 50 percent chance that it will be down. In fact, during most of the trading day, you can expect that the market has a 50–50 chance of moving up X points before falling X points. The odds drift to maybe 60–40 at times during the day, and these brief times offer good trading opportunities. However, the market then quickly gets back to uncertainty and a 50–50 market where the bulls and bears are mostly in balance.

With so many traders trading and using countless approaches, the market is very efficient. For example, if you bought at the market at any point during the day without even looking at a chart, and placed a profit target 10 ticks higher and a one cancels the other (OCO) protective stop 10 ticks lower, you have a 50 percent chance of making a profit. If instead you sold originally and again used a 10-tick stop and profit target, you would still have a 50–50 chance of making 10 ticks on your short before losing 10 ticks on your protective stop. The odds are the same if you picked 20 or 30 ticks or any value for X. There are obvious exceptions, like if you pick a very large value for X, but if your value for X is reasonable based on the recent price action, the rule is fairly accurate.

During the spike phase of a strong trend, the probability may be 70 percent or more that the trend will continue over the next few bars, but this happens only briefly and rarely more than once or twice a day. In general, as a strong breakout trend move is forming, if you choose a value for X that is less than the height of the current breakout, the probability is 60 percent or better that you will be able to exit with X ticks' profit before a protective stop X ticks away is hit. So if a bull breakout has gone four points (16 ticks) so far and is very strong and you pick a value of eight for X, then you probably have about a 60 percent chance of being able to exit with eight ticks' profit before an eight-tick protective stop is hit.

Because of the inherent high level of uncertainty, I often use words like *usually*, *likely*, and *probably* to describe what I think will follow in at least 60 percent of cases. This can be frustrating to readers, but if you are going to make a living as a trader, this is as good as it gets. Nothing is ever close to certain, and you are always operating in a gray fog. The best trades that you will ever see will always be described by uncertain words like these because they are the most accurate descriptions of the reality that traders face.

Everything is relative and everything can change to the exact opposite in an instant, even without any movement in price. It might be that you suddenly see a trend line seven ticks above the high of the current bar and instead of looking to short, you now are looking to buy for a test of the trend line. Trading through the rearview mirror is a sure way to lose money. You have to keep looking ahead, not worrying about the mistakes you just made. They have absolutely no bearing on the next tick, so you must ignore them and just keep reassessing the price action and not your profit and loss (P&L) on the day.

Each tick changes the price action of every time frame chart, from a tick chart or 1 minute chart through a monthly chart, and on all other types of charts, whether the chart is based on time, volume, the number of ticks, point and figure, or anything else. Obviously, a single tick move is usually meaningless on a monthly chart (unless, for example, it is a one-tick breakout of some chart point that immediately reverses), but it becomes increasingly more useful on smaller time frame charts. This is obviously true because if the average bar on a 1 minute Emini chart is three ticks tall, then a one-tick move is 33 percent of the size of the average bar, and that can represent a significant move.

The most useful aspect of price action is what happens after the market moves beyond (*breaks out* beyond) prior bars or trend lines on the chart. For example, if the market goes above a significant prior high and each subsequent bar forms a low that is above the prior bar's low and a high that is above the prior bar's high, then this price action indicates that the market will likely be higher on some subsequent bar, even if it pulls back for a few bars in the near term. However, if the market breaks out to the upside and then the next bar is a small inside bar (its high is not higher than that of the large breakout bar) and then the following bar has a low that is below this small bar, the odds of a failed breakout and a reversal back down increase considerably.

Small patterns evolve into larger patterns that can lead to trades in the same or opposite direction. For example, it is common for the market to break out of a small flag to reach a scalper's profit and then pull back, and the pattern then evolves into a larger flag. This larger flag might also break out in the same direction, but it might instead break out in the opposite direction. Also, a pattern often can be seen to be several different things at the same time. For example, a small lower high might be the second lower high of a larger triangle, and a second right shoulder of an even larger head and shoulders top. The name that you apply is irrelevant since the direction of the subsequent move will be the same if you read the bars correctly. In trading ranges, it is common to see opposite patterns setting up at the same time, like a small bear flag and a larger bull flag. It does not matter which pattern you trade or what name you use to describe it. All that matters is your read of the price action, and if you read well, you will trade well. You will take the setup that makes the most sense, and if you are not fairly certain, you will wait until you are.

Over time, fundamentals control the price of a stock, and that price is set by institutional traders, who are by far the biggest volume players among the traders who are trading for the long term; high-frequency trading (HFT) firms trade larger volume but are intraday scalpers and probably do not significantly affect the direction on the daily charts. Price action is the movement that takes place along the way as institutions probe for value. The high of every bar on every time frame is at some resistance level; the low of every bar is at support; and the close is where it is and not one tick higher or lower, because computers put it there for a reason. The support and resistance may not be obvious, but since computers control everything and they use logic, everything has to make sense, even if it is often difficult to understand. Short-term computer algorithms and the news determine the path and speed, but the fundamentals determine the destination, and an increasing amount of the fundamental analysis is being done by computers as well. When the institutions feel that the price is too high, they will exit or short, and when they feel it is too low (a good value), they will buy. Although conspiracy theorists will never believe it, institutions do not have secret meetings to vote on what the price should be in an attempt to steal money from unsuspecting, well-intentioned individual traders. Their voting is essentially independent and secret and comes in the form of their buying and selling, but the results are displayed on price charts. They can never hide what they are doing. For example, if enough of them are buying, you will see the market going up, and you should look for ways to get long. In the short run, an institution can manipulate the price of a stock, especially if it is thinly traded. However, institutions would make much less money doing that compared to what they could make in other forms of trading, and they don't want to waste their time on small profits. This makes the concern of manipulation of negligible importance, especially in stocks and markets where huge volume is traded, like the Eminis, major stocks, debt instruments, and currencies.

Each institution is operating independently of the others, and none knows what any other is doing. In fact, large institutions have many traders competing against one another; often they are on different sides of a trade without realizing it, and they don't care. Each trader is following his own system and is not interested in what some guy on the ninth floor is doing. Also, every move on the chart is a composite based on the total dollars traded; each trader is motivated by different factors, and there are traders trading on every time frame. Many traders are not even using charts and instead are trading off fundamentals. When I say that the market does something for a reason, it never does something for only one reason. Whatever reason I am giving is just one of the countless reasons behind the move, and I point to that one reason to give some insight into what some of the major traders are doing. For example, if the market gaps up a little on the open, falls quickly to the moving average, and then rallies for the rest of the day, I might say that the institutions wanted to buy lower and were on the sidelines until the market fell to an area of support and then they believed it was likely not to go lower. At that point, they bought heavily. In fact, that might be the logic used by some institutional traders, but others will have countless other reasons for buying at that price level and many of those reasons will have nothing to do with the chart in front of you.

When I look at a chart, I am constantly thinking about the bullish case and the bearish case with every tick, every bar, and every swing. During most of the day, the chance of making a certain number of ticks on a trade is just about the same as the chance of losing the same number. This is because the market is always searching for value and balance and spends most of the day with both bulls and bears feeling comfortable taking positions. Sometimes the odds might be 60–40 in favor of one direction, and in very strong trends the odds can briefly be 80–20 or even higher, but after most ticks during the day, the odds are about 50–50 and uncertainty, value, and balance prevail. Alan Greenspan said that as Fed chairman he was right about 70 percent of the time. This is very revealing because he had so much influence over whether he was right, yet he could only get his winning percentage up to 70. If you make money on 70 percent of your trades where you can never trade large enough volume to increase your chances of success, you are doing extremely well.

Whenever a pundit on television says with certainty that the market is going up and then castigates another panelist with an ad hominem attack, you know that the person is a fool. His arrogance indicates that he believes that his ability to predict is at least 90 percent, but if that were true, he would be so rich that he would not bother being on television. Because most scalps are only about 60 percent certain, that other 40 percent possibility warrants a lot of respect. You should always have a plan in case the opposite happens, since it will happen often. Usually, it is better to get out, but sometimes it is better to reverse. It is always most important to be aware that the exact opposite of what you believe will happen in about 40 percent of your trades. It is worth noting that some traders are so good at reading charts and placing and managing trades that they can win as much as 90 percent of the time, but those traders are rare.

Television analysts always have impressive titles, make very convincing arguments, look impressive, sound professorial, and appear to be dedicating their lives to helping you. However, it is all a sham and you should never forget that it is just television. The purpose of television is to make money for the corporations that own the shows and the networks. The shareholders of those companies are not concerned at all about whether you make money from trade recommendations on the shows. The networks choose analysts based on ratings. They want people who will attract viewers so that they can sell advertising. They invariably choose charismatic people who look so sincere and concerned about your financial well-being that you feel compelled to watch and trust them. And they might be sincere, but that does not mean that they can help you. In fact, they can only hurt you by misleading you into believing that they can solve your financial problems and alleviate the stress that you are feeling as you try to care for your family. They are selling false hope and it is for their benefit, not yours. Remember, no one ever got rich from watching television.

Many television analysts make trade recommendations based on their fundamental analysis, and then describe the trade in technical terms. This is particularly true of forex traders. They will isolate an event, like an upcoming central bank meeting for some country, predict what the outcome will be, and recommend a trade based on that expected outcome. When they describe their trade, they will invariably make it clear that the trade is entirely technical and has nothing to do with the fundamentals. For example, if the EUR/USD is in a bull trend, they will invariably conclude that the meeting will make the Euro stronger against the dollar and recommend buying a pullback, placing a protective stop below the most recent swing low, and going for a profit target that is about twice as large as the stop. No one needs to know anything about that meeting to place that trade. They are simply recommending buying a pullback in a bull trend, and the trade has nothing to do with their analysis or the upcoming meeting. The people who actually influence the direction of the market because of their huge volume, like governments and banks, know far more about the upcoming meeting and the effect any announcement might have, and that is already reflected in the price. Also, these institutions are concerned about many variables that have nothing to do with the meeting. These television pundits are simply trying to impress listeners with their tremendous intellectual capacity to analyze the fundamentals. They want to see themselves as especially bright and insightful. The reality is that they are enjoying pretending to be experts, but are talking nonsense. Their predictive ability based on the fundamentals is pure guesswork and has a 50 percent probability of being correct. Their technical analysis, however, is sound, and if the trade is successful, it is entirely due to their chart reading and in no way related to their fundamental analysis. Stock pundits also regularly make absurd interpretations of the fundamentals, like telling listeners to buy GS tomorrow, even though it has been in a bear trend for six months, because its CEO is strong and he will take action to make end the bear. Well, that CEO was there last week, last month, and six months ago, yet GS has been falling relentlessly! Why should it start to rally tomorrow or over the coming weeks? There is no fundamental reason at all, despite the professorial proclamation by the carnival barker on television whose job is to sell advertising, not to help you make money. Another pundit might recommend ADM or POT because Africa is developing quickly, and the improved quality of life of Africans will create demand for agricultural products. Well, it was growing quickly last month and six months ago, and nothing is different today. Whenever you hear a pundit make a recommendation based on what he proudly considers to be his profound insight, it is far better to assume that he is a fool and is on television only to entertain in order to earn advertising dollars for the network. Instead, simply look at the chart. If the market is going up, look to buy. If it is going down, look to sell. These television analysts always make it sound as if their single piece of fundamental information will control the direction of the market. Markets are far more complex and move for hundreds of reasons, most of which the television analyst has no way of knowing. The fundamentals are already reflected in the price action, and all you have to do is look at the chart to understand how the institutions, who are far smarter than the clown on television and who trade enough dollars to control the direction of the market, view the fundamentals. They analyze all of the data, not just one small piece, and they base their trades on thorough mathematical analysis, not some whimsical, simplistic sound bite. Follow them, not the pundit on television. They will clearly show you what they believe, and they cannot hide it. It is on the chart in front of you. Incidentally, fundamental analysis is basically a form of technical analysis because fundamental traders are making their decisions based on charts. However, their charts are of earnings growth, debt growth, revenue, profit margins, and many other factors. They study momentum, slope, and trend lines so they are really technicians but do not see themselves that way, and many don't trust the technical analysis of price alone.

Why does price move up one tick? It is because there is more volume being bid at the current price than being offered, and a number of those buyers are willing to pay even more than the current price, if necessary, to get their orders filled. This is sometimes described as the market having more buyers than sellers, or as the buyers being in control, or as buying pressure. Once all of those buy orders that can possibly be filled are filled at the current price (the last price traded), the remaining buyers will have to decide whether they are willing to buy at one tick higher. If they are, they will continue to bid at the higher price. This higher price will make all market participants reevaluate their perspective on the market. If there continues to be more volume being bid than offered, price will continue to move up since there is an insufficient number of contracts being offered by sellers at the last price to fill the orders of the buyers. At some point, buyers will start offering some of their contracts as they take partial profits. Also, sellers will perceive the current price as a good value for a short and offer to sell more than buyers want to buy. Once there are more contracts being offered by sellers (either buyers who are looking to cover some or all of their long contracts or new sellers who are attempting to short), all of the buy orders will be filled at the current price but some sellers will be unable to find enough buyers. The bid will move down a tick. If there are sellers willing to sell at this lower price, this will become the new last price.

Because volume controls the direction of the market, beginning traders invariably wonder if market depth can give them an edge in their trading. If they are placing their trades on a price ladder, they can see the volume at every tick for several ticks above and below the current price. They think that since the information is there, there must be some way to use it to get an edge. They forget that the market is controlled by computer algorithms, and the programmers are also after every imaginable edge. When the game centers on quickly processing a lot of information in a fraction of a second in an attempt to make one or two ticks a thousand times a day with just a 55 percent success rate, an individual trader will lose every time. Traders have no way of knowing if what they see is real, or just a trap being set by one computer to trap other computers. There is a reason why you don't hear a lot of professional traders talking about incorporating market depth into their decision making. It is because it is not helpful. Even if traders could process it fast enough, the edge would be tiny compared to the edge that they can have from reading charts. They would be distracted and end up missing lots of other trades with a comparable risk, but a larger reward and winning percentage, and would therefore make less money. Only fight wars that you know you can win.

Since most markets are driven by institutional orders, it is reasonable to wonder whether the institutions are basing their entries on price action or their actions are causing the price action. The reality is that institutions are not all watching Apple (AAPL) or the SPDR S&P 500 exchange-traded fund (SPY) tick by tick and then starting a buy program when they see a two-legged pullback on a 1 minute chart. They have a huge number of orders to be filled during the day and are working to fill them at the best price. Price action is just one of many considerations, and some firms will rely on it more and others will rely on it less or not at all. Many firms have mathematical models and programs that determine when and how much to buy and sell, and all firms continue to receive new orders from clients all day long.

The price action that traders see during the day is the result of institutional activity and much less the cause of the activity. When a profitable setup unfolds, there will be a confluence of unknowable influences taking place during the trade that results in the trade being profitable or a loser. The setup is the actual first phase of a move that is already underway and a price action entry lets a trader just jump onto the wave early on. As more price action unfolds, more traders will enter in the direction of the move, generating momentum on the charts and causing additional traders to enter. Traders, including institutions, place their bids and offers for every imaginable reason and the reasons are largely irrelevant. However, sometimes a reason can be relevant, because it will allow smart price action traders to benefit from trapped traders. For example, if you know that protective stops are likely located at one tick below a bar and will result in losses to traders who just bought, then you should consider getting short on a stop at that same price because you will have a good chance to make a profit off the trapped traders as they are forced out.

Since institutional activity controls the move and their volume is so huge, and they place most of their trades with the intention of holding them for hours to months, most will not be looking to scalp and instead they will defend their original entries. If Vanguard or Fidelity has to buy stock for one of its mutual funds, its clients will want the fund to own stock at the end of the day. Clients do not buy mutual funds with the expectation that the funds will day trade and end up in all cash by the close. The funds have to own stock, which means they have to buy and hold, not buy and scalp. For example, after their initial buy, they will likely have much more to buy and will use any small pullback to add on. If there is none, they will continue to buy as the market rises.

Some beginning traders wonder who is buying as the market is going straight up and why anyone would buy at the market instead of waiting for a pullback. The answer is simple. It is institutions working to fill all of their orders at the best possible price, and they will buy in many pieces as the market continues up. Also, a lot of this trading is being done by institutional computer algorithms and it will end after the programs are complete. Other firms trade programs that buy constantly when the momentum is strong and stop only when the momentum slows. If a trade fails, it is far more likely the result of the trader misreading the price action than it is of an institution changing its mind or taking a couple of ticks' profit within minutes of initiating a program. The programs are statistically based, and for a trend to continue is statistically likely. The trend will continue until it reaches some technical point where the odds are that it has gone too far. It is not as if there is some single trend line or measured move target that all of the software writers will agree on. There are actually countless key technical points on the chart. The market turns when enough of them occur in the same area. One firm's programs will use some, and another firm will use others. If enough firms are betting on a reversal in the same general area, the reversal will occur. At that point, the math favors a reversal; the institutions will take partial profits, and the quantitative analyst (quant) firms will take positions in the opposite direction. These algorithms will continue trading in the opposite direction until the market overshoots again, at which point the math favors a reversal and the quants will once again bet in the opposite direction.

If institutions are smart, profitable, and responsible for every tick, why would they ever buy the highest tick in a bull trend (or sell the lowest tick in a bear trend)? It is because that is what their algorithms have been doing profitably all of the way up, and some are designed to continue to do it until it is clear that the bull trend is no longer in effect. They lose on that final buy, but make enough on all of their earlier trades to offset that loss. Remember, all of their systems lose between 30 and 70 percent of the time, and this is one of those times. There are also HFT firms that will scalp for even a single tick right up to the high tick of a bull trend. The high is always at a resistance level, and many HFT firms will buy a tick or two below resistance to try to capture that final tick, if their systems show that this is a profitable strategy. Other institutions are buying as part of a hedge in another market (stocks, options, bonds, currencies, etc.) because they perceive that their risk/reward ratio is better by placing the hedge. The volume is not from small individual traders, because they are responsible for less than 5 percent of the volume at major turning points.

The only importance of realizing that institutions are responsible for price action is that it makes placing trades based on price action more reliable. Most institutions are not going to be day trading in and out, making the market reverse after every one of your entries. Your price action entry is just a piggyback trade on their activity, but, unlike them, you are scalping all or part of your trade.

Incidentally, if a scalper is using a stop that is larger than his profit target, he has to win on 70 percent or more of their trades to be profitable. Very few traders can consistently win 70 percent of the time, and therefore most traders should never use a stop that is larger than the profit target. However, when traders see a situation where the potential profit is at least as large as the risk and they are at least 60 percent confident about the setup, then they can consider taking the trade. Most traders should start out looking for swing trades where the profit is at least twice as large as the risk. The probability of success is usually only 40 to 50 percent, and there are only a few opportunities a day, but the chance of being profitable long-term is greater. There are times when a swing setup has a chance of success of 60 percent or more, but these are usually during strong breakouts. These are difficult for most traders to take because of the limited time to analyze the trade and the large bars and, therefore, larger risk, but the math is often the best that a trader will ever have.

There are some firms that day trade substantial volume. However, for their trades to be profitable the market has to move many ticks in their direction, and price action traders will see the earliest parts of the move, allowing them to get in early and be confident that the odds of a successful scalp are high. Those firms cannot have the market go 15 ticks against them if they are trying to scalp four or eight ticks. Therefore, they will enter only when they feel that the risk of an adverse move is small. If you read their activity on the charts, you should likewise be confident in your trade, but always have a stop in the market in case your read is wrong or other institutions overwhelm the current move with trades in the opposite direction.

There is often a pullback that tests the entry bar's extreme to the tick. For example, if there is a long entry, the buyers will often place their protective sell stop at one tick below the low of that entry bar just after the bar closes. It is fairly common to see a pullback that comes down exactly to the low of that entry bar but not one tick lower. This means that the stops were not run, and that there must be institutional size volume protecting the stops. Since it is such an obvious price on the chart, they are doing this buying based on price action.

In the 5 minute Emini, there are certain price action events that change the perspective of smart traders. For example, if there is a two-legged pullback (an ABC) in a bull trend and the market then trades above the high of the prior bar, many buyers will be long at one tick above that prior bar's high (a high 2 long entry). If the market then trades below the low of the two-legged pullback, everyone will assume that the market will likely have at least one more leg down. If you are an institutional trader and you bought that high 2, you do not want it to fail and you will buy more all the way down to one tick above that key protective stop price. That institution is using price action to support its long.

HIGH-FREQUENCY TRADING

It is important to realize that a large and increasing part of the daily stock, futures, exchange-traded fund, currency, commodity, and options volume is being executed by high-frequency trading (HFT) firms that have algorithms designed by quantitative analysts called quants. Most of the programmers have master's degrees or PhDs in mathematics, quantitative analysis, engineering, programming, or physics, and the best ones make a $1 million a year for their efforts. Some algorithms hold positions for a fraction of a second, and others for an hour or two. Every imaginable strategy is used, including models based on complex financial analysis of huge volumes of data, to simple statistical aberrations. Every idea has to have sound logic, and back-testing has to confirm that it is effective. Some programmers tweak their programs during the day to give them an edge for the next few hours. Many programs operate in the world of nanoseconds (a billionth of a second), and every advance in hardware and software that reduces the latency between receiving data and getting orders filled is employed. The fastest programming languages and operating systems are also used to reduce the latency. Since their edge is very small and hundreds of millions of dollars are at stake, HFT firms tend to be secretive, stealthy, and filled with smart people.

CBS's *60 Minutes* ran a story on HFT in October 2010 and reported that as much as 70 percent of the volume and over a billion shares of stock daily were being traded by HFT programs. This is somewhat misleading because the HFT firms are only part of the algorithm trading world. There are other programs that are designed for longer-term trading and are also part of that 70 percent. Both the instantaneous high-frequency trading software and the longer-term program trading software are created by quantitative analysts. These quants are mathematicians, and the ones who design the HFT programs care nothing about charts or fundamentals and are interested only in short-term market tendencies based on statistical analysis. Most of them don't even care about 5 minute charts, and their trading has nothing to do with whatever chart you are watching during the day.

In its report, *60 Minutes* interviewed the head of Tradeworx, a small HFT firm of mathematicians and quants that was trading 40 million shares a day on its basket of 4,500 stocks. That means that the firm is averaging 10,000 shares per day per stock. Since the traders are often making only a penny or a fraction of a penny per trade, they hold their positions for only a few seconds to a few minutes, and their position size is probably very small. Computers do all of the trading because the opportunities that they are trading exist for only a fraction of a second and humans are too slow to capture them. Because they are trading 4,500 companies, one of those companies is ranked 4,500th in terms of size and probably average daily volume. This means that some of the companies they are trading trade just a few hundred thousand shares or less a day. If they trade 10,000 shares in that company and 50 other HFT firms also trade 10,000 shares, that would be 5 million shares a day. Because this is more than the total volume traded in that company, it is likely that Tradeworx is often trading 1,000 shares or fewer per trade. The traders are obviously not trading 10,000 shares in every stock, but that is their average, based on the 40 million shares that they trade and Tradeworx's basket of 4,500 stocks. They are probably trading larger volume and more often in companies that have huge daily volume, but they would still have to be trading very small volume on many stocks. Many firms trade with the goal of scalping a penny or less on each trade, holding the trade for a few seconds to a few minutes.

Their programs are based solely on statistics. The edge in trading is always very small, but if it has a high mathematical certainty and you use it thousands of times a day, it theoretically will produce consistent profits. This is the same principle on which casinos make their money. On most games, their edge is only 3 percent or less, but they are more than 99 percent certain that the edge is real and not just a coincidence. If a casino only has one customer, and he bets a billion dollars on a single bet, the casino has a 47 percent chance of going out of business on that bet. However, when thousands of gamblers place small bets every day, the odds are overwhelming that the casinos will consistently make money. The same is true for HFT firms.

One hypothetical strategy that this quant mentioned was buying $5 of every stock that fell 5 percent in the past week and shorting $10 of every stock that went up 10 percent in the past week on the basket of 4,500 stocks. The number of winners is only slightly greater than the number of losers, but when you trade a system with a slight edge often enough, you can generate a consistent profit, just like the casinos. He said that his firm sometimes loses two or three days in a row but has never had a losing month. One person interviewed mentioned that one firm reportedly made money every day for four consecutive years. You have to assume that they test every strategy that they can imagine, based on every piece of data available, including spreads, volumes, related markets, and the overall market, and if the testing shows that they have an edge, then they will trade it until it no longer continues to test well.

These firms get information about order flow a few milliseconds before everyone else and they spend tens of thousands of dollars a month to be as close to the exchange as possible to get their information as quickly as possible, and they also run the fastest computers available. Every extra millisecond that they can buy increases their edge. Their computers place and cancel thousands of order per second to get a sense of the impending market direction, and then they use this information to get in and out as early as possible. The technology is rapidly changing and since computerized trading controls most of the volume, it controls most of the price action, and this will likely always be the case. One important benefit to individual traders is that the huge volume makes liquidity high and allows traders to exit and enter with small spreads, reducing the cost of trading.

Dow Jones & Company now has a news service called Lexicon that transmits machine-readable financial news to its subscribers. Lexicon scans all of the Dow Jones stories about stocks and converts the information into a form that the algorithms can use to make decisions to buy and sell stocks in a fraction of a second. Other algorithms operate on a longer time frame and analyze stock performance and earnings statements, in addition to the news feeds, to make trading decisions. Some use differential evolution optimizing software to generate data that is used to generate other data. They can continue to refine the data until it reaches some level of mathematical certainty, and then the result is used to automatically buy or sell stocks. Some orders are so huge that they take time to place, and algorithmic trading software breaks the orders into small pieces to conceal the trading from traders who would try to capitalize on the incipient trend. Predatory trading algorithms try to unravel what the algorithm trading programs are trying to hide. Everyone is looking for an edge, and more and more firms are using computers to find the edges and place the trades.

A trader cannot possibly analyze a report and all of its implications in time to place a trade on the 5 minute chart. Computers can process information and place orders far faster than an individual trader can, and this gives them a huge edge over individual traders just after a report is released. When a trader's opponent has a huge edge, he is at a big disadvantage, which means that he has no edge. Since his edge can never be large and he should trade only when it is there, he should avoid trading when it is not, especially when a competitor has a particularly large one. However, he can still make money from the report. Since so many firms now have computers that quickly analyze reports and then place trades based on that analysis, all a trader has to do is be able to read a chart to see what the consensus opinion is from all of that analysis. The computers will show you what the report means to the market, and all you have to do is trade in the same direction. Incidentally, computers have an additional edge at the end of the day. When traders have been trading for hours, they naturally become tired, slower, and resistant to taking trades. Computers never get tired and are as effective up to the final seconds of the day as they were at the open. If traders are not at their best, which is often the case in the final hour, they have less of an edge or no edge, and they should take a trade only if both they and the setup are strong.

If you think about it, an inherent problem that HFT firms face is that they can kill the goose that is laying those golden eggs. Their trading is statistically based, and although it is mostly tested over many years, they certainly pay attention to the way that the market has been behaving over the past few weeks. If enough firms make adjustments due to recent price action, there won't be enough volume to take the other side of their trades, and as a result they won't be able to trade the way their algorithms intend and they won't make as much money. They might even lose money. This imbalance results in a change in the price action. For example, if the recent daily range has shrunk to about a third of its long-term average, it cannot last that way for too long. Eventually everyone will figure out how to make money off of the small days, and they will likely all be doing the same thing. At some point, there won't be enough money left to take the opposite side of their trades, and either they won't get filled or they will have to accept worse entries. In either case, that will change the behavior of the market.

Many institutional traders who are working to fill large orders for institutional clients are angry with the high-frequency traders, but I suspect that a lot of it is jealousy. These institutional traders used to be at the top of the food chain and were responsible for all the significant moves in the market. Not anymore. They see the quants consistently making more money, and they are doing it in a way that totally disregards the fundamentals that traditional institutional traders think forms the bedrock of Wall Street. They hate these upstarts coming into their game, disregarding their rules and everything they hold dear, having much better track records, commanding the most awe, and probably becoming more desirable places to work for the very best young, new traders. It is likely that some of their client money is getting diverted to HFT and other program trading firms, and this threatens some of their income. However, the goal is to make money; I am happy to have the added liquidity and I like all of the strong swings that are now common. I even like the tight trading ranges that these quants create, but they are more stressful to trade.

Liquidity means the immediate availability of shares at a fair price, and this means that high-frequency traders are actually helping institutional traders get a good price on their trades. This liquidity used to be provided by order offsetters (market makers), but their role has largely been taken over by HFT firms. Incidentally, just as there are complaints about HFT firms, there used to be complaints about unfair practices of market makers. One big complaint is that they fail to take the other side of trades when the market is crashing, which is the time when most traders desperately need someone to take the other side of a trade. There are other complaints about dark pools, flash trading, crossover networks, front-running, and just about every other aspect of computerized trading, but most of the unfair practices will likely be minimized by the federal government and should not cause a problem for individual traders in the long run.

The quants are providing liquidity to the market and reducing spreads for all traders, but their programs can sometimes contribute to big moves in a matter of minutes if enough of them are doing the same thing at the same time. These scalping programs probably do not have much influence on the swings during the day, which are more the result of institutional orders being filled for clients. Over the long run, fundamentals rule, but over the next few seconds to minutes, program trading often controls the market and it probably has nothing to do with the fundamentals of the market in question. The fundamentals determine the direction and the targets over the next several months, but mathematicians determine the path that the market will follow to that target. Since the algorithms are statistically based, they may in fact enhance support and resistance and trending because of market inertia. Markets tend to keep doing what they are doing, so the program writers will detect recurring behavior and write programs that capitalize on this. Since a trend is likely to continue, the programs will keep taking with-trend positions, and this might make the trend more reliable and have smaller pullbacks. Also, most breakout attempts of trading ranges fail, and they may even be more likely to fail with so much volume betting that they will.

Although markets have inertia, at some point the current price action becomes excessive. For example, if the daily SPY is in a bull channel and it has not touched the moving average for 45 days and it has only done that once in the past 10 years, the current behavior is extremely unusual. Anything that is extreme cannot last long because eventually it will show up as an excess on every imaginable measure of excess, and excess is opportunity. The market is not good at determining how far is far enough, but it is very good at knowing when the market has reached an excess. Once enough firms have decided that there is an excess, they will see it as an edge and place bets on a regression toward the mean. They will bet that the market will go back to doing what it has always done. In the case of that SPY bull, the strong bears will short and add on higher as the number of days away from the moving average becomes even more extreme. Also, the strong bulls will see the unusual behavior and they will begin to take profits and not look to buy again until the market pulls back at least to the moving average. The market can reach extremes in any type of behavior, like the number of consecutive bear trend bars; the number of consecutive days where the range is half of the average or twice the average; the number of consecutive bars with lows, highs, or closes above those of the prior bar; and just about anything else that you can imagine. There are institutions out there that pay attention to any form of extreme behavior and they will fade it. Also, extreme behavior will eventually show up as extreme on every conceivable indicator, so traders basing their decisions on indicators will also begin to bet that the behavior will end. Yes, the extreme will eventually end, but unless you are very confident in your read, do not fade the trend, because the market can sustain its unusual behavior longer than you can sustain your account.

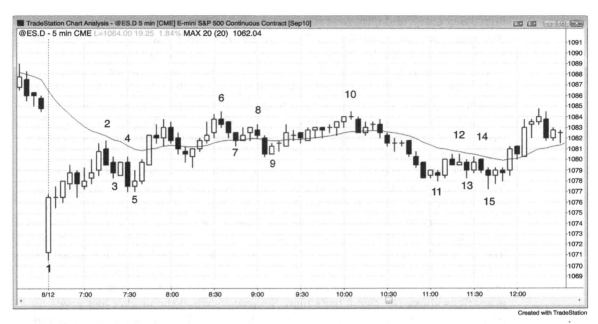

FIGURE PI.1 Two-Legged Pullbacks

Figure PI.1 and all of the charts in the book are available for download at www .wiley.com/go/tradingtrends, and you will be able to zoom in on the charts to see the details.

Two-legged corrections are reliable setups for trades in the direction of the trend. Bar counting is discussed in detail in a later section (in the second book), but since ABC patterns appear on just about every chart, they are worth discussing briefly here. As shown in Figure PI.1, bar 3 was the first leg down after the strong move up to bar 2. That made it the A leg of the ABC pullback. The little move up to the bar 4 high was the B leg, and the move down to the bar 5 low was the C leg. Since most pullbacks are not clear ABC patterns and instead often have just one leg and others have three or four, it is useful to have an alternative way to describe what is happening. Labeling a four-legged pullback as an ABCDE is too awkward to be useful. Instead, when there is a pullback in a bull leg, like to bar 3 in Figure PI.1, then the first bar that goes above the high of the prior bar is a high 1 long entry. Bar 4 is an example, as is the bar after bar 7. If the pullback continues down for a second leg, like it did to bar 5, then the first bar after bar 5 that goes above the high of the prior bar would be a high 2 entry. The bar after bar 5 is an example of a high 2 long entry, as is the bar after bar 9. Bars 5 and 9 were the high 2 buy setups or signal bars. If there was a third leg down in the bull flag, the entry would be a high 3 buy entry, and if there was then a fourth leg down and the market turned up, the entry would be a high 4 long. When the market is in a bear leg, like it was in the move down from bar 10, the first leg up is the A leg of the ABC correction. Bar 12 or the bar before it was that A leg. The pullback from that small leg up was the B leg, which was bar 13. And then the second leg up was the C leg, which ended with the bar before bar 14. This was a sideways ABC, and it is common for the C leg to not surpass the A leg in an ABC pullback. Bar 13 was a low 1 short entry, as it was the first bar that traded below the low of the prior bar in a bear flag. Bar 15 was a low 2 short entry bar.

The big legs are essentially unstoppable, but the small price action is fine-tuned by some institutional traders who are watching every tick or have programs designed to take trades based on small price movements. For example, some Emini traders will try to scalp out with a one-point profit, or four ticks. If they just entered a buy, the market will usually have to move six ticks above the high of the signal bar. They probably entered on a buy stop at one tick above the high of the signal bar, and their profit-taking limit order is four ticks above their entry price. It usually will not get filled unless the market trades one tick higher than their limit order, which is six ticks above the signal bar's high. Sometimes when the market just keeps hitting five ticks but not six (a potential five-tick failure), there will suddenly be a trade of 250 Emini contracts and the price does not tick down. In general, anything over 100 contracts should be considered institutional in today's Emini market. Even if it is just a large individual trader, he likely has the insight of an institution, and as he is trading institutional volume, he is indistinguishable from an institution. Since the price is still hanging at five ticks, almost certainly that 250-lot order was an institutional buy. This is because if institutions were selling in a market filled with nervous longs, the market would fall quickly. When the institutions start buying when the market is up five ticks, they expect it to go more than just one tick higher and usually within a minute or so the price will surge through six ticks and swing up for at least many more. The institutions were buying at the high, which means that they think the market will go higher and they will likely buy more as it goes up. Also, since four-tick scalps work so often, it is likely that there is institutional scalping that exerts a great influence over most scalps during the day.

Traders pay close attention to the seconds before key time frames close, especially 3, 5, 15, and 60 minute bars. This is also true on key volumes for volume bar charts. For example, if many traders follow the 10,000 shares per bar chart for the 10-Year U.S. Treasury Note Futures contract, then when the bar is about to close (it closes on the first trade of any size that results in at least 10,000 shares traded since the start of the bar, so the bar is rarely exactly 10,000 shares), there may be a flurry of activity to influence the final appearance of the bar. One side might want to demonstrate a willingness to make the bar appear more bullish or bearish. In simplest terms, a strong bull trend bar means that the bulls owned the bar. It is very common in strong trends for a reversal bar to totally reverse its appearance in the final few seconds before a 5 minute bar closes. For example, in a strong bear, there might be a long setting up with a very strong bull reversal bar. Then, with five seconds remaining before the bar closes, the price plummets and the bar closes on its low, trapping lots of front-running longs who expected a bull trend reversal bar. When trading countertrend against a strong trend, it is imperative to wait for the signal bar to close before placing your order, and then only enter on a stop at one tick beyond the bar in the direction of your trade (if you are buying, buy at one tick above the high of the prior bar on a stop).

What is the best way to learn how to read price action? It is to print out charts and then look for every profitable trade. If you are a scalper looking for 50 cents in AAPL or two dollars in GOOG on the 5 minute chart, then find every move during the day where that amount of profit was possible. After several weeks, you will begin to see a few patterns that would allow you to make those trades while risking about the same amount. If the risk is the same as the reward, you have to win much more than 60 percent of the time to make the trade worthwhile. However, lots of patterns have a 70 percent or better success rate, and many trades allow you to move your stop up from below the signal bar extreme to below the entry bar extreme while waiting for your profit target to be reached, reducing your risk. Also, you should be trying to enter trades that have a good chance of running well past your profit target and you should therefore only take partial profits. In fact, initially you should focus on only those entries. Move your stop to breakeven and then let the remainder run. You will likely have at least a couple of trades each week that run to four or more times your initial target before setting up a reverse entry pattern.

Fibonacci retracements and extensions are a part of price action, but since most are just approximations and most fail, they only occasionally are helpful in trading. For example, the first pullback in a new trend often retraces about 62 percent of the first leg but not often enough to place a limit order to enter there. That limit order would have you entering in the opposite direction of the market. For example, if the market is falling and you are trying to buy what you hope will become a higher low, the risk/reward ratio is not high enough and the stress is too great to be doing that routinely; however, there are exceptions when it is a sensible strategy. If a Fibonacci number is good, it will be associated with a chart pattern that is reliable and tradable on its own, independent of the Fibonacci measurement or any indicators.

Elliott Wave Theory is also a type of price action analysis, but for most traders it is not tradable. The waves are usually not clear until many, many bars after the ideal entry point, and with so many opposite interpretations at every instant, it requires far too much thought and there is too much uncertainty for most active day traders.

CHAPTER 1

The Spectrum of Price Action: Extreme Trends to Extreme Trading Ranges

Whenever anyone looks at a chart, she will see areas where the market is moving diagonally and other areas where the market is moving sideways and not covering many points. The market can exhibit a spectrum of price behavior from an extreme trend where almost every tick is higher or lower than the last to an extreme trading range where every one- or two-tick up move is followed by a one- or two-tick down move and vice versa. Only rarely will the market exist in either of these extreme states, and when it does, it does so only briefly, but the market often trends for a protracted time with only small pullbacks and it often moves up and down in a narrow range for hours. Trends create a sense of certainty and urgency, and trading ranges leave traders feeling confused about where the market will go next. All trends contain smaller trading ranges, and all trading ranges contain smaller trends. Also, most trends are just parts of trading ranges on higher time frame (HTF) charts, and most trading ranges are parts of trends on HTF charts. Even the stock market crashes of 1987 and 2009 were just pullbacks to the monthly bull trend line. The following chapters are largely arranged along the spectrum from the strongest trends to the tightest trading ranges, and then deal with pullbacks, which are transitions from trends to trading ranges, and breakouts, which are transitions from trading ranges to trends.

An important point to remember is that the market constantly exhibits inertia and tends to continue to do what is has just been doing. If it is in a trend, most attempts to reverse it will fail. If it is in a trading range, most attempts to break out into a trend will fail.

FIGURE 1.1   Extreme Trading Range and Trends

Figure 1.1 has two extreme trends and one extreme trading range. This day began with a strong bear trend down to bar 1, then entered an unusually tight trading range until it broke out to the upside by one tick at bar 2, and then reversed to a downside breakout into an exceptionally strong trend down to bar 3.

Two-legged moves are common, but unfortunately the traditional nomenclature is confusing. When one occurs as a pullback in a trend, it is often called an ABC move. When the two legs are the first two legs of a trend, Elliott Wave technicians instead refer to the legs as waves 1 and 3, with the pullback between them as wave 2. Some traders who are looking for a measured move will look for a reversal back up after the second leg reaches about the same size as the first leg. These technicians often call the pattern an AB = CD move. The first leg down begins with point A and ends with point B (bar 1 in Figure 1.1, which is also A in the ABC move), and the second leg begins with point C (bar 2 in Figure 1.1, which is also B in the ABC move) and ends with point D (bar 3 in Figure 1.1, which is also C in the ABC move).

Some corrections go for a third or even a fourth leg, so I prefer a different labeling system to account for this and discuss it later in the books. In its simplest form, it counts the legs of a pullback. For example, if there is a down leg in a bull trend or in a trading range and a bar then goes above the high of the prior bar, this

Figure 1.1   THE SPECTRUM OF PRICE ACTION   **57**

breakout is a high 1. If the market then has a second leg down and then a bar goes above the high of a prior bar, the breakout bar is a high 2. A third occurrence is a high 3, and a fourth is a high 4. In a bear leg or in a trading range, if the market reverses back down after one leg, the entry is a low 1. If it reverses back down after two legs up, the entry is a low 2 entry and the bar before it is a low 2 setup or signal.

Since measured moves are an important part of trading and the AB = CD terminology is inconsistent with the more commonly used ABC labeling, the AB = CD terminology should not be used. Also, I prefer to count legs and therefore prefer numbers, so I will refer to each move as a leg, such as leg 1 or the first push, and then leg 2, and so forth. After the chapter on bar counting in the second book, I will also use the high/low 1, 2, 3, 4 labeling because it is useful for traders.

Deeper Discussion of This Chart

The day broke out above yesterday's high on the open and the breakout failed, leading to a "trend from the open" bear trend day. This was also a trend resumption bear trend day. Whenever there is a strong trend on the open and then a tight trading range for several hours, the chances for a trend resumption day are good. There is often a false breakout between approximately 11:00 a.m. and noon PST, trapping traders into the wrong direction, and that failed breakout is a great setup for a swing trade into the close.

CHAPTER 2

Trend Bars, Doji Bars, and Climaxes

The market either is trending on the chart in front of you or it is not. When it is not, it is in some kind of trading range, which is composed of trends on smaller time frames. When two or more bars largely overlap, they constitute a trading range. The trading range can have many shapes and many names, like flags, pennants, and triangles, but the names are irrelevant. All that matters is that the bulls and bears are in some equilibrium, often with one side slightly stronger. On the level of an individual bar, it is either a trend bar or a trading range bar. Either the bulls or bears are in control of the bar or they are largely in equilibrium (a one-bar trading range).

The two most important concepts in trading are that there is a mathematical basis for everything, and that at any moment when you are convinced of the market's direction, there is someone equally smart who believes the opposite. Never be convinced of anything, and always be open to the possibility that the market will do the exact opposite of what you believe. Although the market at times is imbalanced and moves strongly up or down for many bars, most of the time it is relatively balanced, even though it might not appear to be so to a beginner.

Every tick is a trade, which means that there was someone who thought that the price was a good value to sell, and someone else who thought it was a good value to buy. Since the market is controlled by institutions and they are smart, both of these traders are smart and were acting rationally, and both have strategies that they have tested and shown to be profitable. One of the most important skills that a trader can develop is the ability to understand whether a trend bar is the beginning or end of a move. If you see a strong bull trend bar only as bullish and a strong bear trend bar only as bearish, you are missing what half of the big players are doing. Around the high of every bull trend bar, there are bulls buying the strength. There are also other bulls who are looking for a pullback and will buy near the low of the bar if the market gets there. However, it is important to realize that there are other bulls who expect the strength to fail and they are using the strength as an opportunity to sell out of their longs and take profits. There are also bears who see the bull trend bar, no matter how strong, as a climactic, failed effort by the bulls, and are shorting around the high of the bar. Some were sitting on the sidelines, waiting for a strong bull trend bar, so that they could short at what they consider to be an overdone rally. Other bears will short below the low of the bar, since they will see this as a sign of weakness that could lead to a tradable reversal. Similarly, there are profit-taking bears and new bulls buying at the bottom of every bear trend bar, no matter how strong the bar appears to be, and there are other bears who are looking to short near its high, and bulls looking to buy above its high.

For a trader, it is most useful to think of all bars as being either trend bars or nontrend (trading range) bars. Since the latter is an awkward term and most are similar to doji bars, it is simpler to refer to all nontrend bars as dojis. If the body appears tiny or nonexistent on the chart, the bar is a doji; neither the bulls nor the bears controlled the bar, and the bar is essentially a one-bar trading range. On a 5 minute Emini chart, a doji body is nonexistent or only a tick or two large, depending on the size of the bar. However, on a daily or weekly Google chart, the body can be 100 ticks (one dollar) or more and still have the same significance as a perfect doji, and therefore it makes sense to refer to it as a doji. The determination is relative and subjective, and it depends on the market and the time frame. In all of trading, close is close enough and perfection is rare. If something closely resembles a pattern, what follows will likely be what would be expected to follow the perfect pattern.

Subdividing bars with small bodies into a variety of subtypes like hanging man, hammer, or harami adds little to a trader. The fundamental issue is whether the bar and market are trying to trend, realizing that most of the time it is something in between. It is far more important to ascertain the strength of any trend than it is to spend time worrying about a precise name for a particular bar. You make money by placing trades, not by worrying about lots of meaningless, colorful names.

If there is a body, then the close trended away from the open and the bar is a trend bar. Obviously, if the bar is large and the body is small, there was not much trending strength. Also, within the bar (as seen on a smaller time frame), there may have been several swings of largely sideways movement, but this is irrelevant because you should focus on only one chart. Larger bodies, in general, indicate more strength, but an extremely large body after a protracted move or a break-out can represent an exhaustive, climactic end of a trend, and no trade should be taken until more price action unfolds. A series of strong trend bars is the sign of a healthy trend and will usually be followed by a further extreme, even if a pullback immediately ensues. Every trend bar is simultaneously (1) a spike; (2) a breakout; (3) a gap (as discussed in book 2, all breakouts are functionally identical to gaps and, therefore, so are all trend bars); and (4) a part or all of a vacuum and a climax (a pause or reversal bar ends a climax after one or consecutive trend bars). One or more of these four characteristics might be dominant in a particular trend bar and each offers trading opportunities, as will be discussed throughout the books. When it is a climax and the start of a reversal, it is due to the vacuum effect. For example, if a buy spike is followed by a reversal, the sharp rally was more than likely due to strong bears stepping aside and bulls waiting to exit longs until the market reached an area where both had been waiting to sell. If instead there is follow-through buying, then the buying was not due to the vacuum effect but rather a combination of strong bulls buying and strong bears believing that the market would rally further. Traders use the overall context to determine which is more likely. Their assessment will lead them to look to buy, sell, or wait. Obviously, every spike that leads to a reversal is a manifestation of the vacuum effect, but I reserve the term for spikes that end in a reversal at an obvious support or resistance level (dueling lines, discussed in book 2). Incidentally, crashes are examples of the vacuum effect. Both the 1987 and 2009 stock market crashes collapsed to just below the monthly trend line, where the strong buyers reappeared and strong bears took profits, leading to a sharp reversal upward. Also, stock traders routinely buy strong bear spikes in bull trends because they see the spike as a value play. Although they usually look for strong price action before buying, they will often buy a stock that they like at the bottom of a sharp sell-off, especially to the area of the bull trend line, even if it has not yet reversed up. They believe that the market is, temporarily, incorrectly underpricing the stock because of some news event, and they buy it because they doubt it will remain discounted for long. They don't mind if it falls a little further, because they doubt that they can pick the exact bottom of the pullback, but they want to get in during the sell-off because they believe that the market will quickly correct its mistake and the stock will soon rally.

Pullbacks, which are discussed in book 2, are often strong spikes that make traders wonder if the trend has reversed. For example, in a bull trend, there might be a large bear trend bar or two that breaks below the moving average and maybe several ticks below a trading range. Traders will then wonder if the always-in direction is in the process of flipping to down. What they need to see is follow-through selling in the form of maybe just one more bear trend bar. Everyone will watch that next bar closely. If it is a large bear trend bar, most traders will believe that the reversal has been confirmed and will start shorting at the market and on pullbacks. If the bar instead has a bull close, they will suspect that the reversal attempt has failed and that the sell-off is just a brief, but sharp, markdown in price and therefore a buying opportunity. Beginning traders see the strong bear spike and ignore the strong bull trend in which it is occurring. They sell the close of the bear trend bar, below its low, any small bounce over the next few bars, and below any low 1 or low 2 sell setup. Smart bulls are taking the opposite side of those trades because they understand what is happening. The market is always trying to reverse, but 80 percent of those reversal attempts fail and become bull flags. At the time the reversal attempt is occurring, the two or three bear bars can be very persuasive, but without follow-through selling, the bulls see the sell-off as a great opportunity to get long again near the low of a brief sell climax. Experienced bulls and bears wait for these strong trend bars and sometimes step aside until one forms. Then they come into the market and buy because they view it as the climactic end of the selling. The bears buy back their shorts and the bulls reestablish their longs. This also happens at the end of a trend when the strong traders are waiting for one large trend bar. For example, in a strong bear trend near a support area, there will often be a late breakout in the form of an unusually large bear trend bar. Both the bulls and bears stopped buying until they saw it form. At that point, both buy the sell climax, because the bears see it as a great price to take profits on their shorts and the bulls see it as a brief opportunity to buy at a very low price.

Sometimes that bear spike can close on its low, and beginning traders are shocked that the market then slowly or quickly reverses back up. How can a large bear trend bar that closes on its low be followed by a small bull inside bar and then a reversal up to a new high of the day? What they don't realize is that on a smaller time frame, that strong bear trend bar had a clear reversal pattern, like maybe a three-push pattern on a 100-tick chart of the Emini. However, even if they watched and traded the smaller time frame chart, they would lose money because the patterns form too quickly for traders to analyze them accurately. Remember, all patterns are the result of computer algorithms, and computers have a huge speed advantage. It is always a mistake to compete against an opponent who has an edge in a game where the margin for error is so small. When speed is critical, the computers have a huge edge, and traders should not trade against them. Instead, they should pick a time frame, like a 5 minute chart, where they have time to carefully process the information.

A trend bar is a critical component of a climax, and a climax is a critical component of a reversal, but traders often incorrectly use the term *climax* as synonymous with reversal. Every trend bar is a climax or part of a climax, and the climax ends with the first pause bar. For example, if there are three consecutive bull trend bars and then the next bar is a small bull trend bar with a prominent tail on the top, an inside bar, a doji, or a bear trend bar, then the climax ended with the three bull trend bars. This three-bar buy climax simply means that the market went too far too fast and that the enthusiasm to buy has quickly decreased to the point that the market has become two-sided. Some bulls are taking profits and would like to buy more at a lower price, and some bears are starting to short. If the bulls overwhelm the bears, the rally will resume, but if the bears overwhelm the bulls, the market will reverse down in a bear trend bar, which will be acting as a bear breakout, and the reversal pattern will be a climactic reversal top. The buy climax is a move up, and the climactic reversal top is the move up followed by the move down. The bull trend bar is acting more as a climax and the bear trend bar is acting more as a breakout, and together they create a climactic reversal top or a buy climax and reversal.

All strong bull trends have strong bull trend bars or consecutive bull trend bars, and each is a buy climax but most do not become the first leg of a climactic reversal. The reversal requires a buy climax and then a bear breakout, which is a strong bear trend bar. The bull and bear trend bars do not have to be consecutive and are often separated by many bars, but both are required to have a climactic reversal. In fact, every reversal at the top of a bull market is a climactic reversal, whether or not it looks like one on the chart in front of you. If the bull reverses with a strong bear reversal bar on the 5 minute chart, it is still a climactic reversal, but only on a smaller time frame. Although it is not worth searching for ever-smaller time frames for that perfect spike up followed by a spike down, it is always there. Also, whenever there is a climax top that takes place over many bars, it is always a single reversal bar on some higher time frame chart, and again it is not worth looking for the perfect time frame just to see the perfect reversal bar. Remember, traders are all looking for an edge and computer charting programs allow traders to quickly create charts based on every conceivable interval, and there will be traders out there basing their decisions on everything imaginable. This includes charts based not only on time but also on the number of ticks, the number of contracts traded, and any combination of these. There will always be someone out there who sees that perfect reversal bar and someone else who sees the spike up and then the spike down, but you do not have to see either if you understand what the chart in front of you is telling you. The opposite is true for climactic bottoms where a sell climax is followed by a reversal up. Climactic reversals are discussed more in Chapters 5 and 6 on signal bars, and again in book 3.

An ideal trend bar is one with a moderate-size body, indicating that the market trended away from the open of the bar by the time the bar closed. The minimum is a close above the open in a bull trend bar, indicated by a white candle body in these books. The bulls can demonstrate stronger control by having the body be about the same size as or larger than that of the median body size over the past five or 10 bars. Additional signs of strength are discussed in another section and include the open being on or near the low, the close on or near the high, the close at or above the closes and highs of several prior bars, the high above the high of one or more prior bars, and the tails being small. If the bar is very large and especially if it develops in a trend, it might represent exhaustion or a one-bar false breakout that is trapping new bulls, only to reverse down in the next bar or two. The opposite is true for bear trend bars.

All trend bars are attempts to break out into a trend, but as discussed in the next chapter, most breakouts fail. Also, all trends begin with a trend bar, which might have a body that might be only a little larger than the bodies of the recent bars. Sometimes it is large and followed by several other trend bars in the same direction, which indicates a stronger trend and one more likely to have follow-through.

When the market is in a trading range or a bear trend and is starting to create a number of bull trend bars, it is a sign of buying pressure and it is an attempt by the bulls to take control of the market and make it bull trend. Traders are buying small pullbacks within the bar because they believe that the market will soon be higher, and there might not be a bigger pullback for them to buy. When they buy in the final seconds of the bar as it is closing, they are afraid that the next bar might open near its low and then rally even more. They feel a sense of urgency and are eager to get long now, rather than wait for a pullback that might not come until after the market is much higher. They are buying below the low of the prior bar and below swing lows, and the market is transitioning into a bull leg or trend. The bears are no longer shorting heavily at the new lows. They are taking profits, and more and more bulls are seeing new lows as a great value and are buying them.

If bear bodies are starting to accumulate in a bull trend or trading range, it is a sign of selling pressure and the bears might soon be able to create a downtrend. For example, if the market is in a bull trend and has had a couple of pullbacks with large bear trend bars, and now has entered a trading range and there have been several swings with prominent bear trend bars, the selling pressure is building and the bears might soon be able to reverse the market into a bear leg or bear trend. Selling pressure is cumulative, and the more bear bodies and the larger the bodies, the more likely it is that the pressure will reach a critical point and overwhelm the bulls and drive the market down. The opposite is true of buying pressure. If there is a trading range or a bear trend and the bull trend bars are becoming larger and more numerous, the buying pressure is building and this makes a rally more likely.

Strong bulls create buying pressure and strong bears create selling pressure. Strong bulls and bears are institutional traders, and the cumulative effect of these strong traders determines the direction of the market. For example, signs of buying pressure in a bear trend include tails at the bottoms of bars, two-bar reversals or bull reversal bars at the bottoms of down swings, and an increasing number of bars with large bull bodies. It is the strong bulls buying at each new low and at the bottom of each bar that moves the close up off the low of the bar. This can only happen if the strong bears no longer feel that there is value in shorting at these lower prices. These bulls are willing to buy more if the market falls further, unlike weak bulls who would exit with a loss. The strong bears at this point are only willing to short higher. How do you know this? If enough of them were willing to short at the bottoms of the bars, they would have been able to overwhelm the bulls and the bars would have been closing on their lows and not in the middle or near the highs.

Whenever traders see signs of buying pressure, they assume that the strong bulls are buying at the lows and the strong bears are no longer willing to short at the lows and now are only willing to sell rallies. So when the strong bulls are buying at the bottom and strong bears are only willing to sell higher, what happens? The market enters a trading range. The strong bears will short at the top and not at the bottom and the strong bulls will buy at the bottom and not at the top. The weak traders usually do the opposite. The weak bulls continue to sell at the lows as they get stopped out, and they buy at the highs as they become afraid that they are missing a new bull trend. The weak bears short at the low, expecting a breakout, and they cover their shorts at a loss at the highs as they become afraid that the market is turning into a bull trend.

Everything is relative and subject to constant reassessment, even to the point of totally changing your opinion about the direction of the market. Remember, you can rarely be 60 percent certain of the market's direction, and that can quickly change to 50–50 or even 60 percent in the other direction.

Yes, every bar is either a trend bar or a doji bar. A doji bar means that the bulls and bears are in balance. As the doji is forming, if you were to look at a small enough time frame, you would see that either the market went down and then up, creating a sell climax, or up and then down, creating a buy climax. As discussed in the section on Climactic Reversals in book 3 on climaxes, a climax does not mean that the market is reversing. It simply means that it went too far and too fast in one direction and now is trying the other way. At that point, the bulls keep buying as they try to generate upside follow-through and the bears keep shorting as they try to create a bear trend, and the result is usually a sideways market. The sideways trading can be as brief as a single bar or it can last for many bars, but it represents two-sided trading and is therefore a trading range. Since all dojis contain two-sided trading and are usually followed at least briefly by more two-sided trading, dojis should be thought of as one-bar trading ranges.

However, sometimes a series of dojis can mean that a trend is in effect. For example, if there is a series of dojis, each with a higher close and most with a high above the high of the prior bar and a low above the low of the prior bar, the market is displaying trending closes, highs, and lows, so a trend is in effect.

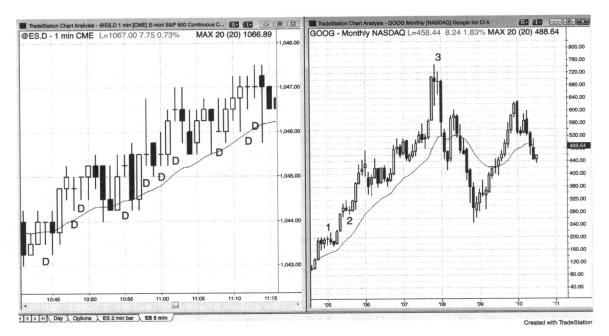

FIGURE 2.1   Dojis Are Rarely Perfect

Figure 2.1 illustrates the shortcoming of restricting the term *doji* to only those bars with the close being at the same price as the open. Since basic price action analysis works on all time frames, it simply does not make sense to restrict the term to a perfect pattern. The 1 minute Emini chart on the left has 10 perfect dojis, despite the bull trend, whereas the monthly chart of Google (GOOG) on the right does not have a single doji. Although several bars look like dojis, even bar 3 with the smallest body still had a close that was 47 cents above its open. Using the classic definition in both cases does nothing to help a trader. In the GOOG chart, bar 3 was a great signal bar that behaved exactly as a doji would be expected to behave, and it should be traded that way. In trading, close is close enough and worrying about perfection can only cost you money.

Deeper Discussion of This Chart

When there is a very large bull trend bar occurring in a bull trend, as in the GOOG chart in Figure 2.1, it may represent the last, desperate buyers buying, either to cover their losing shorts or to get into a very strong bull trend but at a very late stage. It is a buy climax, and after it forms there often is no one left to buy, leaving the bears in the control of the market. The large bear trend bar that followed created the second bar of a reversal.

Figure 2.1 TREND BARS, DOJI BARS, AND CLIMAXES **67**

On some higher time frame, this would be a perfect two-bar reversal. On an even higher time frame, this top would be a large bear reversal bar. After a spike up and a spike down, both the bulls and bears continue to trade as they attempt to create a channel in their direction. This creates a trading range that can be as short as a single bar or it can last many bars. Here, the two-sided trading formed a three-bar lower high. Eventually one side wins.

Figure 2.2

FIGURE 2.2   Intraday Dojis

For trading purposes, it is useful to think of all bars as either trend bars or dojis (or nontrend bars, shown in Figures 2.1 and 2.2 with a D), and the labeling is loose. One bar with a small body could be a doji in one area of price action but a small trend bar in another. The only purpose for the distinction is to help you quickly assess whether one side is in control of the bar or bulls and bears are at a stalemate. Several of the bars in Figure 2.2 could arguably be thought of as both trend bars and dojis.

FIGURE 2.3 Trending Dojis

Individual dojis mean that neither the bulls nor the bears are controlling the market, but trending dojis indicate a trend. They are a sign of building buying pressure and this makes a rally more likely. In Figure 2.3, the 5 minute chart on the right had four dojis in a row, starting at bar 1, each with trending closes, highs, and lows. The 15 minute chart on the left shows that they created a bull reversal bar at what was then a new swing low.

Deeper Discussion of This Chart

The day began with a large gap down in Figure 2.3, which is a bear breakout, and then a large bear trend bar and was therefore likely to be some kind of bear trend day, and traders were looking to get short. The fourth bar of the day in the 5 minute chart on the right was a bull trend bar and an attempt by the bulls to reverse the day, but it failed, trapping bulls in and bears out. The failed breakout failed and this set up a breakout pullback short below that bull trend bar. The moving average (20-bar exponential moving average) gap bar at bar 4 was in a strong bear trend and was a good short for a test of the low of the day; but since the test usually results in a strong pullback or reversal, traders were looking to buy the new low and the later test of the low of the day.

In Figure 2.3, bar 1 was also a trend channel line overshoot on both charts, using the prior two swing lows to create the trend line. The market tried to break out of the bottom of the bear channel and accelerate downward but the breakout failed, as most breakouts do. Failures are especially common with trend channel line breakouts since they are an attempt to accelerate a trend and a trend tends to weaken over time.

Bar 4 was a doji, which is a one-bar trading range but still can be a good setup bar, depending on context. Here, it was a final flag reversal signal bar (an ii flag failed breakout) and a moving average gap bar short setup in a bear trend, and therefore a reliable signal for a test of the bear low. A bear rally to a moving average gap bar usually breaks the bear trend line, and the subsequent sell-off that tests the bear trend's low often is the final leg down before the market tries to reverse. Here, the test of the bar 1 low of the bear trend was a lower low, and traders should expect at least two legs up. If the test was a higher low, then the move up to bar 4 would have been the first leg up and traders should expect at least one more leg up from that higher low.

Figure 2.4   TREND BARS, DOJI BARS, AND CLIMAXES   **71**

FIGURE 2.4   Trend Bars without a Trend

Just like dojis don't always mean that the market is trendless, a trend bar does not always mean that the market is trending. In Figure 2.4, bar 6 was a strong bull trend bar that broke out of a line of dojis. However, there was no follow-through. The next bar extended one tick above the trend bar and then closed near its low. The longs exited at one tick below this bear pause bar and new shorts sold there as well, viewing this as a failed bull breakout. No one was interested in buying without more bullish price action, and this caused the market to drop. The bulls tried to protect the low of the bull breakout bar by forming a small bull trend bar (bar 8 was a setup for a breakout pullback long, although it was never triggered), but the market fell through its low; these new early bulls exited again there, and more new shorts came in. At this point, after the bulls failed in two attempts, they would not be willing to buy without substantial price action in their favor, and both they and the bears would be looking for at least two legs down.

Trend bars can mean the opposite of what they appear to be telling traders. A beginner might have seen the strong trend bar before bar 3 as a breakout into a new bull trend. An experienced trader would have needed follow-through in the form of a second or third bull trend bar before believing that the always-in trade had reversed to up. Experienced traders sold the close of the bar, above the bar, the close of bar 3, and below bar 3. The bulls were scalping out of their longs and the bears were initiating new swing shorts. This same kind of bull trap happened on the bull trend bars that ended bear flags at the bars before bars 7 and 17. The opposite happened at bar 19 where the one of the largest bear trend bars of the day was the beginning of the end of a bear trend. Whenever a large bear trend bar forms in a bear trend that has gone on for 30 or more bars without much of a pullback, it often represents a sell vacuum and an exhaustive sell climax. Sometimes it is the low of the bear trend, and other times, the market falls for a few more bars before trying to reverse. When the strong bulls and bears see some support level and expect it to be tested, they step aside and wait for a large bear trend bar to form. Once it does, they both buy aggressively. The bears buy back their shorts and the bulls buy new longs. Both are expecting a larger correction that should have at least two legs, last at least 10 bars, and poke a little above the moving average. The market might go on to a trend reversal, but traders need to see the strength of the rally before deciding how far they think it will go.

Deeper Discussion of This Chart

Today broke out above yesterday's high, as shown in Figure 2.4, but reversed down in a failed breakout and a trend from the open bear trend. This was basically a bear trend resumption day, although it was a trading range day for the first several hours. The most important trade of the day was the collapse that began at 11:00 a.m. PST. Once the bar 12 breakout formed, traders needed to consider the possibility of a bear trend resumption. When the next bar had an even larger bear body, traders needed to get short. They could even have waited for the next bar, bar 13, which was another strong bear trend bar. Shorting a collapse after a quiet period is very difficult to do because by this point, traders were complacent, expecting the day to remain quiet. However, this was a very high-probability short. Bars 12 to 13 had large bear bodies that did not overlap. They formed a strong bear spike with follow-through for several bars. The odds were high that the market would have some kind of measured move down from the high or open of the first bar to the close or low of the final bar of the spike. Since the bars are large and the market was moving fast, traders were afraid of the risk of a large reversal. The best thing to do is to short at the close of bar 13 or the bar before it and use a protective stop above the high of that signal bar. If you are afraid, just short a very small position to be sure to be in the trade. Once you have another strong bear trend bar, like bar 14, move your stop either to breakeven or to above the high of that bar and hold into the close.

Figure 2.5   TREND BARS, DOJI BARS, AND CLIMAXES   **73**

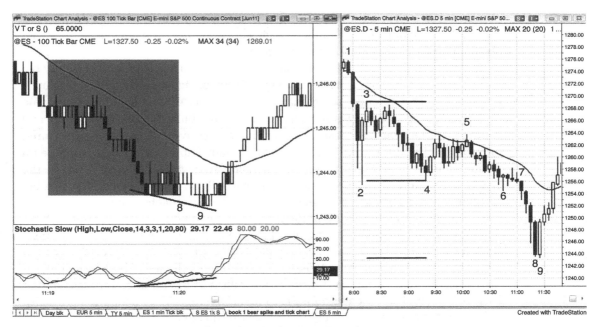

FIGURE 2.5   A Large Bear Trend Bar Can End a Bear Trend

The market was in a strong bear trend on the 5 minute Emini chart on the right in Figure 2.5, but reversed up sharply after the large bar 8 bear trend bar. Bar 9 formed a two-bar reversal at a measured move down from bar 3 to bar 4 (measured moves are discussed in book 2). Could traders have watched a smaller time frame chart and then bought as a small reversal pattern was being triggered? The chart on the left is a tick chart with each bar being 100 ticks. After every 100 trades took place, the bar closed and a new bar began. Bar 8 on the 5 minute chart ended at 11:20 a.m. PST, and bar 8 on the tick chart is made of the final 100 ticks of that 5 minute bar. Bar 9 on the tick chart corresponds to the low of bar 9 on the 5 minute chart. On the tick chart, the market formed a double bottom that broke to the downside at bar 9, but the bear breakout failed and the market reversed up. It occurred with a divergence on the stochastics indicator. This is a very orderly, traditional reversal setup, but there was a problem here that made it untradable. The gray box on the left is the final minute of the 5 minute bar on the right, and it contains 33 bars! That is far too much information for a human to process reliably and then be able to place orders in a timely and accurate way. The markets are controlled by computers, and sometimes prices move very quickly. Trading profitably is always difficult, and it is virtually impossible when speed is critical, because microsecond speed is an edge that only computers have. You cannot hope to make money trading when your opponent has a clear advantage. There were many ways for experienced traders to buy on this 5 minute chart, including buying at the market as bar 8 closed or buying above bar 9, and these are discussed in book 3.

So what took place in the bear spike from bar 7 to bar 9? Each bear body became progressively larger, which is a sign of increasing bear strength. However, it is also a sign of a potential sell climax, as it was here. When a bear trend has gone on for 30 or more bars and is at a support level, both bulls and bears step aside and wait for a large bear trend bar, and then buy aggressively. There was a measured move at the bar 9 low, but there are always many support levels present when a trend reverses, even though most are not visible to beginning traders. Because the strong bulls and bears are waiting for an unusually strong bear trend like this before buying, the absence of buying as the market approaches support leads to a sell vacuum and the formation of the large bear trend bar. Once it forms, the bears quickly buy back their shorts and take their profits, and the bulls initiate new longs. Both understand what is taking place and both expect a large correction or even a reversal, so the bears won't look to short and the bulls won't look to sell out of their longs to take profits until the market rallies at least a couple of legs and at least 10 bars, and at least gets above the moving average. The result often is a sharp rally, and it can begin with a very strong bear trend bar.

Figure 2.6   TREND BARS, DOJI BARS, AND CLIMAXES   **75**

FIGURE 2.6 Trend Transitioning into Trading Range

When bears begin to see a new low as a good place to take profits instead of as a great place to short for a new leg down, and bulls see it as a good price to begin to get long, the market is transitioning from a strong trend into more of a two-sided market. As shown in Figure 2.6, in the bear trend down from bar 2, every time the market fell below the most recent swing low, a bull bar or a bar with a large tail formed within a bar or two. This was a sign of buying pressure, which is cumulative. When there is enough, the bulls can take over a market and create a large bear rally or even a trend reversal.

At the bar 13 top, bear bodies started to accumulate, and this selling pressure was a sign that the market might soon pull back.

CHAPTER 3

Breakouts, Trading Ranges, Tests, and Reversals

Just like a bar can be a trend bar or a trading range bar, any segment of a chart can be classified as trending where either the bulls or the bears are dominant, or two-sided where both the bulls and the bears alternately assume relative control. When the market breaks out into a trend, there is usually a trend bar, which can be small or large, followed by many bars that are trending as the market spikes away from the trading range. One of the most important skills that a trader can develop is the ability to reliably distinguish between a successful and a failed breakout (a reversal). Will the breakout lead to a swing in the direction of the breakout or in the opposite direction? This is discussed in detail in the second book. In thinly traded markets, the breakout can appear as a gap rather than a trend bar, and that is why a trend bar should be thought of as a type of gap (discussed in detail in book 2). At some point, the market begins to have pullbacks and then the trend slows into a shallower slope and becomes more of a channel where a trend line and a trend channel line can be drawn. As the trend continues, the lines should be redrawn to contain the developing price action. Usually the slope becomes shallower and the channel becomes wider.

Some form of this spike and channel behavior happens to some extent every day in all markets. The start of the channel usually becomes the start of an incipient trading range. For example, if there is a spike up (an upside breakout) that lasts several bars, there will then be a pullback. Once the pullback ends and the trend resumes up, it usually does so in a channel rather than a nearly vertical spike, and there is usually more overlap of the bars, more small pullbacks, more bars with tails, and some bear trend bars. The bottom of the channel phase of the trend will usually be tested within a day or two. Once that pullback begins and the market is moving down toward the start of the channel, traders will suspect that a trading range is forming, and they are right. Price action traders will anticipate that trading range as soon as the spike ends and the channel begins, and a few bears will begin scaling into shorts on that first pullback after the spike. Since they are confident that the low of the channel will soon be tested, they will scale in shorts on other pullbacks and above the highs of prior bars as the market continues up. Later in the channel, more bears will scale in above bars. Once the market turns down into a larger pullback that tests the bottom of the channel, they will exit all of their shorts with profits on later entries and at breakeven on their first. Since many traders will cover their shorts around the bottom of the channel, their buying along with bulls returning to buy where they bought earlier (at the bottom of that first pullback after the spike up) will lift the market once again, and the trading range will broaden. After this bounce, the effect of the spike and channel has played out and traders will look for other patterns.

Because channels usually get retraced eventually, it is helpful to look at all bull channels as bear flags and all bear channels as bull flags. However, if the trend is strong, the breakout may go sideways and be followed by more trending. Rarely, the breakout can be in the trend direction and the trend can accelerate sharply. For example, if there is a bull spike and then a bull channel, rarely the market will break out above the trend channel line and the bull trend will accelerate. Usually the breakout will fail within five bars or so and the market will then reverse.

Although most trading ranges are flags on higher time frame charts, and most of them break out in the direction of the trend, almost all reversals begin as trading ranges, which will be discussed in the section on reversals in the third book.

A test means that the market is returning to an area of support or resistance, like a trend line, a trend channel line, a measured move target, a prior swing high or low, a bull entry bar low or a bear entry bar high, a bull signal bar high or a bear signal bar low, or yesterday's high, low, close, or open. Traders often place trades based on the behavior at the test. For example, if the market had a high, a pullback, and then a rally back up to that high, the bulls want to see a strong breakout. If one appears to be developing, they might buy at one tick above the old high or they might wait for a pullback from the breakout and then buy at one tick above the high of the prior bar, expecting a resumption of the breakout. The bears are looking for a reversal. If the rally up to the old high lacks momentum and then the market forms a reversal bar in the area of the old high, they will short below the reversal bar. They don't care if the test forms a higher high, a double top, or a lower high. They just want to see the market reject the prices in this area to validate their opinion that the market is too expensive up here.

A reversal is a change from one type of behavior to an opposite type of behavior, but the term is most often used to describe a change from a bull trend to a bear trend or from a bear trend to a bull trend. However, trading range behavior is arguably opposite to trending behavior, and when a trend is followed by a trading range, the market's behavior has reversed. When a trading range becomes a trend, the market's behavior has reversed as well, but that change is called a breakout. No one calls it a reversal, although it is technically reversing two-sided trading into one-sided trading.

Even though most traders think that a reversal is from a bull trend to a bear trend or a bear trend to a bull trend, most reversals fail to lead to an opposite trend and instead become a temporary transition from a bull or bear trend into a trading range. Markets have inertia and are very resistant to change. When there is a strong bull trend, it will resist change; almost every attempt at a reversal will end up as a bull flag, and the trend will then resume. Each successive bull flag will tend to get larger as the bulls become more concerned at new highs with taking profits and less interested in buying heavily, and the bears will start becoming increasingly aggressive. At some point, the bears will overwhelm the bulls, the trading range will break to the downside, and a bear trend will begin. However, this usually happens after several earlier reversal attempts resulted in increasingly larger bull flags where the bulls overpowered the bears and a bear trend failed to develop. Even though most reversals simply lead to trading ranges, the move is usually large enough to result in a swing trade, which is a large-enough move to create a substantial profit. Even if an opposite trend eventually unfolds, traders will take at least partial profits at the first reasonable targets, just in case the reversal only leads to a trading range, which is usually the case.

Reversals have different appearances, depending on the chart that you are using. For example, if you see a large bear reversal bar on a monthly chart, it might be a two-bar reversal on a weekly chart, and it might be a three-bar bull spike, which is a buy climax, and then a 10-day trading range, and finally a two-bar bear breakout on the daily chart. It does not matter what chart you are using as long as you recognize the pattern as a reversal, and all of these patterns are reversal patterns.

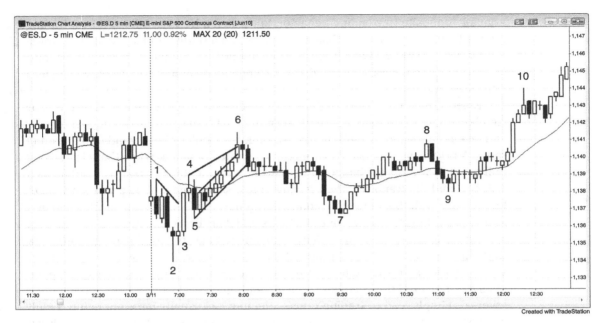

FIGURE 3.1   Breakouts, Trading Ranges, and Tests

The 5 minute Emini chart in Figure 3.1 shows examples of breakouts, trading ranges, and tests. Every swing is a test of something, even though most traders don't see what is being tested. Many of the tests are related to price action on other time frames and other types of charts, and include tests of different types of moving averages, bands, Fibonacci levels, pivots, and countless other things.

The market tested yesterday's low, but the breakout failed and formed a lower low as it reversed up sharply in a spike up to bar 4. Every breakout, whether it is successful or fails, is eventually followed by a trading range, as it was here. A failed breakout to a new low indicates that the bulls and the bears agree that the price is too low. The bears will take profits and not sell very much at these low prices and the bulls will continue to buy aggressively until both believe that the market has reached a new area of equilibrium, which is a trading range.

Bar 1 was the signal bar for the sell-off on the open, and the market should not have been able to go above its high if the bears were still in control.

Bar 4 was a higher high test of the bar 1 high, and the upward momentum was so strong that the market would likely test up at least one more time before the bulls would give up. The double top (double tops and bottoms are rarely exact) resulted in only a one-bar pullback before the breakout above bar 1 succeeded.

Bar 5 tested the high of the bar 2 signal bar and formed a higher low.

Every sharp move and every strong reversal should be thought of as a breakout of something. It does not matter if you view this sharp move up from bar 2 as a breakout above the small bear trend line drawn from bar 1 or as a breakout above the bar 2 reversal bar. What does matter is that during this spike, the market agreed that the price was too low and it was trending quickly to find an area where both the bulls and the bears were comfortable placing trades. This resulted in a channel up from bars 5 to 6, and within the channel, there were many bars that overlapped with the bar before or after. This overlap of bars represents a hesitation by the bulls where the market was now able to trade down for a few ticks and a few minutes before moving higher. Some bulls were taking profits as the market was working higher, and bears were beginning to short. Many were adding to their shorts (scaling in) as the market went up, just as many bulls were taking more and more off (scaling out). This channel is a weaker bull move, and channels are usually the start of a trading range. As you can see, the market retraced back to around the start of the channel by bar 7.

Bar 7 was a higher low test of the bar 5 swing low and a second test of yesterday's low, and the market reversed up in a double bottom.

Bar 8 was a lower high test of the bar 6 high and of yesterday's close, and formed a double top instead of a breakout. It also tested the high of the bear inside bar that followed bar 6, and that bar was the signal bar for the sell-off that followed.

The reversal down to bar 9 tested the moving average and became simply a pullback from the breakout attempt; it was followed by a successful breakout to a new high of the day. Bar 9 also tested the long entry above the bull bar that followed bar 7, and it missed the breakeven stop by a tick. When the bulls are able to prevent their breakeven stop from being hit, they are strong and a new high usually follows.

Deeper Discussion of This Chart

When a chart discussion runs for multiple pages, remember that you can go to the John Wiley & Sons website at www.wiley.com/go/tradingtrends and either view the chart or print it out, allowing you to read the description in the book without having to repeatedly flip pages back to see the chart.

In Figure 3.1, bar 3 was a large bull trend bar that was the start of a bull trend, and it should be thought of as a breakout and a breakout gap.

The market broke below the bull channel into yesterday's close, and a bull channel is a bear flag. The breakout had some follow-through, but there were bull bodies and overlapping bars, indicating that the bulls were active. The market then broke out below yesterday's swing low, and the breakout failed and became the low of the day. If you did not buy the bar 2 reversal up from yesterday's low, the bar 3 strong bull trend bar showed you that the always-in position was up and you should look to buy either at the market or above the bar 5 pullback. *Always in* is discussed in detail in the third book, but it basically means that if you have to be in the market at all times, either long or short, the always-in position is whatever your current position is. This is a very important concept, and most traders should trade only in the always-in direction. The bar 7 double bottom pullback was another chance to get long, hoping for a second leg up into the close.

This type of pattern is a spike and channel bull trend. It is useful here because it shows a market transitioning from one-sided trading (a strong trend) to two-sided trading (a trading range). It does not matter if you view bar 3 alone as the spike or the entire sharp move from bars 2 to 4 as the spike. The market pulled back to bar 5 and then rallied in a less urgent fashion. The bars mostly overlapped one another, and a trader could draw a channel that contained prices fairly well. You could also draw a trend channel line across the highs and highlight a wedge type of channel, which is also discussed later. Some traders would have shorted below the low of bar 4 and then scaled in more shorts at other pullbacks as the market moved up. Other traders would wait for the wedge top, where they would take profits on longs or initiate shorts. As soon as the spike is followed by the pullback to bar 5 and then channel type behavior begins to form, traders will see this bull channel as a possible bear flag and expect that the low of the channel will get tested. In small patterns like this one, the test usually is later in the same day; but in larger patterns, the test might come a day or two later.

The market had the expected two-legged correction from the wedge top to the bottom of the channel, where the bears will take profit on all of their entries. Their earlier entries will be only approximately breakeven trades, but their later entries will be profitable. Also, bulls will again look to buy around the low of bar 5 where they bought earlier at the end of the first pullback, and that becomes the start of the channel. The buying by the bulls and by the short-covering bears usually results in a bounce. That bounce can be a rally from a double bottom (bars 5 and 7) bull flag, or it could be followed by a protracted trading range or even a bear trend.

Also notice that the bar 2 low was the third push down and therefore a wedge reversal.

Bar 6 was a double top bear flag (the first top was the final bar of yesterday) and bars 5 and 7 created a double bottom bull flag. This was followed by the bar 9 double bottom pullback. You could describe the price action between bars 5 and 9 as a triangle that could break out in either direction, but that would overlook the bullishness that the market was showing you.

Bar 7 was a wedge bull flag because it was the third push down from the bar 6 high.

Bar 8 was a final flag reversal after the six-bar bull flag that preceded it.

CHAPTER 4

Bar Basics: Signal Bars, Entry Bars, Setups, and Candle Patterns

Traders look for setups all day long. A setup is a chart pattern composed of one or more bars that leads a trader to believe that an order can be placed that has a good chance of resulting in a profitable trade. In practice, every bar on the chart is a setup because the next bar always can be the start of a strong move in either direction. If the trade is in the direction of the recent or prevailing trend, it is *with trend*, and if it is in the opposite direction, it is *countertrend*. For example, if the recent trend is up and you buy, the setup was a with-trend setup. If instead you shorted, the setup that you used as the basis for your trade was a countertrend setup and your short was a countertrend trade.

A signal bar is always labeled in hindsight, after the bar has closed and after a trade is entered. As soon as your entry order is filled, the prior bar becomes a signal bar instead of just a setup bar and the current bar is the entry bar. The bar after entry is the follow-through bar, and it is always better when there is a second bar in the direction of your entry. Sometimes the market will go sideways for a bar or two before there is a follow-through bar, and this is still good because as long as there is follow-through, the odds of making more from your trade increase.

There are both bulls with buy stops above the high of the prior bar and bears with sell stops below the low of that same bar. There are also bulls with buy limit orders at and below the low of the prior bar and bears with sell limit orders at and above the high of the prior bar. That means that every bar is a signal bar for both long and short trades, with both bulls and bears entering on the breakout of both the top and the bottom. Also, every bar can be thought of as a one-bar trading range. If the next bar goes above or below it, breakout traders will expect this breakout to have enough follow-through for them to make at least a scalper's profit. However, equally smart traders will expect the breakout to fail and will trade in the opposite direction. If the market goes one tick above the high of the prior bar, there will be bulls who will buy on a stop order, and the prior bar is the signal bar for their long. There will also be bears who will short on a limit order at the high of the prior bar, expecting the breakout to fail. They hope that the market will trade below the low of their entry bar on the bar after they short, and their entry bar will then become a signal bar for a short trade. One of the most important things to realize about trading is that no matter how convinced you are that you are right, there is someone just as smart and just as convinced that the opposite will happen.

The single most important skill that a trader can develop is the ability to determine the times when there will be more buyers or sellers above or below the prior bar. Signal bars in the right context are times when there is such an imbalance. For example, when there is a bull signal bar in a pullback in a bull trend, there are probably more buyers than sellers above the bar, so looking to buy above the bar makes more sense than looking to short there. Whenever a trader believes that there is an imbalance, he has an advantage, but it is always very small because there are always smart traders who believe the opposite (someone has to take the opposite side of your trade, or else your order will not get filled). As traders, our edge is our ability to read price action, and the better we become, the greater our edge, and the greater the probability that we can make a living from trading. Here are common signal bars and setups (they are discussed further in the next couple of sections):

Continuation signal in the spike phase of a strong trend: A continuation signal can be buying at the top of a bull trend or selling at the bottom of a bear trend.
- Strong bull trend bar in a bull spike.
- Strong bear trend bar in a bear spike.

Reversal signals: A reversal pattern can be a trend reversal or a pullback that is ending and reversing back into the direction of the trend.
- Reversal bar.
- Two-bar reversal.
- Three-bar reversal.
- Small bar:
  - An inside bar.
  - An ii (or iii) pattern.
  - A small bar near the high or low of a big bar or trading range.
  - An ioi pattern.
- Outside bar and an oo pattern (an outside bar followed by a larger outside bar).
- Double top and bottom.
- Failed reversal attempt, including a reversal bar failure.

- Failed continuation attempt, like buying below a low 1 signal bar in a bear trend that appears to be bottoming or shorting above a high 1 signal bar in a bull trend that appears to be topping.
- Shaved bar: a bar with no tail at either the top or the bottom.
- Trend bar: A bull trend bar can be a sell setup in a rally in a strong bear trend and near the top of a trading range, and a bear trend bar can be a buy setup in a pullback in a strong bull trend and near the bottom of a trading range.
- Any pause or pullback bar in the spike phase of a strong trend.
- All bars in a channel: Buy at or below prior bar, sell at or above prior bar.
- Any bar that forms a higher low in a bull trend and a lower high in a bear trend.

A beginning trader should enter only when the signal bar is also a trend bar in the direction of the trade, and should trade only in the direction of the trend. For example, if they are shorting, traders should restrict themselves to signal bars that are bear trend bars in bear trends, because then the market has already demonstrated selling pressure and the odds of follow-through are higher than if the signal bar had a close above its open. Similarly, when beginners are looking to buy, they should buy only when the signal bar has a close above its open and when there is a bull trend underway.

In general, traders should require signal bars to be stronger for trend reversal entries than for trend pullback and trading range trades. This is because most countertrend trades fail and you need to do everything possible to improve your chances of success. The very strongest trends usually have terrible-looking signal bars, but the trades are still excellent. If a setup is too obvious, the market will quickly correct the discrepancy. The move will be fast and small, as is the case with most scalps. Swing trade setups, in contrast, usually have a probability of success of only 50 percent or less, which is discussed more in the second book. They often look like they are just part of a trading range that will continue for many more bars. Strong trends do everything possible to keep traders out, forcing them to chase the trend as it progresses relentlessly. Second-entry reversal setups at the tops of trading ranges often have signal bars with bull bodies, and buy setups at the bottom often have signal bars with bear bodies. However, since most attempts to reverse a trend fail, traders should consider a reversal trade only if everything looks perfect, including the signal bar, to reduce the chances of failure. Beginners should avoid all but the absolute strongest countertrend trades, and any trader should consider taking one only if the overall chart pattern is supportive of a reversal. At a minimum, traders should wait for a pullback from a strong break of the trend line and take the trade only if there is a strong reversal bar, because most successful reversal trades begin with a strong signal bar. Otherwise, the odds of success are too small and traders will lose over time. Incidentally, the pullback from the trend line breakout can reach a new extreme, like a higher high at the end of a bull trend or a lower low at the end of a bear trend. Because trading countertrend is such a low-probability approach, the best traders will take those trades only when there is substantial evidence that the trend is about to reverse.

Trends tend to continue much longer than most traders believe is possible, and this results in most trades in the opposite direction failing and ultimately just setting up another pullback in the trend and another with-trend entry.

Likewise, if traders are looking to trade with trend, they are eager to enter and will not wait for a strong signal bar to develop. For example, if traders are looking to buy a small pullback to the moving average in a strong trend, and the pullback also is testing a prior swing low, a trend line, and maybe a Fibonacci retracement, the trader will buy even if the signal bar is a bear trend bar. The result is that most successful signal bars in strong trends look bad. As a general rule, the stronger the trend, the less important the appearance of the signal bar is, and the more countertrend that your entry is, the more important it is to see a strong signal bar. In strong trends, most signal bars look bad and very few are trend bars in the direction of the trend.

Almost every bar is a potential signal bar, but the majority never lead to an entry and therefore do not become signal bars. As a day trader, you will place many orders that never get filled. It is usually best to enter on a stop at one tick above or below the prior bar and if the stop is not hit, to cancel the order and look for a new location for an order. For stocks, it is often better to place the entry stop at a couple of ticks beyond the potential signal bar because one-tick traps are common, where the market breaks out by only one tick and then reverses, trapping all of the traders who just entered on stops.

If the entry stop order is hit, you based the trade in part on the prior bar so that bar is called the signal bar (it gave you a signal that you needed to place an order). Often a bar can be a setup bar in both directions, and you will place entry stops beyond both extremes and will enter in the direction of either bar breakout.

Much has been written about candle patterns, and it feels as if their unusual Japanese names must mean that they have some mystical power and that they are derived from special ancient wisdom. This is just what novice traders are looking for—the power of the gods telling them what to do, instead of relying on their own hard work. For a trader, the single most important issue is determining whether the market is trending or in a trading range. When it comes to analyzing an individual bar, the issue is also whether it is trending. If either the bulls or the bears are in control, the candle has a body and is a trend bar. If the bulls and bears are in a state of equilibrium and the body is small or nonexistent, it is a doji. Many candle traders use the term *wick* to refer to the lines that usually extend above and below the bodies, presumably to be consistent with the concept of candles. Others call them *shadows.* Since all of us are constantly looking for reversal bars and reversal bars look more like tadpoles or small fish, a *tail* is a more accurate descriptive term.

You should only think of bars in terms of price action and not a collection of meaningless and misleading candle names (misleading to the extent that they convey imagery of a mystical power). Each bar or candle is important only in relation to price action, and the vast majority of candle patterns are not helpful most of the time because they occur in price action where they have no high-probability predictive value. Therefore, candle pattern names will complicate your trading by giving you too much to think about and they take your mind off the trend.

It is common to see a signal bar beginning to form in an area that is a good location for a trade. Maybe three minutes into the 5 minute bar, it has a great shape, like a bull reversal bar just after breaking out of a final bear flag. Then, with five to 10 seconds before the bar closes, it suddenly increases in size by four or more ticks. When the bar closes, it still has the shape of a good bull reversal bar, but now its high is near the high of the bear flag. You have seconds to decide if you still want to buy above its high with the realization that you would be buying at the top of a bear flag. Until you are consistently profitable and able to read quickly, it is best to not take the trade and to wait for a second entry instead. However, if you are confident that there are lots of trapped bears, then you can take the trade, but the risk is significant whenever there are several large range bars in a row with lots of overlap.

All reversals involve climaxes, but the terminology is often used differently by different traders. Remember, every trend bar is a climax or part of a climax and the climax ends with the first pause bar. For example, if there are three consecutive bull trend bars and then the next bar is a small bull trend bar with a prominent tail on the top, or an inside bar, a doji, or a bear trend bar, then the climax ended with the three bull trend bars.

FIGURE 4.1 A Typical Buy Signal Bar

The 15 minute chart of Visa (V) shown in Figure 4.1 shows a break above the bear trend line and then a two-legged sell-off to a lower low below yesterday's low. The point of this chart is to show what signal and entry bars are, and the particular setup patterns will be discussed later in the book. The first leg was completed by the iii ending at bar 2. Bar 3 was a strong bull reversal bar that reversed both yesterday's low and a test of the bear trend line, setting up a possible long. A buy stop at one tick above this bar would have been filled and then bar 3 became a signal bar (instead of just a setup bar) and the bar in which the trade was entered became the entry bar. There was a decent bull trend bar two bars after entry, and it is a follow-through bar. Since this was a countertrend trade, traders needed a strong bull reversal bar like bar 3 before buying; otherwise the chance of a successful trade would have been significantly less.

Bar 4 was an entry bar off of an ii setup (discussed later) for a second leg up.

Bar 5 was an entry bar off of an inside bar breakout pullback (the market barely broke above the bar 2 iii). The bodies of the two pause bars were each inside bodies, so this setup effectively was the same as an ii pattern.

CHAPTER 5

Signal Bars: Reversal Bars

A reversal bar is one of the most reliable signal bars, and it is simply a bar that reverses some aspect of the direction of the prior bar or bars. If you look at smaller time frame charts, you will see that every bull reversal bar is made up of a bear trend bar and then a bull trend bar, but they don't have to be consecutive. The market had a sell climax followed by a bull breakout (remember, all trend bars are simultaneously spikes, breakouts, and climaxes, but the context determines which property is dominant at the moment). The opposite is true of a bear reversal bar, where there is a smaller time frame bull trend bar, indicating that a buy climax took place, followed by a bear trend bar, indicating that the market broke out to the downside.

Most traders want a reversal bar to have a body in the opposite direction of the old trend, but that is not necessary and there are many other components of a reversal that should to be considered.

The best-known signal bar is the reversal bar and the minimum that a bull reversal bar should have is either a close above its open (a bull body) or a close above its midpoint. The best bull reversal bars have more than one of the following:

- An open near or below the close of the prior bar and a close above the open and above the prior bar's close.
- A lower tail that is about one-third to one-half the height of the bar and a small or nonexistent upper tail.
- Not much overlap with the prior bar or bars.

- The bar after the signal bar is not a doji inside bar and instead is a strong entry bar (a bull trend bar with a relatively large body and small tails).
- A close that reverses (closes above) the closes and highs of more than one bar.

The minimum that a bear reversal bar should have is either a close below its open (a bear body) or a close below its midpoint. The best bear reversal bars have:

- An open near or above the close of the prior bar and a close well below the prior bar's close.
- An upper tail that is about one-third to one-half the height of the bar and a small or nonexistent lower tail.
- Not much overlap with the prior bar or bars.
- The bar after the signal bar is not a doji inside bar and instead is a strong entry bar (a bear trend bar with a relatively large body and small tails).
- A close that reverses (closes below) the closes and lows of more than one bar.

This final property is true of any strong trend bar, such as a strong breakout bar, signal bar, or entry bar. For example, at the bottom of a bear leg, if there is a bull reversal bar and its close is above the close of the past eight bars and its high is above the high of the past five bars, this is usually stronger, depending on the context, than a reversal bar that has a close above only the close of the prior bar and is not above the high of any of the recent bars.

The market can trend up or down after any bar, and therefore every bar is a setup bar for both a long entry and a short entry. A setup bar becomes a signal bar only if a trade is entered on the next bar, which becomes the entry bar. A setup bar in and of itself is not a reason to enter a trade. It has to be viewed in relation to the bars before it and it can lead to a trade only if it is part of a continuation or reversal pattern. One of the most difficult things for new traders is that a signal bar often seems to suddenly appear out of nowhere in the final seconds before the bar closes and at times and locations that just don't make sense until several bars later. A key to trading is to be open to the idea that the market can start a swing up or down on the next bar. Just like the best chess players think several moves in advance, the best traders are constantly thinking about reasons why the market might go up or down on the next bar and next several bars. This puts them in a position to anticipate signal bars so that they are ready to place orders if a good setup quickly develops.

Since it is always wisest to be trading with the trend, a trade is most likely to succeed if the signal bar is a strong trend bar in the direction of the trade. Remember, you are looking for times when there will likely be an imbalance between buyers and sellers above or below the prior bar. A reversal bar in the right context is often such a time, giving traders an edge. Even though you are entering after only a one-bar trend, you are expecting more trending in your direction. Waiting to enter on a stop beyond the signal bar requires the market to be going even more in your direction, increasing your odds of success. However, a trend bar that is in the opposite direction can also be a reasonable signal bar, depending on other price action on the chart. In general, signal bars that are doji bars or trend bars in the opposite direction of your trade have a greater chance of failure since the side of the market that you need to be in control has not yet asserted itself. However, in a strong bull trend, you can pretty much get long for any reason, including buying above the high of a strong bear trend bar, especially if you use a wide enough stop. The stronger the trend, the less important it is to have a strong signal bar for a with-trend trade and the more important it is to have a strong signal bar for a countertrend trade. It is always better to get into a market after the correct side (bulls or bears) has taken control of at least the signal bar. That trend bar will give traders much more confidence to enter, use looser stops, and trade more volume, all of which increase the chances that their scalper's target will be reached.

Reversal bars can have characteristics that indicate strength. The most familiar bull reversal bar has a bull body (it closes well above its open) and a moderate tail at the bottom. This indicates that the market traded down and then rallied into the close of the bar, showing that the bulls won the bar and were aggressive right up to the final tick.

When considering a countertrend trade in a strong trend, you must wait for a trend line to be broken and then a strong reversal bar to form on the test of the extreme, or else the chances of a profitable trade are too small. Also, do not enter on a 1 minute reversal bar since the majority of them fail and become with-trend setups. The loss might be small, but if you lose four ticks on five trades, you will never get back to being profitable on the day (you will bleed to death from a thousand paper cuts).

Why is that test of the extreme important? For example, at the end of a bear market, buyers took control and the market rallied. When the market comes back down to the area of that final low, it is testing to see whether the buyers will again aggressively come in around that price or they will be overwhelmed by sellers who are again trying to push prices below that earlier low. If the sellers fail on this second attempt to drive the market down, it will likely go up, at least for a while. Whenever the market tries to do something twice and fails, it usually then tries the opposite. This is why double tops and bottoms work and why traders will not develop a deep conviction in a reversal until the old trend extreme has been tested.

If a reversal bar largely overlaps one or more of the prior bars or if the tail extends beyond the prior bars by only a couple of ticks, it might just be part of a trading range. If so, there is nothing to reverse, because the market is sideways and not trending. In this case, it should not be used as a signal bar and it even might turn into a setup in the opposite direction if enough traders are trapped. Even if the bar has the shape of a perfect bull reversal bar, since no bears were trapped there will likely be no follow-through buying, and new longs will spend several bars hoping that the market will come back to their entry price so they can get out at breakeven. This is pent-up selling pressure.

When the signal bar is large and it has a lot of overlap with the prior two or three bars, it is part of a trading range. This is a common situation in bull and bear flags, and it traps overly eager with-trend traders. For example, consider a market that has been in a trading range day until it reverses up strongly to just above the moving average. Then it goes sideways for three bars and forms a strong bull reversal bar. If the entry would be maybe a tick or so below the top of the bull flag, it is tempting to buy; but about 60 percent of the time, this is a bull trap and the market will turn down soon after entry.

How much overlap is acceptable? As a guideline, whenever the midpoint of a bull reversal bar is above the low of the prior bar in a possible bull reversal (or if the midpoint of a bear reversal bar is below the high of the prior bar in a possible bear reversal), the overlap might be excessive and be indicating that a trading range is developing instead of a tradable reversal. This is far more important when you are looking to enter countertrend (attempting to pick the reversal of a trend), instead of with trend at the end of a pullback, when you have to be much less fussy about perfect setups.

If the body is tiny so that the bar is a doji but the bar is large, it usually should not be used as a basis for a reversal trade. A large doji is basically a one-bar trading range, and it is not wise to buy at the top of a trading range in a bear trend or sell the low of a trading range in a bull trend. It is better to wait for a second signal.

If a bull reversal bar has a large tail at the top or a bear reversal bar has a large tail at the bottom, the countertrend traders lost conviction going into the close of the bar and the countertrend trade should be taken only if the body looks reasonably strong and the price action is supportive (like a second entry).

If the reversal bar is much smaller than the prior several bars, especially if it has a small body, it lacks countertrend strength and is a riskier signal bar. However, if the bar has a strong body and is in the right context, the risk of the trade is small (one tick beyond the other side of the small bar).

In a strong trend, it is common to see a reversal bar forming and then seconds before the bar closes the reversal fails. For example, in a bear trend, you could see a strong bull reversal bar with a big down tail, a last price (the bar hasn't closed yet) well above its open and above the close of the prior bar, and the low of the bar extending below or overshooting a bear trend channel line, but then in the final few seconds before the bar closes, the price collapses and the bar closes on its low. Instead of a bull reversal bar off the trend channel line overshoot, the market formed a strong bear trend bar and all of the traders who entered early in anticipation of a strong bull reversal are now trapped and will help drive the market down further as they are forced to sell at a loss.

A big bull reversal bar with a small body also has to be considered in the context of the prior price action. The large lower tail indicates that the selling was rejected and the buyers controlled the bar. However, if the bar overlaps the prior bar or bars excessively, then it might just represent a trading range on a smaller time frame, and the close at the top of the bar might simply be a close near the top of the range, destined to be followed by more selling as the 1 minute bulls take profits. In this situation, you need additional price action before entering a countertrend trade. You don't want to be buying at the top of a flag in a bear trend or selling at the bottom of a bull flag.

Computer programs allow traders to use charts based on a wide range of characteristics of price action. Traders use every time frame imaginable as well as charts where each bar is based on any number of ticks (each individual trade of any size is one tick) or contracts traded as well as many other things. Because of this, what appears to be a perfect reversal bar on a 5 minute candle chart might not look anything like a reversal bar on many other charts. And even more important is that every reversal on any chart is a perfect reversal bar on some other chart. If you see a reversal setting up but there is no reversal bar, don't waste your time looking around at dozens of charts for one where there is a perfect reversal. Your goal is to understand what the market is doing, not to find some perfect pattern. If you see that the market is trying to reverse, even if it is doing so over a dozen bars, you need to find some way to enter the market, and that has to be your focus. If you waste time searching other charts for a perfect reversal bar, you are allowing yourself to be distracted from your goal and you are likely not mentally prepared at the moment to be trading.

Most reversal bars on the daily chart come from trending trading range days (discussed in Chapter 22) on the intraday charts, but a few come from climactic intraday reversals. Whenever traders see a trending trading range day, they should be aware that it might have a strong reversal later in the day.

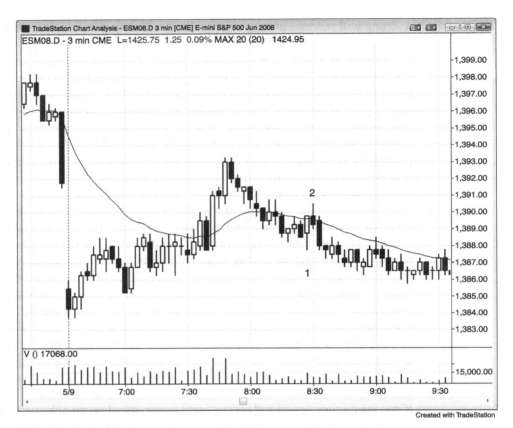

FIGURE 5.1   Reversal Bar in a Trading Range

As shown in Figure 5.1, reversal bar 1 largely overlapped the four prior bars, indicating a two-sided market so there was nothing to reverse. This was not a long
setup bar. Reversal bar 2 was an excellent bear signal bar because it reversed the
breakout of reversal bar 1 (there were trapped longs here off that bull reversal bar
breakout) and it also reversed a breakout above the bear trend line down from the
high of the day. The trapped longs were forced to sell to exit, and this added to
the selling pressure of the shorts. Astute traders knew that there were more sellers
than buyers below the low of bar 2, and shorted there, expecting at least enough
follow-through selling to be able to make a scalper's profit. When the market is in
a trading range in a downswing, it is forming a bear flag. Smart traders will look to
sell near the high, and they would buy near the low if the setup was strong. As trite
as the saying is, "Buy low, sell high" remains one of the best guiding principles for
traders. When I say buy low, I mean that if you are short, you can buy back your

Figure 5.1   SIGNAL BARS: REVERSAL BARS   **95**

short for a profit, and if there is a strong buy signal, you can buy to initiate a long position. Likewise, when the market is toward the top of the range, you sell high. This selling can be to take your profit if you are long, or if there is a good short setup, you can sell to initiate a short position.

Deeper Discussion of This Chart

The market broke below yesterday's low in Figure 5.1, but the breakout failed and reversed up into a trend from the open bull day. The bull trend ended with a strong breakout that failed at 7:48 a.m. PST with a moving average gap bar short setup. The move down to bar 1 was a tight bear channel, and the first breakout above a tight channel usually reverses within a bar or two. At that point, it might form a lower low or higher low pullback from the breakout and then the rally will resume, or the breakout will simply fail and the bear trend will resume, as it did here.

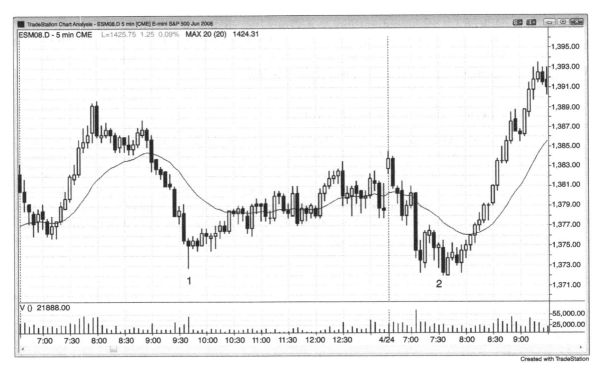

FIGURE 5.2   Reversal Bar with Big Tail and Small Body

Reversal bars with big tails and small bodies must be evaluated in the context of the prior price action. As shown in Figure 5.2, reversal bar 1 was a breakout below a prior major swing low in a very oversold market (it reversed up from a breakout below the steep trend channel line of the prior eight bars). There had also been very strong bullish activity earlier in the day, so the bulls might return. Profit takers would want to cover their shorts and wait for the excess to be worked off with time and price before they would be eager to sell again.

The next day, reversal bar 2 overlapped about 50 percent of the prior bar and several of the bars before that, and it did not spike below a prior low. It likely just represents a trading range on the 1 minute chart, and no trades should be taken until more price action unfolds.

Although a classic reversal bar is one of the most reliable signal bars, most reversals occur in their absence. There are many other bar patterns that yield reliable signals. In almost all cases, the signal bar is stronger if it is a trend bar in the direction of your trade. For example, if you are looking to buy a possible reversal at the bottom of a bear trend, the odds of a successful trade are significantly increased if the signal bar has a close well above its open and near its high.

Figure 5.2   SIGNAL BARS: REVERSAL BARS   **97**

Deeper Discussion of This Chart

Today (the most recent day on the chart), shown in Figure 5.2, broke out above yesterday's trading range, but the breakout failed and the day became a trend from the open bear. The second breakout below yesterday's low also failed and became the low of the day.

When the market goes sharply up and then down, it usually enters a trading range, and the bulls and bears then fight for control of the market. The move to the new low of the day accelerated at the end. There were a couple of large bear trend bars, which were consecutive sell climaxes. This usually is followed by at least two legs and 10 bars up. Because the sell-off to a new low had no follow-through, it was simply due to a sell vacuum and not strong bears. The strong bulls expected the market to test below the low of the day, so they simply stopped buying until the target was reached. Their lack of buying during the several bars leading to bar 1 caused the market to collapse. It did not make sense for them to buy just above the low when they believed that the market was going to fall below the low. Why buy when you can buy lower if you just wait for a few minutes? However, once it reached their buy zone, they bought relentlessly, and the market rallied in a bull channel into the close.

FIGURE 5.3 Reversal Bars Can Be Unconventional

A bear reversal bar does not have to have a high that is above the high of the prior bar, but it does need to reverse something about the price action of the prior bar or bars. In Figure 5.3, bar 29 was a strong bear trend bar in a bull leg, so its body reversed the direction of the market. Its close reversed the closes of the prior 13 bars and the lows of the prior 12 bars, which is unusual but a sign of strength. All of the traders who bought on the close of bar 24 and during any of the next 12 bars now quickly were holding losing positions and if they did not exit as the bar was forming, they would likely have exited on its close or once the next bar traded below its low. The strongest bulls hold through pullbacks and will hold until they believe that the trend has flipped. A single strong reversal that reverses many closes and lows, like bar 29, can flip the always-in direction. It can also lead those strong bulls to believe that the market will likely trade low enough so that they could exit their longs and then look to buy again much lower, probably as much as a measured move down based on the height of the bar. These disappointed bulls will look for any opportunity to exit their longs. They expect to get out with a loss at this point, but would like to get out with as small a loss as possible and will place limit orders above the close of bar 29 and above the high of prior bars. Some traders will see the prior bar as a high 1 buy setup, but this is a situation where traders believe that the always-in direction has reversed to down. They therefore think that high 1 and

Figure 5.3   SIGNAL BARS: REVERSAL BARS   **99**

high 2 entries will fail to yield even a scalper's profit. Both the bulls and bears will place limit orders to sell above these high 1 and high 2 signal bars (entering on limit orders on high or low 1 and 2 signals that you expect them to fail is discussed in book 2). The bulls will be relieved to get out with a smaller loss, and the bears see this as a great opportunity to short above the high of the prior bar in a new bear trend (it might be a bear channel), but if the market falls below the high 2 buy signal bar's low, even the most diehard bulls will give up, and the market will often break out into a bear spike and then at least a measured move down.

If there is no pullback that would allow the trapped bulls to exit with a smaller loss within a few bars, they will exit at the market and on the closes of bars that have bear closes, and on stops below the low of the prior bar. Bears understand what is happening and will look for those same opportunities to sell, but their selling will be to initiate shorts, not to exit longs. The bulls who held through the close of bar 29 are the swing bulls, because they were willing to hold through pullbacks. Swing traders are generally the strongest participants, because many are institutions with deep pockets and have the ability to tolerate pullbacks. Once these strongest bulls decide that the market will fall further, there is no one left to buy, and the market usually has to fall for about 10 bars and two legs to some support level before they will consider buying again. They will not buy until a strong buy setup appears, and if one does not come, they will continue to wait. Here, there were not enough bars left in the day for them to look to buy again, and therefore there were not enough buyers left to lift the market before the close of the day.

Bar 29 was a signal bar, and many traders shorted below its low. It was also an entry bar, and many traders shorted during it as it fell below the low of the prior bar and as it was expanding down, because they believed that the breakout above the trading range of the past 12 bars was failing. It was also a breakout bar because it broke out of that trading range to the downside. It formed a reversal with bar 27 or with the entire bull spike from bar 26 to bar 29. From the inset, you can see that it was part of a large reversal bar on the 15 minute chart.

Bar 21 reversed the closes of the prior three bars but since it was in a steep bear channel, it was safer to wait to buy a breakout pullback after the market broke above the channel. Also, it overlapped the prior two bars and might be forming a trading range instead of a reversal. Bar 23 was a reasonable breakout pullback signal bar, since the market just made two attempts to sell off and both failed (bar 11 and the bar before bar 23). Because the day had such a strong rally in the first couple of hours, the market was likely to try to rally again after a pullback. This increased the chances of success for traders who bought above bar 21, especially since it tested the initial breakout above the opening range (the high of bar 1) and reversed up.

Bar 21 was signal bar but the bar that followed was a doji bar, which shows a lack of urgency by the bulls. Bar 25 was also a signal bar and the next bar was a doji inside bar. Whenever the bar after the signal bar is a small doji bar, the market lacks urgency for a reversal. If the bar is an inside bar, like after bar 25, it is usually better to not take the trade unless the setup is otherwise especially strong. If the doji is the entry bar like after bar 21, you have a few choices. You can try to get out at breakeven or with a one-tick loss, or, if the setup otherwise looks good, you can keep your stop below your signal bar. Since this looked like a good setup, it made sense to hold long with a stop below the signal bar.

The bar after bar 19 was a doji, but bar 19 was a weak signal. When the entry bar after a weak signal is also weak, it is better to try to get out around breakeven.

In general, raising the stop to just below a doji entry bar is not a good choice because the odds are 50–50 it will get hit. If that is what you are inclined to do, it is probably better to try to get out around breakeven. Whenever there is a doji bar within a few bars of a reversal, the market has about a 50 percent chance of trading below it. Also, when you are trading reversals, you are trading countertrend and the odds of a pullback are high. If you take the trade and it looks strong, you have to be willing to allow pullbacks or else you should not take the trade. If the setup instead is weak, you want a very strong entry bar and if you do not get one, consider trying to get out with a scratch (breakeven or maybe a one- or two-tick loss).

There was a strong bull trend bar two bars after bar 13, and since it is a reversal bar, it can be viewed as a signal bar. It was followed by an inside bar, which can be thought of as a breakout pullback. However, since that strong bull signal bar has so much overlap with the two prior bars, it probably had a 60 percent chance of being a bull trap, which it turned out to be. Bull flags just above the moving average where there are three or more large bars that mostly overlap are usually traps. The same is true for a bear flag just below the moving average where there are three or more large bear bars that largely overlap. Even if there is a strong bear trend bar for a signal bar, the odds are that a short below will result in a loss.

Between bars 10 and 15 there were several bars with strong bear bodies and this was a sign of selling pressure. The pressure is cumulative, and it eventually led to a sell-off.

CHAPTER 6

Signal Bars: Other Types

Remember, a signal bar is a setup bar that led to an entry. However, not all trades are worth taking, and just because a stop was triggered and turned the prior bar into a signal bar, that does not make the trade worth taking (for example, many signals in a tight trading range, which is described later, are best avoided). All signal bars are meaningless in the absence of price action that indicates that the breakout of the bar will likely go far enough for at least a profitable scalp.

STRONG TREND BAR

A very important signal bar is a strong trend bar, especially during the spike phase of a trend. For example, if the market just broke above a bottom at an area of major support on a major news item that will affect the market for days, traders will look for any reason to get long. One common approach is to wait for a bar to close and if the bar is a strong bull trend bar, traders will buy at the market as soon as the bar closes. Many will try to quickly place a limit order at the price of the close, and if their order is not filled within a few seconds, they will change it to a market order. Other traders will enter on a stop at one tick above the high of the bar. This urgency results in a series of bull trend bars and an increasingly larger bull spike.

REVERSAL PATTERNS

Traders are always looking for a change of direction, and they rely on reversal patterns as the earliest sign that a change might be taking place. The risk is to the opposite end of the bar and the reward is often several times greater. For example, if a trader buys on a stop at one tick above a bull reversal bar that is eight ticks tall, he might put a protective stop at one tick below the bar and the total risk would then be 10 ticks. However, the trader might be planning on taking profits at 20 or more ticks above the entry.

When there is a strong trend that might be reversing into a trading range or into an opposite trend, traders will want a strong reversal setup, which is often simply called a reversal. This is because trends are resistant to change and if traders are to bet on a move in the opposite direction, they will want a strong sign that the market is about to reverse. However, if there is a strong trend and then a pullback, traders are so confident that the trend will resume that they will not require a strong reversal setup at the end of the pullback. In fact, the majority of signal bars for trend pullback trades look weak. If a pullback setup looks perfect and easy, it usually means that the trend is not strong. So many traders would take it that it often becomes the final flag in the trend, leading to a bigger correction. Trends require traders to keep missing entries so there is a constant tension, a constant desire to get in, and one of the ways that trends accomplish this is through weak signal bars. For example, if there is a two-legged pullback to the moving average in a strong bull trend, traders might be willing to buy above the high of the prior bar even if it is a bear trend bar and not a strong bull reversal bar. They are afraid that the pullback will reverse back into the direction of the bull trend and the rally might quickly accelerate. They wanted a pullback so they could buy at a lower price, and now that they have one, they want to be sure that they buy before the breakout from the bull flag goes very far. All traders have this sense of urgency, which is why the rally to a new high is often very fast. Traders who did not take the trade because the signal looked weak will remain eager to buy, and many will keep buying in small pieces all the way up, just to be certain that they have at least a small position. Trapped shorts keep waiting for a deeper correction and a clearer buy signal to let them out with a smaller loss, but one never comes and they have to keep buying back their shorts in pieces as the trend continues higher. Most trends eventually have at least a minor climax before a deeper correction comes, and the climax is usually due to the weak traders finally entering late and the last traders on the wrong side finally exiting. When no traders are left on the wrong side, the sense of urgency disappears and the market usually enters a trading range, at least for a while.

Besides a classic reversal bar, other common reversal setups (some are two- or three-bar patterns) include the following.

Two-Bar Reversal

Two-bar reversals are one of the most common reversal setups and therefore are very important. It is useful to think of every reversal as a type of two-bar reversal because the phrase reminds traders that the market made a strong move in one direction and then a strong move in the opposite direction. The strongest moves usually begin with either a reversal bar or a two-bar reversal for the signal. This is why it is so important to be ready to place a trade when the setup occurs at a time when a strong move might follow. Two-bar reversals have many variations and are a part of every reversal, but they may not be apparent on the chart you are using. However, as long as you understand that the market is reversing, it is not necessary to look at many types of charts to find a perfect two-bar reversal or a perfect reversal bar, although they both are present in every reversal.

The best-known version is a pair of consecutive 5 minute trend bars of approximately the same size but opposite directions. A long setup is a bear trend bar immediately followed by a bull trend bar, and a bear setup is a bull trend bar immediately followed by a bear trend bar. These two bars create a 10 minute reversal bar, but the reversal bar is evident on the 10 minute chart only 50 percent of the time because only half of the 5 minute two-bar reversals will end at the same time as the 10 minute bar. The other half will result in some other usually less clear reversal on the 10 minute chart.

It is important to realize that all climactic reversals, all reversal bars, and all two-bar reversals are exactly the same and all are present at all reversals, and you will be able to see them if you look at enough different types of charts. If you think about it, even a classic reversal bar is actually a two-bar reversal on some smaller time frame or on some other type of chart, like a tick or volume chart that uses the right number of ticks or shares per bar. Also, the two bars in opposite directions do not have to be consecutive, and most of the time they are not. However, if you look at all possible higher time frame charts, you will be able to find one where the setup actually is a perfect two-bar reversal. You can almost always find one where it becomes a single reversal bar. Always be open to all possibilities because you will then find many more setups that you understand and have confidence to trade. The key is to recognize that a reversal is taking place, and you need to be aware of the many ways that it can appear. A bear reversal always has a bull trend bar, which is acting as a buy climax, followed before long by a bear trend bar, which is acting as a breakout to the downside. A bull reversal is the opposite, with a bear trend bar that is acting as a sell climax and then a bull trend bar that is acting as a bull breakout.

A reversal bar can be the second bar of a two-bar reversal. When it overlaps more than about 75 percent of the prior bar, it is better to regard the two bars as a two-bar reversal setup rather than as a reversal bar. If you do so, the odds of a successful reversal trade are higher. For example, if the market is rallying and forms a bear reversal bar with a low that is one tick above the low of the prior bar, this is often a bear trap. The market frequently falls one tick below the bear reversal bar but not below the bull trend bar that preceded it, and then rallies to a new high within a couple of bars. This happens much less often if that bear entry bar falls below the low of both bars and not just below the low of the bear reversal bar. When the reversal bar overlaps the prior bar by too much, they form a two-bar trading range and the breakout entry is beyond the entire trading range. Since the trading range is only two bars long, the entry is beyond both bars, not just the second bar.

If that bear reversal bar falls below the prior bull trend bar, treat it like an outside bar, even if its high is below the high of the bull trend bar. In general, it is then better to wait for a pullback to a lower high before going short. Otherwise you are shorting so far below the top of the bull leg that there is too much risk that you might be shorting at some support level, like the bottom of a developing trading range, and the market might rally.

There is a special type of two-bar reversal that signals a trade in the opposite direction. If there is a two-bar reversal that is sitting on or touching the bottom of the moving average and the two bars almost entirely overlap one or more prior bars, the breakout usually fails. If the market is in a strong trend, however, the signal will usually work, since almost any with-trend entry works in a strong trend. When there is not a strong trend, the signal usually fails even if there is a perfect two-bar reversal. Any three or more large, overlapping bars will do. For example, if there is a two-bar bull reversal just above the moving average and the bars are relatively large and mostly overlap a third or fourth bar, do not buy above the high of the signal bar. The market has formed a small trading range, and traders who are confident in their read of the overall price action can often short the market at or above the bull signal bar for a scalp down.

Three-Bar Reversals

A three-bar reversal is just a variation of a two-bar reversal where there are three consecutive bars, with the first and third being the bars of a two-bar reversal and the middle bar being an unremarkable bar, like a small bar or a doji. This creates a 15 minute reversal bar when the third 5 minute bar closes at the same time as the 15 minute bar. When that happens, it is likely more reliable because it would then bring in traders who are trading off of 15 minute charts. In the two out of three times that it does not, the 5 minute signal usually results in some other 15 minute reversal pattern. When looking for any 5 minute reversal entry, it is helpful to think about whether there are three consecutive bars that might also be forming a 15 minute reversal bar. If so, this should give you more confidence in your trade since a higher time frame signal is more likely to be followed by a larger move, and you might be more comfortable swinging more of your position and using a wider profit target. In general, traders should view them as simple two-bar reversals and not worry about whether they are also creating a 15 minute reversal bar.

Small Bars

A bar that has a small range compared to the prior bars can be a reversal signal bar. Here are common examples:

- An inside bar, which is a bar with a high below the high of the prior bar and a low at or above the low of the prior bar, or a low above the low of the prior bar and a high at or below the high of the prior bar. It is more reliable if it is small and has a body in the opposite direction of the current trend and less reliable if it is a large doji bar. In fact, a large doji is rarely a good signal bar even if it is an inside bar, and since it is a one-bar trading range, it is usually followed by more two-sided trading.
- An ii (or iii) pattern, which is two consecutive inside bars with the second being inside of the first (an iii is made of three consecutive inside bars).
- A small bar near the high or low of a big bar (trend bar or outside bar) or trading range (especially if its body is in the direction of your trade, indicating that your side has taken control).
- An ioi pattern, which is an inside bar followed by an outside bar and then another inside bar (inside-outside-inside). If it occurs in an area where a breakout seems likely, traders can enter on the breakout of that second inside bar. These are often breakout mode setups, meaning that the move can be in either direction, and it is often prudent to place a sell stop below and a buy stop above that second inside bar and enter in the direction of the breakout. The unfilled order then becomes the protective stop.

Note that doji bars are rarely good signal bars because they are one-bar trading ranges and when the market is in a trading range, you should not be looking to buy above the high or go short below the low. They can be decent signal bars for reversal trades if they occur near the high or low of a trading range day, or if they are a with-trend setup in a strong trend. In a trading range, it can be fine to sell below a doji if the doji is at the high of the range, especially if it is a second entry. The bigger trading range trumps the tiny trading range represented by the doji bar, so selling below the doji bar is also selling at the top of a large trading range, which is usually a good trade.

Outside Bar

An outside bar is a bar with either its high or its low beyond that of the prior bar and the other extreme of the outside bar at or beyond the prior bar's extreme. See Chapter 7.

Micro Double Bottom

A micro double bottom is consecutive or nearly consecutive bars with identical or nearly identical lows. When it forms in a bear spike and it is a bear trend bar closing on or near its low and then a bull trend bar opening on or near its low, it is a one-bar bear flag. If the lows are identical, consider selling at one tick below the low. At all other times, it is more likely a reversal pattern, since most small bull reversals come from some type of micro double bottom (discussed in book 3).

Micro Double Top

A micro double top is consecutive or nearly consecutive bars with identical or nearly identical highs. When it forms in a bull spike and it is a bull trend bar closing on or near its high and then a bear trend bar opening on or near its high, it is a one-bar bull flag. If the highs are identical, consider buying at one tick above the high. At all other times, it is more likely a reversal pattern, since most small bear reversals come from some type of micro double top (discussed in book 3).

Reversal Bar Failure

A reversal bar failure is the bar after a reversal bar that breaks out of the wrong side of the reversal (e.g., if there is a bear reversal bar in a bull trend and the next bar trades above its high instead of below its low).

Shaved Bar

A shaved bar has no tail at one or both of its extremes. It is a setup only when it forms in a strong trend (e.g., in a strong bull trend, if there is a bull trend bar with no tail on its top or bottom, then it is a buy setup).

Exhaustion Bar

An unusually large trend bar in the direction of the trend can often represent an emotional exhaustion of a trend. All trend bars are spikes, breakouts, gaps, and climaxes or exhaustion bars, and sometimes the exhaustive component can be the dominant feature.

Trend Bars

Besides being signal bars for with-trend entries in strong trends, trend bars can also be signal bars for reversal trades, like a pullback reversing back in the direction of the trend, and for reversal trades in trading ranges. For example, if there is a strong bull trend and at least 20 consecutive bars have been above the moving average, and the market drifts sideways to the rising moving average, look to buy the close of the first small bear trend bar with a close that is only a tick or two below the moving average. Also, look to buy above its high. You are expecting the sideways to down correction to end and reverse back into the direction of the trend.

If there is a clearly defined trading range with multiple reversals and there is a two-legged, two bull trend bar spike to a slightly new high in the middle of the day, this is often a good signal to go short at the market, especially if you can scale in higher and especially if it is a part of another pattern, like if it is at the top of a small wedge or if it is a test of a bear trend line. Also, if there is a two-legged sell-off in the trading range that forms a bear trend bar that closes below an earlier swing low in the trading range in the bottom half of the range, this can also be a signal to buy at the market, especially if you can add on lower or if it is part of another pattern, like the bottom of a wedge bull flag.

ALL BARS IN A CHANNEL

When there is a strong bull channel, bulls will place limit orders to buy at or below the low of the prior bar, and bears will place limit orders to short at or above the high of every bar and above every swing high. Bulls will also place buy stop orders above the highs of pullback bars, and the bears will place sell stop orders below the lows of bars at the top of the channel. The opposite is true in a bear channel.

There are many types of small bars and many different situations in which they occur, and all represent a lack of enthusiasm from both the bulls and the bears. Each has to be evaluated in context. A small bar is a much better setup if it has a body in the direction of your trade (a small reversal bar), indicating that your side owns the bar. If the small bar has no body, it is usually better to wait for a second entry since the probability of a successful trade is much less and the chance of a whipsaw is too great.

An inside bar does not have to be totally inside (high below the prior bar's high, low above the prior bar's low). One or both of its extremes can be identical to that of the prior bar. In general, it forms a more reliable signal when it is a small bar and when its close is in the direction of the trade you want to take (it is always better to have bull signal bars when you are looking to buy and bear signal bars when you are looking to sell).

When an inside bar occurs after a big trend bar that breaks out of a trading range, it could be simply a pause by the trend traders, but it could also be a loss of conviction that will lead to a reversal (failed breakout). A reversal is more likely when the small bar is an inside bar and it is a trend bar in the opposite direction of the large breakout bar. A with-trend inside bar increases the chances that the breakout move will continue, especially if the market had been trending in that direction earlier in the day (for example, if this might be the start of the second leg that you were expecting).

Small inside bars after breakout trend bars are somewhat emotional for traders because they will consider entering in either direction on a stop and will have to process a lot of information quickly. For example, if there is a bull breakout during a down day, the trader will often place an order to buy at one tick above the high of the inside bar and a second order to sell at one tick below its low. Once one order is filled, the other order becomes the protective stop. If the order was filled on a breakout failure (i.e., on the sell order), the trader should consider doubling the size of the buy stop order, in case the failed breakout becomes a breakout pullback (opposite failures means that both the bulls and the bears were trapped, and this usually sets up a reliable trade). However, if the trader was first filled on the buy (with trend) order, he usually should not reverse on the protective stop, but might if the day had been a bear trend day. Once there has been a second or third bar without a failure, a failure that then occurs has a higher chance of simply setting up a breakout pullback entry in the direction of the new trend rather than a tradable failure. In general, good traders make quick, subjective decisions based on many subtle factors and if the process feels too confusing or emotional, it is better to not place an order, especially complicated orders like a pair of breakout orders or an order to reverse. Traders should not invest too much emotion in a confusing trade because they will likely be less ready to take a clear trade that may soon follow.

An inside bar after a swing move might mark the end of the swing, especially if its close is against the trend and other factors are in play, like a trend line or trend channel line overshoot, an ABC two-legged correction (a high or low 2), or a new swing high in a trading range. Also, any small bar, whether or not it is an inside bar, near an extreme of any large bar (trend bar, doji, or outside bar) can set up a reversal, especially if the small bar is a small reversal bar. In general, traders should be looking to buy low and sell high. In a trading range (a trading range day or a trading range in a trend day), the only small bar entries should be fades at the extremes. For example, if a small bar is a swing high, or follows a bear trend line test or a bull trend channel line overshoot and reversal, only look for a short entry. If it is a swing low, only look for a buy.

In a trend (even one during a trading range day), a small bar can set up an entry in either direction. For example, if there is a strong bull move and no prior break of a significant bull trend line, an inside bar near the high of a large bull trend bar or a small bar that extends above the high of the trend bar should only be viewed as a buy setup. If it is an inside bar, especially if it is a bull trend bar, it is a great long setup. If it is simply a small bar that extends above the high of the bull trend bar, it might be a safe long setup if the trend is strong enough. In general, it would be better to wait for a pullback, unless the small bar is a bear reversal bar, in which case it could trap bears and it might make sense to buy on a stop at one tick above its high.

An ii pattern is an inside bar that follows a larger inside bar. It is two in a row with the second being inside the first and of the same size or smaller (an iii is even stronger, with three in a row). After a protracted move, especially if there has been a trend line break, a with-trend breakout from an ii pattern is often just a scalp and has a good chance of reversing before or after the profit target is reached (a final flag, as described in book 3). However, a countertrend breakout (or a reversal from a final flag) often leads to a large reversal. The pattern often develops in a final flag because it finally indicates balance between the bulls and the bears; the strength of the weaker side has caught up to that of the stronger side, at least temporarily. As such, if the with-trend side takes control, the odds are high that the countertrend side will try to take it back after the with-trend breakout. The stop on an ii pattern is beyond the opposite side of both bars (not just the second bar, which technically is the signal bar), but sometimes you can use a smaller stop (beyond the second of the two bars instead of beyond both bars) if the bars are relatively large. After the entry bar closes, tighten the stop and consider reversing at one tick beyond the entry bar. Keep looking to reverse on any failure in the next several bars since failures are common soon after ii breakouts, especially if the pattern forms in the middle of the day's range.

A 5 minute ii pattern is often a 1 minute double bottom pullback in a bull trend or a double top pullback in a bear trend (described in book 2), which are reversal patterns and might explain why a small ii can lead to a large countertrend move.

When there is a strong bull trend, there will sometimes be two consecutive bars with identical highs, and usually with small tails at the tops of the two bars. This is a two-bar double top buy setup and is a double top on the 1 minute chart. Place a stop to go long at one tick above the high of the bars because you will be buying a failed double top and there will be protective stops there from traders who shorted it, adding fuel to the move. Likewise, in a strong bear trend, look to short on a stop at one tick below a two-bar double bottom sell setup.

Two-bar reversal setups go by several names, and each is an overlapping pair of trend bars with opposite directions and bodies of about the same size. In a two-bar reversal top setup, the first bar is a bull trend bar and the second is a bear trend bar, and this combination is a sell setup if the market is not in a trading range. A two-bar reversal bottom is a bear trend bar and then a bull trend bar and forms a buy setup. They are each basically a two-bar reversal pattern and they correspond to a 10 minute reversal bar (just imagine how the two 5 minute bars would look when combined into a single 10 minute bar).

A two-bar reversal can be a continuation pattern (a one-bar flag) or a reversal pattern, depending on the context. For example, if the market is in a strong bear spike and then has a bear bar and then a small bull trend bar with a low that is close to the low of the bar before it, this is a two-bar reversal. However, since the market is in a steep trend, you should never look to buy above it. Instead, you should view the bull bar as a one-bar bear flag and consider shorting below it. In contrast, if the identical two-bar pattern formed in a bull trend at the end of a two-legged pullback to the moving average, this is a two-bar reversal and a good setup for a buy setup. The pullback is ending and reversing back into the bull trend.

When a trend bar in a strong trend has a shaved body (no tail at one or both ends), it usually indicates that the market is one-sided and strong. However, a shaved top on a 5 minute bull trend bar in a runaway bull trend is stronger than a shaved bottom, because the extreme strength is right into the close of the bar and it is more likely to continue the strength that occurred five minutes earlier. Therefore, a shaved top is a good setup for a long. If the bar has a one-tick tail at its high or a shaved bottom, it is still strong, but in general that alone would not be reason enough to buy above its high. Also, the bar has to be analyzed in context. If the bar is in a trading range, it would be foolish to buy above its high, because trading ranges tend to test the extremes repeatedly and you should not be buying near the high when the odds of the bar being a test are greater than the odds of the bar being a successful breakout. Similarly, a bear trend bar with a shaved bottom in a runaway bear trend is a setup to short at one tick below its low.

When the market is quiet and the volume is low, shaved tops and bottoms are sometimes common and are not a sign of strength. When you see many shaved tops and bottoms in an hour or so and they are in a trading range, be very selective about trading. Each of those bars is a trap, fooling traders into believing that there is strength when there is none.

Not all small bars are good fade setups. There is one particular situation where they should not be used as signal bars, and that is when the bar is a small doji (small relative to the recent bars), especially if it has no body, it is near the moving average, and it occurs approximately between 10:00 a.m. and 11:00 a.m. PST. These have a very high failure rate and always require more price action before placing a trade.

Although most large trend bars that are with trend are strong, if a bar is unusually large, it often represents a climactic exhaustion (a buy climax). For example, in a bull trend, it often means that the last buyers bought and they bought in a panic because they just had to get in at any price, or if they were short, they just had to buy back their losing shorts at any price. If there are no more buyers, the market will go down. Any standard reversal setup can serve as a signal bar, but a second entry with a strong reversal bar is always the safest setup when trading countertrend.

Big trend bars on breakouts often fail on the next bar, trapping traders into the wrong side of the market. This is especially common on quiet trading range days, when the market is always surging to the top and bottom of the range and fooling naïve traders into expecting a successful breakout.

Figure 6.1   SIGNAL BARS: OTHER TYPES   **111**

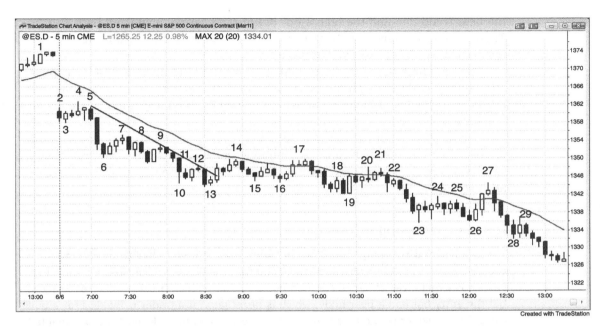

FIGURE 6.1 Small Signal Bars

A small bar can be a with-trend or countertrend setup. In a trend, a small bar on a pullback is only a with-trend setup. As shown in Figure 6.1, bars 7, 9, 12, 14, 17, and 21 were small bars in pullbacks and the only trade they offered was a short on a stop at one tick below their lows. Even though they were mostly doji bars, they were with trend and therefore reasonable shorts. Most signal bars in a strong trend look weak, and that is one of the reasons why the trend just keeps working lower. Bears are eager to short and bulls want to exit with a smaller loss, and both keep waiting for a strong sell setup. This would make them confident that the market is not going to rally and that they need to get out immediately. The perfect setup never comes, and the bears are trapped out and the bulls are trapped in. This creates a constant sense of tension and urgency that keeps driving the market down. Both keep selling in small pieces all day long, just in case their perfect setup never comes . . . and it usually doesn't. The setups never look strong, so it is easy for traders to assume that the trend is weak and that there will soon be a good rally that will allow them to sell at a better price. They see the market staying below the moving average, but it never falls fast enough to make them panic, so they keep hoping for a bigger rally to sell. The weak signal bars are an important ingredient in strong trends.

A small bar can also set up a countertrend trade against a trend if it occurs at a swing low and there are other reasons for trading countertrend, like a prior trend line break. Bar 16 was a small bear bar that set up a long after a break above the bear trend line and the high 4 bottom of the bear channel from bars 7 to 13. There was a two-legged pullback from the bar 14 test of the moving average, and the market was likely to have a second leg up.

The only time that a trader should sell a small bar at a low is in a bear trend, and preferably during a strong bear spike. Bar 29 was not particularly small, but it was an inside bar, which functions like a small bar, and it was a bear trend bar, making it a safe short at the low of the day.

Bar 13 was the middle bar of a three-bar reversal up, and bar 17 was the middle of a four-bar reversal down. All multiple bar reversals are just variations of two-bar reversals. There were several other reversals on the chart, as there are on all charts.

Deeper Discussion of This Chart

The day began with a large gap down in Figure 6.1, so traders had to be looking for a possible trend from the open up or down and they needed to watch closely for a setup. Bar 3 was a bull reversal bar and a good buy setup for a failed breakout and reversal up, but the entry bar had a bear body, which is never good if a trader is looking for a bull trend. This failed breakout failed and became a breakout pullback short setup, and it led to a resumption of the bear breakout. Longs exited on the reversal down below bar 4 and many reversed to short. The next bar was also a doji bar and now the market was in a tight trading range on a large gap down day. This was a great breakout mode pattern for a big trend up or down. Bar 5 went one tick above that doji and likely trapped premature bulls who did not wait for a breakout above the bar 4 top of the opening range. The best trade of the day was the short below bar 5 or on the next bar as it broke below the low of the tight trading range, or on its close when it was clear that the market was always in short. The spike down to bar 6 had three large bear trend bars and was likely to be followed by a measured move down, probably in a bear channel. The trend went much further than that.

Bar 13 was a small bull inside bar at a new swing low and a reversal up from a low 2 final flag short, and the second leg down of a second leg down, making it a high 4 long setup. It was also the third or fourth push down (depending on how you want to count the pushes) in a bear channel in a spike and channel bear. The spike was made of three bear trend bars that started at bar 5. Channels often end on the third push and are usually followed by a two-legged move sideways to up, as happened here. The correction often reaches the top of the channel, but here the bear trend was so strong that the correction could only go sideways and not up. That usually means that lower prices will follow.

Bar 16 was a high 2 buy setup in a developing trading range after a relatively strong move up to bar 14 that was strong enough to break the bear trend line. This strength made a second leg up likely.

Figure 6.1   SIGNAL BARS: OTHER TYPES   **113**

Bar 14 was close to being a 20 gap bar short setup since the prior 20 bars all had highs below the moving average. Close is close enough, and a test of the bear low was likely. The rally to bar 14 was also the first breakout of a tight channel and was therefore likely to be followed by at least a test down.

Bar 17 was an actual 20 gap bar short setup. The market traded below it and then above it and then it sold off to a new low of the day. Bar 17 was a doji moving average gap bar short setup but with the move up from bar 16 being a strong bull spike, most traders would have waited for a second signal before shorting. The entry was below the outside up bar that followed bar 17. The entry bar was a strong bear trend bar and it became the first bar in a strong bear spike.

There are many micro double top and bottom reversal patterns on all charts, and these are discussed in book 3 in the chapter on reversals. Bars 20 and 21 formed an example of a micro double top reversal pattern.

FIGURE 6.2 A Reversal Bar Can Be a Continuation Setup

When a trend is strong, the market often trades below instead of above a bull reversal bar or above instead of below a bear reversal bar. As shown in Figure 6.2, on this 5 minute chart of Baidu, Inc. (BIDU), bar 3 was the third attempt to reverse the market up and it was a strong bull reversal bar. However, instead of moving above it, the market broke out below it. Perhaps there were early longs who entered on the reversal bar before it triggered a buy signal (the next bar did not trade one tick above its high), and these overly eager bulls were now trapped. They would exit at one tick below the bull reversal bar, which was where smart traders went short.

The opposite happened at the bar 6 bear reversal bar, where traders who shorted before the market traded below the low of the bar were trapped and had to cover on the next bar as it traded above the bear reversal bar. A reversal bar alone is not enough reason to enter, even if it is in an area where a reversal might reasonably take place.

Figure 6.3   SIGNAL BARS: OTHER TYPES   **115**

FIGURE 6.3 A Big Trend Bar Can Indicate Exhaustion

An unusually large trend bar that forms in a trend that has lasted for 10 or more bars usually means that the market is exhausted and will correct for at least 10 bars, and sometimes it leads to a reversal.

In Figure 6.3, bar 3 was a huge trend bar that collapsed below the low of the open and through a trend channel line and was followed by a bull inside bar with a shaved top, meaning that buyers were aggressively buying it right into its close. This is a great setup for a long. The large bear trend bar was acting as a sell climax, and the breakout above the bull inside bar was a bull breakout. This is a spike down and then a spike up, which is a reversal, and if you looked at various higher time frame charts, you could find one or more where this bottom was a perfect two-bar reversal and others where this formed a single reversal bar.

Bar 4 was a bear reversal bar but the bar 5 short entry bar immediately reversed up above the bar 4 high, running the stops on those shorts. It is important to note that shorting below the bar 4 bear reversal bar would not have been a wise decision because the upward momentum was too strong. There were 11 consecutive bull trend bars, so traders should not be shorting below the first bear bar. Buying above the bear reversal bar or above the bar 5 bull outside up bar was a reasonable trade since there were stopped-out bears who would wait for more price action before looking to short again. If the bears were not ready to short, the bulls could push the market higher.

Deeper Discussion of This Chart

The day opened with a strong bull trend bar on a gap down in Figure 6.3, but it immediately reversed down in a breakout pullback short setup. With the large tails and bodies of the first two bars and the small gap down on the open, the odds of more sideways action were high and it would be better to wait and not take the short trade. However, this was followed by a two-bar reversal signal for a failed breakout setup and a possible low of the day. There was a four-bar bull spike but no follow-through. At some point over the next couple of hours, traders would have taken at least partial profits and may have exited the balance on a breakeven stop during the late sell-off, if they did not reverse to short.

Bar 3 was also the bottom of a spike and channel bear trend, and the reversal should test the bar 2 start of the channel, which it did. The five-bar sell-off down to bar 1 was the spike, and the channel down began at the pullback to bar 2. The sell-off down to bar 3 was climactic because it had about a dozen bars with lows and highs below those of the prior bar. The actual number is not important. What is important is that there were many bars, and the more there are, the more unsustainable and therefore climactic the behavior is. A large bear trend bar like bar 3 after a strong bear trend is a sell climax. This usually leads to a two-legged sideways to up correction, and less often to a trend reversal like the one that developed here.

The failed bar 4 reversal bar was a failed low 2 buy setup. The low 2 trapped naïve traders who sold under the reversal bar but failed to wait for a prior demonstration of bearish strength. You should not sell in a strong bull trend if the market is in a tight channel where there has not been a prior bull trend line break.

The four-bar spike up to the 7:05 bar could have been followed by a channel up. The spike down to bar 1, however, created the possibility that there might be a channel down instead, which was the case. It was appropriate to buy the pullback that ended around 8:45, expecting the spike up, and equally appropriate to reverse to short below the bear inside bar that followed bar 2.

Note that none of the dojis before and after bar 1 are good signal bars, because they are in the middle of the day's range and next to a flat moving average.

The swing high that occurred five bars before bar 1 formed a three-bar reversal, which would look like a 15 minute reversal bar with a one-tick-tall bull body on the 15 minute chart since the third bar closed at the same time as the 15 minute bar.

Figure 6.4

SIGNAL BARS: OTHER TYPES **117**

FIGURE 6.4 A 15 Minute Reversal on 5 Minute Chart

Note that 15 minute reversals can be seen on a 5 minute chart. In Figure 6.4, the 15 minute chart on the left had several reversal bars and the corresponding three-bar patterns were within the boxes on the 5 minute chart on the right. In general, a 15 minute reversal is more likely to result in a longer move than a 5 minute reversal is. When you are looking to take a 5 minute trade, if you see three-bar combinations that also create 15 minute reversals, you usually can feel more confident about your trade.

In general, it is a good idea to look at any trend bar that is followed within the next 10 bars or so by an opposite trend bar with a close near the open of the first bar as a reversal. The reversal will be a two-bar reversal on some higher time frame chart, and a reversal bar on an even higher time frame chart.

Deeper Discussion of This Chart

The market broke below the moving average in Figure 6.4, and the breakout failed and led to a trend from the open bull trend. Bar 3 was a moving average gap bar in a strong trend, and the move down to bar 3 broke the bull trend line. A moving average gap bar often leads to the final leg of the trend before a larger correction. Bar 4 was a two-bar reversal short setup at the higher high.

FIGURE 6.5 Three-Bar Reversals

Some three-bar patterns on the 5 minute chart do not create good reversals on the 15 minute chart, but they still lead to acceptable reversals. In Figure 6.5, the 5 minute chart on the right had a couple of three-bar patterns that looked like they should form perfect 15 minute three-bar reversals. However, since the third bar in both cases closed at 25 minutes after the hour instead of at 30 minutes after the hour, when the 15 minute bar closed, the 15 minute pattern did not show the same strength. Traders could trade the 5 minute pattern if it was a perfect 15 minute reversal and buy at one tick above the high of the three bars, or earlier if there was an earlier 5 minute entry. For example, in the second example on the 5 minute chart, the second and third bars formed a two-bar reversal, so it would be acceptable to enter at one tick above the two-bar reversal instead of two ticks higher, above the top of the three bars. In general, traders should not spend time looking for three-bar reversals, because they occur only a couple of times a day and you should not risk missing other more common setups.

Bar 2 was the first bar of a two-bar reversal, and you could find some time frame where the three large bear trend bars that led to the bottom and the two large trend bars that followed bar 2 comprised a two-bar reversal, like the 15 minute chart on the left. You could also find a chart where those bars created a perfect single reversal bar. Because of this, all reversal setups are closely related. Don't be too

Figure 6.5　　　　　　　　　　　　　　　　SIGNAL BARS: OTHER TYPES　**119**

particular and don't lose sight of the goal. You are trying to see when the market is trying to reverse and then look for some way to get in once you believe the reversal will likely have follow-through.

Deeper Discussion of This Chart

The market broke below yesterday's low with a small gap in Figure 6.5, and the first bar was a failed breakout buy setup for a possible trend from the open bull trend. When the reversal is within a steep bear channel like this, it is better to wait for a pullback after the reversal up before buying. There was a higher low a few bars later, but the bars were sideways and had big tails, so bulls should wait for more strength. Instead, there was a low 2 short that was also a breakout pullback short, but most traders prefer to wait for the breakout of the entire opening range when the opening range is a small trading range that is less than about a third of an average day's range. The large bear trend bar that broke out below the low of the opening range shows that most traders waited for that breakout before going short.

Bar 2 was a two-bar reversal for an opening reversal long. It followed a one-bar final flag, and there was earlier buying strength in the strong first bar of the day.

FIGURE 6.6 Two-Bar Reversal

A two-bar reversal is a setup composed of two bars and the entry is one tick beyond both. In Figure 6.6, even though bar 5 was a bear trend bar, its low was one tick above the low of the bar before it. When a reversal bar almost entirely overlaps the bar before it, it should be considered to be a two-bar reversal setup. Here, for example, the safest short entry was below the lower of either bar 5 or the bar before it. The market fell one tick below bar 5, but it formed a double bottom with the low of the bar before it. Traders who thought that it was safe to short below a large bear bar were stopped out with a loss.

Bar 3 was a similar situation, and if a trader was thinking of shorting, it would be safer to short below the low of the bar before it and not just below the bar 3. In any case, this was a risky short since the market had been trending up strongly for nine bars. It would be much better to not short and instead look to buy a pullback, like above the bar 4 two-bar reversal.

Bar 1 was the second bar of a two-bar buy reversal where the second bar was above the high of the first bar. The entry is above the high of that second bar.

Bar 2 was a two-bar reversal where the highs of both bars were the same.

Figure 6.6   SIGNAL BARS: OTHER TYPES   **121**

Deeper Discussion of This Chart

There was a large gap down and a bull trend bar in Figure 6.6. The market then formed a two-bar reversal down that did not trigger a short and instead became a two-bar reversal up. The long above bar 1 had good follow-through two bars later. Since this was a possible trend from the open bull trend and there were signs of buying strength, traders should rely on their initial stop below the low of the day until after the higher low. Once the market turned up from the higher low with a strong bull trend bar, they could move their stop up to below the higher low and hold long into the close.

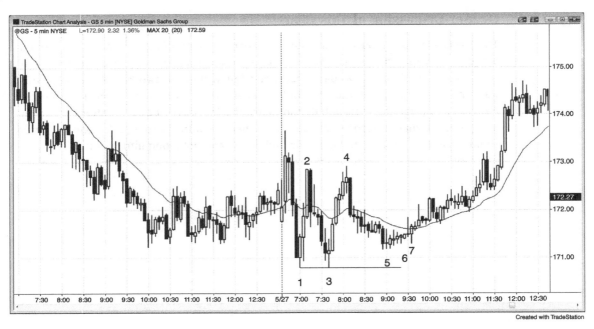

FIGURE 6.7 First Hour Reversal

Always be ready for a reversal in the first hour or so. Goldman Sachs Group (GS) was in a bear trend yesterday and had a strong rally off the open today so traders were looking for a pullback to a lower low or higher low and a possible trend reversal. As shown in Figure 6.7, there was a lower low at bar 1, which was tested by bar 3 and they created a double bottom. This was followed by a higher low at bar 5, and bulls were looking for a buy setup for a possible new bull trend. Bar 5 was an inside bar and the bar after it was inside of bar 5, with its low above the low of bar 5 and its high below the high of bar 5. This is an ii setup, and traders would buy on a stop at one tick above the second bar. Bar 6 was a second ii setup since it was an inside bar and the bar before it was also an inside bar.

Deeper Discussion of This Chart

There was a tricky open in Figure 6.7, and when in doubt, stay out. The market broke above the trading range of the final couple of hours of yesterday, but the breakout failed on the third bar. The market then broke out below the trading range and that breakout failed and reversed up at bar 1. Bar 3 was an acceptable double bottom long setup, but traders who waited could buy the double bottom pullback above bar 6.

This was a double bottom pullback buy setup. Double bottom pullbacks have a pullback that typically extends more than 50 percent and often almost the entire way

Figure 6.7 SIGNAL BARS: OTHER TYPES **123**

to the double bottom. This double bottom was exact to the tick. The higher low often forms a rounded bottom, and traditional stock traders would describe it as an area of accumulation. The name is irrelevant; what is important is that the market failed to put in a lower low on this second attempt down (bar 3 was the first), so if it can't go down, the bears will step aside and the market will probe up (in search of sellers willing to sell at a higher price). Instead of finding sellers, the market found buyers willing to buy at the higher price.

Bar 7 set up a third entry on the back-to-back, opposite failures. The market failed on the upside breakout above bar 6 and then failed on the downside on the next bar, meaning that both the bulls and bears were trapped. Bar 7 became just a pullback from the breakout above bar 6 and is therefore a breakout pullback long setup.

Bar 4 was a double top bear flag short setup. The rally on the open was followed by a lower high at bar 2, which was tested by bar 4, creating a double top. Since the double top was below the high of the open, there is a possible bear trend and any pullback in a bear trend should be thought of as a bear flag.

FIGURE 6.8 Bars That Are Tiny Can Still Be Helpful

Sometimes the bars are so tiny that they appear to be insignificant but they still can be telling you something that is very important. In Figure 6.8, the bar 2 signal bar was a tiny bar (11 cents in a $185 stock), but if you look at a line chart of the closes, the small higher low was clear at point 2.

Bar 2 was the second half of a reversal setup, and the large bear trend bar that formed three bars before bar 1 was the start of the down part of the reversal. You could find some higher time frame chart where this collection of 10 bars formed a two-bar reversal.

Figure 6.8   SIGNAL BARS: OTHER TYPES   **125**

Deeper Discussion of This Chart

The day opened on the high tick in Figure 6.8 and had a two-bar spike down as it broke out of a two-bar bear flag from yesterday's close. The market tried to reverse up on the fourth bar but there was no long entry since it was an outside up bar without follow-through. The shorts would hold with a stop above the signal bar or maybe above the outside up bar. The next bar was a bear inside bar that set up a low 2 short entry in a trend from the open bear trend.

The bull reversal bar three bars before bar 2 was a riskier entry since the market had been in a tight bear channel for the seven prior bars. It is safer to wait for the breakout from the channel and then buy the breakout pullback. This pullback was more of a sideways pause and it ended with the bar 2 higher low buy signal. Second entries in general are more reliable. It was very close to being an iii pattern, which often leads to reversals at the ends of swings.

Bar 1 was not a good setup for the reversal up from the final flag breakout because the signal bar was a doji. Instead, you should wait for a bull trend bar for a signal bar when bottom picking in a strong bear trend. Also, the prior four bars were bear trend bars, so there was too much downward momentum to be buying the first attempt to reverse, especially when the signal bar is a doji, which does not represent strong buying.

FIGURE 6.9   An ii Pattern Is a Smaller Time Frame Reversal

Because an ii pattern always represents a clear reversal setup on a smaller time frame chart, you never have to check that chart to confirm it. In Figure 6.9, on the 5 minute chart on the right, there were two ii patterns (the first is an iii). These often are clearer reversal patterns on smaller time frame charts, like the 1 minute chart on the left. The bar 1 iii on the 5 minute chart was a higher low that was tested repeatedly on the 1 minute chart. The bar 2 ii on the 5 minute chart was a higher low after a higher low, so the market was making trending higher lows, which is a component of a bull trend.

In both cases, the bull trend bar at the end of the ii pattern was a great setup for a long entry. Even though small bars have less directional significance, it is always better to have the final one be a trend bar in the direction of your intended entry.

Bar 2 on the 5 minute chart formed a reversal with the bear trend bar that formed two bars earlier.

Deeper Discussion of This Chart

The bar 1 setup on the 1 minute chart in Figure 6.9 was a double bottom pullback buy pattern, and the bar 2 setup was a failed low 2.

Figure 6.10   SIGNAL BARS: OTHER TYPES   **127**

FIGURE 6.10 Two-Bar Double Bottoms and Tops

Double bottoms and tops can be as small as two consecutive bars and still be important.

In Figure 6.10, bar 1 was a micro double bottom bear flag setup, since it is a bear trend bar immediately followed by a bull trend bar in a bear spike and they have identical lows. Sell at one tick below its low. You could also sell below the low of the one-bar pullback on the next bar, giving you an earlier entry.

Bar 2 was another example.

Bar 3 was a micro double top entry bar for a long trade, since the bear trend bar is a one-bar bull flag in a bull spike (a high 1 buy setup in a bull spike). It is also a micro double bottom and a two-bar reversal with the bar before it. Traders could therefore also buy above the high of bar 3, although this is a riskier entry since it is four ticks worse. Also, buying above a large bar after a breakout of three overlapping bars is risky because those three bars might be the start of a trading range.

Deeper Discussion of This Chart

The first bar of the day in Figure 6.10 broke out below yesterday's low and the breakout failed. Since the market was still within the trading range from the final hour of yesterday and the two-bar reversal up on the open had large bars, this would force traders to buy at the top of a trading range that had many bars with large tails. Instead, traders should wait. The move up to the moving average was a bear flag and it broke out at 7:15 a.m. PST, but the breakout failed and reversed up on the next bar in a two-bar reversal, which was a reasonable buy.

At 8:50 a.m. there was a double bottom pullback long setup.

Figure 6.11   SIGNAL BARS: OTHER TYPES   **129**

FIGURE 6.11   A Strong Two-Bar Reversal

Although it is usually better to not buy the first reversal attempt in a strong bear trend, a strong two-bar reversal can be a reliable buy setup after a sell climax. As shown in Figure 6.11, Lehman Brothers Holdings (LEH) had a two-bar reversal bottom on a test of the bear trend channel line and after consecutive sell climaxes. The sell-off was climactic because it was unsustainable behavior. Sixteen of the prior 17 bars each had a high that was below the high of the bar before. Also, there were three occurrences of a large bear trend bar that followed a series of smaller bear trend bars. A climax is usually followed by a two-legged correction that lasts for many bars (at least an hour on a 5 minute chart).

Bar 1 was the first bar of a two-bar reversal. It is usually risky to buy the first reversal in a strong bear trend, but after several signs of climactic behavior and a very strong two-bar reversal, this was a reasonable buy setup. Bar 1 was another large bear trend bar and therefore another sell climax, and the second bar was a strong bull trend bar. It was large and it opened on its low and closed on its high.

Deeper Discussion of This Chart

The market in Figure 6.11 opened with a breakout of a bear flag over the last 90 minutes of yesterday and it tested yesterday's low. The third bar tested the moving average and the next bar set up a low 2 short for a possible trend from the open bear and breakout pullback short. Many traders waited for the breakout below the first bar of the day to go short, and this resulted in a bear trend bar that became the first bar of a three-bar bear spike. Traders could also get short below the bear flag that followed.

Bar 1 had a big range and followed a strong bear leg, and it was therefore a sell climax. There was another large bear trend bar four bars earlier and it, too, was a sell climax. When a trend is particularly strong, it often will not correct until after a second sell climax, and rarely after a third.

The small inside bar that formed two bars before bar 1 turned into a one-bar final flag.

There were three large consecutive bear trend bars with very little overlap off the open, and they constitute a spike down. A strong spike down is commonly followed by a bear channel and then a pullback and sometimes a reversal. That initial spike down was followed by a sideways low 2 and then even stronger selling. Even though this follow-through selling was almost vertical, it should be thought of as the bear channel that followed the initial spike down. That low 2 is a type of final flag, even though the market fell far before trying to pull back.

Spike and climax bears (a type of spike and channel bear trend) usually test to around the start of the channel within a day or two, but when the selling is this strong, they may not, and a higher time frame pattern might be controlling the market. For example, the entire sell-off down to bar 1 might be a large spike on the 60 minute chart and the trading range that followed might become the pullback that leads to a large bear channel move down to much lower prices.

Figure 6.12   SIGNAL BARS: OTHER TYPES   **131**

FIGURE 6.12   Two-Bar Reversal Buy Climax

The first attempt to reverse a strong bull channel can be a reliable short if it is at the end of a buy climax and the two-bar reversal is strong.

In Figure 6.12, bar 4 was a large two-bar reversal top on a break above yesterday's high and a bull trend channel line, and after the breakout of a small flag (bar 3). When two bars overlap so much, the chances of a profitable trade are greater if you short below the lower of the two bars and not below the other (bar 4 in this case). Also, the second bar had a large bear body, and when a bull trend is strong, you should short only below a strong bear bar and never below a strong bull bar.

Bar 1 and the bear bar before it did not provide a good two-bar reversal buy setup because there was too much downward momentum in those two large bear trend bars on their breakout from the lower high. The bars barely overlap one another and they have small tails.

This was immediately followed by another two-bar reversal buy setup (back-to-back patterns happen occasionally), but four overlapping bars after a spike down there is a bear flag and you should not buy at the top of a trading range in a bear trend, especially just below the moving average. Two-bar reversals are countertrend signals only if there is a reason to expect a reversal.

Bar 2 is an acceptable entry bar for a short based on the two-bar reversal top created by the prior two bars. It was reversing the small correction up to the moving average. However, whenever there is a two-bar reversal sell setup just below the moving average and the bars are relatively large and overlap one or more other bars, you usually can buy at or below the low of the signal bar for a long scalp. This is a small trading range and it is usually better to buy at the bottom of a small trading range.

Bar 4 was the first bar of a two-bar reversal.

Deeper Discussion of This Chart

The bar 4 two-bar reversal in Figure 6.12 followed a small final flag at bar 3, and it was the third push up after the bull spike that began at 9:10 a.m. Spike and channel patterns often correct after three pushes up. The spike is the first push and then there are often two more spikes followed by a correction that usually tests to around the bottom of the channel.

The first bar of today was a breakout below the double bottom bull flag of the final 90 minutes of yesterday. Traders could have shorted below the double bottom on a stop or below the ii breakout pullback setup three bars later.

There was a large two-legged move down from yesterday's high that ended in a triple bottom on today's open. There was a second chance to go long on the higher low at 9:05 a.m. PST, after the initial strong leg up that tested the high of the open. This was also a breakout pullback buy setup (even though the market had not yet broken out above the high of the open).

Bar 1 was an up bar, and it was followed by a down bar and then a second up bar that tested the moving average. This is a small two-legged correction to the moving average and therefore a low 2 short setup. There were also trapped bulls who bought above the back-to-back two-bar reversal bottom attempts, and once the low 2 triggered, they would exit their longs with a loss. Their selling adds to the selling of the new bears and increases the chance of success. Also, since they just lost, they will be hesitant to buy, and the losses of buyers increase the chance of a successful short scalp.

A series of overlapping bars is a tight trading range, which is a magnet, and breakouts often fail and the market is drawn back into the tight trading range. This is because both bulls and bears feel that there is good value in that range. When the market drifts toward the bottom of the range, the bulls feel that there is even better value and they buy more aggressively. The bears prefer to short in the middle or top of the range. Their absence at the bottom of the range and the increased buying by the bulls lifts the market back up. The opposite happens at the top of the range, where bears become more aggressive and the buyers stop buying and wait for slightly lower prices. The entire

Figure 6.12   SIGNAL BARS: OTHER TYPES   **133**

process is amplified on a breakout. Here, the bears were able to overwhelm the buyers and break the market to the downside. However, instead of finding new sellers down there who could push the market down further, the buyers saw these lower prices as an even better value than that in the tight trading range. The result was that the market was pulled back into the range.

The market later tried to break out of the top and again was pulled back into the range. However, there will always be an successful breakout eventually.

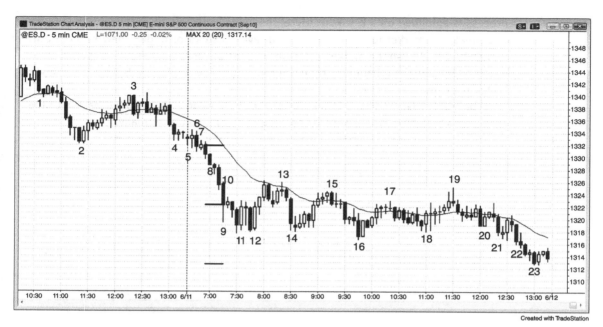

FIGURE 6.13 No Tails Means Strength

A bar with no tail at either end in a strong trend is a sign of strength, and traders should enter with trend on its breakout. In Figure 6.13, bar 8 was a bear bar in a strong bear trend, and it had no tail at both its high and its low, indicating severe selling pressure (they sold it from start to finish). It was likely that there would be more selling to come. Traders have to be fast in placing their sell stop orders because the market is moving fast. Alternatively, they can just short at the market or on a one- or two-tick bounce using a limit order.

The bar after bar 10 had a shaved top in a bear trend but since the market was not in free fall at this point, that alone was not enough reason for a short.

The bar after bar 16 was a bull trend bar with a shaved top and bottom, but it was not in a bull trend and therefore it does not function as a buy setup based solely on the absence of tails.

The bar after bar 17 and the bar before bar 20 were not shaved bar sell setups because they were not in a free-fall bear trend.

There were many two-bar reversal setups on this chart, as there are on all charts.

Deeper Discussion of This Chart

There was a quiet open in Figure 6.13 that continued the tight trading range of the close of yesterday. Bar 8 was a two-bar breakout and traders could have shorted on the close

Figure 6.13   SIGNAL BARS: OTHER TYPES   **135**

of the bar because of a likely trend from the open bear trend, or below bar 10, the first pause, or on the bar 13 double top bear flag test of the moving average.

Bar 11 was the second bar of a two-bar reversal and the market might have been trying to turn up after the sell climaxes. The next bar was a doji inside bar and a low 1 short setup. However, when there is a bear flag where the signal bar mostly overlaps with the two prior bars and the market might be in a trading range, the odds are high that the short will fail and will become a bear trap. Do not take these short signals.

The three-bar rally from bar 12 led to a 20 gap bar short, but since the upward momentum was strong, it was better to wait for a second signal, which occurred at bar 13.

Bar 19 was a moving average gap bar short and it led to a new low of the day. It was also a failed breakout above the bars 15 and 17 swing highs and a test of the top of the trading range. It is common for a trend day to have a strong countertrend move between 11:00 a.m. and noon PST, trapping traders into the wrong direction as it did here. It is important to realize this so that you will be mentally prepared to take the with-trend trade, which was a short here.

Since the bar before bar 10 was a large range bar in a trend that had gone on for a while, it is a sell climax and the market might try to correct sideways to up soon. The first pause in a strong trend is usually a successful short scalp, even in a strong bear trend, but it might become a final flag and lead to a correction up (the breakout below its low may reverse up within a bar or two). Whenever there is a strong spike down, it is usually followed by a measured move down based on some aspect of the spike, usually the distance from the open or high of the first bar to the close or low of the last bar of the spike. The low of the day was a perfect measured move down from the open of the first bar to the close of the final bar. Traders should continue to hold short at least until the market reaches the general area of these targets.

Bar 16 was a large bull inside bar reversing up from a new low of the day, and the market was now in a trading range. It was also a high 2 in a trading range and therefore an acceptable long setup. The high 1 formed two bars earlier.

The two-bar spike down into the close of yesterday led to the bear channel that ended on the bar before bar 11 today. However, the entire channel was steep enough to likely function as a spike on either the 15 or 60 minute chart, and the market might be in the process of channeling down into the close of the day.

The bar 21 strong bear trend bar or the bar before bar 20 might have served as a small spike down that led to the bear channel into the close of the day.

FIGURE 6.14 Signal Bar Examples

Apple (AAPL) demonstrated many common signal bars on the 5 minute chart shown in Figure 6.14. Even though bar 1 was a Hammer doji bar at the bottom of a swing down and it would make many candle worshipers want to buy, especially since it was a double bottom with the first bar of the day, this was a bad setup for price action traders. It was the third overlapping doji, meaning that the market traded both up and down in all three bars. This was an area of two-sided trading and therefore a trading range, and whenever there is a trading range just below the moving average, the odds favor a downside breakout. There are always sellers on any test of the moving average from below, and there was not enough room between the high of the bar and the moving average to make even a scalper's profit. If you were to buy above bar 1, you would have to pay attention to the size of the bars, all of which had relatively large ranges. This increases the risk of the trade because your protective stop location should be in part determined by the size of the current bars. If you wanted to keep your risk the same on all of your trades, you would have to trade fewer shares.

Bar 2 was a much better reversal bar setup because it had a decent-size bull body and it was the second attempt to reverse up from below yesterday's low and

Figure 6.14   SIGNAL BARS: OTHER TYPES   **137**

from a new low of the day (bar 1 was the first attempt). The bull bodies of the first two bars of the day showed some prior bull strength. The tail at the top showed some weakness, but this was erased by the trend bars that followed it.

Bar 2 was the second bar of a two-bar reversal and the middle of a large two-bar reversal on some higher time frame chart. You can find a chart where the bar before or after formed a two-bar reversal, and you could find an even higher time frame chart where the two bars before and the two bars after formed a two-bar reversal. As with all two-bar reversals, you can find an even higher time frame chart where the five bars formed a single bull reversal bar.

Bar 3 was an outside up bar (an outside bar with a bull body) after a pause bar, which followed the breakout to a new high of the day, and was an entry bar for the purchase above the high of the small bar. Outside bars in new trends often trap traders out of great trades because they happen so quickly. Many traders don't have enough time to reverse their perspective fast enough from bearish to bullish, and then they have to chase the market up. The bar before bar 3 was a doji, so it was not a strong setup for a short, even though the market might reverse down after a breakout to a new high of the day. Only scalpers and weak shorts would be shorting below its low because of the signs of bull strength that were accumulating. The bar before that doji had the largest bull body of the day and closed on its high, and it was also the third consecutive up bar. All three bars had decent-size bodies, and the second and third did not overlap more than half of the prior bar. It was likely that traders were aggressively looking to buy any pullback and had limit orders to buy both below the low and above the high of the doji, and the buying was so strong that both sets of buy orders were filled in one bar.

Bar 4 was a bear doji at a new high, but the upward momentum was so strong and the reversal bar was so weak that a short could be considered only on a second entry. This was the first bear body after seven consecutive bull bars and the market rarely reverses very far on the first attempt, especially when the signal bar has a close in the middle instead of at its low. The bears were not even strong enough to close the bar on its low so they will unlikely be able to push the market down very far before the bulls overwhelm them again.

Bar 5 was another outside up bar that tested the moving average and the breakout from the opening range, and it was the end of first pullback in a strong up move.

Bar 6 was a bear reversal bar and a second entry short setup (the first was two bars earlier) after taking out the bar 4 swing high and yesterday's high. Since the bears had enough strength to test the moving average with bar 5 and the bull trend is even more overdone, the bears should be able to correct to the moving average or even below it this time. As a trend wears on, the bulls typically will want deeper pullbacks before looking to buy again.

Bar 7 was an entry bar on an ii short setup at a time when you were expecting a test of the moving average. Both ii bars had bear bodies, which increases the chance of success for a short trade. Although a bull body on a bear entry bar is not good and the bar after it traded above it, the market did not trade above either of the ii bars where the protective stop would be. If you are going to take a trade in a tight trading range, you have to give it a little room. That entry bar became a small bull reversal bar, but small reversal bars are rarely good and when one forms in a tight trading range, it should not be looked at as a reversal bar because there is nothing to reverse. The ii breakout reversed back up a couple of bars later, which is expected when an ii is in the middle of the day's range. Also, the market completed its goals of two legs down and a penetration of the moving average.

Bar 8 was a doji bar at close to a double top in what was now a trading range. Doji bars are never good signal bars for shorts in strong bulls, but they are acceptable signal bars for shorts in trading ranges, depending on the context. Since the market was testing the top of the range, it was an acceptable signal bar for a short since the market might test the bottom of the range.

Bar 9 was a two-bar reversal after a new swing low and test of the bar 5 low. The entry was above the high of the higher of the two bars, which would be above bar 9. However, this is risky because there will always be shorts at the moving average when the market tests it from below. Also, the two bars are large, forcing buyers to come in too high above the low of a down leg. When the risk is greater, it is better to not take the trade and to wait for a strong setup.

Bar 10 was a two-bar reversal following four bear trend bars with good-size bodies, small tails, and very little overlap, and therefore a good short setup in a strong bear trend.

Bar 11 was a bull reversal bar after a third push down and it was an attempt to hold above the low of the day. The bear trend had gone on for a long time and there were many pullbacks along the way, so the odds were high for a test of the moving average. Since it is countertrend, you have to be willing to allow for pullbacks in the move up to the moving average, so do not tighten your stop too soon.

Deeper Discussion of This Chart

The market broke below the moving average on the open in Figure 6.14, but the breakout failed with a strong bull reversal bar. The second bar had a bull body but it also had prominent tails and it failed to get above the moving average. There was also no follow-through buying on the third bar, which also tested the moving average and failed to get above it. Bulls should have considered exiting their longs and waiting since the market was now in a small tight trading range below the moving average and the bars were large with tails. A tight trading range below the moving average usually breaks out to the downside, but there was no reliable short setup. Instead, traders should wait for a better setup. Bar 2 was a strong bull reversal bar that set up a long of the failed breakout of that tight trading range, which became a final flag.

Figure 6.14   SIGNAL BARS: OTHER TYPES **139**

Once the market broke above the opening high, a measured move up was likely.

Bar 2 was also a bear micro wedge that overshot the trend channel line that could be drawn across the bottoms of the prior three bars. Notice how there is a tail at the bottom of the bar that followed bar 1. That means the buyers came in around the low of the bar. The bears were hoping to find sellers on the breakout below the low of the bar and for the close to be well below the low of the bar, but instead there were some buyers. This happened on the next bar as well and even more so with bar 2. The bears were finally able to drive the price even further below the low of the prior bar, but the bulls became especially aggressive and reversed the market and closed the bar above its open and near the top of the bar. Although micro wedges by themselves don't usually lead to major reversals, the other factors at work here created the low of the day.

Bar 2 along with the bar before it and the bar after it also created a three-bar reversal and a 15 minute reversal bar because the bar before it would have the same open as the 15 minute bar, the bar after it would have the same close as the 15 minute bar, and that close is above the open. The next bar would then trigger a 15 minute long entry.

The move down from bars 4 to 5 had several overlapping bars and could be a final flag. Bar 5 and the bar that followed it both had very large bodies and small tails and therefore formed a two-bar buy climax. When a climax occurs after a trend has been going on for many bars, the odds of a two-legged sideways to down correction lasting at least 10 bars increase. The next bar was a bear inside bar after a buy climax and might become a one-bar final flag.

Bar 6 was the second leg up from the bar 5 first pullback and from the bar 2 low, and second legs are often reversals. Also, it was a low 4 and a wedge with the three pushes being bar 4, the bar after bar 5, and bar 6. It was additionally a larger wedge with the three pushes being the third bar of the day, bar 4, and bar 6. With this many factors operating, a trader should expect at least two legs down. It also followed two buy climaxes, the first being the two-bar climax of bar 5 and the next bar and the second being the bar before bar 6. A second consecutive buy climax usually results in at least a two-legged correction that penetrates the moving average and lasts at least an hour.

The two-legged pullback that followed the bar 6 short penetrated the moving average and ended with a moving average gap bar. Since it formed in a strong trend, a test of the trend's high was likely. It was also a wedge bull flag buy setup with the first push down being the bar before bar 6 and the second push down being the third bar after bar 6. A moving average gap bar often leads to the final leg of the trend before the market has a larger pullback and even a reversal.

Bar 8 was a lower high or double top after a moving average gap bar, which always breaks the trend line, and therefore a possible trend reversal. There is a good risk/reward setup for a swing down, and shorts should swing part of their position. It also formed a one-bar final flag reversal, and a micro double top reversal with the tails at the top of either of the two bars before it.

Bar 9 was a wedge bull flag with the three pushes down from bar 8, but because the sell-off was in a relatively tight bear channel and the market might have reversed into a bear trend, it is better to wait to see if there will be an acceptable breakout pullback buy setup. Five bars later, there was an outside up bar but that is not an acceptable long entry in either a trading range or a bear trend, and therefore buyers would have to wait some more. Bar 9 was also an attempt to form a double bottom bull flag with bar 5, at a price level where the market found buyers earlier in the day. Finally, it was the end of a large two-legged correction from the bar 6 high and therefore a high 2 long and probably a clear high 2 long on a higher time frame chart, like the 15 minute chart.

Bar 10 was a breakout pullback from the breakout below the bar 9 wedge bull flag low and the failed high 2, and it followed a breakout below the double top bear flag that formed after bar 9. The four-bar breakout was a spike down, and the market bounced back up to test the bar 10 top of the channel by the close. There was a double top bear flag short setup with the high of bar 10 and the bar that formed four bars later. All breakouts are spikes and climaxes, and there was a second sell climax two bars before bar 11; a second consecutive sell climax usually leads to at least a two-legged pullback. A breakout spike often leads to a measured move down. Take the number of ticks between the open of the first of the four bars and the close of the fourth bear bar and project down from the top of the first pullback (the high of bar 10).

Bar 11 was similar in appearance to bar 1, which earlier found buyers in this price area and they may be willing to buy again. Since there has not yet been a break of the bear trend line, the odds of a trading range are greater than the odds of a significant reversal. The move down from bar 6 was in a channel, and a bear channel should be thought of as a bull flag, so there might be a strong move up before long. Also, the entire move down from bar 6 is a complex two-legged move with the second leg down beginning at bar 8; it might be a simple two-legged correction on a higher time frame chart, like the 60 minute chart.

Bar 11 was a micro double bottom reversal with the tail of the bull doji bar that preceded it.

Figure 6.15   SIGNAL BARS: OTHER TYPES   **141**

FIGURE 6.15 One-Bar Bear Flag

A bull reversal bar in a bear spike can be a one-bar bear flag. In Figure 6.15, bar 8 was a break below a bull reversal bar (failed reversal bar) in a strong bear trend and is a great short because the early bulls who bought will be trapped and forced to sell below its low.

Bars 8 through 14 created a two-bar reversal on a higher time frame chart and a single reversal bar on an even higher time frame chart.

Bars 9 and 10 formed a small double bottom and bar 11 was the entry bar for the long, but a doji is not a good signal bar for a countertrend trade against a strong trend. There were no prior bull pullbacks in the sharp sell-off, and since the first pullback in a strong trend usually fails, smart traders expected this bottom to fail. They placed sell stop orders to go short exactly where the losing longs would sell out of their positions, which was one tick below bar 11.

A doji is a one-bar trading ranges and bars 9 and 10 created a pair of large dojis with a small doji in between. These three bars formed a small sideways trading range in a strong bear trend, which is a bear flag, so a downside breakout was likely. Since bar 11 was the second attempt to rally (the first attempt was two bars earlier but it could not even get above the bull doji just before it), the longs would almost certainly exit below bar 11 and not look to buy again until the market moved down for a bar or two. As these longs sold their positions, their selling added to the selling pressure from the smart traders who expected this weak bottom to fail and therefore shorted below bar 11. The only traders willing to buy just bought and lost, so the market became briefly one-sided and destined to fall.

Deeper Discussion of This Chart

Bar 7 formed a micro double bottom with the tail at the bottom of the large bear bar two bars earlier (the bottoms do not have to be exactly at the same price). Since the market was in a bear spike, selling the breakout below the bar 7 double bottom low was a reasonable short. This is different from the bar 18 micro double bottom (with the tail of the doji bar two bars earlier), which was in a pullback from a four bar bull spike, and not in a bear spike. It was reasonable to buy above bar 18 (most minor bull reversals come from some type of micro double bottom, as discussed in book 3 in the chapter on reversals), but not good to short below it. Bar 11 formed a micro double top with the high of the bar two bars earlier, and became a low 2 bear flag sell signal bar.

Bar 15 strongly broke above the bear trend line in Figure 6.15, and the gap down opening to bar 16 was a higher low buy setup for an expected second leg up. The market broke below the moving average and below the double bottom bull flag of the final hour of yesterday and the breakout failed.

Bar 18 was a breakout pullback long for the breakout of the bull flag from bar 15 to bar 16.

Bar 6 and the next bar were large bear trend bars that broke out below the bars 2 and 4 double bottom. The tails were small and the bodies were large, and more selling was likely. Every large bear breakout is a sell climax but that does not mean that the market will reverse. This breakout looked strong and the bulls could generate only a two-bar pause after the sell climax before they were overwhelmed again by the bears. A breakout is not only a climax but a spike as well, and when the breakout is strong like this, it is usually followed by a channel down before a tradable bottom develops. Bears will be aggressively shorting every pause and every little pullback until a possible bottom forms. The bottom will usually be at some measured move target, and the first one to consider is a measured move down from the top to the bottom of the trading range before the breakout. Next, look at the open of the breakout bar to the close or low of the final strong bear trend bar of the breakout, which might be the bar before bar 7 or the bar before that. It turns out that the bear trend bottomed at a measured move using a projection down from the top of the spike to the low of the third and final bear bar of the spike. You should also look for other possible measured move projections as well, because if the market tries to reverse within a couple of ticks of one of these magnets, it should increase your confidence to take the trade. However, you cannot take the countertrend trade on a measured move alone since most fail and you have to keep looking at others. The odds of success are too small. However, if there are other reasons to take the trade, like a trend channel line overshoot and reversal or a final flag reversal, the odds of success increase considerably.

Figure 6.15   SIGNAL BARS: OTHER TYPES   **143**

After a strong spike down, the most likely follow-up will be some type of channel down and eventually a test up to the top of the channel. Traders would keep shorting all the way down the channel and then buy at the bottom for the pullback to the top of the channel.

Bar 8 and the bar after it were large bear trend bars with little overlap and therefore constituted a second sell climax. Although a second sell climax usually leads to two legs sideways to up and lasts at least 10 bars, the move down to bar 9 was so steep that buyers were unwilling to buy and sellers were still willing to sell more.

Bar 11 was the end of a four-bar barbwire pattern, and barbwire after a long trend often becomes a final flag, which was the case here. Traders were expecting any breakout below the small tight trading range to soon fail and the market to be pulled back into the range. Because of this, they would likely only scalp the short below bar 11 instead of holding it for a swing down. The two bars after bar 11 were again large bear trend bars and formed a third spike, which is always also both a breakout of something (here, barbwire and therefore a potential final flag) and a climax. A third consecutive sell climax is fairly unusual and the odds were therefore high that there would be at least a two-legged sideways to up correction lasting at least 10 bars. This is even more likely after a final flag breakout and a measured move.

Even though the bar 12 signal bar at the low had a bear body, its close was above its midpoint so the buyers showed some strength. It was also the third push down after the spike breakout (bars 7 and 9 were the first two), and the channels that follow spikes often end with a third push. In the context of a final flag, a third consecutive sell climax, a wedge bottom, and a measured move, it was a good setup for a rally. The first objectives were tests of the top of the barbwire around the bar 11 high and a test of the moving average. Another objective was a two-legged move sideways to up lasting about 10 bars or about an hour. The final objective was a test of the top of the channel after the initial spike, and that was the top of the bar 7 bull bar. Although the move up to bar 15 had two legs, it was mostly contained in a channel and therefore more likely to be a complex first leg in a larger two-legged pattern, which it was. The second leg up began on the bar 16 open of the following day.

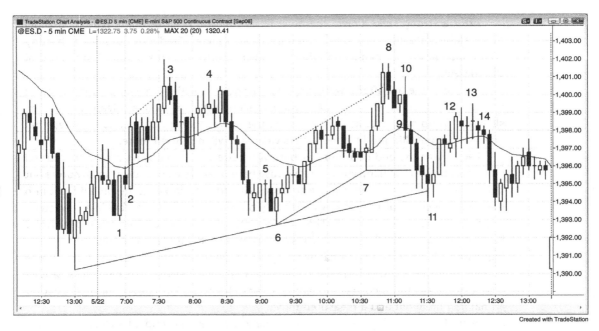

FIGURE 6.16   Good Setups Are Common

There are many good setups every day on every chart, and the more experience you have in spotting them as they form, the better chance you have of being able to profit from them.

In Figure 6.16, bar 1 was a two-bar reversal buy setup after taking out the low of the open, and it was a higher low compared to yesterday's low.

The small bear reversal bar before bar 2 tested the moving average and was an attempt to make the two-bar reversal fail. It failed and became just a pullback from the breakout above bar 1. When the market is trying to go up, it is good to buy above pullbacks.

Bar 3 was a bear inside bar after an attempt to break above a bull trend channel line and yesterday's high. This set up a short because if the market traded below its low, traders would think that the breakout had failed and there should be a pullback.

Bar 4 was a doji bar after two other dojis, and a bar with a tiny body and a micro wedge top made of dojis is rarely a reliable setup. The overlapping dojis represent two-sided trading and therefore uncertainty. However, the three tails on the tops of the bars were a sign of building selling pressure. A second entry setup came two bars later in the form of a two-bar reversal, and the short entry was below the lower of the two bars. That entry below that bear trend bar was also a break below a micro double bottom formed by that bear bar and the doji bar two bars earlier.

Figure 6.16   SIGNAL BARS: OTHER TYPES   **145**

Bar 5 was a failed upside breakout above an ii.

Bar 6 was a bull reversal bar and a second attempt to rally on a test of the low of the day.

Bar 7 was a doji but it was a pullback to the moving average with a bull body after a strong move up, and it was the second attempt to rally (the first was the bar before it).

Bar 8 was a bear inside bar, but it followed three strong bull trend bars. With that much upward momentum, it is better to wait for a second entry before shorting.

Bar 8 was a two-bar reversal and in the middle of a two-bar reversal on a higher time frame chart. The bull component of that higher time frame reversal was formed by the three bull trend bars before bar 8, and the bear component was the series of bear trend bars that ended at bar 11. Some higher time frame charts would use all of those bars, and others would use most of the trades that took place during those bars.

Bar 9 was a bull reversal bar but it was relatively small compared to recent bars and therefore less likely to lead to a successful long. It was better to wait for a second entry but one never came. Instead, the longs who bought above bar 9 were immediately trapped as the market reversed into an outside down bar. Selling below the bar 9 low was acceptable because it would be capitalizing on those longs who would have to sell out of their now losing positions. However, a trader would have to think quickly to realize this and place an order.

Bar 11 was an ioi and a second-entry long setup on the push below the bar 7 swing low. On trading range days, the market often reverses breakouts above and below prior swing points, and second signals are especially reliable. The first signal was two bars earlier, but the downward momentum at that point was so strong that it would have been unwise to buy there. Bar 13 was a risky long entry because whenever there are three or more overlapping, relatively large bars sitting on the moving average, the bull breakout is usually a trap.

Deeper Discussion of This Chart

On the open in Figure 6.16, the market continued the rally from yesterday's close, pulling back to the moving average and setting up a moving average pullback short. However, the upward momentum was strong, so it was better not to take the first entry short and instead to wait to see if there would be a second. The market fell below the open of the day, and the breakout to the new low failed. This reversal up was a possible low of the day, and it formed a double bottom with the first bar of the day and a higher low.

Bar 1 was a failed low 2 buy setup with the low before yesterday's close being the first push down.

Bar 2 was a strong follow-through bar for the long entry above bar 1, and it became a large breakout bar after the failed low 2. A failed low 2 usually is followed by either one more push up and a wedge bear flag short setup, or two more pushes up and a low 4 short. If the breakout is strong, as it was here, the low 4 is more likely. Since it was such a strong spike up, a channel up was also likely. The channel assumed the shape of a wedge. Once either a wedge or a channel reverses, the first target is a test of the start of the pattern.

Bar 3 was the expected low 4 short setup after the failed low 2. It was also the setup for a reversal down from two wedge tops. The smaller one had the bar after bar 2 as the first push, and the second push up occurred three bars later. The larger wedge began with the second bar of the day and the second push was the bar after bar 2. Both wedges should be followed by at least two legs sideways to down and they should test the start of each wedge. The test of the start of the smaller wedge occurred three bars after bar 3. It had two small legs, with the tail of the doji that formed two bars after bar 3 being the first leg down. The bar bounced up into its close and the second push down came on the next bar. This was a double bottom bull flag with the swing low that formed three bars after bar 2, and this is a common setup when the market tests the bottom of a channel or wedge.

These two small legs were just the first leg down for the larger wedge top, and bar 6 was the end of the second leg and the reversal up from the test of the bottom of that wedge and a five-tick failed breakout.

Bar 5 was the third small sideways bar after a sell-off, and any sideways pattern after a move can become a final flag, as it did here. Because it did so with a five-tick failure, there were trapped bears who bought back their shorts above bar 6, adding to the buying pressure. Bar 6 also formed a double bottom bull flag with the low of bar 1, leading to the expected bounce. It also was the setup for the long from the wedge bull flag that had its first push down three bars after bar 3 and its second push down three bars before bar 5.

Bar 7 was a wedge bull flag in a strong up move. The first push down was the bar just before 10 a.m. PST, and the second push down ended two bars before bar 7. Even though dojis in general are not reliable signal bars, they can be for pullbacks in trends or in strong legs in trading ranges.

Bar 8 was an inside bear trend bar that was the end of the second leg up in a trading range day and a test of the high of the day, both of which often lead to a reversal. It also followed a trend channel line breakout and the third push up in a bull channel (bar 5 was the first).

Bar 11 was technically a high 3, but should be expected to behave like a high 2, since the bar 10 outside bar bull trap should be considered the start of the downswing (not the bar 8 actual swing high).

Figure 6.17   SIGNAL BARS: OTHER TYPES   **147**

FIGURE 6.17 A Bear Reversal Bar Can Lead to a Bull Flag

A bear reversal bar in a bull trend is not enough reason to go short and it sometimes becomes a bull flag. In Figure 6.17, the bar after bar 1 was a strong bear reversal bar but it followed five strong bull trend bars. In the absence of no prior strength by the bears, it was not a short setup. Only a second entry could have been considered, which was a short below bar 2. However, bar 2 was a doji and there were four largely overlapping bars in a strong bull trend. Rather than short, it was better to wait for a pullback to buy. The two-bar reversal at the moving average four bars later was a good setup.

Although buying above a bear trend bar in a bull spike is often a good trade, buying above the bear trend bar here or above the bull reversal bar that followed it was risky. Bar 1 was a large bull trend bar after several other bull trend bars and it was therefore climactic. There was too much risk of a sideways to down correction after a buy climax. If you look at the highs of the bars up to bar 1, the slope was increasing. This parabolic curvature is also a sign of climactic behavior and that makes the risk of a correction significant. Buying a pullback or looking for a short was a safer approach.

Bar 4 was a two-bar reversal following a breakout below two small doji bars and the bar 3 breakout below a seven-bar horizontal bear flag near the moving average. Because the trend down for the past 15 bars or so had only very small pullbacks, this was a scalp long at best, despite the large outside up bull trend bar.

Bar 5 was a small bull reversal bar with a close near its high and it was the third push down in the past six bars, so buyers were starting to come in. Although the market was still in the bear channel of the past couple of hours, this is a good long scalp setup.

Bar 6 was a large bear trend bar with a big bottom tail and a close above the midpoint of the bar, which can be enough of a show of strength by bulls to reverse the market, especially after a collapse at the end of the bear trend. It was also an overshoot of several bear trend channel lines (not shown). With four large bear trend bars in a row, only a second-entry long can be considered, which came on the bar 7 outside up bar. The bar 7 low was a small higher low, which is the start of the second leg up. It is acceptable to buy above bar 6 but better to buy above the high of a bull bar, like the bar after bar 6, and best to buy at a second signal. Bar 7 was that second signal and you could buy either as soon as it went outside up, because it went above the high of that strong bull bar that followed bar 6, or above the high of bar 7.

Deeper Discussion of This Chart

In Figure 6.17, the market opened with a gap up and a bull trend bar, creating a bull spike, and then pulled back a little on the second bar, trading as low as below the middle of the first bar. This was the only pullback before the market went parabolic, creating a gap spike and channel bull trend and a trend from the open bull trend. *Parabolic* means that the trend accelerated after already being strong. Here, if you draw a trend channel line across the highs of the first three bars, highlighting the slope of the trend, you will see that the fourth bar broke above that trend channel line. If you continue to draw trend channel lines across the highs of successive bars, you will see that the lines get steeper, and then flatter at the high. This is a parabolic shape, and a parabolic move is a type of buy climax. Since the market was still in a trend from the open bull trend, you should not sell the first attempt at a pullback, because the first pullback is almost always followed by a test of the high within a few bars.

As strong as the upward momentum was, traders should always be aware that the market can reverse at any time, especially in the first hour. The market often races to some magnet that often is not evident, and once it is tested, the market is then free to do anything, including reverse.

Whenever there is any type of climax, once the market begins to correct, it usually corrects in two legs and for at least 10 bars.

Just before bar 3, there was a seven-bar horizontal bear flag, and tight trading ranges after a trend has gone for 10 or more bars often become final flags. There was a low 2 short signal with a bear signal bar, but because of the possibility of a final flag reversal, it is better to only scalp the short. The breakout of the bear flag was the large bar 3 bear trend bar, which is always a spike and a sell climax. When a sell climax forms after a

Figure 6.17   SIGNAL BARS: OTHER TYPES   **149**

protracted trend, it can fail and lead to a two-legged sideways to up correction lasting about ten bars. However, there has been no significant sign of strength in the bear trend, so if the market does try to reverse, it is better to look only for a scalp.

The spike was followed by a wedge bear flag that was formed by the doji after bar 3, the outside up bar after bar 4, and the small doji two bars later. It can also be viewed as a low 2 short, with bar 4 being the first push down and the short being below the small bull inside bar four bars later.

The move consisting of four strong bear trend bars down to bar 6 was another spike and therefore another sell climax, and it was the third push down after the bar 3 spike. Channels that follow spikes often end with three pushes, but when the downward momentum is so strong, it is better to wait for a second signal before looking to buy, and this occurred with bar 7. A bear channel is a bull flag, so the market should rally once it breaks above the bear channel. Also, it should test the start of the channel after the bar 3 spike down, but sometimes the rally will not be completed until the next day.

FIGURE 6.18 Weak Reversal Bars Need More

When a reversal bar is not particularly strong, it can still be a good setup if there is an additional reason to take the trade.

In Figure 6.18, bar 1 was a relatively small bar after a big bear trend bar broke out of a large flag, and might have been setting up a failed breakout of the flag. It was also an exact test of the earlier low. On a trading range day with bar 1 setting up these two reversals, it was a reasonable long setup, especially since the next bar created a two-bar reversal buy setup. The rally up from bar 1 and the sell-off down to the same price area the next day formed a two-bar reversal top on some higher time frame chart, and a single reversal bar on an even higher time frame chart.

Bar 2 was a small bear reversal bar after a large bull trend bar that broke out of a small trading range. This was an acceptable failed breakout short signal bar.

Deeper Discussion of This Chart

The market broke out above yesterday's high in Figure 6.18, but the breakout failed and led to a trend from the open bear day.

Figure 6.18   SIGNAL BARS: OTHER TYPES   **151**

Bar 2 was a final flag sell setup after the failed breakout from a tight trading range. Tight trading ranges after 10 or more bars of a swing often become final flags. It also was a double top bear flag with the 7:30 a.m. PST high. Remember, close is close enough. The bear trend that followed was huge and the market closed 30 points lower, but the rest of the day is not shown because it would shrink this bull trend bar to the point of looking unremarkable instead of how it appeared in real time.

FIGURE 6.19 Shaved Bars Can Be Meaningless

Shaved tops and bottoms are not always a sign of strength. When many shaved tops and bottoms occur close together, traders should be very careful because they may represent low volume in a trading range instead of strength in a trend. In the first cluster of four shaved tops in Figure 6.19 (indicated by "s"), the bear trend was still strong. However, in the second cluster, the market was in a trading range and they may just indicate that the volume was low. Be very careful about trading under these circumstances.

Deeper Discussion of This Chart

The market broke out above yesterday's high with a gap up in Figure 6.19, but the first bar was a bear trend bar and therefore a sign of weakness by the bulls. The market could have traded down in a failed breakout but instead broke to the upside with a strong bull trend bar. This could have led to a strong trend from the open bull day but instead was followed by a large bear trend bar. This set up a two-bar reversal for a failed breakout short, but the short was never triggered and the longs were still holding their positions. The market then broke to the upside out of the ii pattern; however, the breakout failed, setting up a failed breakout short and a possible high of the day.

Figure 6.19   SIGNAL BARS: OTHER TYPES   **153**

When there are several bars with large ranges that form a tight sideways trading range, entering on a breakout is risky because most breakouts will fail due to the magnetic effect of a tight trading range. The market broke out to the upside and then to the downside, and then rallied off the moving average back into the range. The spike down to the moving average was followed by a lower pullback that formed a lower high and then it evolved into a double top bear flag. The pullback to test the high of the day had low momentum, indicated by many overlapping bars, several bear bars, and many bars with tails. That is not how a strong bull leg looks.

CHAPTER 7

Outside Bars

I f the high of the current bar is above the high of the previous bar and the low is below the low of the previous bar, then the current bar is an outside bar. Outside bars are complicated to read because both the bulls and the bears were in control at some point within the bar or the prior bar, and there are many subtleties in their analysis. The increased size of the bar means that bulls and bears are willing to be more aggressive, but if the close is near the middle, it is essentially a one-bar-long trading range. In fact, by definition, since an outside bar totally overlaps the prior bar, every outside bar is a part of a trading range, which is two or more bars that largely overlap. At other times, they can act as reversal bars or trend bars. Traders must pay attention to the context in which they occur.

Traditional technical analysis teaches that outside bars are setup bars for a breakout in either direction, and that you should put an entry stop above and below. Once filled, double the size of the unfilled stop and make it a reversal order. However, it is almost always unwise to enter on a breakout of a 5 minute outside bar, especially if the outside bar is large, because of the greater risk that the distant stop entails. Sometimes they occur when you are looking for a major reversal and you are very confident that there will be a large, strong reversal. When that happens, it makes sense to enter as soon as the bar takes out the extreme of the prior bar. If you are less certain, you can wait for the bar to close and then enter on the breakout of the outside bar. If you did enter on the breakout of an outside bar and the protective stop is too large, consider using a money stop (like two points in the Emini) or trading fewer contracts. Since an outside bar is a one-bar trading range and it is better to not buy at the top of a sideways market or sell below it, it is usually best to not enter on a breakout of the bar.

Outside bars can be reliable entry bars if the bar before them was a good signal bar. For example, if a trader is looking to buy at the bottom of a bear swing and the market forms a strong bull reversal bar but the next bar trades below the bar, the trader should consider leaving the buy stop in the market. If the bar suddenly reverses back above the bull signal bar, the buy stop will be triggered and the current bar will become an outside bar and an entry bar. In general, traders should not enter a reversal trade on an outside bar unless the bar before it was a decent signal bar.

Sometimes you have to enter on an outside bar (not on its breakout) because you know that traders are trapped. This is especially true after a strong move. If an outside bar occurs as the second entry in a strong reversal from a trend line break or trend channel line overshoot, it can be an excellent entry bar. For example, if the market just sold off below a swing low for the second time and reversed up from a trend channel line overshoot, you are likely looking to buy and you keep moving a buy stop order to one tick above the prior bar's high until you get filled. Sometimes the fill will be on an outside up bar. This is usually a good reversal trade and it is due to strong buyers.

If an outside bar is in the middle of a trading range, it is meaningless and should not be used to generate trades, unless it is followed by a small bar near the high or low of the outside bar, setting up a fade. An outside bar in a trading range just reaffirms what everyone already knows—that both sides are balanced and both will sell near the top of the range and buy near the bottom, expecting a move toward the opposite end of the outside bar. If the market instead breaks out in the other direction, just let it go and look to fade a failed breakout of the outside bar, which commonly happens within a few bars. Otherwise, just wait for a pullback (a failed breakout that fails is a breakout pullback setup).

If the bar after the outside bar is an inside bar, then this is an ioi pattern (inside-outside-inside) and can be a setup for an entry in the direction of the breakout of the inside bar. However, take the entry only if there is a reason to believe that the market could move far enough to hit your profit target. For example, if the ioi is at a new swing high and the second inside bar is a bear bar that closes near its low, a downside breakout could be a good short since it is likely a second entry (the first entry probably occurred as the outside bar traded below the low of the bar before it). If it is in barbwire (a tight trading range), especially if the inside bar is large and near the middle of the outside bar, it is usually better to wait for a stronger setup.

When a with-trend outside bar occurs in the first leg of a trend reversal and the prior trend was strong, it functions like a strong trend bar and not a trading range type of bar. For example, in a bear trend, if there is a strong reversal up, traders might start looking for more of a rally. Many traders will be looking to buy above the high of a higher low, and fewer traders will short below the low of the prior bar. If the bulls are especially aggressive, they will buy below the low of the prior bar instead of waiting to buy above its high, and they will keep buying for the next several minutes as more and more traders see that the bulls have taken control of the market. This will make the bar extend above the high of that prior bar. Once it does, it becomes an outside up bar and those bears who just shorted below the low of the prior bar will likely cover and not be eager to short again for at least a couple of bars. With very few bears and many aggressive bulls, the market is one-sided and likely to go up at least for a bar or two. Everyone suddenly agrees about the new direction and therefore the move will have so much momentum and extend so far that it will likely get tested after a pullback, creating a second leg up. This higher low, and not the actual bear low, is the start of the up leg because it is when the market suddenly agreed that the next leg is up and not down. There will usually be two legs up from the bottom of the outside bar. Although the swing up will appear as three legs up from the actual bear low on the chart, it functionally is only two legs up since the market did not agree about the bull move until the higher low formed rather than at the actual low. This is where it became clear that the bulls had seized control.

Why is the move often strong? The old bears who shorted below the low of the prior bar, in what they thought would be just another bear flag, became trapped. Then their entry bar quickly reversed to an outside bar up, trapping the bears in and trapping the bulls out. Many bulls were trapped out because they don't like entering as outside bars are forming since many outside bars just lead to trading ranges. Invariably, the market will trend up hard for many more bars as everyone realizes that the market has reversed and they are trying to figure out how to position themselves. The bears are hoping for a dip so they can exit with a smaller loss, and the bulls want the same dip so they can buy more with limited risk. When everyone wants the same thing, it will not happen because both sides will start buying even two- or three-tick pullbacks, preventing a two- or three-bar pullback from developing until the trend has gone very far. Smart price action traders will be aware of this possibility at the outset, and if they are looking for a two-legged extended up move, they will watch the downside breakout of that bear flag carefully and anticipate its failure. They will place their entry orders just above the high of the prior bar, even if it means entering on an outside bar up (especially if it is the entry bar for the shorts).

If you think about this from an institution's perspective, you will want the bear flag short to trigger so that there will be longs who are trapped out and who will chase the market up, and also new shorts who will be trapped in and will have to cover if the bear breakout fails. This is an ideal situation for the institution that wants and expects a rally. So, as an institution, what can you do to contribute to this? Don't buy aggressively until after the trap. In fact, you try to create the trap by selling until the short entry is triggered and then you buy aggressively as all those bear traders get short and the longs exit with losses just below the low of the prior bar. You take the opposite side of their positions and buy heavily below the low of the prior bar! Once you've trapped them all, you can buy aggressively all the way up; they will chase the market up once they see the trap, and this will propel the market upward with everyone in agreement that the market is heading higher.

The single most important thing to remember about outside bars is that whenever a trader is uncertain about what to do, the best decision is to wait for more price action to develop.

Figure 7.1   OUTSIDE BARS   **159**

FIGURE 7.1   Outside Bars Are Tricky

Outside bars are risky, and traders have to pay careful attention to the price action that led to them.

In Figure 7.1, bar 1 was an outside up bar in a strong bear trend, so traders would be looking to enter only on a downside breakout. You could either short below bar 1 or wait to see what the breakout bar looks like after it closes. Here, it was a strong bear trend bar, and trapped longs will likely exit below such a strong bear trend bar. Because of this, it makes sense to short below the low of that bear bar.

Bar 5 was an outside down bar but the market was basically sideways with lots of overlapping bars, so it was not a reliable setup for a breakout entry. The inside bar that followed it (ioi) was too large to use as a breakout signal, because you would be either selling at the bottom of a trading range or buying at the top and you only want to buy low or sell high.

Deeper Discussion of This Chart

The market broke out below yesterday's low in Figure 7.1, and the first bar was a bear trend bar and the first bar of a trend from the open bear trend. Bar 1 and the bar before it formed the first pullback, and there is usually at least a scalp down after that first pullback. There was a two-legged pullback to the moving average at bar 3, which was also a 20 gap bars short setup.

Figure 7.2

OUTSIDE BARS **161**

FIGURE 7.2 An ioi Pattern

Outside bars are tricky because both the bulls and bears were in control at some point during the bar or during the prior bar, so the movement over the next few bars can have further reversals. In Figure 7.2, bar 1 was an outside bar that formed an inside-outside-inside (ioi) pattern. The bar 2 breakout of the inside bar following bar 1 failed, which is common, especially when the inside bar is large. This is because longs were forced to buy near the top of the ioi pattern, which is a trading range, and that is never a good thing, particularly when the market is falling.

Bar 2 was a small bar near the top of the trading range, which is a good area in which to look for a short entry. Since traders expected bulls to exit with a loss below the low of bar 2, their entry bar, they shorted at one tick below bar 2, which was a failed ioi breakout at the top of a trading range. Since the ioi bars were so large, there was plenty of room below bar 2 for at least a scalp down.

Bar 4 was almost an outside up bar, and in trading if something is almost a reliable pattern, it will likely yield the reliable result. Bar 4 was the third bull trend bar in the prior five bars, and therefore was reversing up from a third push down. It was also the strongest, with the biggest range and smallest tails, indicating that the bulls were gaining strength.

Bar 5 was an outside bar followed by a small inside bar near its high. Again, this yielded a great short with minimal risk, especially since the inside bar was a bear bar.

Deeper Discussion of This Chart

The first bar in Figure 7.2 broke out above yesterday's high and the breakout failed. The bar became a strong bear trend bar and it set up a trend from the open short.

Bars 8 and 9 formed a small double bottom, which was not the downward momentum that traders were expecting after the bar 7 bear breakout bar. This loss of downward momentum was followed by the bar 10 double bottom pullback long.

Bar 9 was also a high 2 long on the two-legged pullback from the rally up from bar 4. This formed a higher low on the day after the break of the bear trend line, setting up a possible trend reversal.

Figure 7.3　　　　　　　　　　　　　　　　　　　　OUTSIDE BARS　**163**

FIGURE 7.3　Outside Bars Depend on Context

Outside bars have to be evaluated in context. In Figure 7.3, the doji inside bar after bar 1 was not a good short signal bar since there were three sideways bars and bar 1 just reversed the bear bar before it. The odds were that the market would go sideways or up for at least a bar or two after that opening reversal, especially with a relatively flat moving average. There was room up to the moving average for a scalp, and it is best to buy above bull bars. The inside bar was a pause and therefore a type of pullback after the reversal up, so buying above its high and above the bar 1 high was reasonable. A trader could place a buy stop one tick above bar 1, and when bar 2 traded below the inside bar it was wise to keep the stop in place. The logic behind the long remained, and now there were trapped shorts who had made the mistake of selling below a weak signal bar and would cover above the signal bar. This made entering long on bar 2 as soon as it went outside up a good trade. As long as the bar before the outside bar is a decent signal bar, entering on the outside bar can be a sensible trade.

Bar 3 was a bear reversal bar near the moving average and an acceptable short, but it was small compared to the bull bodies of bars 1 and 2 so the market might form a higher low and then rally some more, which often happens when there is a strong outside trend bar at a possible trend reversal. Therefore, whether or not traders shorted below bar 3, they had to be ready to buy a higher low, and the small bull ii two bars later was a good signal.

Bar 4 was an outside bar, but the market was sideways for five bars. Therefore it was just part of the trading range and not a signal bar.

Bar 5 was an even larger outside bar, forming an oo or outside-outside pattern. This is usually just a larger trading range. Here, the bar had a large bear body and closed below the low of bar 4; traders who mistakenly shorted below the bar 4 outside bar were trapped. In general, it is not good to short a breakout of a trading range when many of the bars in the trading range are relatively large and have big tails, because the odds that the breakout will fail are high. The small bull doji bar that followed was a good signal bar for a failed reversal long.

Bar 6 set up a short following the breakout of the top of an outside up bar.

Bar 7 broke to a swing high and reversed down as an outside bar that closed on its low. This is an instance where there were trapped bulls and a strong bear reversal after a rally. However, this was a trading range day and any time a leg lasts more than five bars, traders will be looking for a reversal ("Buy low, sell high" on trading range days). Although it was acceptable to short as the bar traded below the small bear bar before it, it would be better to sell below the low of bar 7 since you would be shorting below a strong bear reversal bar as it is getting some follow-through.

Deeper Discussion of This Chart

The market broke out to the downside with a large gap down and a bear trend bar in Figure 7.3, but instead of trading down and creating a trend from the open bear trend, the breakout to the downside failed and the market reversed up into a trend from the open bull day.

Bar 2 was an outside bar up and a possible low of the day since the market was reversing up from a big gap down. This means that it was on bar 2 that the market decided that the trend was up and therefore it should be considered the start of the move up. Although bar 3 was a low 2 short, it was seen by the market as just a low 1 because it was the first pullback in the move up from the bar 2 start of the rally, and therefore likely to just lead to a higher low. Traders were expecting it to fail, and it does not matter whether you see the move up as a failed low 2 or a failed low 1 because both are good buy setups in a possible bull trend.

Bar 5 was a breakout of a barbwire pattern; most breakouts from barbwire fail, so traders should look for the fade setup. Barbwire is an area of intense uncertainty and two-sided trading. Bulls buy aggressively near the low and stop buying near the high. Bears sell aggressively near the high but stop shorting near the low. There are large buy and sell programs at work here, as can be seen by the good volume being traded during each bar. Both bulls and bears are comfortable trading here, and if one side is able to

Figure 7.3   OUTSIDE BARS   **165**

briefly overwhelm the other and create a breakout, usually the magnetic effect of the pattern will pull the market back. Once the market broke to the downside, the bulls, who were happy to buy higher in the middle of that trading range, were even happier buying lower. Also, the bears, who were happy selling at the top of the trading range, would be quick to buy back their shorts if there was not immediate follow-through on the breakout. These factors led to the high probability that the breakout would fail and get pulled back into the barbwire, as was the case here. Sometimes the market then breaks out of the other side and other times the trading range continues. Eventually there will be a move out of the pattern.

The first bar of the day and the first several bars often foreshadow what the next few hours, and often the entire day, will look like. The day started with a two-bar reversal, and then a doji, which is an intrabar reversal, and then an outside up bar reversal. There was then a bear reversal and several small bars with tails, indicating uncertainty. Multiple reversals, big tails, and uncertainty are all characteristics of trading range days, which was what the day became. With that suspicion early on, traders were more comfortable placing trades in both directions, scalping a larger portion of their positions, and less inclined to swing.

At 11:25 a.m. PST, there was a bull outside bar that formed a two-bar reversal, and therefore, created a buy setup. This pattern also formed a micro double bottom with the doji bar before it.

FIGURE 7.4   An Outside Bar as an Entry Bar

An outside bar can sometimes be a reasonable entry bar. In Figure 7.4, bar 3 was an outside up bar and an acceptable entry bar because it was a reversal up after a two-legged correction in a strong bull trend, and there was a bull trend bar a couple of bars earlier, showing strength. Traders would buy as soon as the bar went above the high of the prior bar, but it would be safer to wait a few more ticks until it went above the high of that bull trend bar from two bars earlier. Buying above a bull bar usually has a higher chance of leading to a profitable trade. Finally, traders could wait for the close of the outside up bar to see if it closed near its high and above the prior bar, which it did. Once they see that strength, they could buy above the high of the outside bar.

Bar 6 was an outside down bar and five of the six prior bars had bear bodies. It closed on its low, and aggressive traders could have shorted below it after such bear strength, especially since it trapped bulls into buying the old bull trend, which now may be over.

Deeper Discussion of This Chart

The market in Figure 7.4 broke out below the trading range of the final hour of yesterday. The first bar was a bull trend bar but it had a large tail on the top, indicating that the

Figure 7.4   OUTSIDE BARS   **167**

bulls were not strong enough to close the bar on its high. You could either buy above this bar or wait. The second bar was a setup for a breakout pullback short for a trend from the open bear day. The move down to bar 1 was a parabolic sell climax and therefore a possible low of the day. Since the selling was strong, it would be better to wait for a second signal before buying, and it came eight bars later in the form of a higher low and a failed breakout of a bear flag.

The sell-off to bar 3 broke a major trend line, alerting traders to short a test of the bar 2 high. The bar before bar 3 was a moving average gap bar buy setup in a strong trend, so buying above it, even with an outside up bar, was a good trade. The move down to a 20 gap bars setup almost always breaks a trend line, and the move up from the bar usually tests the high of the trend with either a higher high or a lower high. If there is then a reversal down, it usually leads to at least two legs lasting at least 10 bars and often a trend reversal.

Bar 3 was also the second bar of a two-bar reversal with the bear bar before it and with the bear bar from two bars earlier, so many bulls bought above the high of bar 3.

Bar 4 was a large bull trend bar (climactic) that formed a higher high, and it was followed by a strong bear inside bar that was the signal for the short. Traders were expecting two legs down from such a strong setup. As such, smart traders will be watching for the formation of a high 1 and then a high 2 and readying themselves to short more if these long setups fail and trap the bulls.

Bar 5 was a short setup for a failed high 1, and bar 6 was a great bull trap. It was a failed high 2, and the long entry bar reversed into an outside bar down, trapping longs in and bears out. This outside bar acted like a bear trend bar and not just an outside bar. Because it was an outside bar, the entry bar and its failure happened within a minute or two of each other, not giving traders enough time to process the information. Within a bar or two, they realized that the market in fact had become a bear trend. The longs were hoping for a two- or three-bar pullback to exit with a smaller loss, whereas the bears were hoping for the same rally to allow for a short entry with a smaller risk. What happened was that both sides started selling every two- or three-tick pullback, so a two- or three-bar rally did not come until the market had gone a long way.

Note that the high 2 long was a terrible buy setup because five of the six prior bars were bear bars and the other bar was a doji. A high 2 alone is not a setup. There first has to be earlier strength, usually in the form of a high 1 leg that breaks a trend line, or at least an earlier strong bull trend bar.

CHAPTER 8

The Importance of the Close of the Bar

A 5 minute bar usually assumes something similar to its final appearance seconds to a minute or more before the bar closes. If you enter before the bar closes, you might occasionally make a tick or so more on your trade. However, once or twice every day, the signal that you thought was going to happen does not and you will lose about eight ticks. That means that you need about eight early entries to work as planned for every one that does not, and that simply won't happen. You can enter early with trend in a strong trend and you will likely be fine. However, when there is a strong trend, you have so much confidence in the signal that there is no downside to waiting for the bar to close and then entering on a stop beyond the bar. You cannot be deciding on every bar if an early entry is appropriate, because you have too many other important decisions to make. If you add that to you list of things to think about, you will likely end up missing many good trades every day and forgo far more in missed opportunities than you could gain on an occasional successful early entry.

This holds true for all time frames. For example, look at a daily chart and you will see many bars that opened near the low but closed in the middle. Each one of those bars was a strong bull trend bar with a last price on the high at some point during the day. If you bought under the assumption that the bar was going to close on its high and bought near the high and instead it closed in the middle, you would realize your mistake. You are carrying home a trade that you never would have entered at the end of the day.

There are two common problems that regularly occur on the 5 minute chart. The most costly is when you try to pick a bottom in a strong trend. Typically you will see a lower low after a trend line break and traders will be hoping for a strong reversal bar, especially if there is also a bear trend channel line overshoot. The bar sets up nicely and is a strong bull reversal bar by the third minute or so. The price is hanging near the high of the bar for a couple of minutes, attracting more and more countertrend traders who want to get in early so that their risk will be smaller (their stop will be below the bar), but then with one to five seconds remaining before the bar closes, the price collapses and the bar closes on its low. All of those early longs who were trying to risk a tick or two less end up losing two points or more. These longs let themselves get trapped into a bad trade. A similar situation happens many times a day when a potential signal bar is forming just before the bar closes. For example, a trader might be looking to short below a bear reversal bar that has seconds to go before it closes, and the current price is on the bottom of the bar. With less than a second before the bar closes, the close bounces up two or three ticks from the low of the bar, and the bar closes off its low. The market is telling the trader that the signal is now weaker, and the trader needs to avoid getting trapped into trading based on the expectation and hope that she had just three seconds ago.

The other common problem is getting trapped out of a good trade. For example, if you just bought and your trade has had three to five ticks of open profit but the market just can't hit six, allowing you to scalp out with four ticks of profit, you start to become nervous. You look at the 3 or 5 minute chart with about 10 seconds before its bar closes and it is a strong bear reversal bar. You then move your protective stop up to one tick below that bar, and just before the bar closes, the market drops and hits your stop, only to pop up several ticks in the final two seconds of the bar. Then, within the first 30 seconds of the next bar, the market quickly goes up to six ticks where smart traders took partial profits while you are sitting on the sidelines. Good entry, good plan, bad discipline. You just let yourself get trapped out of a good trade. If you had followed your plan and relied on your initial stop until the entry bar closed, you would have secured your profit.

There is one other point about bar closes. Pay very close attention to the close of every bar, especially for the entry bar and the bar or two later. If the entry bar is six ticks tall, you would much prefer seeing the body suddenly increase from a body that was two ticks to one that was four ticks in the final seconds of the bar. You will then likely reduce the number of contracts that you will scalp out. This is true for the next couple of bars as well. If there are strong closes, you should be more willing to swing more contracts and hold them for more points than if these bars had weak closes.

Another reason why the close is important is that many institutional traders place orders based on value and not price action, and when they look at charts, the charts are line charts, which are based on the close. They would not look at charts at all if the charts did not influence their decision making, and the only price they are considering is the close, which increases its importance.

Figure 8.1   THE IMPORTANCE OF THE CLOSE OF THE BAR   **171**

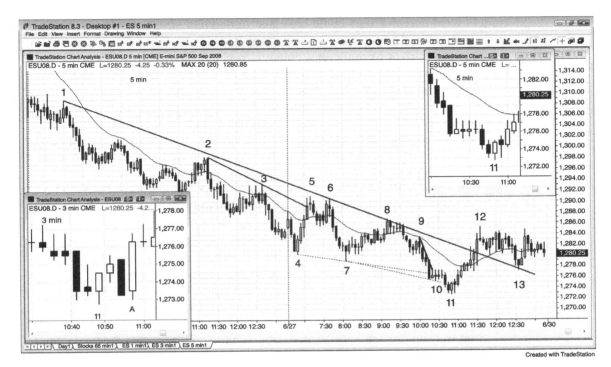

FIGURE 8.1 Smaller Time Frame Charts Result in More Losses

Smaller time frame charts allow for smaller stops but have a greater risk of stopping a trader out of a good trade. In Figure 8.1, the insert on the left shows that traders using the 3 minute chart were stopped out, but traders who relied on the 5 minute chart did not get stopped out.

The 5 minute Emini had been in a strong bear trend for weeks and was now starting to have bigger pullbacks. Each new lower low was being bought, and the longs were profitable countertrend trades. The bulls were more confident and the bears were becoming more willing to take profits. The thumbnail on the left is a 3 minute chart and the one on the right is a close-up of the 5 minute chart.

Bar 11 was a strong bull reversal bar and a two-bar reversal, and it was the second attempt to reverse up from a lower low (the ii after bar 10 was the first) and it was the third push down on the day (a possible wedge bottom). This was a high-probability long, but the stop would have had to be beneath its low, three points below the entry price. This was more than what was typically required in the Emini (two points worked recently and when the average daily range had been about 10 to 15 points), but that was what the price action showed was needed. If traders were nervous, they could have just traded half size, but they must take a strong setup like this one and plan on swinging half.

This is a perfect example of a common problem that traders face when they try to reduce risk by watching a smaller time frame chart. The risk is smaller but the probability of success also drops. Since there are more trades on a 3 minute chart, there is more risk of missing the best ones, and this can lead to the overall profitability of 3 minute trades being less for many traders.

Just like on the 5 minute chart, the 3 minute chart also had a reversal bar at bar 11. However, the stop below the entry bar was hit by a bear trend bar with a shaved top and bottom, indicating strong sellers. At this point, it would have been very difficult to reconcile that with the 5 minute chart where the stop had not been hit. The large size of the stop required on the 5 minute chart would make traders more willing to exit early and take a loss. If traders were also watching the 3 minute chart, they almost certainly would have exited with a loss and would have been trapped out of the market by that strong bear trend bar. The next bar on the 3 minute chart was a very strong outside bull trend bar, indicating that the bulls were violently asserting themselves in creating a higher low, but most of the weak hands who were stopped out would likely be so scared that they would not take the entry, and instead wait for a pullback.

Stop runs on the 3 minute chart are much more common than on the 5 minute chart at important reversals, and smart traders look at them as great opportunities. This is because they trap weak longs out of the market, forcing them to chase the market up. It is always better to just watch and trade off one chart because sometimes things happen too quickly for traders to think fast enough to place their orders if they are watching two charts and trying to reconcile the inconsistencies.

Deeper Discussion of This Chart

Bar 5 broke above a trend line in Figure 8.1, and bar 8 exceeded another by a fraction of a tick. Both breakouts failed, setting up with-trend shorts.

CHAPTER 9

Exchange-Traded Funds and Inverse Charts

Sometimes the price action becomes clearer if you change something about the chart. You can switch to a bar or line chart, a chart based on volume or ticks, or a higher or lower time frame, or you can simply print the chart. Several exchange-traded funds (ETFs) are also helpful. For example, the SPDR S&P 500 ETF (SPY) is almost identical in appearance to the Emini chart and sometimes has clearer price action.

Also, it can be helpful to consider the chart from an opposite perspective. If you are seeing a bull flag but something doesn't seem quite right, consider looking at the ProShares UltraShort S&P 500 (SDS), which is an ETF that is based on the inverse of the SPY (but with twice the leverage). If you look at it, you might discover that the bull flag that you were seeing on the Emini and SPY might now look like a rounding bottom on the SDS. If it does, you would be wise not to buy the Emini flag and instead to wait for more price action to unfold (like waiting for the breakout and then shorting if it fails). Sometimes patterns are clearer on other stock index futures, like the Emini Nasdaq-100, or its ETF, the QQQ, or its double inverse, the QID, but it is usually not worth looking at these and it is better to stick with the Emini and sometimes the SDS.

Since an ETF is a fund, the firm that runs it is doing so to make money and that means that it takes fees from the ETF. The result is that the ETFs don't always track exactly with comparable markets. For example, on triple witching days, the SPY will often have a much larger gap opening than the Emini, and the gap is due to a price adjustment to the SPY. It will still trade pretty much tick for tick with the Emini throughout the day, so traders should not be concerned about the disparity.

FIGURE 9.1 The Emini and the SPY Are Similar

As shown in Figure 9.1, the top chart of the Emini is essentially identical to that of the SPY (the middle chart), but the price action on the SPY is sometimes easier to read because its smaller tick size often makes the patterns clearer. The bottom chart is the SDS, which is an ETF that is the inverse of the SPY (with twice the leverage). Sometimes the SDS chart will make you reconsider your read of the Emini chart.

Figure 9.2   EXCHANGE-TRADED FUNDS AND INVERSE CHARTS   **175**

FIGURE 9.2   SPY Adjustment on Triple Witching Days

As shown in Figure 9.2, on a triple witching day the SPY's price gets adjusted, and this often results in a gap opening that may be much larger than that on the Emini (the SPY is on the left and the Emini is on the right). However, they then pretty much trade tick for tick, like on any other day, so don't be concerned by the gap and just trade the price action as the day unfolds.

CHAPTER 10

Second Entries

Analysts often say that bottoms on the daily chart usually require a second reversal off the low to convince enough traders to trade the market as a possible new bull trend. However, this is true of tops as well. A second entry is almost always more likely to result in a profitable trade than a first entry.

If the second entry is letting you in at a better price than the first, be suspicious that it might be a trap. Most good second entries are at the same price or worse. A second-entry trader is someone entering late, trying to minimize risk, and the market usually makes him pay a little more for that additional information. If it is charging you less, it might be setting you up to steal your money in a failed signal.

Traders looking for second entries are more aggressive and confident and will often enter on smaller time frame charts. This usually results in traders on the 5 minute charts entering after many other traders have already entered, making the entry a little worse. If the market is letting you in at a better price, you should suspect that you are missing something and should consider not taking the trade. Most of the time, a good fill equals a bad trade (and a bad fill equals a good trade!).

If you are fading a move, for example shorting the first reversal in a strong bull trend where the move had about four consecutive bull trend bars or two or three large bull trend bars, there is too much momentum for you to be placing an order in the opposite direction. It is better to wait for an entry, not take it, wait for the trend to resume for a bar or two, and then enter on the market's second attempt to reverse.

FIGURE 10.1   Second Entries

There were many second-entry trades today (see Figure 10.1), and all but one were at the same price or a worse price than the first entry. Look at the bar 10 long. The market is letting you buy at one tick better than the traders who bought at bar 9. In general, the "good fill, bad trade" maxim applies. Whenever the market is offering you a bargain, assume that you are reading the chart incorrectly; usually it is better not to take the trade. Even though bar 10 was a second entry, the momentum down was strong, as seen by the tight bear channel down from bar 8. Before taking a countertrend trade, it is always better to see some evidence in the preceding several bars that the bulls were able to move more than just a couple of ticks above the prior bar.

As discussed in book 3, most tops occur from some type of micro double top, like bar 1 and the bear reversal bar from two bars earlier, and most bottoms occur from some type of micro double bottom, like bar 18 and the bar before bar 17.

Figure 10.2   SECOND ENTRIES   **179**

FIGURE 10.2   In Strong Moves, Wait for Second Reversals

When the momentum is strong, it is better to wait for a second reversal setup before trading countertrend (see Figure 10.2).

Bar 1 followed five bull trend bars, which is too much upward momentum to be shorting the first attempt down. Smart traders would wait to see it the bulls would fail in a second attempt to rally before going short, and this happened on the second short entry at bar 2.

Bar 3 was a first entry long on a new low of the day, but after six bars without a bullish close it makes more sense to wait for a second long entry, which occurred on bar 4.

Bar 5 followed four bear trend bars, which is too much downward momentum to buy. A second entry never developed, so smart traders averted a loss by waiting.

Bar 10 followed six bars with higher lows and only two bars with small bear bodies, indicating too much bullish strength for a short. There was a second entry at the bar 11 bear reversal bar.

Deeper Discussion of This Chart

The market in Figure 10.2 broke above the bear channel into yesterday's close, but the breakout failed at the moving average, setting up a short. Today the market broke out below yesterday's low, but the breakout failed on the reversal up on the fourth bar of the day. This reversal can be thought of as a breakout pullback to a lower low after the first bar broke above the small bear channel.

The market failed to put in a higher high and instead the trending bear channel continued. Traders should have shorted below the bar 6 double top because the attempt to become a trend from the open failed as the market failed to break above a prior lower high. The trend of lower highs and lows was continuing.

The pullback from the bear spike that ended on the bar before bar 3 formed a low 4 short setup that triggered with a bear trend bar at 9:35 a.m. PST. The bear breakout grew into a four-bar bear spike.

Bar 5 was a high 2 but it followed four bear trend bars and therefore should not be bought.

Bar 6 was the start of a four-bar bear spike.

The bar 7 ii was a possible final flag.

Bar 7 led to a two-bar bear spike. All three-bear spikes in this channel down from that low 4 short constitute consecutive sell climaxes, and once there are three, the odds of at least a two-legged rally are high.

Traders could have gone long on bar 9 after the bar 8 reversal bar, expecting at least two legs up after a final flag and protracted bear trend. Bar 8 was a micro double bottom (a buy setup) since the market went down on bar 8 and it also went down two bars earlier (bear bar).

Bar 10 was a low 1 but there was too much bullish strength for a short, and it made more sense to look to buy a higher low or even on a limit order below the prior bar. With this much upward momentum, the market was very likely to at least test the high of the leg up.

Bar 11 was a doji reversal bar after a big bull trend bar. A big bull trend bar after five to 10 bar bull trend bars is a buy climax and is likely to be followed by about 10 or more sideways to down bars before the bulls return. It is also in the area of the final lower high of the bear trend, creating a potential double top bear flag. With the bulls as strong as they were, most traders assumed that the market would have a higher low, but they used the double top bear flag as an area to take profits. Some bear scalpers shorted there, expecting at least a test down to the moving average. With so many bull trend bars in that rally, it was likely that the market would form a higher low since buyers were clearly aggressive.

CHAPTER 11

Late and Missed Entries

If you look at any chart and think that if you had taken the original entry you would still be holding the swing portion of your trade, then you need to enter at the market. The market has a clear always-in position, and you need to participate in the trend, because the probability of making a profit is high. However, you should enter only with the number of shares or contracts that you would still be holding had you taken the original entry, and you should use the same trailing stop. Your stop will usually be larger than what you would use for a scalp, and you therefore need to trade a smaller position to keep your dollar risk the same. For example, if you see a strong trend underway in GS, and had you taken the original entry with 300 shares you now would only be holding 100 shares with your protective stop $1.50 away, you should buy 100 shares at the market and place a $1.50 protective stop. Logically, it doesn't make any difference whether you are buying a swing-size portion now or holding a swing position from an earlier entry. Although it might be easier emotionally to think of the trade with the open profit as risking someone else's money, that is not the reality. It is *your* money, and what you are risking is no different from buying now and risking the same $1.50. Traders know this and will place the trade without hesitation. If they do not, then they simply do not believe that they would still be holding any shares had they entered earlier, or they need to work on this emotional issue.

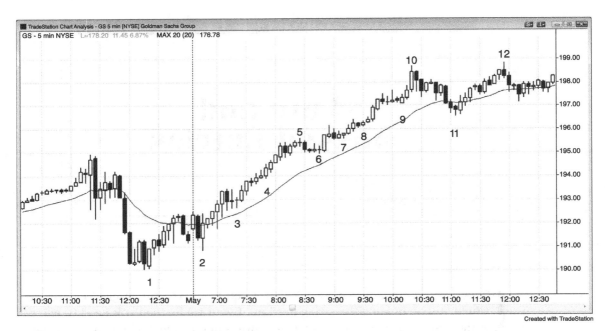

FIGURE 11.1   Consecutive Trend Bars in a Trend

Once the market starts forming four or more consecutive bull trend bars that are not too large and therefore possibly climactic, traders should buy at least a small position at the market instead of waiting for a pullback.

As shown in Figure 11.1, GS had a strong two-legged sell-off into the close yesterday but a strong bull reversal bar at bar 2. It was setting up a higher low test of the bear low and a bull trend day.

If traders began watching this chart at around bar 4, they would have seen a series of bull trend bars and a strong bull trend. They would probably have wished that they had at least the swing portion of their position still working. If they normally trade 300 shares and at this point would have only 100 shares left from that entry above bar 3, they should buy 100 shares at the market. Also, they should use the same stop that they would have used had they entered above bar 3. Since they would have only the swing portion remaining, they should use a breakeven stop or maybe risk about 10 cents below the bar 3 high. They should also look for pauses and pullbacks to add on. After adding on above bar 6, they could move the stop for the entire position to one tick below the bar 6 signal bar and then trail it up.

Entering late while using the original stop is absolutely identical to being long the swing portion of the original position, using the same protective stop.

Figure 11.1   LATE AND MISSED ENTRIES   **183**

Deeper Discussion of This Chart

The first bar of the day in Figure 11.1 broke above the closing swing high, setting up a small double top bear flag short at the moving average. However, this second attempt to break below the bear flag that began at bar 1 failed. Bar 2 reversed strongly up and formed a two-bar bull reversal. The next bar was a bull inside bar and was a good signal bar for the trend from the open bull. It also reversed up from the breakout below the small double bottom formed by the final four bars of yesterday.

The sell-off to the bar 11 moving average gap bar broke the bull trend line and should be expected to lead to a higher high or lower high test of the bull high. Normally, the market would then form a larger or more complex correction. However, the rally up to bar 10 was in such a tight channel that it showed that the bulls were exceptionally strong. The entire rally was probably a spike on a higher time frame chart, and it would probably be followed by a channel up on that chart before there was much of a correction on the 5 minute chart. Also, the bar 11 moving average gap bar was also a 20 gap bar pullback. After the first new high following a 20 gap bar pullback, the market usually pulls back and then tests the high again, so this moving average gap bar would likely function more like a 20 gap bar setup than a typical moving average gap bar setup.

CHAPTER 12

Pattern Evolution

It is important to remember that the current bar can always be the start of a big move in either direction, and you have to watch carefully as the price action unfolds to see if a pattern is changing into something that will lead to a trade in the opposite direction. Patterns frequently morph into other patterns or evolve into larger patterns, and both can result in trades in the same or in the opposite direction. Most of the time, if you read the price action correctly, the original pattern will provide at least a scalper's profit. Likewise, the larger pattern should as well. It does not matter whether you label the larger pattern as an expanded version of the original pattern. Names are never important. Just make sure that you read correctly what is in front of you and place your trade, ignoring the pattern that completed a couple of bars earlier.

The most common example of a morphed pattern is a failure, where a pattern fails to yield a scalper's profit and then reverses into a signal in the other direction. This traps traders on the wrong side of the market, and as these traders are forced to exit with losses, they will then provide the fuel that will drive the market to at least a scalper's profit in the opposite direction. This can happen with any pattern, since all can fail. If the failure just goes sideways for a number of bars and then a new pattern develops, it makes more sense to simply regard the new pattern as being independent of the first. Ignore the first one because there will not be many trapped traders left who will drive the market as they are forced to exit with losses.

Although it is not important at this point to be familiar with all of the patterns in the book, in later chapters you will see common examples of pattern evolution. An expanding triangle sometimes expands from five legs to seven. A micro trend line breakout usually fails and then has a breakout pullback. When a final bear flag fails to reverse the market, it usually morphs into a breakout pullback sell setup. It then often enlarges into a wedge reversal setup, or into a larger trading range that often becomes a larger final flag. A bull spike and channel trend pattern usually evolves into a trading range and then a double bottom bull flag. In the first hour, double top bear flags often evolve into double bottom bull flags and vice versa. If you are aggressively trading the market in question, you should look to take both entries, and swing part of them, because a big move is common from either the first or second of these patterns.

Figure 12.1   PATTERN EVOLUTION   **187**

FIGURE 12.1   Setups Can Evolve into More Complex Patterns

Reliable patterns fail about 40 percent of the time and often evolve into larger patterns that set up entries in either direction. Figure 12.1 is the 5 minute EWZ, which is the iShares MSCI Brazil Index Fund. Here, the low 2 short setup below bar 2 failed but the pattern evolved into a larger wedge top with an entry below the bar that followed bar 3.

The bar 19 low 2 bear flag evolved into a more complex low 2 short setup below the bar 21 two-bar reversal. The first push up was bar 18.

Deeper Discussion of This Chart

The high 2 after bar 6 in Figure 12.1 evolved into a wedge bull flag above bar 8 at the moving average. It was also a spike and channel bear where bar 8 was the third push down in the channel, which is often the end of the channel.

The low 2 at bar 10 was likely to fail since the spike up to bar 9 was strong. The low 1 entry was two bars before bar 10. The pattern became a failed low 2 buy at bar 11 and then a spike and channel top at bar 12, where the channel ended in the third push up, which is common.

The bar 15 high 2 failed and the pattern turned into a second attempt to reverse down at a new high of the day. The entry was below the high 2 entry bar that followed bar 15.

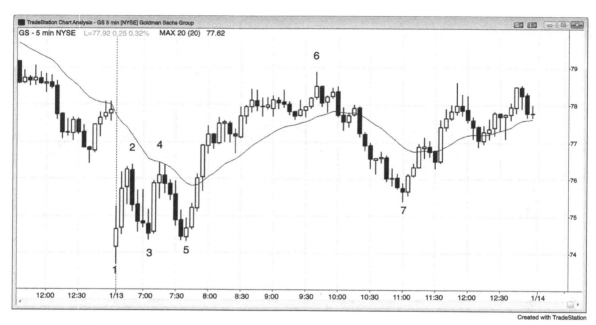

FIGURE 12.2   Breakout Mode in the First Hour

In the first hour, it is common to see both a double top and a double bottom, putting the market in breakout mode. In Figure 12.2, the double top in GS evolved into a double bottom bull flag. This is a common pattern, and you should take both entries (short below bar 4 and then go long above bar 5) and swing part because a big move commonly follows either the first or the second pattern. Remember, one extreme usually forms in the first hour, which means that the market will then usually move away from that price for much of the next couple of hours, and possibly all day if the day becomes a trend day. Here, GS had a large gap down that broke below a trend channel line from yesterday and reversed up on the first bar of the day. The market formed a low 2 and a double top bear flag at the falling moving average at bar 4, only to reverse up at the bar 5 double bottom bull flag. The market then ran up $3 to the bar 6 high of the day.

Deeper Discussion of This Chart

Large gap openings often lead to trend days in either direction. With the first three bars strongly up in Figure 12.2, a bull trend was more likely, especially after a reversal up from the overshoot of the bear trend channel from yesterday. However, the bear trend tried to reassert itself at the moving average but when the market came down to bar 5, it again found strong bulls in the area of the low of bar 3. The bar 4 second attempt to

Figure 12.2   PATTERN EVOLUTION   **189**

create a bear trend day failed, and the market then proceeded to create a bull channel once the bar 5 second attempt to form a bottom succeeded.

The market had bull spikes up to bar 2 and bar 4 and bear spikes down to bar 3 and bar 5. This often results in a trading range as the bulls and bears continue to trade in an attempt to generate a channel in their direction. Here, the market formed a very strong five-bar bull spike up from bar 5 and then a three-push channel up to bar 6. Some traders will look at this chart and say that the move up to bar 2 was a spike and the trading range to bar 5 was a pullback that led to a channel up to bar 6. Other traders will say that the spike up from bar 5 was the dominant feature of the day and that the bull channel began once that five-bar bull spike ended. There is no one clear answer and both traders have valid interpretations. The important thing is to see that the bull spikes up from bar 1 and bar 5 were stronger than the bear spikes down from bar 2 and bar 4, and therefore the odds favored a bull channel.

This could have been a trend from the open bull trend day but instead became a trending trading range day. Bar 7 tested down into the lower trading range and then reversed up into the close, near the high of the higher trading range.

PART II

Trend Lines
and Channels

Although many traders refer to all lines as trend lines, it is helpful to traders to distinguish a few subtypes. Both trend lines and trend channel lines are straight, diagonal lines that contain the market's price action, but on opposite sides, forming a channel. In a bull trend, the trend line is below the lows and the trend channel line is above the highs, and in a bear trend, the trend line is above the highs and the trend channel line is below the lows. The lines defining the channel most often are parallel or roughly parallel, but are convergent in wedges and most other triangles, and divergent in expanding triangles. Trend lines most often set up with trend trades, and trend channel lines are most helpful finding tradable countertrend trades. Curved lines and bands are too subjective and therefore require too much thought when you are trying to place trades quickly.

A channel can be up, down, or sideways, as is the case in a trading range. When the channel is sideways, the lines are horizontal and the line above is the resistance line and the line below is the support line. Some stock traders think of a resistance line as an area of distribution, where traders are exiting their longs, and support lines as an area of accumulation, where traders are adding to their longs. However, with so many institutions now shorting as much as they are buying, a resistance line is just as likely to be where they are initiating a new short as it is that they are exiting or distributing their longs. Also, a support line is just as likely to be an area where they are exiting or distributing their shorts as it is a place where they are initiating longs.

FIGURE PII.1   Lines Highlight Trends

Lines can be drawn to highlight the price action, making it easier to initiate and manage trades (see Figure PII.1).

Line 1 is a trend channel line above an expanding triangle, and line 2 is a trend channel line below an expanding triangle. Because the channel was expanding, there was no trend and therefore no trend line.

Line 3 is a trend line below the bars in a bull trend and is a support line, but line 10 is a trend line above the highs in a bear trend and is a resistance line.

Line 4 is a trend channel line in a bull trend and is above the highs, and line 9 is a trend channel line in a bear trend and is below the lows.

Lines 5 and 6 are horizontal lines in a trading range, which is just a horizontal channel. Line 5 is above the highs and is a resistance line and line 6 is below the lows and is a support line.

The channel formed by lines 3 and 4 is convergent and rising and therefore a wedge.

Lines 7 and 8 are trend lines in a small symmetrical triangle, which is a convergent channel. Since there is both a small bear trend and a small bull trend within a symmetrical triangle, the channel is made of two trend lines, and there is no trend channel line. A convergent triangle can be subdivided into symmetrical, ascending, and descending types, but since they all trade the same way, these terms are not necessary.

Deeper Discussion of This Chart

The first bar of the day broke above yesterday's high in Figure PII.1, but the breakout failed. Since the final six bars of yesterday were bull trend bars, only a second-entry short could be considered, but there was no reasonable signal. The market entered a small trading range for the first seven bars, and therefore the market was in breakout mode. Traders would buy on a stop at one tick above the high and go short at one tick below the low of the opening range. The market broke to the upside and a minimal target was a measured move up equal to the height of the expanding triangle.

CHAPTER 13

Trend Lines

A bull trend line is a line drawn across the lows of a bull trend, and a bear trend line is drawn across the highs of a bear trend. A trend line is most helpful when looking for entries in the direction of the trend on pullbacks and in the opposite direction after the trend line is broken. Trend lines can be drawn using swing points or best fit techniques such as linear regression calculations or simply quickly drawing a best approximation. They also can be created as a parallel of a trend channel line and then dragged to the trend line side of the bars, but this approach is rarely needed since there is usually an acceptable trend line that can be drawn using the swing points. Sometimes the best fit trend line is drawn just using the candle bodies and ignoring the tails; this is common in wedge patterns, which often do not have a wedge shape. It is not necessary to actually draw the line when it is obvious. If you do draw a line, you usually can erase it moments after you verify that the market has tested it, because too many lines on the chart can be a distraction.

Once a trend has been established by a series of trending highs and lows, the most profitable trades are in the direction of the trend line until the trend line is broken. Every time the market pulls back to the area around the trend line, even if it undershoots or overshoots the trend line, look for a reversal off of the trend line and then enter in the direction of the trend. Even after a trend line breaks, if it has been in effect for dozens of bars, the chances are high that the trend extreme will get tested after a pullback. The test can be followed by the trend continuing, the trend reversing, or the market entering a trading range. The single most important point about a trend line break is that it is the first sign that the market is no longer being controlled by just one side (buyers or sellers) and the chances of further two-sided trading are now much greater. After every trend line break, there will be a new swing point on which to base a new line. Typically, each successive line has a flatter slope, indicating that the trend is losing momentum. At some point, trend lines in the opposite direction will become more important as control of the market switches from the bears to the bulls or vice versa.

If the market repeatedly tests a trend line many times in a relatively small number of bars and the market cannot drift far from that trend line, then either of two things will likely happen. Most of the time, the market will break through the trend line and attempt to reverse the trend. However, sometimes the market does the opposite and moves quickly away from the trend line as traders give up trying to break through it. The trend then accelerates rather than reverses.

The strength of the trend line break provides an indication of the strength of the countertrend traders. The bigger and faster the countertrend move, the more likely that a reversal will occur, but there will usually first be a test the trend's extreme (for example, in the form of a lower high or a higher high in the test of the high of the bull trend).

It is helpful to consider a gap opening and any large trend bar to be effectively breakouts and each should be treated as if it is a one-bar trend, since breakouts commonly fail and you need to be prepared to fade them if there is a setup. Any sideways movement over the next few bars will break the trend. Usually, those bars will be setting up a flag and then be followed by a with-trend move out of the flag, but sometimes the breakout will fail and the market will reverse. Since the sideways bars broke the steep trend line, you can look to fade the trend if there is a good signal bar for the reversal.

Figure 13.1   TREND LINES   **197**

FIGURE 13.1   All Trend Lines Are Important

Which trend lines were valid? Every one of them that you can see has the potential to generate a trade. Look for every swing point that you can find and see if there is an earlier one that can be connected with a trend line, and then extend the line to the right and see how price responds when it penetrates or touches the line. Notice how each successive trend line tends to become flatter until some point when trend lines in the opposite direction become more important.

In actual practice, when you see a possible trend line and you are not certain how far it is from the current bar, draw it to see if the market has hit it and then quickly erase the line. You don't want lines on your chart for more than a few seconds when trading, because you don't want distractions. You need to focus on the bars and see how they behave once near the line, and not focus on the line.

As a trend progresses, countertrend moves break the trend lines and usually the breakouts fail, setting up with trend entries. Each breakout failure becomes the second point for the creation of a new, longer trend line with a shallower slope. Eventually a failed breakout fails to reach a new trend extreme. This creates a pullback in what may become a new trend in the opposite direction, and this allows for the drawing of a trend line in the opposite direction. After the major trend line is broken, the trend lines in the opposite direction become more important, and at that point the trend has likely reversed.

Figure 13.1 illustrates one of the most important points that everyone needs to accept as reality if they are to become successful traders—most breakouts fail! The market repeatedly races toward a trend line with very strong momentum, and it is easy to get caught up in the strength of the bar and overlook what just took place over the past 20 bars. For example, when the market is trending up, it has many very strong sell-offs that quickly drop to the bull trend line. This makes beginners assume that the market has reversed and they sell just above, at, or below the trend line, believing that with so much downward momentum, they will ride that wave to a big profit and be entering the new bear trend near the very beginning. At the very worst, the market might bounce a little before having at least a second leg down that would allow them to get out at breakeven. When they are making their decision to trade against the trend with the hope that a new trend is starting, all they are considering is the reward that they stand to gain. However, they are ignoring two other essential considerations for every trade: the risk and the probability of success. All three must be evaluated before placing a trade.

While beginners are shorting on those strong sell-offs near the bull trend line, experienced traders are doing the opposite. They have limit orders to buy at and just below the trend line, or they will buy there with market orders. The market usually has to go at least a little below the trend line during a sharp sell-off to find information. It needs to know if there will be more sellers or more buyers. Most of the time, there will be more buyers and the bull trend will resume, but only after there has been a big break below the trend line and then another rally that tests the old bull high by forming either a higher high as it did here, or a lower high.

Figure 13.2

TREND LINES **199**

FIGURE 13.2 Monthly Trend Lines

Trend lines are important on all time frames, including the monthly chart of the Dow Jones Industrial Average (INDU). Note in Figure 13.2 how the 1987 crash at bar 3 ended on a test of trend line B drawn from bars 1 and 2. The 2009 bear market reversed up from trend line A, drawn from the 1987 crash and the 1990 low, but since the 2009 bear trend was so strong, there is a reasonable chance that the market will again test line B. It is unlikely that the market will come all the way back to the line C breakout, which coincided with the Republican takeover of the House and Senate in 1994. Normally, when a breakout is followed by a protracted trend, it is unlikely to be touched again, but it usually gets tested. Since we never adequately tested it, it may remain as somewhat of a magnet, drawing the market down. However, it was many bars earlier and likely has lost some or all of its magnetic pull.

Incidentally, the market's direction is usually only about 50 percent certain because the bulls and bears are in balance most of the time. However, when there is a strong trend, traders can often be 60 percent or more certain of the direction. Since the 2009 crash was so strong, it is probably 60 percent certain that its low will be tested before the all-time high is exceeded. Bears will probably start looking at the current bear rally as a potential right shoulder of a head and shoulders top, a double top with the 2007 high, or an expanding triangle top (if the market reaches a new all-time high). Price action traders see each of these as simply a test of the top of the 12-year-long trading range.

FIGURE 13.3   Trend Line Created as Parallel

A trend line can be drawn using a parallel of a trend channel line, but this rarely provides trades that are not already apparent using other more common price action analysis.

In Figure 13.3, a bear trend channel line from bars 1 to 4 was used to create a parallel, and the parallel was dragged to the opposite side of the price and anchored at the bar 2 high (because this then contained all of the prices between the bars 1 and 4 beginning and end of the trend channel line).

Bar 6 was a second attempt to reverse the break above that line and therefore a good short setup.

The trend line created as a parallel to the bar 1 to bar 4 trend channel line was almost indistinguishable from the trend line created from the highs of bar 2 and

Figure 13.3   TREND LINES   **201**

bar 5 (not shown) and so added nothing to a trader looking for a short. It is shown only for completeness.

Deeper Discussion of This Chart

Bar 6 in Figure 13.3 was also a failed overshoot of the bars 3 and 5 trend channel line, making the bar 6 short an example of a dueling lines trade. This is where a trend channel line in a pullback or a leg of a channel intersects the channel's trend line. Here, the pullback to the trend line was in the form of a wedge bear flag created by bars 3, 5, and 6.

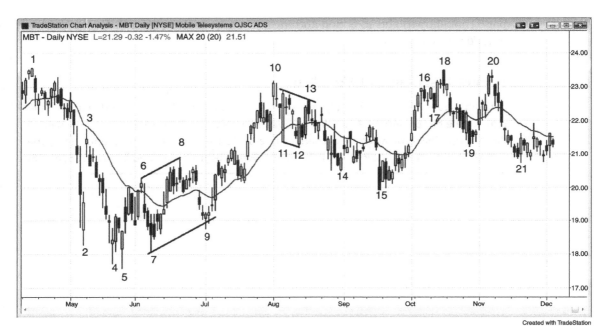

FIGURE 13.4 Trend Channel Line Creating a Channel

After the first couple of pushes, sometimes the trend channel line that they generate can be used to create a channel. Figure 13.4 is the daily chart of the Russian
communications company Mobile Telesystems (MBT).

The push up to bar 6 was strong and there was a second strong move up to
bar 8. After the wedge bottom at bar 4, the market might have been developing a
trend reversal and a bull channel. Traders could have used the trend channel line
from bar 6 to bar 8 to create a parallel, and then they could have dragged it to
the bar 7 swing low in between them to create a channel. Traders then watched the
sell-off from bar 8 to see if it was followed by a reversal up at the bottom of the
channel. The bar 9 bull reversal bar was the buy setup.

Similarly, bar 10 was in the area of the bar 1 high, so traders were aware of a
possible double top. The market gapped down on bar 11 and had a second leg down
to the bar 12 low. Traders could have drawn a trend channel line across their lows
and then they could have dragged it to the high in between them, which happened
to be the top of bar 11. They would then wait for a rally off the bar 12 low to see
if it found resistance at the top of this potential new bear channel. When they saw
the strong bear reversal bar at bar 13, they could have shorted, expecting that the
market might have been in the process of channeling down.

Figure 13.5

TREND LINES   **203**

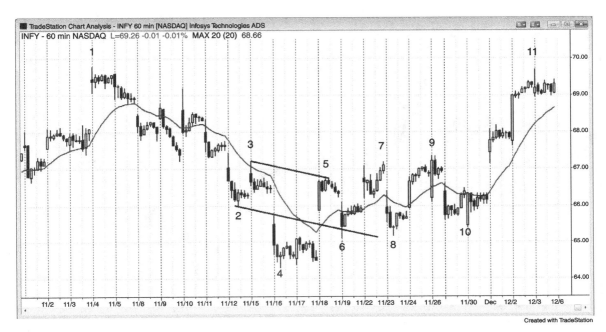

FIGURE 13.5   Head and Shoulders Using Trend Channel Line

As shown in Figure 13.5, when a possible head and shoulders pattern is setting up (the area around bar 4 is the head), a trend channel line drawn across the neckline (bars 3 and 5) and dragged to the left shoulder (bar 2) sometimes gives an approximation of where the right shoulder might form (bar 6). When the market falls to that level, traders will begin to look for buy setups, like the strong bull inside bar that followed the bar 6 sell climax. This is of minor importance since the most recent bars are always much more important in deciding where to enter. This is the 60 minute chart of Infosys Technologies (INFY), one of the leading software companies in India.

FIGURE 13.6   Trend Channel Line Creating a Channel

In Figure 13.6, the dotted trend channel line that runs from the bar 3 low to just below the bar 5 low was created as a parallel of the dotted bear trend line drawn across the highs of bars 1 and 4. Although neither bar 5 nor bar 6 touched it, they were close enough and many bulls would have been satisfied that the bottom of the channel was adequately tested and therefore the market could be bought. However, many traders prefer to see a penetration of the channel before looking for a reversal up that should penetrate the top of the channel as a minimum target.

When a trend channel line is so steep that it is tested but not broken, it is wise to look for other possible ways to draw the line. Maybe the market is seeing something that you have not yet seen. Since the bear trend began in earnest with the bar 2 large bear trend bar, it is reasonable to consider that as a starting point for a trend line. If you draw a trend line from bars 1 to 4 and then create a parallel and drag it to the bar 3 low, you would discover that bar 6 was the second reversal up from an overshoot of the bottom of that channel (bar 5 was the first). The market, as expected, rallied and broke above the top of the channel. It then pulled back and ran even further up.

Figure 13.6   TREND LINES   **205**

Deeper Discussion of This Chart

Today broke above yesterday's high with a gap up in Figure 13.6, and the breakout failed. The market trended down for four bars, creating a trend from the open bear trend. Bar 2 was the first pullback, and that is usually a reliable entry into the bear trend. It was a breakout to the downside and therefore a spike down and was followed by a bear channel that ended with three pushes down to bar 3. Since a spike and channel pattern is a type of climax, the reversal usually has two legs up and the rally usually tests the top of the channel where it often sets up a double top bear flag short, as it did here.

Bar 4 was another spike down, and there was an even larger bear spike eight bars later. It was followed by a bear channel, and the top of that channel was tested by a bull spike and channel that ended just after 12:00 p.m. PST. There was then a four-bar sell-off that tested near the bottom of that bull channel, setting up a double bottom bull flag, and it was followed by a strong rally that tested the bar 4 high. This was a potential double top bear flag setup going into the next day.

The average daily range was about 20 points, so once the market got down to about 20 points below the open, this gave traders another reason to look for a bounce.

FIGURE 13.7 Repeated Tests of a Trend Line

As shown in Figure 13.7, the dotted bear trend line was repeatedly tested about 15 times and eventually the bulls gave up. The trend line was a best fit line across the highs to illustrate all the tests of the resistance line. The bulls finally stopped trying. They sold out of their longs, adding to the selling pressure, and stopped looking to buy again until the market fell for many more bars. The market was therefore very one-sided and the bears were able to accelerate the trend downward. Usually when the market repeatedly tests a trend line and is unable to fall from it, it breaks above it. Other times, like here, it accelerates downward and ends in a climax around the bottom of a channel. The trend line drawn across the highs of bars 3 and 15 contained all of the highs and therefore was a reasonable choice for the top of the channel. A parallel was anchored to the bar A low, and both bars B and C broke through the bottom of the channel and reversed up. Once the reversal was confirmed by the two-bar reversal at bar C and the bar after, the first objective of the rally was a test above the top of the channel. There was a breakout on bar D, then a one-bar pause, which is a type of pullback. Instead of finding resistance and sellers at the bear trend line, the market found strong buying and had a strong bull breakout above the bear channel.

Figure 13.7   TREND LINES   **207**

Deeper Discussion of This Chart

Today tested the moving average in Figure 13.7, and then broke out below yesterday's swing low. Traders could short below the first bar, since it was a low 2 short (it was a small two-legged pullback to the EMA) or below the fourth bar of the day. However, the second, third, and fourth bars were large and almost entirely overlapping, and this is a sign of uncertainty, one of the hallmarks of a trading range. This makes shorting below that fourth bar more likely to be followed by a breakout that would not go far before getting pulled back by the magnetic force of that tight trading range.

The market remained in a trading range for several hours and then broke down to a new low of the day. The two-sided forces continued to control the market and the market reversed up into the close, ending the day about where it began.

CHAPTER 14

Trend Channel Lines

In a bull or bear channel, the trend channel line is on the opposite side of the price action from the trend line and has the same general slope. In a bull trend, a trend line is below the lows and a trend channel line is above the highs, and both are rising up and to the right. A trend channel line is a useful tool for fading a trend that has gone too far, too fast. Look for an overshoot that reverses, especially if it is the second penetration that is reversing.

A trend channel can have roughly parallel lines, or the lines can be convergent or divergent. When they converge and the channel is rising or falling, the channel is a wedge and this often sets up a reversal trade. In general, any channel that is sloping up to the right can be thought of as a bear flag and it is likely that there will be a breakout through the bottom of the channel. The breakout can lead to a trend reversal or to a trading range that can break out to the upside or the downside. Sometimes the market will accelerate to the upside and break out of the top of the channel. When this happens, it is usually a climactic rally that leads to a reversal back into and often through the bottom of the channel, but sometimes it can be the start of another leg up in an even stronger bull trend.

Similarly, a channel that slopes down to the right can be thought of as a bull flag and the market will likely break out of the channel to the upside. This can be the start of a trend reversal or a trading range. If the market falls through the bottom of a falling channel, the breakout will usually fail within about five bars and lead to a reversal, but it can also be the start of a new, stronger bear leg.

A trend channel line can be created as a parallel of a trend line that is then dragged to the opposite side of the price action. It can also be drawn across spikes on the opposite side of the channel, or it can be drawn as a best fit line, like a linear regression line or by simply visually drawing a best fit line. In a bull trend, a trend line is drawn across two lows. If that trend line is used to create a parallel that will be used for a trend channel line, drag the parallel line to the opposite side of the trend. You want it to contain (be above) the highs of all of the bars located in between the two bars used to create the trend line, so drag it to the high of whatever bar will leave it touching that bar alone. Occasionally you will get a better sense of the trend if you anchor the line to a bar that is outside of the two bars. Always do whatever best highlights the trend.

Sometimes there will be a single spike up within an otherwise fairly tight channel, and when that is the case, it is usually best to ignore it and use the other bars for the location of the trend channel line. However, be aware of the possibility that the market might ultimately decide that the channel line should instead be across that spike up. If the market begins to have wider swings and they all are stopping at the top of the channel that uses that one spike as the anchor for the trend channel line, then you should use that wider channel.

A trend channel line can also be created on its own, rather than as a parallel of the trend line. In a bear swing, a trend line will be downward sloping and above the highs. The trend channel line will have a similar slope, but draw it between any two swing lows in the bear swing. It is most useful if it contains (is below) all of the other bars in the swing, so choose the bars that will give that result.

Trend channel line overshoots are closely related to wedges and should be viewed and traded as if they are one and the same. Most wedges have failed trend channel line breakouts as the trigger for a reversal trade, and most trend channel line overshoots and reversals are also wedge reversals, although the wedge may not be obvious or have a perfect wedge shape. The wedges are less obvious and less likely to be present when the trend channel line is constructed as a parallel of a trend line, but wedges are still often present.

When a channel has a wedge shape, it is due to urgency. For example, in a wedge top, the slope of the trend line is greater than the slope of the trend channel line. The trend line is where the with-trend traders enter and the countertrend traders exit, and the opposite happens at the trend channel line. So if the slope of the trend line is greater, that means that the bulls are buying on smaller pullbacks and the bears are exiting on smaller sell-offs. What first distinguishes a wedge from a channel where the lines are parallel is the second pullback. Once the second push up has begun to reverse down, traders can draw a trend channel line and then use it to create a parallel line. When they drag that parallel line to the bottom of the first pullback, they have created a trend line and a trend channel. That tells bulls and bears where support is, and bulls will look to buy there and bears will look to take profits there. However, if the bulls begin to buy above that level and the bears exit their shorts early, the market will turn back up before it reaches the trend line. Both are doing so because they feel a sense of urgency and are afraid that the market will not drop down to that support level. This means that both feel that the trend line needs to be steeper and that the trend up is stronger.

Once the market turns up, traders can redraw the trend line. Instead of using the parallel of the trend channel line, they now can draw a trend line using the bottoms of the first two pullbacks. They now see that it is steeper than the trend channel line above and they begin to believe that the market is forming a wedge, which they know is often a reversal pattern. Traders will draw a parallel of that new steeper trend line and drag it to the top of the second push up, in case the market is forming a steeper parallel channel instead of a wedge. Both the bulls and the bears will watch to see whether the original trend channel line will contain the rally or the new, steeper one will be reached. If the original one contains the rally and the market turns down, traders will think that although there was more urgency in the buying on the second pullback, that urgency did not continue on the third push up. The bulls took profits at the original, shallower trend channel line, which means that they exited earlier than they could have. The bulls were hoping that the market would rally to the steeper trend channel line but now are disappointed. The bears were so eager to short that they were afraid that the market would not reach the steeper, higher trend channel line so they began to short at the original line. Now it is the bears who have a sense of urgency and the bulls who are afraid. Traders will see the turn down from the wedge top and most will wait for at least two legs down before they look for the next major pattern to buy or sell.

Once the market makes its first leg down, it will break below the wedge. At some point, the bears will take profits and the bulls will buy again. The bulls want to cause the wedge top to fail. When the market rallies to test the wedge top, the bears will begin to sell again. If the bulls begin to take profits, they believe that they will be unable to push the market above the old high. Once their profit taking, combined with the new selling by the bears, reaches a critical mass, it will overwhelm the remaining buyers and the market will turn down for that second leg. At some point, the bulls will return and the bears will take profits, and both sides will see the two-legged pullback and wonder if the bull trend will resume. At this point, the wedge has played itself out and the market will be looking for the next pattern.

Why do so many reversals occur after a trend channel line overshoot when everyone knows that it commonly leads to a reversal? Won't early entrants prevent the line from ever being reached? Common wisdom is that novice traders on the wrong side hold their losing positions until they cannot stand any more pain, and then suddenly all of them exit at once, creating a blow-off or a parabolic climax. For example, in a bull channel, the market works its way up to some resistance level, even if it is not very apparent or impressive, and pokes through it, causing the last shorts to no longer be willing to take the pain. They suddenly give up. As soon as these last shorts cover in unison, many euphoric, inexperienced bulls see the upsurge and buy into it, adding to the sudden, sharp move that breaks above the trend channel line. This spike up causes more remaining shorts to cover, and the impressive upsurge causes more naïve bulls to initiate new longs, with the process feeding on itself. But then there are not enough shorts left who will cover and move the market higher, and those euphoric bulls who were trading on emotion rather than logic will panic when the market suddenly stops accelerating up, pauses, and starts to turn down. They suddenly realize that they bought at the high of a possible climax and will be quick to exit. With no more buyers left and with trapped new longs panicking to sell out of their positions, the market suddenly becomes one-sided and dominated by sellers so that it can only go down. That is the conventional logic and it is not important whether it is true. In fact, it is likely not a meaningful component of a reversal in a huge market like the Eminis where institutions dominate and most of the trading is probably computer generated. Smart traders won't trade countertrend until either there is a pullback from a strong trend line break or there is a reversal from a trend channel line overshoot. For example, in a bull trend, smart money will keep buying until they drive the price above the bull trend channel line and then they will take profits. There may be a couple of failed attempts to reverse, and the market may continue to rally at an accelerated pace, creating steeper trend channel lines. Incidentally, if you find yourself redrawing trend channel lines repeatedly, this is usually a sign that you are on the wrong side of the market. You are looking for a reversal but the trend keeps getting stronger. You should be trading with the trend instead of intensely looking for a reversal.

Eventually the market will agree on which trend channel line is the final one and you will see a convincing reversal. Be patient and trade only with trend until then; never trade against the trend until it has clearly reversed. At the same time as the profit takers are taking profits, many will reverse and many other traders who were already flat will initiate shorts. Other smart traders will wait for a reversal on the charts and there will be traders entering on reversals on all types of charts (1 to 5 minute, and volume charts and tick charts of any size).

Once they believe that the top is in, this smart money won't be looking to buy any longer. They are short and most of these traders will hold through a new high, despite an open loss on their current position, believing that the top is in or close to in. In fact, many will add on above the high, both to get a better average price for their shorts and to help push the market down. The big players are only thinking short and won't be scared out except by the rare occurrence of a failed second entry or a huge failure (for example, maybe three points above their entry in the Emini). There are no buyers left, so the market only has one way to go.

Although you do not need to look at volume when deciding whether to place a trade since it is so unreliable, it is often huge at key turning points, especially at bottoms. Every trade is between one or more institutions buying and one or more selling. The major buyers at a market bottom are the profit taking bears and the new longs. Why would a firm ever sell at the bottom tick of a bear market? Every firm uses strategies that they have carefully tested and found to be profitable, but all lose money on 30 to 70 percent of their trades. The firms selling at the low tick are the ones who were selling at the low tick all the way down in the bear, making profits on many of their earlier entries, and they simply continue to use those strategies until it is clear that the trend has reversed. So, yes, they lose on that short at the final low tick of the bear, but make enough from all of their earlier shorts to end up profitable. There are also HFT firms that will scalp for even a single tick right down to the low tick of the bear. Remember, the low is always at a support level, and many HFT firms will short a tick or two above support to try to capture that final tick, if their systems show that this is a profitable strategy. Other institutions sell as part of a hedge in another market (stocks, options, bonds, currencies, etc.) because they perceive that their risk/reward ratio is better if they place the hedge. The volume is not from small individual traders, because they are responsible for less than 5 percent of the volume at major turning points. The reversal at an overshoot happens because it is such an entrenched part of institutional trading psyche that it has to happen. Even if institutions do not look at charts, they will have some other criterion that tells them that the market has gone too far and it is time to exit or reverse, and this will invariably coincide with what price action traders are seeing. Remember, price action is the inescapable footprint of what is happening to price as a huge number of smart people are independently trying to make the most money they can in the market. In a big market, the price action cannot be manipulated and will always be basically the same.

One final minor observation is that the slope of the final flag of a trend often provides an approximation of the slope of the new trend. This has limited value to a trader because there will be other much more important factors involved in the decision leading up to placing a trade, but it is an interesting observation.

FIGURE 14.1   Testing a Trend Channel Line

A trend channel line points in the direction of the trend but is on the opposite side of the trend from the trend line. Extend it to the right and watch how the price acts when it penetrates the channel line. Does it reverse or does the trend accelerate, ignoring the line?

Trend channel lines are commonly drawn in one of two ways. The first way is to draw it as a parallel line (dashed lines in Figure 14.1) of a trend line (solid lines), drag it to the opposite side of the action, and place it to touch a swing point located between the two bars used to create the trend line. Choose the point that will result in all of the bars between the trend and channel lines being contained between the lines. The second type (dotted lines in Figure 14.1) of a trend channel line is drawn across swing points and is independent of any trend line. You can also simply draw a best fit, but these are usually not helpful in trading.

Figure 14.2

TREND CHANNEL LINES **215**

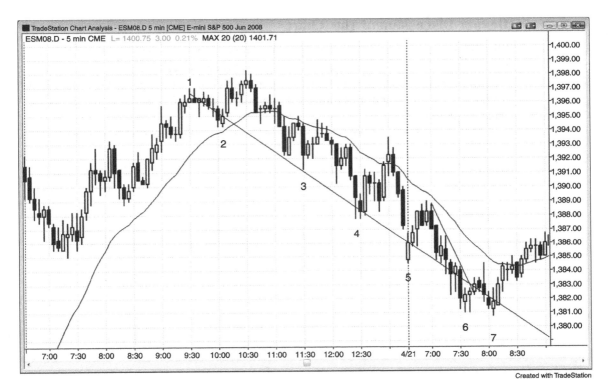

FIGURE 14.2 Slope of the Final Flag

The slope of the final flag of the bull trend provided direction for the subsequent bear trend in Figure 14.2. A linear regression trend line drawn between bars 1 and 2 became a rough bear trend channel line for the sell-off that extended into the next day. It is possible that it contributed to the buying at bar 7, but bar 7 was a buy simply based on the break of the trend line drawn over the first hour of trading, and the second attempt to reverse the breakout below the bar 5 low of the open. It is usually far better to place orders based on the most recent price action if it provides a justification for a trade than to look back 30 or more bars.

In hindsight, the bull trend effectively ended at bar 1, even though the market made a higher high after bar 2. The move down to bar 2 was the first leg down in the bear channel.

Deeper Discussion of This Chart

The market was in a bear channel in Figure 14.2 for the final couple of hours of yesterday, so the odds of a successful first attempt to reverse upward were not great. The breakout below the trend channel line reversed up with the first bar of the day, which was a bull trend bar, but the failed breakout went only a few bars before setting up a breakout pullback short.

Figure 14.3

TREND CHANNEL LINES **217**

FIGURE 14.3 Lengthy Trend Channel Line

In Figure 14.3, the trend line from bars 2 and 3 was used to create a parallel that was dragged to bar 1 and extended to the right. This trend channel line was not penetrated by bar 6. Also, it was anchored to bar 1, which was not in between bars 2 and 3 (the bars used to create the original trend line). However, traders should always be looking at every possibility. Had there been a penetration and reversal, the chances of a two-legged rally off the bar 5 low would have been improved.

The simple trend channel line created from the bars 1 and 5 lows was penetrated by bar 6, but this was not an ideal trend line to use as a basis for a countertrend trade since bars 1 and 5 were far apart and bars 5 and 6 were close together. Trend lines work best when they are tested by a third leg. Here, bars 5 and 6 were essentially still part of the same leg (three pushes down, bars 4, 5, and 6). The trade was still worth taking because bar 6 was small, so the risk/reward ratio was good. This was also a shrinking stair pattern down (discussed later, but it is a series of lower lows where each successive breakout is smaller than the prior one), which indicated waning bearish momentum and supported a long.

Deeper Discussion of This Chart

The large gap down in Figure 14.3 was a breakout, as all large gaps are, and the day started as a trend from the open bear day. The small opening range put the market in breakout mode, and there was a large bear breakout bar. However, an unusually large bear trend bar forming after a bear trend has gone a long way usually is a sell climax that will be followed by at least a two-legged sideways to up correction that lasts at least 10 bars. Bar 1 was a strong bull reversal bar that set up the failed breakout long. There was a two-legged sideways correction that ended with the bar 3 failed breakout of a tight trading range, and it formed an approximate double top with bar 2. Even though most of the trading was sideways, the day still opened near its high and closed near its low. This was a trending trading range day with upper and lower trading ranges.

CHAPTER 15

Channels

When trading is mostly confined to between a pair of lines, it is in a channel. The market is always in some kind of channel if you look hard enough to find one, and it usually is simultaneously in several, especially if you look at other time frames. A trend channel is a channel that is diagonal and is contained by a trend line and a trend channel line. For example, a bear channel has a descending trend line above (a bear trend line) and a descending trend channel line below (a bear trend channel line). A trading range is contained between a horizontal support line below and a resistance line above. Sometimes a trading range can be slightly rising or falling, but if so, it is better to think of it as a weak trend channel.

Triangles are also channels, since they are areas of price action contained between two lines. Since they have either higher highs or lower lows, or both in the case of an expanding triangle, they have some trending behavior in addition to their trading range behavior. An expanding triangle is contained between two diverging lines, both of which are technically trend channel lines. The line below is across lower lows, so it is below a bear trend and therefore a trend channel line, and the line above is across higher highs and therefore a bull trend channel line. A contracting triangle is contained between two trend lines, since the market is both in a small bear trend with lower highs and a bull trend with higher lows. An ascending triangle has a resistance line above and a bull trend line below, and a descending triangle has a support line below and a bear trend line above. A wedge is an ascending or descending channel where the trend line and trend channel line converge, and it is a variant of a triangle. An ABC correction in a bull trend is a small bear channel, and when it is in a bear trend it is a small bull channel.

Although the moving average often functions as support or resistance in a strong trend and many traders create curved channels and bands based on the moving average and many other factors, straight trend lines and trend channel lines consistently provide more reliable setups and profitable trades.

A bull channel can be in a trading range, a bull trend, a bear trend, or at a possible bottom of a bear trend as the market begins to reverse up. When it is in a trading range, traders can consider buying when in the lower half of the range, but the odds of success become less as the channel progresses into the upper half of the range. When a channel is in a bull trend, higher prices are more certain, and traders should look to buy near the bottom of the channel. The chance of a successful long remains good until the channel begins to have prominent selling pressure, or until it approaches significant resistance. When a channel is especially tight, meaning that the trend line and trend channel lines are close together and the pullbacks are small, it is a sign that the trend is strong, and it can be a spike on a higher time frame chart. A broader channel may follow, which might reach a measured move target, based on the height of the tight channel. A channel that is so tight that it has no pullbacks or only one or two tiny pullbacks is a micro channel, which is discussed in the next chapter.

When a bull channel forms in a bear trend, it is a bear flag, and traders should look to short near the top, or on the pullback from a downside breakout. Sometimes when a bear trend begins to reverse up, the first five to 10 bars are in a weak bull channel, with lots of overlapping bars and one or more attempts to break below the bear flag, but these fail and quickly reverse up. After a failed low 2 or low 3, the market then sometimes breaks out to the upside from the bear flag, the market suddenly becomes always-in long, and a bull reversal begins. When traders suspect that a bear flag might be the start of a bull trend, many will buy below the low 1, 2, or 3 signal bars, expecting them to fail and for the market to reverse up.

As a channel is forming, traders are uncertain if there will actually be a channel or just a two-legged move and then a reversal. In fact, you usually cannot even draw channel lines until after the market begins to reverse from the two-legged move and the reversal fails, and the third leg begins. For example, if the market just completed two legs up and has started to reverse, many traders will short the reversal if the rally is not a strong bull trend. However, if the leg down ends and is comparable in size to the first leg down (the leg after the first leg up), and then it reverses up again, traders will now begin to assume that a bull channel is underway rather than a reversal down into a bear leg. Once that second leg ends, traders will draw a trend line from the bottom of the first leg down to the bottom of this second leg and extend it to the right. They will look to buy whenever the market again comes back to the trend line. They will also create a parallel of the line and drag it to the top of the first leg up, and this is their first creation of a channel. Whenever the market rallies up to that trend channel line, traders will take profit on their longs, and look to short. Since a bull channel needs at least those first two legs down to confirm the existence of the channel and the market will usually then test above the top of the second leg up, bull channels usually have at least three pushes up. Traders will usually not look for a reversal and a downside breakout of the channel until after that third leg up forms. However, once it does, especially if there is an overshoot of the trend channel line and a strong bear reversal bar, traders will short aggressively because the odds of a successful downside breakout have increased. Because of this, many bull channels end after a third push up. Likewise, many bear channels end after a third push down.

Why does the market race toward the top and bottom of the channel? This is because of a vacuum effect. For example, if there is a bull channel and there is a leg that is approaching the trend channel line above, the traders believe that the market will likely touch that line and may even go a tick or two above it. Since they believe that the market will go at least a little higher than it is right now, they will hold back on their selling. The bulls want to sell out of their longs eventually to take profits, and the bears want to sell to initiate new shorts. The current relative absence of selling creates a buy imbalance, and whenever there is any imbalance, the market moves quickly. The result is that there is often a large bull trend bar or two that form as the market tests the top of the channel. This often attracts overly eager bulls to buy at the top of the spike since they think the market is forming a new, stronger bull leg. However, most breakout attempts fail, and this one will likely fail as well. Why? Because of the institutional traders. The strong bears want to short, but they believe that the market will touch that upper trend channel line, so they wait. Once the market is there, they short heavily and overwhelm the bulls. They like to see a strong bull trend bar because they believe that the market will go lower and there is no better price to short than at the point of maximum bullishness. The market might pause for a small bar at the top of the bull trend bar as both the bulls and the bears decide if the breakout will fail, but it will usually then quickly fall since both the institutional bulls and bears know that the odds are strongly in favor of all breakout attempts failing.

So what do those strong institutional bulls do? They stop buying and they quickly sell out of their longs, capturing a brief windfall profit. They know that this opportunity will likely be brief because the market does not stay at an extreme for long, so they exit and they won't look to buy again for at least a bar or two. The relative absence of these institutional bulls and the aggressiveness of the institutional bears force the market down quickly to the bottom of the channel, where the opposite process begins. Both the bulls and the bears expect the trend line below to be tested; the bears will keep shorting until the market gets there and then they will buy back their shorts as they take their profits, and the bulls won't buy until the market gets there. This creates a brief, sharp move down that will entice beginning traders into shorting, expecting a bear breakout, but they are doing the exact opposite of the institutions. Remember, your job is to follow what the institutions are doing. You should not be doing what you hope they will soon do, and you should never do the exact opposite of what they are doing. Each of these small pullbacks is a micro sell vacuum. Once the market gets close to the bottom of the channel, both the bulls and the bears expect the market to reach the bull trend line and they stop buying until it gets there. Once there, the bulls buy to initiate new longs and the bears take profits on their short scalps. Both expect a new channel high and a test of the top of the channel, where the process begins again. This takes place in all channels, including in trading ranges and triangles.

Even in a trend channel, there is two-sided trading taking place and this is trading range behavior. In fact, a trend channel can be thought of as a sloping trading range. When the slope is steep and the channel is tight, it behaves more like a trend, and trades should be taken only in the direction of the trend. When the slope is less steep and there are broad swings within the channel, some lasting five or even 10 bars, the market is behaving more like a trading range and can be traded in both directions. As with all trading ranges, there is a magnetic pull in the middle of the trading range that tends to keep the market in the range. Why does the market stay in a channel and not suddenly accelerate? Because there is too much uncertainty, like with all trading ranges.

For example, in a bull channel, the bulls want to buy more, but at a lower price. The weak shorts want a sell-off so they can exit with a smaller loss. Both the bulls and the weak bears are concerned that there may not be a pullback that will allow them to buy all of the shares that they want to buy (the weak shorts are buying back their losing short positions) at a better price, so they continue to buy in pieces as the market goes up, and this adds to the buying pressure. They buy even more aggressively on any small dip, like with a limit order below the low of the prior bar or at the moving average or near the trend line that forms the bottom of the channel.

In general, when a channel is beginning it is better to trade with the trend, and as it is approaching a target area and as it develops more two-sided trading, experienced traders will often to start trading countertrend. So at the start of a bull channel, it is better to buy below the lows of bars, but as the channel reaches resistance areas and starts to have more overlapping bars, bear bars, deeper pullbacks, and prominent tails, it is better to consider shorting above bars instead of buying below bars.

However, for traders just starting out, whenever they see a channel, they should trade only with the trend, if at all. Trading channels is very difficult because they are always trying to reverse, and have many pullbacks. This is confusing to beginning traders and they often take repeated losses. If there is a bull channel, they should only look to buy. The most reliable buy signal will be a high 2 with a bull signal bar at the moving average where the entry is not too close to the top of the channel. This kind of perfect setup does not occur often. If traders are just starting out, they should wait for the very best setups, even if that means missing the entire trend. More experienced traders can buy on limit orders below weak sell signals and near the moving average and near the bottom of the channel. If traders are not consistently profitable, they should avoid taking any sell signals in a bull channel, even if there is a small lower high. The market is always-in long and they should not be looking to short, even though there will be many signals that look acceptable. Wait for the market to become clearly always-in short before looking to short. That will usually require a strong bear spike that breaks below the channel and below the moving average and has follow-through, and then has a lower high with a bear signal bar. If the setup is any weaker than that, beginners should wait and only look to buy pullbacks. Do not fall into the regression toward the mean mind-set and assume that the channel looks so weak that a reversal is long overdue. The market can continue its unsustainable behavior much longer than you can sustain your account as you bet against that very weak-looking trend.

Many bulls will be scaling into their long positions as the market goes up, and they will be using every conceivable logical approach to do this. Some will buy on a pullback to the moving average, or below the low of the prior bar, or on pullbacks at fixed intervals, like every 50 cents below the most recent high in AAPL. Others will buy as the market appears to be resuming the channel up, like every 25 cents above the prior low. If you can think of an approach, so can some programmer, and if she can show that it is effective mathematically, her firm will probably try trading it.

With both the bulls and trapped bears wanting lower prices but afraid that they will not come, both continue to buy until they have nothing left to buy. This always happens at some magnet like a measured move or a higher time frame trend line or trend channel line. Since channels usually go much further than what most traders expect, the trend usually continues up beyond the first one or more obvious resistance levels until it reaches one where enough strong bulls and bears agree that the market has gone far enough and will likely not go much higher. At that point, the market runs out of buying pressure and the strong bulls take profits and sell out of their longs, and the strong bears come in and sell more aggressively. This results in a reversal into a deeper correction or into an opposite trend. The bull trend often ends with a breakout of the top of the channel as the last desperate bears buy back their shorts in despair, and the weakest bulls who have been waiting and waiting for lower prices finally just buy at the market. The strong bears expect that and will often wait for the strong breakout and then begin shorting relentlessly. They believe that this is a brief opportunity to short at a very high price and that the market won't stay here for long. The strong bulls see the spike up as a gift and they exit their longs and will now buy again only after at least a two-legged pullback lasting at least 10 bars. They often will not buy until the market gets down to the beginning of the channel, where they originally bought into a profitable trade. The strong bears know this and will look to take profits exactly where the strong bulls will be buying again; the result usually is a bounce and then often a trading range as both sides become uncertain about the direction of the next move. Uncertainty usually means that the market is in a trading range.

Or at least that is the conventional logic, but it is probably more complicated, sophisticated, and unknowable. All institutions are familiar with this pattern, and you can be certain that their programmers are constantly looking for ways to capitalize on it. One thing an institution might do is try to create a buy climax. If it has been buying all the way up and is ready to take profits but it wants to be sure that the top is in, it could suddenly buy a final big piece with the realization that it might even take a small loss on it, but with the goal of creating a climactic reversal on the charts. If the firm is successful, and it might be if several other institutions are running programs that are doing similar things, it can exit all of its longs, most with a profit, and then even reverse to short, confident that the sellers now control the market.

Does this happen with every climax? It is unknowable and irrelevant. Your goal is to follow what the institutions are doing, and you can see it on the charts. You never have to know anything about the programs behind the patterns, and the institutions themselves never know what types of programs the other institutions are running. They only know their own programs, but the market rarely goes far unless many institutions are trading in the same direction at the same time, and they have to be trading with enough size to overwhelm the other institutions that are doing the opposite. The only time that the vast majority of the institutions are on the same side is during the spike phase of a strong trend, and that occurs in fewer than 5 percent of the bars on the chart.

It is not just bulls and weak shorts who are placing trades as the channel continues up. Strong shorts are also selling as the market moves higher, scaling into their positions, believing that the upside is limited and ultimately their trade will be profitable. Their selling begins to create selling pressure in the form of more bars with bear bodies, larger bear bodies, tails on the tops of the bars, and more bars with lows below the low of the prior bar. They are looking for a downside breakout of the channel and maybe even a test to the beginning of the channel. Since they want to short at the best possible price, they are selling as the market is going up rather than waiting for the reversal. This is because the reversal might be fast and strong and then they would end up shorting much further below the top of the channel than they believe is likely to be profitable.

They have several ways to add to their short position, like selling on a limit order above the high of the prior bar or above a minor swing high in the channel, at every test of the top of the channel at the trend channel line, at measured move targets, at a fixed interval as the market goes up (like every 50 cents higher in AAPL), or on each potential top. Once the market reverses, they might hold their entire position with the expectation of a significant reversal, or they might exit at a profit target, like on a test of the trend line at the bottom of the channel or even at the entry price of their first short, which is often near the start of the channel. If they do that, their first entry will be a breakeven trade and they will have a profit on their higher entries.

If you are scaling into shorts in that bull channel, it is best to do this only in the first two-thirds of the day. You do not want to find yourself heavily short in a bull channel with your breakeven entry so far below that you don't have enough time left to get out without a loss, never mind with a large profit. In general, if you are trading a channel in the second half of the day, it is far better to only trade with the trend, like buying below the low of the prior bar, or above every bull reversal bar at the moving average.

If the market continues higher than the shorts believe is likely, they will buy back their entire position at a loss, and this is probably a significant contributor to the climactic upside breakout that sometimes comes at the end of a channel. They no longer expect a pullback any time soon that would allow them to buy at a better price, and instead buy at the market and take losses on all of their short entries. Since many are momentum traders, many will switch to long. All the momentum-trading bulls will aggressively buy as the market accelerates upward because they know that the math is on their side. The directional probability of the next tick being higher and not lower is more than 50 percent, so they have an edge. Even though the breakout might be brief and the reversal sharp, their buy programs will continue to buy as long as the logic supports doing so. However, this is like musical chairs; as soon as the momentum music stops, everyone quickly grabs a chair, which means that they exit their longs very quickly. As they are selling out of their longs, there are aggressive bears shorting as well and this can create a strong imbalance in favor of the bears. If the bears take control, the sell-off will usually last at least 10 bars and there will usually be a reversal back below the trend channel line and into the channel, and then a breakout of the downside of the channel.

The television pundits will attribute the sharp upside breakout to some news item, and there are always many to choose from, because they see the market only from the perspective of a traditional stock trader who trades on fundamentals. They don't understand that many things that happen, especially over the course of an hour or so, have nothing to do with fundamentals and are instead the result of large programs doing the same thing at once with no regard for the fundamentals. Once the market quickly reverses on the climactic blow-off, they move on to the next story. They never address the fact that they just gave a report that was foolishly naïve, and they remain completely oblivious to the powerful technical forces that drive the market in the short run. Every few years there is an exceptionally huge intraday move, and that is pretty much the only time that they will acknowledge that technical factors were at work. In fact, they invariably blame it on programs, as if the programs suddenly briefly appeared. There is nothing to blame. The vast majority of all intraday price movement is due to programs, yet the reporters don't have a clue. All they see are earnings reports, quarterly sales, and profit margins.

Since a channel is a sloping trading range, just like with other trading ranges, most attempts to break out of either the top or the bottom fail. Yes, one side is stronger, but the principle is the same as for any trading range. For example, in a bull channel, both bulls and bears are active but the bulls are stronger and that is why the channel is sloping up. Both the bulls and the bears are comfortable placing trades in the middle of the channel, but when the market gets near the top of the channel, the bulls become concerned that the upside breakout will fail; and as soon as they think that a failure is likely, they will sell out of some of their longs. Also, the bears were comfortable shorting in the middle of the channel and will short even more aggressively near the top, at a better value. When the market gets near the bottom of the range, the bears are less interested in shorting at these lower prices and the bulls, who were just buying moments ago at higher prices, will buy even more aggressively here. This leads to a bounce up off of the trend line. The market usually pokes below the channel one or more times as it is forming, and you have to redraw the trend line. The result is usually a slightly broader and flatter channel. Ultimately, the downside breakout will be strong enough to be followed by a lower high and then a lower low, and when that happens, traders will begin to draw a bear channel, even if the bull channel still exists, albeit much wider.

It is important to realize that most bull breakouts of bull channels fail. If the bulls are able to create a bull breakout and they can overwhelm the bears, they usually will be able to do so for only a few bars. At that point, the bulls will see the market as too overdone and will take profits; they won't want to buy until the market has corrected for a while. The magnetic effect of the middle of the channel will usually pull the market back into the channel and cause the breakout to fail, making the breakout a buy climax. Once back in the channel, the market usually pokes through the bottom of the channel as its minimum objective. The buy climax usually leads to a two-legged correction that lasts about 10 bars and usually breaks below the channel. Once the downside breakout happens, if the selling continues the next objective is a measured move equal to about the height of the channel. The bears also know that the buy climax will likely be followed by a correction and they will short aggressively. With the bulls selling out of their longs, there is strong selling pressure and the market corrects down and can even become a bear trend.

Sometimes an upside breakout of a bull channel is strong and does not fail within a few bars. When this is the case, the market will usually rally to a measured move target, and the breakout will become a measuring gap. For example, if the bull channel has a wedge shape, and breaks to the downside, but the downside breakout fails within a few bars, and then the market races up and breaks above the top of the wedge, the rally will usually reach a measured move up that is equal to about the height of the wedge. The trend bar or bars that break above the wedge then become a measuring gap. Gaps, measured moves, and breakouts are discussed in book 2.

If instead of an upside breakout, there is a downside breakout but without a failed upside breakout, buy climax, and bear reversal, the market usually goes sideways for a number of bars. It may form a lower high and then a second leg down, or the trading range might become a bull flag and lead to a resumption of the bull trend. Less commonly, there is a strong spike down and a strong bear reversal. The opposite of all of this is true for bear channels.

Since a trend channel is simply a sloping trading range, it usually functions like a flag. If there is a bull channel, no matter how steep or protracted, it usually will have a downside breakout at some point and therefore can be thought of as a bear flag even if there was no bear trend preceding it. At some point, the strong bulls will take profits and they will be willing to buy again only after a significant pullback. That pullback often has to go all the way to the beginning of the channel, where they began buying earlier, and this is part of the reason why channels often lead to a correction all the way to the bottom of the channel, where there is usually a bounce. The strong bears are as smart as the strong bulls, and generally just when the strong bulls stop buying, the strong bears begin to aggressively short and will not be shaken out higher. In fact, they will see higher prices as an even better value and they will short more. Where will they take profits on their shorts? Near the bottom of the channel, just where the strong bulls might try to reestablish their longs.

Because a bull channel behaves like a bear flag, it should be traded like a bear flag. Similarly, any bear channel should be viewed as a bull flag. There may or may not be a bull trend that precedes it, but that is irrelevant. Sometimes there will be a higher time frame bull trend that might not be evident on the 5 minute chart, and when that happens, the bear channel will appear as a bull flag on that chart. Although a higher time frame trend might increase the chances of a bull breakout and the chances that the breakout will be strong and go further, you will so often see huge bull breakouts from bear channels that it is not necessary to look for a higher time frame bull trend to trade the channel like a bull flag. The opposite is true of bull channels, which are functionally bear flags.

Since a bull channel is a bear flag, there is usually a bear breakout eventually. Sometimes, however, there is a bull breakout above the channel. In most cases, this breakout is climactic and unsustainable. It might last for just a bar or two, but sometimes it lasts for five or more bars before the market reverses down. Less often, the bull trend will continue in a very strong trend. If it reverses, it usually reenters the channel, and with any channel breakout that reenters the channel, it usually tests the opposite side of the channel. After a failed breakout of the top of a bull channel, since this is a type of climax, the reversal should have at least two legs down and last at least 10 bars, and it often becomes a trend reversal. The opposite is true of a downside breakout of a bear channel. It usually is a sell climax and reverses back above the channel and has at least two legs up.

All channels eventually end in a breakout, which can be violent or have very little momentum. Trend channels usually last much longer than what most traders suspect and they often trap traders into prematurely taking reversal trades. Most channels usually have at least three legs before they end. This is especially clear in triangles, and in wedges in particular. With triangles, the breakout is usually imminent but the direction is often not clear.

The steeper the slope and the closer together the lines are, the stronger the channel is and the stronger the momentum is. When a channel is steep and tight, it is a special type of channel called a tight channel. When it is horizontal, it is a tight trading range, which is discussed in book 2. When a channel is strong, it is risky to trade the first breakout against the trend, and it is likely that the entire channel will be a spike on a higher time frame chart. So if there is a steep bear channel and most of the pullbacks within the channel have been only a single bar, it is better not to buy one of those breakouts above the prior bar, even if it breaks above the bear trend line. Instead, it is better to wait to see if there is a breakout pullback, which can be a lower low or a higher low. If there is and the reversal up looks strong (for example, maybe there were two or three good-sized bull trend bars within the past several bars), then you can consider buying the breakout pullback. If there is no pullback and the market races upward, then the odds of even higher prices are good and you can wait for any pullback, which should come within five bars or so. The odds of the long being profitable are better if the rally up goes above the moving average and that first pullback stays above the moving average. This is a sign of strength. If the first pullback forms below the moving average, the bulls are weaker and the chance of a second leg up is less. If the market continues to sell off after the upside breakout, the breakout failed and the bear trend is resuming.

The strength of a channel is especially important when the market might be in the process of reversing. For example, if there is a strong bull trend and then there is a strong sell-off that breaks well below the bull trend line, traders will study the next rally carefully. They want to see whether that rally will simply be a test of the bull high or will instead break out strongly above the high and be followed by another strong leg up in the bull trend. One of the most important considerations is the momentum of that test of the bull high. If the rally is in a very tight, steep channel with no pullbacks and very little overlap between the bars, and the rally goes far above the bull high before having any pause or pullback, the momentum is strong and the odds are increased that the bull trend will resume, despite the strong sell-off and breakout below the bull trend line. Usually the first breakout of a tight, prolonged channel will fail. The trend will then resume and often break out to a new extreme and reach a measured move equal to about the height of that initial breakout.

By contrast, if the rally has many overlapping bars, several large bear trend bars, two or three clear pullbacks, maybe a wedge shape, and a slope that is noticeably less than the slope (momentum) of the original bull trend and of the sell-off, the odds are that the test of the bull high will result in either a lower high or a slightly higher high and then another attempt to sell off. The market might be reversing into a bear trend, but at a minimum a trading range is likely.

Whenever there is a breakout of any channel and then a reversal back into the channel, the market will try to test the other side of the channel, and will usually try to break out of it, at least by a little. If there is a successful breakout of the channel in either direction, the next minimum objective is a measured move equal to about the height of the channel. For example, a double top is a horizontal channel and if there is a successful breakout of the downside, the minimum target is a measured move equal to the height of the channel. However, the breakout can become a trend reversal and the move can be much greater. If instead the breakout is to the upside, the target is again a measured move up equal to the height of the double top. If AAPL is forming a double top and the top of the pattern is $5.00 above the bottom, the initial target of any breakout to the upside is $5.00 above the top. If the breakout instead is to the downside, the initial objective is $5.00 below the low of the pattern. The same is true for a wedge bottom. The first objective is a test of the top of the wedge. If the market continues up, the next target is a measured move up. If the rally continues, the market might then be in a bull trend. Even when a channel is sloping, the initial objective is a move equal to the height of the channel. In a bull channel, for example, pick any bar and look at the channel lines directly above and below. Simply measure how far apart they are to get the measured move projection. The measured move targets are only approximate, but the market often hits them exactly and then pauses, pulls back, or reverses. If the market goes much beyond the target, a new trend is likely underway.

As with all breakouts, three things can then happen: it can be successful and be followed by more trading in that direction; it can fail and become a small climactic reversal; or the market can just go sideways and the pattern can evolve into a trading range. Most breakouts have an attempt to reverse within a few bars. If the reversal bar is strong compared to the breakout bar, the odds of a failed breakout and a successful reversal are good. If the reversal bar is weak compared to the breakout, the odds are that the reversal attempt will fail and set up a breakout pullback within a bar or two, and the breakout will resume. If the breakout and the reversal are about equally strong, traders will then look at the bar after the reversal signal bar. For example, if there is a strong bull trend bar that breaks out of a bull flag, and the next bar is an equally impressive bear reversal bar, the bar that follows becomes important. If it trades below the bear reversal bar, the breakout has failed, at least for the moment. If it then has a strong bear close and is a strong bear trend bar, the chance that the reversal will continue down increases. If instead it is a strong bull reversal bar, chances are that the failed breakout will not succeed, and this bull reversal bar then becomes a signal bar for a breakout pullback buy at one tick above its high. Breakouts are discussed in book 2.

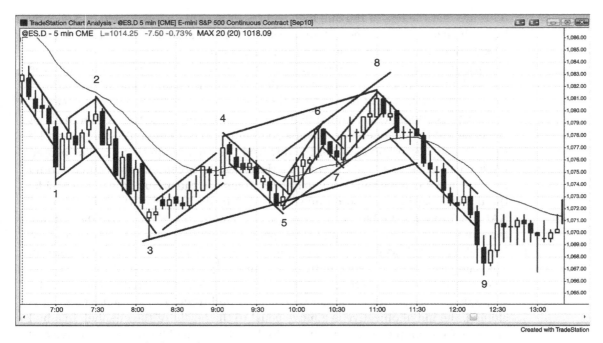

FIGURE 15.1 Nested Channels

Channels are common on all charts, and some smaller channels are nested inside of larger channels. In Figure 15.1, notice that the lines do not always have to be drawn to contain all of the highs and lows in the channel. Drawing them with best fit lines helps to make the channel behavior clearer and often makes it easier to anticipate signals. Since most trading is institutional and placed by computer programs, it is reasonable to assume that each small, tight channel is due to program trading. Since there are so many firms running programs all day long, a channel probably can develop only when several firms are running programs in the same direction and with enough volume to overwhelm the programs that are trying to make the market move in the opposite direction. For example, in the channel down from bar 4, there were enough sell programs going on to overpower any buy programs, and the market moved down. When the buy and sell programs are largely in balance, the market moves sideways in a tight trading range, which is a horizontal channel.

Bull channels are indistinguishable from bear flags, and bear channels should be thought of as bull flags. When the channel is tight like from bars 2 to 3, buyers should wait until there is a failed breakout and reversal up before looking for longs, as occurred at bar 3. They could also wait for a pullback after the breakout, like the buying above the high of the small bar that formed five bars after bar 3.

Figure 15.1

CHANNELS **231**

Until either of these develop, traders should only be shorting. When a channel has broader swings like the channel from bars 3 to 8, trades can be taken in both directions, since it more clearly resembles a sloping trading range and trading ranges are two-sided markets that give both buy and sell signals.

Most of the channels in the chart were tight, and since several had no pullbacks or small (only one- to three-tick) one-bar pullbacks and lasted about 10 bars or less, they were also micro channels.

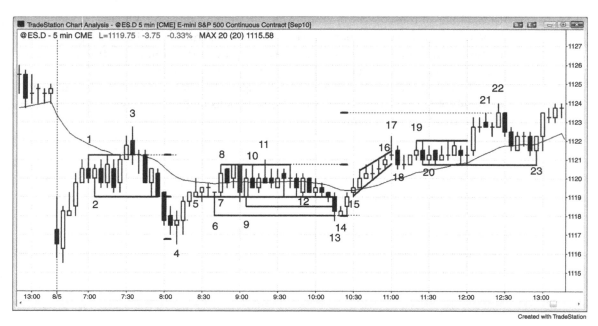

FIGURE 15.2 Failed Channel Breakouts

When there is a breakout of a channel and then a reversal back into the channel, the market usually tests the opposite side of the channel and often breaks out of the other side, at least minimally. If the breakout has follow-through, the first target is a measured move equal to the height of the channel. In Figure 15.2, bar 3 broke out of the top of a trading range and reversed back down. After breaking through the bottom of the channel, the bar 4 low was one tick below a perfect measured move.

Bar 11 broke above the top of a trading range and then the market tested the bottom of the range with bar 13. Sometimes there are several bars to choose from when drawing the lines, and it is usually worth being aware of all of the possibilities because you may not know which is best until several bars later. The widest channel is the most certain.

The bull inside bar that followed the bar 13 breakout set up a failed breakout buy. Since the market was again reversing into the channel, the first target was a test of the top of the channel. The breakout of the top was successful and the next target was a measured move up. Bar 22 went one tick above that target. Sometimes a trend will begin and carry much further.

Bar 17 broke above a bull micro channel or wedge and reversed back down on the next bar. Since the channel was so tight, the objective of testing the lower end of the channel was met on that next bar, but there was not enough room for a profitable short and no trade should be taken.

Figure 15.2   CHANNELS   **233**

The measured move up for the breakout of the channel formed by bars 19 and 20 was at the same price as the measured move up from the trading range defined by bars 6 and 10. When multiple targets are around the same price, any reversal there has an increased chance of success. Bar 21 was a valid short setup but it failed on the bar after entry. There was a second entry below bar 22 and the market tested the bottom of the channel. There, it formed a bull reversal bar and the market then tested the top of the channel.

Deeper Discussion of This Chart

The market broke below a closing trading range with a large gap down in Figure 15.2, but the first bar was relatively large and had good-sized tails above and below. This is trading range behavior and not a good signal bar for a trend from the open buy or short. The second bar was a strong bull reversal bar and signaled a long for a failed breakout and a trend from the open bull trend. The market entered a tight trading range just below the moving average, and it became a final flag with a failed breakout and reversal down. Although traders could short as soon as bar 3 went below the low of the prior bar, it was safer to wait until the bar closed to confirm that it would have a bear body, and then short below its low.

The rally to bar 1 was in a micro channel, so the bar 2 downside breakout was likely to not go very far without a pullback. When the market moved above the high of the bar 2 breakout bar, the breakout failed. At that point, the market went sideways as traders fought for control. The bears were looking for a higher high or lower high pullback from the bar 2 breakout, and the bulls simply wanted a failed breakout and then another leg up.

The bears won and the market fell in a micro channel down to bar 4, where the process reversed. Bar 5 was the signal bar for the failed breakout, but the four-bar bull spike was strong enough for traders to believe that the market would likely test higher, which it did in the move up to bar 8.

The move from bar 14 to bar 17 was another bull micro channel, and bar 18 was the breakout. The market then went sideways before the small trend resumed in the move up to bar 22.

FIGURE 15.3 Bull Channels in Bull and Bear Markets

A bull channel can occur in any type of market. In Figure 15.3, the 5 minute Emini chart on the left had a bull channel in a strong bull trend, where the market gapped up and became a trend from the open bull trend day. The pullbacks were small, and the market worked higher all day. Because the day was a strong bull trend day, traders were buying small pullbacks, like at and below the low of the prior bar.

The bull channel in the middle chart was a wedge bear flag in a bear trend, and traders should not have been looking for longs. They could have shorted below the ii pattern at bar 18, or on any of the several following bars, as the market became always-in short.

The bull channel on the right was a small bear flag in an overdone bear trend. It formed after the large bear trend bar on the open, which was the third push down. Bar 26 (see insert) set up a strong two-bar reversal up from yesterday's low. Even though the channel from bar 26 to the bar before bar 29 was a bear flag, traders believed that the market was reversing up, and bought below the lows of the prior bars, expecting the low 1 and low 2 sell setups to fail. Bar 29 was a strong bull trend bar that broke out of the top of the bear flag and turned the market into a clear always-in long. Not all bear flags break out to the downside. Some become the final flag of the bear trend, break out to the upside, and lead to a bull trend, as happened here.

Figure 15.4

CHANNELS **235**

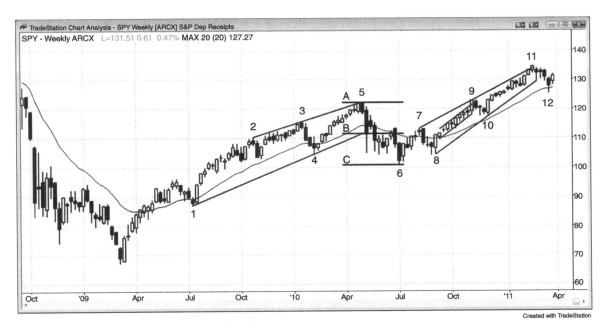

FIGURE 15.4 Channel Breakout and Measured Move

When the market successfully breaks out of any channel, the first target is a measured move. In Figure 15.4, a weekly chart of the SPY, the trend line was drawn across the lows of bars 1 and 4 and the trend channel line drawn from the highs of bars 2 and 3 was touched at bar 5. This is a bull channel and the lines are slightly convergent. Horizontal line A is across the bar 5 high and line B is the bottom of the channel directly below bar 5. Line C is a measured move down from lines A to B. Bar 6 found support at the measured move and a rally followed.

A similar target would have been projected using an Andrew's Pitchfork, but since basic price action analysis gives the same result, it is all that you need. There were probably countless reasons why bears were taking profits around the bar 6 low and why aggressive bulls were buying. None of them is important since there is never any way to know how many dollars are being traded for each reason. All that you know is that the chart is the distilled result of all of those dollars being traded for countless reasons, and understanding recurring patterns puts you in a position to know when to take profits and when to consider reversal trades.

The move down to bar 1 was the first breakout below a tight, strong bull channel and was therefore likely to fail. When a first breakout fails and the trend resumes, it often extends up to a measured move that is approximately equal to the height of that initial reversal attempt. Here, the rally extended much further.

The channel that began after the bar 1 bull spike was also very tight, and the spike down to bar 4 was the first strong breakout. The reversal failed and the trend resumed. The bulls tried to extend the rally for about a measured move up. That measured move was equal to the height of bar 3 to bar 4, added to the top of bar 3, but the market did not quite reach the target.

The rally to bar 7 broke above the two-legged bull flag down to bar 6, and bar 8 was the breakout pullback. It was also the start of another bull channel, and the move down to bar 12 broke below the channel, reaching about a measured move down, based on the height of the channel and the height of the first leg down (bar 11 and the bar after it). Bars 3, 5, and 7 formed a head and shoulders top, and like most reversal patterns, became a large bull flag and not a reversal.

Deeper Discussion of This Chart

The bar before bar 6 in Figure 15.4 was a breakout pullback short setup and a low 2 short at the moving average. The bar after bar 5 had a large tail, as did several of the next bars, and that trading range below the moving average was a barbwire pattern, which often becomes a final flag, as it did here.

There was a one-bar spike up on the low of the chart, which was followed by a very tight channel. In fact, there were three or four tight channels in the rally (some traders saw the second spike from bar 1 to bar 3 as a single steep channel or spike, and others saw it as two). When a channel is tight, it often functions like a spike, and is followed by a channel. The pullback to bar 1 was followed by a two-bar spike and then another channel that again was so tight that it was likely to function as part of the initial spike. After the pullback from bar 2, the channel up had several bear bodies, which was a sign of building selling pressure. The result was a strong four-bar bear spike down to bar 4. The selling pressure was building, and bulls were likely to take profits on the test of the high. Although the channel up from bar 4 was tight and therefore possibly another spike, a spike can also function as a climax. This was the third or fourth consecutive buy climax (every spike, whether it is one bar or many bars, is a climax), and it followed a strong bear spike. Consecutive climaxes usually lead to a larger correction, as they did here.

Figure 15.5   CHANNELS   **237**

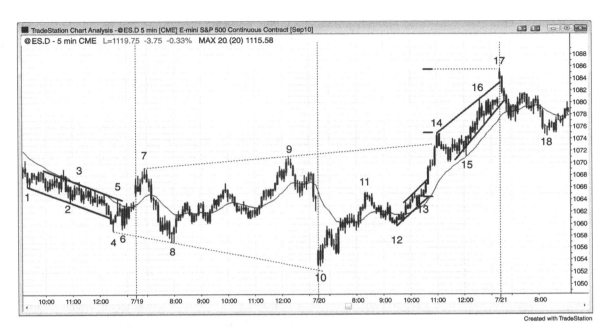

FIGURE 15.5   Climactic Bear Breakout of Bear Channel

A bear channel that breaks out of the bottom of the channel can be followed by an even stronger bear trend, but the breakout usually soon becomes a climax and is typically followed by at least two legs up, as shown in Figure 15.5. Bar 4 broke below the bear channel but became a sell climax, as expected, and was followed by a two-legged rally that ended at bar 7.

There was a bull spike up to bar 14 that was followed by a pullback to bar 15, and then a wedge-shaped channel developed. The market broke out to the upside on the gap up to bar 17, but this breakout was just a buy climax that reversed back into the bull channel and then broke out of the downside. The correction had two legs, ending at bar 18. Many channels have three pushes in them before reversing, and bars 14, 16, and 17 were three pushes up.

The small bull channel that started at bar 12 broke out to the upside, and the breakout was very strong. All breakouts are climaxes, but climaxes don't always lead to reversals. Some can become very strong breakouts, like this one. Once they finally finish correcting and the trend then resumes, it usually does so with less momentum (the slope is less) and there are usually more overlapping bars, which is a sign of increased two-sided trading.

When a bull trend is strong, traders will buy tests of the moving average, like at bars 13 and 15. The moving average therefore contains the trend, and functions like the lower line of a channel. You can write indicators to create a parallel of the trend line and place it above the highs, creating a channel, but usually curved channel lines or bands of any type do not provide as many reliable trades as do straight channel lines.

Deeper Discussion of This Chart

The strong move up from bar 13 to bar 14 in Figure 15.5 was almost vertical, and all strong bull breakouts should be thought of as spikes up and as buy climaxes. When the spike is composed of two or more large bull trend bars, it is particularly strong and more likely to have some type of measured move up before there is a significant correction. Measured moves using the open or low of the first bar of the spike and the close or high of the last bar often are good areas for the bulls to take partial or full profits and sometimes are good areas for bears to initiate shorts. Bar 13 had no tail on the bottom and closed near its high; it was the first of many bull trend bars, so it is the bottom of the spike. The height of the spike using the open of bar 13 and the high of the bar 14 top of the spike projected a measured move up to the exact high of the channel, the bar 17 high.

Bar 7 was a second-entry moving average gap bar short in a bear trend, which often leads to the final leg in the bear trend before a larger reversal develops. The rally to bar 7 broke the bear trend line and was followed by a lower low trend reversal at bar 8.

Bar 10 was another lower low in what at that point was a trading range, but it was also an expanding triangle bottom. Expanding triangles often rally to a new high and set up an expanding triangle top. The market attempted to do that at bar 14, but the momentum was so strong that anyone thinking about shorting would have to wait for a second entry, which never set up. It was far better to be looking to buy a pullback than to consider taking a short after such a strong bull breakout. The expanding triangle top failed, as expected, and the breakout of the top of the trend channel line and the bar 9 high of the prior day was followed by a two-legged sideways breakout pullback correction to the moving average at bar 15.

Figure 15.6

CHANNELS **239**

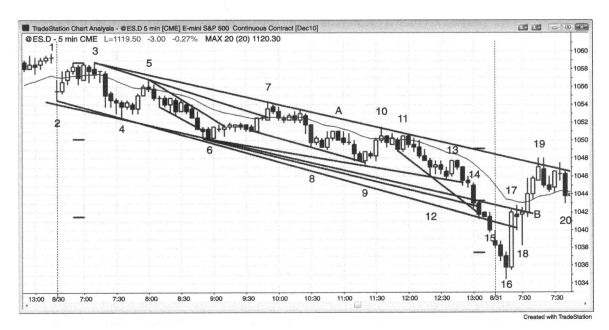

FIGURE 15.6 Reversals at Lines

Once the market appears to be trending, look for all possible trend lines and trend channel lines because they are areas where the market might reverse. Traders will use every technique to draw the lines, like connecting swing points, creating parallels, and using best fit lines. Figure 15.6 shows some of the more obvious lines, but there were many others. Some would have been based on related markets like the cash index, and others were based on other types of charts like volume and tick charts. The shorts can take partial profits on the tests of the bottom of the channels near the trend channel lines, and aggressive bulls can initiate long scalps there. At the top of the bear channel, bulls will take profits on their scalps and bears will initiate shorts for swings and scalps.

The line A bear trend line created by the bar 3 to bar 7 high was tested to the tick six bars after bar 7 and again at bar 10 and bar 11, and it contained all of the upside price action. This made it clear that it was important today. Because it was important, creating a parallel (line B) and anchoring it at a swing low that contained all of the sell-offs would likely create a channel that traders would feel was significant. Bar 6 was the logical choice for the anchor.

Once bar 14 broke below the bottom of the channel, traders would look at a measured move down using the height of the channel at the time of the breakout for a possible measured move projection. The move was exceeded on the open of the next day. When a bear channel breaks out of the downside instead of the top, even if the breakout is sharp as it was here, it usually goes only a few bars before reversing. Once it reversed back into the channel on bar 17, the objective was a poke above the channel, which occurred at bar 19.

The sell-off from bar 13 to bar 16 had 10 bear trend bars with little overlap and large bodies with small tails, all signs of bear strength. This was unsustainable behavior and therefore climactic; it had to be an unusually large bear trend bar on some higher time frame chart, although nothing is gained by looking for the perfect higher time frame chart. Any large bear trend bar is a spike, a breakout, and a sell climax. The strong move up to bar 19 had to create a two-bar reversal with that sell-off from bar 13 on some higher time frame chart, and even a bull reversal bar on an even higher time frame chart. Never lose sight of the big picture, and don't become frightened by an unusually strong sell-off. Yes, a huge bear spike is a strong sell climax and will often be followed by a protracted bear channel, but it can also represent exhaustion and lead to a big reversal, as it did here.

The market usually races to the top and bottom of the channel due to the vacuum effect. For example, bar 7 was a strong bull trend bar and there was another strong bull bar two bars earlier. Weak bulls saw a three-bar spike and a strong reversal up on the day and bought as bar 7 was forming and on its close and on the high 1 three bars later. Strong bulls instead exited their longs on the test of the top of the bear channel.

So why was the market vacuumed up with such force on a bear trend day when bears clearly controlled the day? It was because the bears believed that the trend line was going to get tested, so as the market got closer and closer to it, they became more confident that the price would soon reach the bear trend line. There is no incentive for them to short when they believe they can short at an even better price a few minutes later. This absence of the strongest of the bears creates an updraft that sucks the market up quickly to the trend line. The momentum traders kept buying until the momentum stopped and since there were fewer bears willing to short, the market quickly moved up to a price that represented value to the bears. Once there, the bears, who had been waiting for the test, shorted aggressively. They had been able overwhelm the bulls all day, as seen by the bear trend day, and both the bulls and bears knew that the bears were in control. There was a bear channel and the market was spending most of the day below the moving average.

Since everyone except novice traders knew that the odds strongly favored the failure of any attempt to break above the trend line, it was a great location to put on shorts. Also, shorting when the bulls were at their strongest gave the bears a great entry. They saw the market as overextended and not likely to go much higher. Since they believed that the market might not go another tick higher, they finally came back into the market and shorted heavily and relentlessly, even though they were on the sidelines for several bars. The bulls used the test as a place to take

Figure 15.6   CHANNELS   **241**

profits on their scalps. Both the bulls and the bears knew that the market would be at the top of the channel only briefly, so both acted quickly. The bulls quickly scalped out of their longs because they did not want to risk the market reversing down quickly below their average entry price, and the bears began shorting heavily and continued to short all the way down to the test of the bottom of the channel. There, some took partial profits and others continued to hold short until they saw a strong trend reversal, which did not come until the next day.

Deeper Discussion of This Chart

The market formed a wedge bear flag with bars 2, 4, and 6 in Figure 15.6, and once the market broke below the flag, it fell to a measured move down, reaching the target three bars before the close.

The day opened with a small gap down but the first bar was a doji and therefore a weak setup for a failed breakout long. By bar 3, the day was a trading range so it was acceptable to short below the bar 3 low 2, especially since the high or low of the day usually forms in the first hour and this was a possible high of the day. The market might have been forming a lower high and was failing to hold above the moving average.

Bar 5 was a test of the breakeven stops of the traders who shorted below bar 3, and set up another low 2 short at the moving average. The market was forming lower highs and lows and might have been in the early stages of a bear trend.

FIGURE 15.7   Channels Are Always Trying to Reverse

When the market is in a channel, the reversal setups often don't look quite right. That is because they are not reversal setups, but just the beginning of flag pullbacks. In Figure 15.7, the Emini completed a wedge bull flag down to bar 12, which poked a couple of ticks below an earlier low on the 60 minute chart (insert) and set up a large double bottom bull flag. Traders saw the market as flipping to always-in long on the bar after bar 12, on bar 14, or on the breakout above the bar 18 signal bar for the bull breakout of a small triangle (bars 15, 17, and 18 were the three pushes down).

A bull trend is either in a spike or in a channel. Since the market was not in a strong spike, traders assumed that it was in a bull channel, which meant that there would be pullbacks. Anything that looked like a low 1 or low 2 signal bar was then a buy signal. Instead of shorting below those bars, there would likely be more buyers at and below the lows of the signal bars. This is what happened with the low 1 short signal bar that followed bar 17. Traders bought the breakout below the bear inside bar, because they saw the market as always-in long and in a bull channel, and not in a bear leg. They wanted to buy at and below the low of the bar before bar 18, expecting the low 2 sell signal to fail. However, the bulls were so eager to get long that they placed their buy limit orders one tick above the low of the bar. They were afraid that there would not be enough bears left to push the market below the low of the sell signal bar, and they did not want to get trapped out of what they saw as

Figure 15.7   CHANNELS   **243**

the early stage of a bull trend. They saw the market as always-in long, and believed that the bears were wrong and that any sell signal would fail. They expected any sell-off, along with any opportunity to buy on a markdown in price, to be brief. They were happy to see any bear trend bar, especially a low 1 or low 2 that might trap bears, who would then be forced to buy back their losing shorts as the market reversed up. These bears would then be buyers, helping to lift the market, and they would be hesitant to short again for at least a few bars. This would make the market one-sided in favor of the buyers, giving them at least a scalper's profit, and possibly a swing profit.

Because the three pushes up to bar 16 were in a tight bull channel, many traders saw that wedge as a single spike up and were looking for a bull channel to follow after a pullback. Since the three prior pullbacks in the rally were between five and nine ticks, bulls would have placed limit orders to buy pullbacks of about that size. The pullback to bar 20 was seven ticks, the pullback to bar 22 was eight ticks, and the pullback to bar 24 was also eight ticks. Other traders just buy with limit orders at one to three ticks below the low of the prior bar in a channel, risking to below the most recent swing low. For example, they bought as bar 20 fell below the small doji before it, or below bar 19, and had their protective stops below bar 17. To a beginner, this is counterintuitive, but to experienced traders, this is an opportunity. They know that 80 percent of attempts to break below the bottom of the channel will fail, so buying as the market is making an attempt is likely to be a good trade.

Bears who saw the entire move up from bar 12 as an overdone bear rally were unhappy with how weak the short signals were at bar 13, the bar before bar 15, bar 16, the bar after bar 19, the bar before bar 21, bar 23, and the bar after bar 25. Whenever the market is working higher in a relatively tight channel, all of the sell signals tend to look bad, because they are not really sell signals—they are just the start of small bull flags. Since the strong bulls are buying below the lows of the prior bars and on limit orders that are located between maybe five and 10 ticks below the most recent swing high, it is a low-probability bet to short exactly where the strong bulls are buying. In a tight bull channel, it is rarely wise to short below the low of a bar unless there has been a strong climactic reversal after a breakout of the top of the channel, and even then it is often better not to short below a bar until after a sell-off that is then followed by a lower high. Remember, the market is always-in long and it is always better to only buy until the market flips to always-in short. It is easy to look at the channel and see it as weak, and to look at the sell-off down to bar 12 and assume that the bears will return, but you have to trade the market in front of you, not the one that just ended or the one that you think should soon begin.

When a channel has relatively small bars, bars with prominent tails, and trend bars in the opposite direction, there is significant two-sided trading taking place, even though the channel is a trend. This creates an opportunity for countertrend scalpers. The channel up from bar 18 is an example. Bears will short the closes of bull trend bars above prior swing highs, like the bar after bar 22, and the closes of small bull bars that follow, like bar 23, for scalps. Many are willing to scale in higher (scaling into trades is discussed in book 2). For example, if they shorted the close of the bull trend bar after bar 20 and one or more of the closes of the small bull bars that followed, or a point or so above their first entry, they would then take profits on their entire position at their original entry. That original entry would then be a breakeven trade and their later entries would give them a scalper's profit. These profit-taking bear scalpers bought back their shorts on the low of bar 22, since its low fell below the entry price of their first entry (the close of the bull trend bar after bar 20). That bar was also a test of the moving average, so there were also bulls who bought the test, in addition to the profit-taking bear scalpers who exited because the market reached whatever profit target they were using, such as the close of the bull trend bar after bar 20, the moving average, a breakout test of the 16 high, or five ticks below the high of the doji bar after bar 20 (as discussed in book 2, that was a weak buy signal bar, so bears would have shorted with a limit order at its high, and they would have scalped out one point lower; this meant that the market had to fall five ticks, which it did at the bar 22 low). There are always many different traders entering or exiting at every tick all day long for every conceivable reason. The more reasons that line up in the same direction, the more likely the market will trend.

Figure 15.8

CHANNELS **245**

FIGURE 15.8 Entering on Limit Orders in Channels

In addition to entering on stops, entering on limit (or market) orders can be an effective approach whenever the market is in any type of channel, including triangles and trading ranges. In Figure 15.8, the market had eight consecutive bull trend bars in the strong bull spike up to bar 3, so the market was likely to have a test of the high after a pullback. Although bears shorted below the bar 3 bear reversal bar, bulls were scaling in on limit orders below the low of the bar. Some bought on a limit order at the low of bar 3, but because the next bar was a strong bear trend bar, there were far more sell orders. Other bulls bought on a limit order at one tick above the moving average, since the market might have only touched the moving average and not filled a buy limit order exactly at the moving average. Some bulls scaled in lower, maybe buying more at one-point intervals. If they did, they could have then put a limit order to exit both positions at the entry price of the first order, at or just below the low of bar 3. They would have been filled on bar 5, would have broken even on the first entry, and would have made a profit on their second. This profit taking by these bulls contributed to the bear reversal bar at bar 5.

Traders saw the doji inside bar after the bear trend bar that followed bar 3, and many thought that this was not a good short setup. Since they believed that shorting below the bar would likely not yield a profitable scalp, some traders instead bought on a limit order at or one or more ticks below its low. This buying contributed to the tail at the bottom of bar 4. Bar 4 was the fourth consecutive down bar, which is enough bearish momentum to make traders hesitant to buy above its high, even though they believed the market would test the bar 3 high. They expected the first attempt up would likely fail and they preferred to wait for a two-legged pullback to buy. Bears realized this and thought that the traders who bought above bar 4 would likely lose money. This made shorting on a limit order at or just above the high of bar 4 a reasonable scalp. They exited with a one-point profit as bar 6 fell five ticks below the high of bar 4. Why was the low of bar 6 exactly five ticks below the high of bar 4? In large part because those short scalpers became buyers as they took their profits down there, and their buying helped create the tail at the bottom of bar 6.

Since most traders still believed that the market should test the bar 3 high, they were still looking to buy. Since the market clearly became always-in long in the spike from bar 1 to bar 3 and there was not yet a clear flip to short, the always-in position was still long. Therefore, they did not believe that shorting below the low of bar 5 was a good trade. Given that they thought it would be a losing trade, many traders did the opposite and bought on a limit order at or below the low of bar 5. Their buying, in addition to the buying by the shorts who were taking profits from their scalp down from above bar 4, created the tail at the bottom of bar 6.

Bar 6 was a two-legged sideways correction down from the bar 3 high, and many traders bought above bar 6 on a stop for the test of the bar 3 high. At the same time, many of the traders who bought below bar 5 sold out for a profitable scalp on the rally.

Although the market formed a double top at bar 7, many traders did not expect a trend reversal and instead expected a trading range and then a bull channel because that is what usually happens after such a strong spike on a day where a strong case could be made that bar 1 was likely going to remain as the low of the day. Bar 7 formed a two-bar reversal with the bar before it and the better entry is below the lower of the two bars. The problem with entering below the low of the bar 7 bear bar is that the market often has a one-tick bear trap. This means that it falls one tick below the bear bar but not below the low of both bars of the two-bar reversal, and then the rally resumes. This risk is less if you enter below the low of both bars, and that is why the market reversed up six ticks later. The bears bought back their shorts on a profit-taking limit order located five ticks below the signal bar low, which usually requires the market to fall six ticks. The bar 8 low was exactly six ticks below the bottom of the two-bar reversal.

If this was a strong bear trend, traders could short on a stop below the prior swing low at bar 4. Since most traders thought that the low of the day was in and that the market would likely form a bull channel, they thought that shorting below

Figure 15.8   CHANNELS   **247**

the bar 4 low was a bad idea. This means that buying below its low might be a good long, especially if the traders could scale in lower if need be. Also, since the market was likely to form a channel that could last for hours and the market might not again come down to this level, these bulls could swing some or all of their positions.

Other bulls saw bar 8 as the second leg down from bar 3 (bar 4 was the first leg down) and they bought above the high of bar 8 on a stop. The bar after bar 8 was a doji bar, which indicates that the market is still two-sided. Bar 8 was not a strong bull reversal bar, and the two-bar spike down from bar 7 made traders wonder if the market might be reversing. Traders had to decide if they thought that bar 9 was going to be the lower high pullback that would lead to a bear channel, or if always in was still long and that the market was in the early stages of a bull channel.

The traders who thought that the bottom was in believed that bar 9 was a bad short setup and they placed limit orders to buy at and below the low of bar 9. Many of these bulls would have added on if the market fell below the bar 8 low. The bears who shorted below bar 9 bought back their shorts when the market reversed above the bar 10 entry bar. Bulls also bought, believing that this failed short was more evidence that a bull channel was forming.

Channels have lots of pullbacks along the way, and the bulls would not let themselves be stopped out by a pullback. Instead, they would buy on a limit order at or below the low of the prior bar, like below bars 9 and 11. Since channels have two-sided trading, as long as the channel is not too tight and too steep, bears will short at or above swing highs. For example, they would have shorted as bar 12 went above the bar 7 high and some would have added on one point higher. This in part was the reason that the high of bar 13 was exactly five ticks above bar 7. They would also have shorted on the move up to bar 17 as the market went above the bar 13 high. Some bears would even have shorted the sharp rally up to bar 30 as it moved above the bar 17 high and they would have added on one point higher. They could have bought back both shorts at the original entry price as the market fell to bar 31. Their original short would have broken even and their add-on would have made a one-point profit.

The bulls would have looked at the rally up to bar 29 as having trending highs, lows, and closes, and therefore would have believed that it was strong. Some would have bought more on a stop at one tick above the bar 17 high. They could have exited with a profit on bar 30. Whenever a breakout trade results in a profit, it is a sign that the trend is strong. However, it is not absolute and if the market is mostly in a trading range, as it was today, there may not be follow-through.

There was two-sided trading throughout the day and both bulls and bears were entering on limit orders and on stops. For example, once the always-in position flipped to short at the bar 17 wedge top (wedge reversals are discussed later), bears began shorting above the high of the prior bars, like above bars 18, 20, and the bar after bar 24. Bulls were buying below prior swing lows, like below bars 20 and bar 23. There were many other setups during this day, as there are on all days, but the purpose of this chart is not to show every possible trade. Instead, it is to make the point that when the market is in a bull channel, bulls are buying below the low of the prior bar and bears are selling above swing highs. In bear channels, they do the opposite—bulls buy below swing lows and bears short above the high of the prior bar.

CHAPTER 16

Micro Channels

A micro trend line is a trend line on any time frame that is drawn across from 2 to about 10 bars where most of the bars touch or are close to the trend line and the bars usually are relatively small. Typically a trend channel line can be drawn along the opposite ends of the bars as well, and the result is a very tight channel called a micro channel. Unlike a conventional channel where pullbacks are common, a micro channel progresses with no pullbacks, or rare, small pullbacks, making it an extremely tight channel.

The more bars, the stronger the bars (like bars with big trend bodies in the direction of the micro channel), and the smaller the tails, the stronger the micro channel, and the more likely that the first pullback will fail to reverse the trend. A micro channel can last for 10 or more bars, and other times it will run for about 10 bars, have a small pullback, and then resume for another 10 bars or so. It does not matter whether you view the entire channel as one big micro channel (a micro channel is a type of tight channel), two consecutive micro channels separated by a small pullback, or a large tight channel, because you will trade it the same way. The trend is very strong and traders will look at reversal attempts to fail and become pullbacks and for the trend to continue.

Ten years ago, traders saw micro channels as a sign of program trading. Now, since most trading is done by computers, it adds nothing to say that micro channels are signs of program trading, because every bar on the chart is due to program trading. A micro channel is just one particular type of program trade, and it is likely due to many firms running programs simultaneously. One or more firms will start it, but once the momentum is underway, momentum programs will detect it and begin trading in the same direction, adding to the strength of the trend. Once the trend begins breaking above resistance levels, breakout programs will start trading. Some will trade in the direction of the trend and others will begin to scale in against the trend, or scale out of longs that they bought lower.

Eventually one of the bars penetrates through the trend line or the trend channel line, creating a breakout. Bull and bear micro channels can develop in bull or bear trends, and in trading ranges. The environment in which they occur determines how to trade them. Both bull and bear channels can have breakouts to the upside or the downside. As with all breakouts, three things can then happen: it can be successful and be followed by more trading in that direction, it can fail and become a small climactic reversal, or the market can just go sideways and the pattern can evolve into a trading range.

As with any breakout, traders will trade either in the direction of the breakout, expecting follow-through, or in the opposite direction, if they expect the breakout to fail. Breakouts, failed breakouts, and breakout pullbacks are closely related and are discussed in book 2. As a guide, traders compare the strength of the breakout with that of the reversal attempt. If one is clearly stronger, the market will likely go in that direction. If they are equally strong, the trader needs to wait for more bars before deciding where the market is likely to go next.

When a bear micro channel forms in a bull trend, it is usually a bull flag, or the last leg of a bull flag, and traders will look for a signal bar and then place a buy stop above its high to enter on the breakout of the bear micro channel and of the bull flag. When a bull micro channel forms in a bear trend, it is usually a bear flag or the final leg of a bear flag and traders will short below any signal bar.

If instead of a bear micro channel forming in a bull flag, the micro channel is a rising micro channel (a bull micro channel) in a bull trend, the first downside breakout (the first pullback) will usually not go far, and it will be bought aggressively. The more bars in the bull micro channel, the more likely that the bear breakout will not reverse the bull trend. For example, if there is a five-bar bull micro channel in a bull trend, there will probably be far more buyers at and below the low of that fifth bar than sellers. If the market trades below that fifth bar, the bar creates a bear breakout of the bull channel. However, it is unlikely to lead to more than a bar or two of selling because the bulls will be eager to buy the first pullback from the strong micro channel bull trend. Remember, many traders have been watching the rally for five bars, waiting for any pullback to buy. They will be eager to buy below the fifth bar and above the high of the pullback bar, which is a failed breakout buy signal bar (a high 1 buy setup). If the market triggers the long but creates a bear reversal bar within a bar or two, this then sets up a micro double top sell signal. It can also be thought of as a pullback from the breakout below the bull micro channel, even if its high is above the highest bar in the micro channel. It would then be simply a higher high reversal, which is a micro version of a major trend reversal (reversals are discussed in book 3).

It is important to realize that traders do not have to wait for a pullback to get long. Many experienced traders understand what is happening after the second or third bar of the bull micro channel in a bull trend. They think that the market is in the early stages of a very strong buy program where momentum buy programs are also buying aggressively. These traders will try to copy what the computers are doing and will buy every bull close, and place limit orders one or two ticks below the close of every bar, and one or two ticks above the low of the prior bar. If the biggest pullback in the micro channel has been five ticks, they will place limit orders to buy any three- or four-tick pullback. They expect that the first time a bar falls below the low of the prior bar will attract even more buying, so they know that their most recent buy will likely be profitable, despite the pullback. Since they made money all the way up, they are not worried about getting out at breakeven or with a small loss on their final entry when a pullback finally does come.

As with any channel, a bull micro channel can form in a trading range, or within a bull or bear trend. When it is in a bull trend, higher prices are more certain, and traders should look to buy near the middle or bottom of the prior bar. When the micro channel is especially tight, it can be a spike on a higher time frame chart; a broader channel may follow, and it might reach a measured move target based on the height of the tight micro channel. When a bull micro channel is in a bear trend, it is a bear flag, and traders should look to short the downside breakout or the pull-back from a downside breakout. When a bull micro channel forms after a possible low in a bear trend, it can become the final flag in the bear trend and break out to the upside instead of to the downside, and the breakout can be the spike that leads to a bull trend. When a bull breakout occurs, it usually follows a failed low 1, 2, or 3.

A micro channel is a sloping tight trading range, and therefore it has a strong magnetic pull that tends to prevent breakouts from going very far. It is also often tight enough to sometimes act as a spike, and it can be followed by a broader channel, creating a spike and channel trend. When there is a breakout from a micro channel, it is usually just for a bar or two and is mostly due to profit taking. For example, if there is a bull micro channel (an upwardly sloping micro channel) and a bar trades below the low of the prior bar, that is a breakout below the micro channel. This is primarily due to bulls taking profits, although there are some bears who are shorting. Within a bar or two, other buyers come in, some bears exit, and the market usually trades above the high of the prior bar. Some traders will see this as a failed breakout of the micro channel, and they will buy as the market goes above the high of the prior bar. For them, this is a high 1 buy setup. Others will assume that the trend is reversing down; they will wait for the market to form either a higher high or lower high breakout pullback over the next couple of bars, and then they will short below the low of the prior bar. The overall context can give a clue to which outcome is more likely. For example, if the market is in a strong bear trend and the bull micro channel is just a pullback, the odds favor that the breakout below the micro channel will be followed by more selling. If the market trades above the breakout bar, bears will place stop orders to short below the low of the prior bar. If instead the bull micro channel is forming as a breakout from a trading range in a bull market, the odds favor the breakout below the micro channel becoming a pullback in the bull trend, and bulls will place buy orders at one tick above the high of the prior bar.

A breakout of the trend line sets up a with-trend entry. For example, if there is a bull micro channel and the market is always-in long, and then there is a bar with a low below the micro bull trend line, then buying the high of that bar can be a reliable trade. This is a tiny but strong one-bar bull flag (a high 1 buy setup) and it is a failed breakout buy signal. It might be a two-legged correction on a smaller time frame chart; however, it is better to not look, because you will find yourself with too much information to process in a short time and you will likely mismanage or not take the trade.

If the bull micro channel is within a trading range or in a bear trend instead of in a strong bull trend, you have other things to consider before buying above the failed bear breakout. If the channel is at the top of a trading range, it is often better not to buy the failed breakout and instead to wait to see if the reversal back up stalls and becomes a higher high pullback from the breakout. If it only goes up for a bar or two and then forms a bear reversal bar, this can be a reliable short setup when it is near the top of a trading range (a micro double top, discussed in book 3). If the bull micro channel is a bear flag just below the moving average, you should only look to short, since the odds are that the shorting by the bears will overpower the bulls who bought the pullback. Wait for the breakout below the channel and then for the failure and one more push up. If that reversal back up forms a bear reversal bar at the moving average within a bar or two, this is usually a reliable breakout pullback short setup (a low 2). The market broke out of the downside of the bull micro channel and then pulled back to a small higher high. Finally, if it reversed back down, it set up a breakout below what has become a bear flag.

As with any breakout below a bull channel, there might be a pullback and then a resumption of the selling. That pullback can be a lower high or a higher high (a higher high means that the high of the bar goes above the high of the most recent swing high, which is likely the highest bar in the bull channel). Because most attempts at reversing a trend fail, the odds are in favor of the bear breakout failing and becoming just a pullback in the bull trend, followed by the bull trend resuming. Traders should place an order to go long at one tick above the high of the breakout bar, in case the bear breakout fails and the bull trend resumes.

However, they must be aware that their long might be a bull trap, trapping them into a losing long trade. Remember, although most attempts to reverse a trend fail, some succeed. Instead of the breakout to the downside failing, the market might be just briefly pulling back from the bear breakout and forming a small higher high or lower high before the selling resumes. This could be followed by a successful trend reversal into a bear leg or trend. Because of this, the trader has to be prepared to reverse to short below his long entry bar, if the overall price action makes a reversal seem appropriate. In this case, this is a breakout pullback short setup. Whenever a breakout fails, this failure sets up a trade in the direction of the original trend. If that also fails, then it becomes a breakout pullback from the original bear breakout (opposite failures create a breakout pullback) and a second attempt to reverse the trend to down.

If the breakout pullback short triggers (by the bar going one tick below the low of the prior bar, which is usually the bull breakout bar), look at the size of the bodies of the recent few bars. If the bars are bull or bear trend bars, then this second failure has high odds of being a successful second entry short. Remember, the first failure was when the bears lost on the failed downside breakout, trapping them out of their short trade. The second failure was when the bulls were trapped into their losing trade, which was set up by the failed bear breakout below the channel. If the market now turns down again, you have just had bears trapped out and bulls trapped in. In general, if both sides get trapped in or out, the odds of success of the next setup increase. If the bars have more of a doji look, then the market will likely enter a trading range, but the odds still favor a downside breakout. If you are not certain, then wait because it is likely that most traders will not be certain and a trading range will usually follow.

Although the vast majority of micro trend line breakouts are one- and two-legged pullbacks on the 1 minute chart, you should avoid trading off that chart because you will likely lose money. Most traders are unable to take all of the signals and invariably pick too many losers and not enough winners. The best trades often set up fast and trigger quickly and are therefore easy to miss. Many losing trades are often slow to set up and give traders plenty of time to enter, trapping them in the wrong direction.

That bull micro channel could instead have a breakout to the upside, above the trend channel line, in an attempt to form an even steeper bull trend. If it fails and there is a strong bear reversal bar, this buy climax is a potential short setup.

When a micro trend line extends for about 10 or more bars, the odds increase substantially that there will soon be a tradable reversal. This type of trend is unsustainable and therefore a type of climax, which is usually followed eventually by a pullback or a reversal. After such climactic behavior, be ready to take a breakout pullback entry. This is the second attempt to reverse the trend, with the original trend line breakout being the first.

A micro trend line break is important not only when the micro trend line is part of a micro channel, but also whenever there is any strong trend underway. If there is a strong bear trend with large bear trend bars and little overlap between consecutive bars and there are no pullback bars for four or five bars, you are likely eager to get short. Look for any bear micro trend line and then sell below the low of any bar that pokes above any bear micro trend line. Any poke through it is a setup for a failed breakout short entry. Enter at one tick below the bar that breaks above the bear micro trend line (a low 1 short setup).

Small, steep trend lines, even drawn using two consecutive bars, often provide setups for with-trend trades. If the trend is steep, sometimes a small pullback bar or a pause bar can penetrate a tiny micro trend line. When it does, it can become a signal bar for a with-trend entry. Some of the penetrations are smaller than one tick in the Eminis, but are still valid.

When there is a trend and then it has a pullback, it is common to see a micro trend line in the pullback. For example, in a pullback in a bull trend, if there is a bear micro trend lasting about three to 10 bars, and then there is a break above that bear micro trend line, this theoretically sets up a short on the failed breakout. Since this is occurring during a bull trend and it almost always happens above or near the moving average, you should not be shorting this pattern. You would find yourself holding a short at the bottom of a bull flag near a rising moving average in a bull trend, which is a very low-probability trade. As this short will likely fail, you should anticipate this and be ready to buy the failure, getting in exactly where the trapped shorts will get out. Your long will be a breakout pullback buy since the market broke above the bear micro trend line and then pulled back to either a small lower low or a higher low, and then the market resumed in the direction of the breakout, which is also the direction of the major trend of the day.

It is critical to remember that micro trend lines should only be used to find with-trend setups. However, once the trend has reversed, for example after a bull trend line break and then a reversal down from a higher high, you should be looking for micro trend line short setups, even if they are at or just above the moving average.

As with any chart pattern, a micro channel's appearance is different on both smaller and higher time frame charts. Even though the trend bars in a micro channel or any other type of tight channel are usually not large and there is usually a lot of overlap between adjacent bars, the trend is strong enough to be a large trend bar or a series of trend bars on a higher time frame chart. This means that it often functions as a spike, and is often followed by a broader channel, like any other spike and channel trend. Also, even though there are no pullbacks in the micro channel, there are many pullbacks if you look at a small enough time frame chart.

Figure 16.1   MICRO CHANNELS **255**

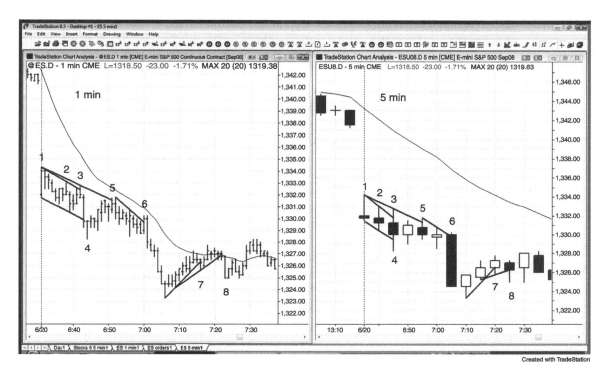

FIGURE 16.1 Micro Trend Lines

Small trend lines can generate many scalps during the day, especially on the 1 minute chart, which is seldom worth trading. In Figure 16.1, the chart on the left is a 1 minute Emini chart and the numbers correspond to the same bars on the 5 minute chart on the right. Both show that failed breakouts from tiny trend lines can result in profitable fades. There are other trades on the 1 minute chart that are not shown because the purpose of this figure is only to show how 5 minute micro trend lines correspond to more obvious, longer trend lines on the 1 minute chart, so if you can read the 5 minute chart, you do not have to additionally look at the 1 minute chart to place your orders. Many of these trades could have been profitable scalps on the 1 minute chart.

Note that several breaks of micro trend lines on the 5 minute chart are easy to overlook and are less than one tick in size. For example, bars 3, 5, 6, and 7 were failed micro trend line breaks on the 5 minute chart that would have been invisible to most traders, but the one at bar 5 was particularly significant and led to a good short scalp. It was the second failed attempt to break above a bear trend line (bar 3 was the first).

The failed breakout below the bull micro channel at bar 7 was a risky long and a scalp at best. Since it was a bear flag pullback to the moving average, it was better to expect the move up to stall and become a breakout pullback sell setup, which it became here.

Price action trading works even at the tiniest level. Note how bar 8 on the 1 minute chart was a higher high breakout test (it tested the high of the bar that formed the low of the bear trend) long setup and that although the market came down to test the bar 8 signal bar low two bars after entry, the protective stop below the signal bar would not have been hit. Also note that there was also an even smaller major reversal in this segment of the 1 minute chart. There was a tiny bull trend, indicated by the bull micro trend line up from the low of the chart, then a break of the trend line at bar 7, and then a higher high test of the tiny bull trend extreme. Since the pattern is so small, the trend reversal down to bar 8 was just a scalp, as expected.

On the 5 minute chart, bar 8 did not set up a long. Why? Because it was a pullback in a bear trend. You should not be buying the top of a pullback in a bear trend day. Instead, once you see the micro trend line buy trigger, get ready to short its failure, entering exactly where the trapped longs will be forced out with their losses.

Figure 16.2   MICRO CHANNELS   **257**

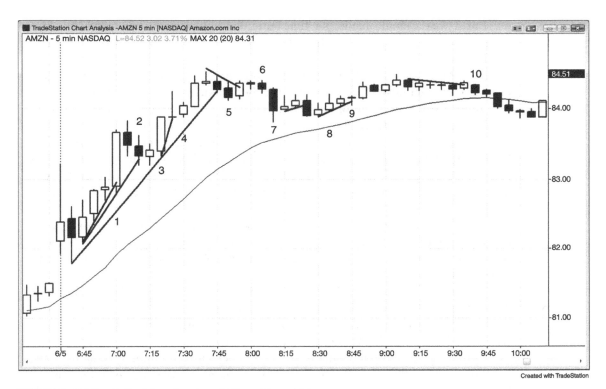

FIGURE 16.2 Failed Breakouts of Micro Trend Lines

Even trend lines created using just two or three consecutive bars in a steep trend can set up with trend entries when there is a small break that immediately reverses. Each new break becomes the second point in a longer, flatter trend line until eventually trend lines in the opposite direction become more important, and at that point the trend has reversed.

In Figure 16.2, bar 1 dipped below a three-bar trend line and reversed up, creating a long entry at one tick above the prior bar.

Bar 2 dipped below a six-bar trend line. Traders would have placed buy stops above its high. When not filled, they would move their buy stops to the high of the next bar and would have been filled on bar 3. This was a high 1 buy entry, and most bear breakouts of bull micro channels in a bull trend fail and become high 1 buy setups. Since the micro channel is usually breaking above something, like a prior high, as it did here when it moved above the first bar of the day, the high 1 is usually also a breakout pullback buy setup. Incidentally, the bar before bar 2 was a possible short setup based on a failed breakout of a micro trend channel line (not shown) that is a parallel of the three-bar micro trend line leading up to bar 1. The upward momentum was too strong for a short without a second entry, but this illustrates how micro trend channel lines can set up countertrend trades.

Bar 4 was a small inside bar that extended below a two-bar trend line (the penetration is not shown). The buy is on a stop at one tick above the high of the small inside bar.

Bar 5 broke the major trend line of the day (any trend line lasting about an hour or so is more significant), so traders would be thinking that a two-legged pullback was more likely. After the break above the bear trend line on the bar following bar 5, a short would be triggered on the bar 6 lower high. When bars are small doji bars like those following bar 5, it is usually best to wait for bigger trend bars before taking more trades, but these trend line reversals still led to profitable scalps of 30 to 50 cents in Amazon (AMZN). Since bar 5 was the first breakout of a fairly tight bull channel, it is better not to short it and instead to wait for a breakout pullback to short.

Bar 6 was a reasonable lower high breakout pullback short entry for a scalp down toward the moving average. This was not a good trend reversal trade because there had yet to be a test of the moving average followed by a test of the bull trend high.

Bar 6 was a micro trend line short in a bull trend, which is a bad trade when it occurs close to the moving average. Here, however, there was plenty of room down to the moving average; in addition, it was following a wedge top and therefore would likely be part of a two-legged correction down.

Unlike a conventional channel, where pullbacks are common, in a micro channel the lack of pullbacks is one of its defining characteristics. For example, in the bull micro channel that started on the bar before bar 8, the first leg ended with the small bar 9 pullback. Some traders saw the next four bars as part of the same channel, with bar 9 as a pullback, and other traders saw bar 9 as the start of a second micro channel. It really does not matter, because the sideways move to bar 10 broke below both.

Deeper Discussion of This Chart

The market gapped up in Figure 16.2 and therefore broke out above the close of yesterday and the first bar was a bull trend bar. The body was reasonably strong and there was a tail below, both showing buying pressure. Yesterday closed with some bull bodies, again showing strength by the bulls, so this bar was not a strong signal bar for a short on the basis of a possible failed breakout setup. The second bar had a bear body and dipped below the low of the first bar and was a reasonable breakout pullback long setup for a possible trend from the open bull day. There were four bull trend bars, creating a spike up, but the final one had a large range and might indicate some exhaustion. This led to the first pullback long setup, and bar 3 was a strong entry bar. This was also a breakout pullback long from the breakout above the opening high. Since the first bar of the day was unusually large, it could and did lead to about a measured move up.

Figure 16.3   MICRO CHANNELS   **259**

FIGURE 16.3 Micro Trend Lines in Strong Trends

Small trend lines in strong trends, even when drawn using adjacent bars, often have failed breakouts that set up good with-trend entries. Many of these are two-legged pullback setups (ABC corrections) on 1 minute charts, but you don't need to look at the 1 minute chart when you see the false breakouts on the 5 minute chart.

When trading, you do not have to actually draw the trend lines on the chart very often because most trends are visible without the help of the drawn lines.

There were many good with-trend entries in AAPL on this 5 minute chart in Figure 16.3 based on failed breakouts of micro trend lines. When the trend is steep, you should only be looking to trade with the trend and you should not be trading small reversals. For example, even though bar 3 broke above a bear micro trend line, the bear trend was actually a bull flag in a strong bull trend where the market has been above the moving average for more than 20 bars. You should only be looking to buy and not short, especially not just above the moving average.

Bar 2 was a breakout below a bull micro channel in a strong bull trend, and it should be expected to fail. This set up a reliable high 1 buy setup.

Bars 10 and 12 were first breakouts above steep, tight channels and therefore not good long entries. Although bar 12 was the second breakout to the upside on the way down, the move down from bar 10 lasted several bars and was steep; it therefore created a new small micro channel, and bar 12 was the first attempt to break out of the new channel (both bars 10 and 12 were low 1 sell signal bars).

Bar 9 was a bear reversal bar and a signal bar for the downside breakout of the small triangle. A triangle is a mostly sideways trading range with three or more pushes in one or both directions. The bar before bar 9 was the third of three small pushes down, and was the point at which the trading range became a triangle. Since the market was in such a tight bear channel from the first bar of the day, it was unreasonable to believe that the triangle would be a reliable buy setup. In fact, most traders did not see the pattern as a triangle yet, and were continuing to look for shorts. Once the bar 9 bear reversal bar formed the third push up, traders were confident that the pattern was a triangle in a bear trend, and a reliable sell setup. Even though bar 9 had a bull body, it was a small doji and therefore did not have much buying pressure. However, it was still a reversal bar since it closed below its midpoint. Bar 9 would have been a stronger signal if it had bear body.

The tight bear channel that ended three bars after bar 8 had several smaller micro channels within it. It does not matter whether a trader sees the tight channel as a large micro channel with a couple of small pullbacks, three consecutive micro channels, or as a large tight bear channel, because he would trade the market the same way. The move down is very strong and is probably a strong spike on a higher time frame chart. Smart traders were looking for any pullback to short, expecting that any pullback would simply be profit taking by the bears, and would be followed by lower prices and not a trend reversal. In a strong trend such as this, traders will short above the high of the prior bar and below the low of any pullback, like below bars 9, 10, and 12.

Many bull trends that have only small pullbacks but result in large profits have low probability short setups. For example, both bars 10 and 12 were doji bars in areas of other bars with tails, and therefore were signs of two-sided trading. When the market begins to develop signs of two-sided trading, it often is evolving into a trading range, which means shorting near its low and hoping for a breakout of the developing trading range is a low probability short. The probability of a successful swing down might be only 40 percent. However, since the reward is several times the risk, the trader's equation is still very positive. Traders who prefer to take only high probability trades would not have shorted below bars 10 or 12, and instead would have waited for high probability reversals to buy (like the bull reversal bar after a series of sell climaxes at the low of the day; reversals are discussed in book 3), or pullbacks to short (like the bar 9 triangle), or strong bear spikes to short (like

Figure 16.3

MICRO CHANNELS **261**

the bar 11 close, since it was a breakout below a wedge bottom; the low of the bar before bar 11 and the high of bar 12 formed a measuring gap, which is discussed in book 2).

Deeper Discussion of This Chart

In Figure 16.3, yesterday closed with a strong bull trend bar breakout of a largely horizontal bull flag after a protracted bull trend. This was a final flag short setup and it triggered on the first bar of today. Traders could short below the bull trend bar or below the first bar, which had a small bear body, or below the bottom of the final flag. The entry bar was a large bear spike and was followed by a tight and therefore very strong bear channel. The day was a trend from the open bear trend day.

The first reversal attempt of micro channels is due to profit taking. For example, when the bear bar before bar 2 fell broke below the bull micro channel, it was due mostly to bulls taking profits. Other bulls were eager to get long, since this was in a bull trend, and bought using limit orders as that bear trend bar fell below the low of the prior bar, and others bought one to several ticks below. Some bought on the close of the bear bar, expecting it to become a failed breakout. Limit order entries are discussed in book 2. Traders who prefer stop entries bought above the bar 2 two-bar reversal, which was a high 1 and a breakout pullback buy setup.

FIGURE 16.4 Micro Trend Lines Are Just Trend Lines on Smaller Time Frames

What appear as micro trend line setups on a 5 minute chart are usually 3- to 10-bar pullbacks on the 1 minute chart (see Figure 16.4). The 1 minute Emini provided entries on trend line tests and trend channel overshoots and reversals all day long. Many of the penetrations were less than one tick but still meaningful. The lines shown are just some of the ones that could be drawn on this chart; there are many others. Just because it looks easy when you look back at a 1 minute chart at the end of the day does not mean that it is easy to make money trading the chart in real time. It is not. Invariably the best setups look bad but set up and trigger too fast to take them, whereas the losers give you plenty of time to get in. The result is that you end up taking too many bad trades and not enough good ones to offset your losses and you lose money on the day.

Each successive trend line in Figure 16.4 gets shallower until trend lines in the other direction dominate the price action.

A micro channel is usually a trend bar (a spike) on some higher time frame chart, and a channel with many pullbacks on a smaller time frame chart.

Figure 16.5   MICRO CHANNELS   **263**

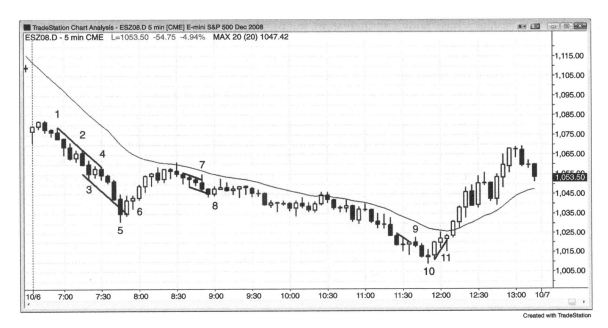

FIGURE 16.5 Micro Trend Lines When the Dow Is Down 700 Points

There were many micro trend line and channel trades in the Eminis on the day charted in Figure 16.5 (only four are shown), a very unusual day when the Dow was down over 700 points but rallied into the close to make back half of the loss.

Bar 5 was a micro trend channel overshoot that became the first bar of a two-bar reversal. The channel line was a parallel of the bars 1 to 4 micro trend line. You could also have drawn the channel line using the lows (the low of the bar after bar 1 and the low of bar 3). There was a great ii setup where both bars had bull closes, which is always desirable when fading a strong bear trend. The bar after bar 5 formed a two-bar reversal with bar 5.

When a micro channel starts having five to 10 bars like the channel from the open that ended at bar 5, you can just as accurately simply refer to it as a channel. The term does not matter because a micro channel is simply a channel and the only reason to distinguish it from larger channels is because micro channels often set up reliable with-trend scalps in trends.

Bars 7 and 9 were micro trend line failed breakout short scalps and both were quickly followed by buy scalps as the failures failed, creating breakout pullback buy setups (even though both were lower lows). Bar 7 was the first breakout above the micro channel and therefore not a good long setup. Instead, it became an outside down entry for a short. You could also have waited for bar 7 to close to be sure that it had a bear body and then short the breakout below the bar 7 outside down bar for a scalp.

Bar 11 was a classic trap to get you out of a strong rally. If you exited, you needed to buy again on the high 1 above the bar 11 micro trend line false breakout. Bar 9 was a breakout above the bear micro channel, and bar 10 was a lower low breakout pullback, so traders were wondering if a larger rally was likely. Bar 10 had a small bear body and the next bar was a strong bull trend bar. The following bar also had a bull body. The buying pressure was building, and that made that third bull bar a weak low 1 sell setup. Traders expected it to fail and bought at and below its low. They did not know that a bull trend would follow, but believed that the market would rally enough for at least a long scalp. Within a bar or two after bar 11, traders saw the market as always-in long, and swung the remainder of their longs, and even added to them.

Many of the bars today had a range of over 6 to 8 points. It would be prudent to reduce your position size to half or less, and increase your stop to 4 points and your profit target to 2 points. Otherwise, it was just another well-behaved price action day.

Deeper Discussion of This Chart

The day opened with a large gap down in Figure 16.5, but the first bar was a strong bull reversal bar and therefore set up a trend from the open buy signal based on the failed breakout below the close of yesterday. The third bar was a strong bear bar and therefore a spike down, but the market might just be forming a higher low before the rally resumes. Instead, the market traded above the higher low and then reversed down in an outside bar down (bar 1), triggering a breakout pullback short entry. The gap down was the breakout, and the failed breakout and attempt to rally failed and became a breakout pullback for a resumption of the bear breakout. Traders reversed to short as the bar went outside down. Other traders shorted below the low of the outside down bar, and others shorted below the low of the bull reversal bar (the first bar of the day). The day became a large trend from the open bear day as the market traded in a tight channel down to bar 5. The channel was so tight that it was effectively just a spike. The market pulled back to the moving average and then a bear channel unfolded down to the bar 10 low of the day.

Most failed micro trend line trades are low 1 entries in bear trends and high 1 entries in bull trends. Bar 9 was a low 1 sell setup. Bar 11 was a high 1 buy setup; it was the first higher low in the new bull leg, and a higher low after a possible trend reversal into a bull is a good buy setup. The low 1 signal bar before bar 11 was a doji bar and it followed two bull trend bars. The first was a strong bull trend bar that might have turned the always in direction to long (it was a two-bar reversal with the bar after bar 9, after the bar 9

Figure 16.5   MICRO CHANNELS   **265**

one-bar final flag). Aggressive bulls would have bought with limit orders at the low of the low 1 signal bar, expecting the short to fail.

Breakout pullback trades that have higher highs or lower lows are small final flag reversals. For example, bar 9 was a breakout above a micro trend line, and the breakout failed and sold off to a lower low at bar 10. Bar 10 can be thought of as a pullback from the bar 9 breakout, and it pulled back to a lower low, which breakout pullbacks sometimes do. Since it reversed up, bar 9 became a one-bar-long final flag.

The sell-off down to bar 5 was in a tight channel, but it was so strong that it had to be a spike down on a higher time frame chart. The market then rallied to the moving average, where there was a 20 gap bars sell signal. This was followed by a long channel down to bar 10, completing the bear spike and channel pattern. The first target of the reversal was the top of the first strong buy setup, which was the bar 5 two-bar reversal. After that, the next target was the start of the bear channel, which was the moving average test at 8:30.

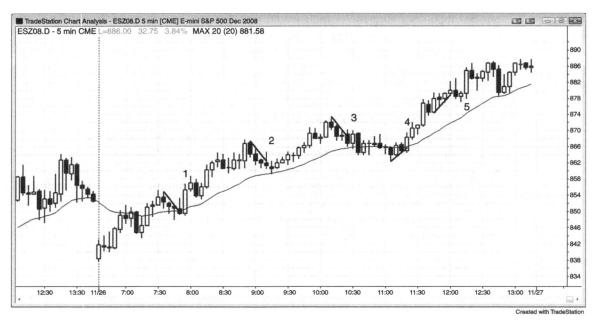

FIGURE 16.6   Micro Trend Lines in a Bull Trend

On a strong bull trend day, shorts should be avoided, including micro trend line shorts, especially near or above the moving average. In Figure 16.6, shorting on bars 1, 2, and 3 would have been selling against the bull trend in the area of the moving average or above the moving average. Yes, the downward-sloping micro trend line indicated that there was a small bear trend, but each occurred as part of a pullback in a very strong bull trend, and you should have been only looking to buy. These were bull flags and they were above the moving average, which is a sign of bull strength. There had been no break of a significant bull trend line followed by a reversal down from a higher high or lower high test of the bull high. The only value of bear micro trend lines on a bull trend day is to alert you to buy the breakout pullback that will form as the micro trend line short fails. In other words, don't short on bars 1, 2, and 3, and instead go long where those shorts would have covered. The failure would form a small lower low (like after the bars 2 and 3 failed micro trend line breakouts) or a small higher low (like on the bar 1 failed breakout), and would just become a pullback in the bull breakout of the bear micro trend line (a breakout pullback long setup).

With-trend micro trend line entries are high-probability trades, like the longs at bars 4 and 5.

Deeper Discussion of This Chart

The chart in Figure 16.6 shows a trend from the open bull day, so shorts should be avoided, including micro trend line shorts, especially near or above the moving average. The market broke out below the moving average but immediately reversed up in a failed breakout. The bears tried to turn the rally into a breakout pullback short at the moving average, but the rally had several strong bull bodies, which meant that traders should short only on a second entry. There was none. The sell-off was brief and became a higher low.

CHAPTER 17

Horizontal Lines: Swing Points and Other Key Price Levels

Most days are trading range days or have a lot of trading range activity. On these days you will find that horizontal lines across swing highs and lows often serve as barriers that result in failed breakouts and then reversals. Expect swing high breakouts to fail and form higher high reversal setups, and swing low breakouts to fail and form lower low reversal setups. Sometimes the failure fails, which is a breakout pullback setup, and the market makes a second more extreme higher high or lower low. A fade of a second higher high or lower low setup is even more likely to be successful, because they are second attempts to reverse the market and second signals are good setups on trading range days.

On trend days, horizontal lines should generally be used only to enter on pullbacks. For example, if there is a strong upside breakout of a trading range on a bull trend day, there might be a pullback to the area of breakout level after a few bars. If there is a bull reversal setup on the test, this is a good breakout pullback buy setup.

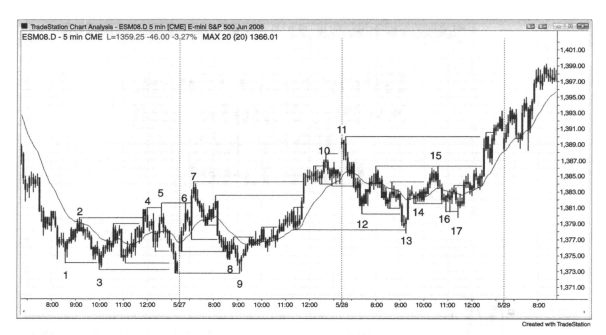

FIGURE 17.1 Breakouts Can Set Up Reversals

Most days are not strong trend days, and on these days traders should be looking at all prior swing highs and lows to see if the market creates failed breakouts, which can lead to reversal entries. Second signals are the best. A second higher high or lower low is a more extreme point on a trading range day where the middle of the day acts like a magnet, and this further extreme is therefore more likely to yield a scalper's profit. For example, in Figure 17.1, bar 5 was a second higher high over bar 2.

Bar 9 was a second attempt to reverse up after falling below the low of the open, and a double bottom with the low of the day before.

Deeper Discussion of This Chart

Bar 5 was also the third push up from the bar 3 low in Figure 17.1. Even though it did not have a wedge shape, three push patterns usually behave like wedges and can be considered to be variations of wedges.

Bar 9 was the seventh point of an expanding triangle bottom (even though it was a double bottom with yesterday's low and not a lower low, close is close enough) and bar 11 was an expanding triangle top. It was also a smaller expanding triangle where bar 10 was the second push up and it was about five bars after the first.

Bar 13 was a large double bottom pullback. There were multiple bottoms to choose from for labeling the double bottom, and bars 3 and 9 might have been the best. It was also a high 2 buy setup since it was at the bottom of two large, complex legs down. Since bars 9 to 11 formed a bull channel, which is a bear flag, bar 13 was a failed breakout of that bear flag. It was also a large wedge bull flag where the small swing low before or after bar 10 was the first push down and bar 12 was the second.

Bar 15 was a double top bear flag. It failed as a large bull breakout bar went above its high, and the market became noticeably more bullish.

Bar 17 was a second lower low below bar 14 and a lower low below bar 16. It was also a wedge bull flag with bars 14 and 16, and a breakout pullback to a higher low following the breakout above the bull flag of bars 11 to 13.

FIGURE 17.2   Don't Fade Strong Trends

On strong trend days, consider fading swing highs in bull trends and swing lows in bear trends only if there was first a good trend line break and a strong reversal bar. In Figure 17.2, both days were strong trend days with one extreme near the open and then no moving average pullback for over two hours (20 gap bar pullback setups). Bar 4 was a bear reversal bar and a reversal down from the breakout above a trading range following a small reversal up from a breakout below. Also, bar 8 was the first bar of a small two-bar reversal and there was a higher low above bar 7. However, since these are countertrend and there was only minimal countertrend momentum on the trend line breaks, these trades are not strong and should only be scalps. Do not take them if they are distracting you from the with-trend entries, where you should swing much of your position.

Deeper Discussion of This Chart

In Figure 17.2, today opened with a breakout below the bull channel of the final hour of yesterday. A bull channel should always be thought of as a bear flag. The first bar had a bear body, indicating strength by the bears on the open; but the next bar reversed up in an attempt to form a failed breakout and a trend from the open bull day. Instead, the failed breakout failed and led to a breakout pullback short below the fourth bar and again below the low of the opening range. There was a strong two-bar bear spike followed by a protracted bear channel.

Bars 1 and 5 formed a double bottom bull flag, and bar 9 was part of a double top bear flag. Bar 8 was another small double bottom bull flag. Remember, a double bottom bull flag is often just a higher low that is a double bottom.

Bar 4 was a possible top of a channel in a spike and channel bull day, and the market tested down to the bar 1 beginning of the channel. This set up a double bottom bull flag buy setup.

Both bars 5 and 13 were moving average gap bar setups. They were after 11:30 a.m., when there is often a strong countertrend move that traps traders out of the trend and into the wrong direction. This sets up a reliable with-trend trade that usually results in a new extreme and often lasts into the close.

PART III

Trends

A trend is a series of price changes that are mostly either up (a bull trend or a bull) or down (a bear trend or a bear). This is very important when it comes to trading because a trader usually should not be looking to buy unless the market is at least forming a higher low and should not be looking to short unless the market is at least forming a lower high. A trend can be as short as a single bar (remember, a trend bar is made up of a trend on a smaller time frame) or longer than all of the bars on your screen. Trends can be loosely classified into four overlapping and often interchangeable categories: trend, swing, pullback, and leg. The distinctions are just guidelines because each of the three smaller versions is a different version on different time frames. For example, a pullback in a bull trend on a 60 minute chart might be a strong bear trend on a 1 minute chart. Also, each category will contain one or more of the smaller versions. A trend might be made of 10 swings, each containing one to four pullbacks, and each pullback might have one to four legs. Every upswing and downswing of any size is commonly referred to as a leg, so the distinctions are not very important, but each term carries a subtle distinction with it.

At its simplest, a trend is present when the chart on your computer screen starts at one of the two left-hand corners and ends at the diagonally opposite corner of the screen without huge fluctuations in between. For example, if the bars on the left are near the lower left-hand corner of your monitor and the bars on the right are near the upper right-hand corner and there are not many large upswings and downswings in the middle of your screen, then this is a bull trend. Your personal radar can tell you if the market is more likely in a trend instead of in a strong leg within a trading range. If you have a sense of uncertainty, the market is more likely in a trading range. If instead you have a sense of urgency and you are hoping for a pullback, then the market is more likely in a trend.

Trends can be very steep, with a series of trend bars with large bodies, very little overlap between adjacent bars, and small tails. This is the spike phase of a trend, and it can be as brief as a single bar. It is when the market becomes clearly always-in long in the eyes of most traders if the trend is a new bull trend, or always-in short in the case of a new bear trend. The market eventually begins to have some two-sided trading in the form of pullbacks, and the trend then transitions into the channel phase, which can last far longer than most traders expect is possible. Trends can have small spikes with big or small channels, or big spikes with big or small channels. The spikes can have some overlap between the bars and look more like a tight channel, and the channels can be steep with very little overlap between adjacent bars and look more like a large spike. The key point is that most trends tend to be very strong when starting out and then lose momentum as they mature, and the market eventually has larger pullbacks and evolves into a trading range. The trading range is simply a pullback on a higher time frame chart. At some point, the market breaks out into a spike in the opposite direction, and then the market reverses into a trend in the other direction.

A chart only shows one or two trends. If more than two trends are present on a chart, it is preferable to describe the trends by using one of the other three classifications because the two-sided action creates different trading opportunities. Both swings and legs are smaller trends, and there are at least two on the chart. The term *swing* is used when there are two or more smaller trends on the chart, even though the overall chart might be sideways.

A leg is any smaller trend that is part of a larger trend; it can be a pullback (a countertrend move), a swing in a trend or in a sideways market, or a with-trend move that occurs between any two pullbacks within a trend.

A pullback is a temporary countertrend move and is part of a trend, swing, or leg. For example, a bull pullback is a sideways to downward move in a bull trend, swing, or leg that will be followed by at least a test of the prior high. Any bar or series of bars that represents any pause or loss of momentum is a pullback, even if there is no actual backward movement. This includes a single inside bar, which obviously does not extend below the low or above the high of the prior bar. When it is a single bar, the bar is a pause bar or a pullback bar. These one-bar pullbacks are made up of a series of small swings on a smaller time frame chart. However, you might have to go all the way down to a 1 minute chart or a 100 tick or smaller chart to see them. This is a waste of time for a trader, but it is helpful to be aware of the reality because it provides a rationale for considering placing a trade.

Within any trend, there are a number of smaller opposite trends, some lasting for only one or two bars. All of them should be considered as likely to fail and therefore setups for trades in the direction of the larger trend. In a bull trend, the swings should be trending upward, meaning that each pullback should be above the prior pullback and result in a new high (trending highs and lows, or trending swings). All moves with strong momentum usually have at least a test of the extreme following a pullback (all strong moves usually have at least two legs, even if the second one falls short and reverses).

All trends, no matter how small, must first break a trend line from the prior trend or a support or resistance line from a prior trading range, and then have trending swings (e.g., a series of higher highs and lows in a bull trend). Absent either of these, there is no trend. The best risk/reward ratio occurs when you enter on the first pullback after a trend line break, before there is a clearly established trend. As a possible trend day is unfolding, traders should look for signs of strength, each of which increases the odds that the trend will continue.

Why is it important to recognize the existence of a trend? Because then most of your trades should be in that direction and you must try to take every with-trend entry and rarely take countertrend entries. Depending on how you define a trend and a reversal attempt, about 80 percent of attempts to reverse a trend will fail. Markets have inertia and tend to continue what they have just been doing. Because of this inertia, it makes far more mathematical sense to wait for the reversal attempt to fail and become simply a pullback in the trend and then enter in the direction of the trend. Incidentally, market inertia also means that if a market is in a trading range, it will resist breaking into a trend and about 80 percent of breakout attempts will fail.

The earlier you see the trend, the more money you stand to make. Focusing on the countertrend setups will likely make you miss the much more profitable but often scarier with-trend entries. The with-trend entries are scary because the market always looks overdone and it's hard to imagine that selling near the low of an overdone bear or buying near the high of an overdone bull could ever be profitable. However, that is exactly why it is! For example, in a bear trend, no one is sure if there is going to be a bounce where they can sell at a better price but everyone is sure that the market will be even lower very soon. Because of this, everyone is selling at the market or on tiny pullbacks, and larger pullbacks just don't materialize. The longs need to get out at any price and the bears want to get in at any price, because both believe the market is heading lower and they don't want to risk missing it while they wait or hope for a bounce.

When a trend is especially strong, there is usually follow-through over the next one or more days. For example, if today was a huge bull trend day, especially if it was a reversal or a breakout and a possible start of a big move, the day will usually close near its high and the next day will also usually have a close above its open. This may continue for several days in a row. The opens often have sharp sell-offs that trap bulls out and bears in but usually find support at the 15 or 60 minute moving average or at some other support level (these are discussed in the section on support and resistance in book 2).

A trend is an area of relative certainty, where the odds are greater than 50–50 that the market will move X ticks further before it moves X ticks in the opposite direction. A trend is a series of spikes alternating with small trading ranges, and during each brief spike phase, the odds are better than 50–50, but in each trading range phase, uncertainty increases and the odds hover around 50–50 again. One of the difficulties in trading a trend is that the spike phases are often brief, and by the time you realize that one exists, there may not be enough ticks left with those increased odds to make a profit. Before you know it, a trading range forms and the odds are back to 50–50. One of the best ways to trade a trend is to anticipate when the next spike will begin and to enter on a stop as it is starting. That way, you can catch a spike with maybe a 60 percent probability or even higher of making X ticks before losing X ticks, and if you become proficient at this, you will be a successful trader.

Big traders don't hesitate to enter a trend during its spike phase, because they expect significant follow-through, even if there is a pullback immediately after their entry. If a pullback occurs, they increase the size of their position. For example, if there is a strong bull breakout lasting several bars, more and more institutions become convinced that the market has become always-in long with each new higher tick, and as they become convinced that the market will go higher, they start buying. This makes the spike grow very quickly. They have many ways to enter, like buying at the market, buying a one- or two-tick pullback, buying above the prior bar on a stop, or buying on a breakout above a prior swing high. It does not matter how they get in, because their focus is to get at least a small position on, and then look to buy more as the market moves higher, or if it pulls back. Because they will add on as the market goes higher, the spike can extend for many bars. A beginning trader sees the growing spike and wonders how anyone could be buying at the top of such a huge move. What they don't understand is that the institutions are so confident that the market will soon be higher that they will buy all the way up, because they don't want to miss the move while waiting for a pullback to form. The beginner is also afraid that his stop would have to be below the bottom of the spike, or at least below its midpoint, which is far away. The institutions know this, and simply adjust their position size down to a level where their dollars at risk are the same as for any other trade.

In every trend, no matter how strong, the market eventually pulls back a little. For example, if there is a strong bull breakout, or a trend from the open bull, where there is a bull spike made of four consecutive large bull trend bars with small tails, and then the fifth bar falls below the low of the prior bar, this is a pullback. If everyone is looking to buy a pullback, why would one ever develop? It is because not everyone is looking to buy. Experienced traders who bought early on look for price levels to take partial profits (they will begin to scale out of their longs), and sometimes they will sell out of their entire positions. These are not the bulls who are looking to buy a few ticks lower on the first pullback. The traders who are taking partial or full profits are afraid of a reversal, or of a deeper pullback, which would allow them to buy again many ticks lower. If they believed that the pullback was only going to last for a few ticks, and then the bull was going to resume, they never would have exited. They always take their profits at some resistance level, like a measured move target, a trend line, a trend channel line, or at the bottom of a trading range above the market. Most of the trading is done by computers, so everything has a mathematical basis, which means that the profit-taking targets are based on the prices that anyone can see on their screens. With practice, traders can learn to spot areas where the computers might take profits, and they can take their profits at the same prices, expecting a pullback to follow.

Sometimes the spike will have a bar or a pattern that will allow aggressive bears to take a small scalp, if they think that the pullback is imminent and that there is enough room for a profitable short. However, most traders who attempt this will lose, because most of the pullbacks do not fall far enough for a profit, or the trader's equation is weak (the probability of making their scalp times the size of the profit is smaller than the probability of losing times the size of their protective stop). Also, traders who take the short are hoping so much for their small profit that they invariably end up missing the much more profitable long that forms a few minutes later.

Some traders don't like to buy spikes because they don't like to risk too much. They prefer to feel like they are buying at a better price (a discount). These value bulls will only buy pullbacks and will wait for one to form. Other bulls who missed the initial buy or did not buy enough during the spike eagerly wait for the first pullback to buy or to add to their positions. They place limit orders at and below the low of the prior bar, hoping for a small dip, so that they can get long. Because of this, the first pullback usually only falls below the low of the prior bar by a few ticks. When the bulls are particularly aggressive, they will buy above the low of the prior bar, and what appeared to be a bar that would become a pullback bar might instead not fall below the low of the prior bar.

If the bulls holding profitable longs think that the bull spike is weakening and that the next bar will trade below the low of the current bar, some will sell out of their longs at the market. Others will wait for the bar to close, and if the bar is not another strong bull trend bar, they will sell at the close of the bar, realizing that they might be selling too early, but happy with being able to sell at a high price. Eventually, there will be a true pullback bar, with a low below the low of the prior bar. Once there is, other bulls will place stop orders to buy above its high, because this bar is a high 1 buy setup in a strong bull spike and therefore a high probability buy setup. Some traders prefer to buy on stops above bars and not limit orders below bars because they want the market going in their direction when they enter, so that they will have the wind at their backs instead of in their faces. They are willing to exchange some of their potential profits for a higher probability of success. Both approaches are reasonable, if the trader's equation is favorable for their trades. Bull trends on higher time frame charts tend to have rallies in the final 30 to 60 minutes of trading on the 5 minute chart. Some of the buying is from mutual funds and some is from short covering, but much of it is simply statistically based program trading where the programmers have testing that shows that buying into the close in a bull trend is a profitable strategy. The strong finish often pushes the close above the open of the day. The result is a bull trend bar on the daily chart. When the market is in a bull trend, look for buy setups in the final hour. Likewise, when the daily chart is in a bear trend, look for sell setups in the final hour, as the 5 minute chart will often sell off into the close, causing the bar on the daily chart to be a bear trend bar.

The most recent bars are at the top of your computer screen in a bull trend and at the bottom in a bear trend, and psychologically there does not appear to be any more room for the market to go further. The result is that many traders won't take a great buy signal at the top of a bull trend or sell signal at the bottom of a bear trend and will instead look for reversals. But that computer screen illusion has nothing to do with the market and if you can add space above or below the chart, there suddenly will be lots of room for the trend to run. The market draws in countertrend traders, and if you enter in the direction of the trend exactly where they exit at a loss, they will drive the market in your direction, even though the market looks so overextended.

A move above a prior swing high in a bull trend will lead to predominantly one of three outcomes: more buying, profit taking (by far the most common possibility), or shorting. When the trend is strong, strong bulls will buy the breakout above the old high (they are "pressing," or adding to, their longs) and there will be a measured move up of some kind. For example, if a bull trend forms a wedge top, but then breaks above the top of the wedge, if enough bulls are pressing their long, the market will often go up for a measured move that is equal to the height of the wedge. The bears will quickly see how strong the breakout is and will buy back their shorts. This urgent short covering adds fuel to the breakout and contributes to the size of the bull spike. The strong bears who were shorting during the wedge top will now see that their premise is wrong. They will expect about a measured move up and will quickly buy back their losing shorts and not consider shorting again for several bars and probably not until the market tests some resistance area, like the measured move target. This often leads to a strong bull breakout lasting one or more bars, with follow-through over the next several bars. If the move up is very strong, the bears might not look to sell again for dozens of bars and possibly even for the rest of the day.

Whenever the market goes up far enough above the breakout to enable a trader to make at least a profitable scalp before there is a pullback, then assume that there was mostly new buying at the high. If it goes sideways, assume that there was profit taking and that the bulls are looking to buy again a little lower. If the market reverses down hard, assume that the strong bears dominated at the new high and that the market will likely trade down for at least a couple of legs and at least 10 bars.

In the absence of some rare, dramatic news event, traders don't suddenly switch from extremely bullish to extremely bearish. There is a gradual transition. A trader becomes less bullish, then neutral, and then bearish. Once enough traders make this transition, the market reverses into a deeper correction or into a bear trend. Every firm has its own measure of excess, and at some point enough firms decide that the trend has gone too far. They believe that there is little risk of missing a great move up if they stop buying above the old high, and they will buy only on pullbacks. If the market hesitates above the old high, the market is becoming two-sided, and the strong bulls are using the new high to take profits.

Profit taking means that traders are still bullish and are looking to buy a pullback. Most new highs are followed by profit taking. Every new high is a potential top, but most reversal attempts fail and become the beginnings of bull flags, only to be followed by another new high. If a rally to test the high has several small pullbacks within the leg up, with lots of overlapping bars, several bear bodies, and big tails on the tops of the bars, and most of the bull trend bars are weak, then the market is becoming increasingly two-sided. The bulls are taking profits at the tops of the bars and buying only at the bottoms of the bars, and the bears are beginning to short at the tops of the bars. Similarly, the bulls are taking profits as the market approaches the top of the bull trend, and the bears are shorting more. If the market goes above the bull high, it is likely that the profit taking and shorting will be even stronger.

Most traders do not like to reverse, so if they are anticipating a reversal signal, they prefer to exit their longs and then wait for that signal. The loss of these bulls on the final leg up in the trend contributes to the weakness of the rally to the final high. If there is a strong reversal down after the market breaks above the prior high, the strong bears are taking control of the market, at least for the near term. Once that happens, then the bulls who were hoping to buy a small pullback believe instead that the market will fall further. They therefore wait to buy until there is a much larger pullback, and their absence of buying allows the bears to drive the market down into a deeper correction, lasting 10 or more bars and often having two or more legs.

There is one situation where the breakout in a bull trend is routinely met by aggressive shorts who will usually take over the market. A pullback is a minor trend in the opposite direction, and traders expect it to end soon and for the larger trend to resume. When there is a pullback in a strong bear trend, the market will often have two legs up in the minor bull trend. As the market goes above the high of the first leg up, it is breaking out above a prior swing high in a minor bull trend. However, since most traders will see the move up as a pullback that will end very soon, the dominant traders on the breakout will usually be aggressive sellers, instead of aggressive new buyers or profit-taking longs, and the minor bull trend will usually reverse back down into the direction of the major bear trend after breaking out above the first or second swing high in the pullback.

The same is true of new lows in a bear trend. When the bear trend is strong, strong bears will press their shorts by adding to their positions on the breakout to a new low and the market will continue to fall until it reaches some measured move target. As the trend weakens, the price action at a new low will be less clear, which means that the strong bears are using the new low as an area to take profits on their shorts rather than as an area to add to their shorts. As the bear trend further loses strength, eventually the strong bulls will see a new low as a great price to initiate longs and they will be able to create a reversal pattern and then a significant rally.

As a trend matures, it usually transitions into a trading range, but the first trading ranges that form are usually followed by a continuation of the trend. How do the strong bulls and bears act as a trend matures? In a bull trend, when the trend is strong, the pullbacks are small because the strong bulls want to buy more on a pullback. Since they suspect that there may not be a pullback until the market is much higher, they begin to buy in pieces, but relentlessly. They look for any reason to buy, and with so many big traders in the market, there will be some buying for every imaginable reason. They place limit orders to buy a few ticks down and other limit orders to buy a few ticks above the low of the prior bar, at the low of the prior bar, and below the low of the prior bar. They place stop orders to buy above the high of the prior bar and on a breakout above any prior swing high. They also buy on the close of both any bull or bear trend bar. They see the bear trend bar as a brief opportunity to buy at a better price and the bull trend bar as a sign that the market is about to move up quickly.

The strong bears are smart and they see what is going on. Since they believe, just like the strong bulls, that the market is going to be higher before long, it does not make sense for them to be shorting. They just step aside and wait until they can sell higher. How much higher? Each institution has its own measure of excess, but once the market gets to a price level where enough bear firms believe that it might not go any higher, they will begin to short. If enough of them short around the same price level, more and larger bear trend bars form and bars start to get tails on the tops. These are signs of selling pressure and they tell all traders that the bulls are becoming weaker and the bears are becoming stronger. The strong bulls eventually stop buying above the last swing high and instead begin to take profits as the market goes to a new high. They are still bullish but are becoming selective and will buy only on pullbacks. As the two-sided trading increases and the sell-offs have more bear trend bars and last for more bars, the strong bulls will want to buy only at the bottom of the developing trading range and will look to take profits at the top. The strong bears begin to short at new highs and they are now willing to scale in higher. They might take partial profits near the bottom of the developing trading range if they think that the market might reverse back up and break out to a new high, but they will keep looking to short new highs. At some point, the market becomes a 50–50 market and neither the bulls nor bears are in control; eventually the bears become dominant, a bear trend begins, and the opposite process unfolds.

A trend that has gone on for 30 or more bars will often have an unusually strong breakout, but it can be an exhaustive climax. For example, in a protracted bull trend, all strong bulls and bears love to see a large bull trend bar or two, especially if it is exceptionally large, because they expect it to be a brief, unusually great opportunity. Once the market is close to where the strong bulls and bears want to sell, like near a measured move target or a trend channel line, especially if the move is the second or third consecutive buy climax, they step aside. The absence of selling by the strongest traders results in a vacuum above the market, which creates one or two relatively large bull trend bars. This bull spike is just the sign that the strong traders have been waiting for, and once it is there, they appear as if out of nowhere and begin their selling. The bulls take profits on their longs and the bears initiate new shorts. Both sell aggressively at the close of the bar, above its high, at the close of the next bar (especially if it is a weaker bar), and at the close of the following bar, especially if the bars are starting to have bear bodies. They also sell below the low of the prior bar. When they see a strong bear trend bar, they sell at its close and below its low. Both the bulls and the bears expect a larger correction, and the bulls will not consider buying again until at least a 10-bar, two-legged correction, and even then, only if the sell-off looks weak. The bears expect the same sell-off and will not be eager to take profits too early.

Weak traders see that large bull trend bar in the opposite way. The weak bulls, who had been sitting on the sidelines hoping for an easy pullback to buy, see the market running away from them and want to make sure they catch this next leg up, especially since the bar is so strong and the day is almost over. The weak bears, who shorted early and maybe scaled in, were terrified by the rapidity with which the bar broke to a new high. They are afraid of relentless follow-through buying, so they buy back their shorts. These weak traders are trading on emotion and are competing against computers, which do not have emotion as one of the variables in their algorithms. Since the computers control the market, the emotions of the weak traders doom them to big losses on big bull trend bars at the end of an overdone bull trend.

Once a strong bull begins to have pullbacks that are relatively large, the pullbacks, which are always small trading ranges, behave more like trading ranges than bull flags. The direction of the breakout becomes less certain and traders begin to think that a downside breakout is about as likely as an upside breakout. A new high is now a breakout attempt above a trading range, and the odds are that it will fail. Likewise, once a strong bear trend begins to have relatively large pullbacks, those pullbacks behave more like trading ranges than bear flags, and therefore a new low is an attempt to break below a trading range and the odds are that it will fail.

Every trading range is within either a bull trend or a bear trend. Once the two-sided trading is strong enough to create the trading range, the trend is no longer strong, at least while the trading range is in effect. There will always be a breakout from the range eventually, and if it is to the upside and it is very strong, the market is in a strong bull trend. If it is to the downside and strong, the market is in a strong bear trend.

Once the bears are strong enough to push a pullback well below the bull trend line and the moving average, they are confident enough that the market will likely not go much higher and they will aggressively short above the old high. At this point, the bulls will have decided that they should buy only a deep pullback. A new mind-set is now dominant at the new high. It is no longer a place to buy, because it no longer represents much strength. Yes, there is profit taking by the bulls, but most big traders now look at the new high as a great opportunity to initiate shorts. The market has reached the tipping point and most traders have stopped looking to buy small pullbacks and instead are looking to sell rallies. The bears are dominant and the strong selling will likely lead to a large correction or even a trend reversal. After the next strong push down, the bears will look for a lower high to sell again or to add to their short positions, and the bulls who bought the pullback will become concerned that the trend might have reversed or at least that there will be a much larger pullback. Instead of hoping for a new bull high to take profits on their longs, they will now take profits at a lower high and not look to buy again until after a larger correction.

There will still be bulls who bought much lower and want to give the bull trend every possible chance to resume. Traders know that most reversal attempts fail, and many who rode the trend up will not exit their longs until after the bears have demonstrated the ability to push the market down hard. Many longs bought puts to protect themselves in case of a severe reversal. The puts allow them to hold on to give the bull trend every possible chance to resume. They know that the puts limit their losses, no matter how far the market might fall, but once they see this impressive selling pressure, they will then look for a rally to finally exit their longs, and as that rally begins, they will take profits on their puts. Also, most of their puts expire within a few months, and once expired, the traders no longer have downside protection. This means that they cannot continue to hold on to their positions unless they keep buying more and more puts. If they believe that the market will likely fall further and not rally again for many months, it does not make sense to continue to pay for ongoing put protection. Instead, they will look to sell out of their positions. Their supply will limit the rally, and their selling, added to the shorting by aggressive bears and the profit taking by bulls who saw the sell-off as a buying opportunity, will create a second leg down.

These persistent bulls will each have a price level on the downside that, if reached, will make them want to exit on the next rally. As the market keeps working lower, more and more of these bulls will decide that the bull trend will not resume anytime soon and that the trend might have reversed into a bear trend. These remaining die-hard longs will wait patiently for a pullback in the bear swing to exit their longs, and their positions represent a supply that is overhanging the market. They sell below the most recent swing high because they doubt that the market will be able to get above a prior swing high, and are happy to get out at any price above the most recent low. Bears will also look for a pullback from each new low to add to their shorts and place new shorts. The result is a series of lower highs and lows, which is the definition of a bear trend.

If the market enters a bear trend, the process will reverse. When the bear trend is strong, traders will short below prior lows. As the trend weakens, the bears will take profits at new lows and the market will likely enter a trading range. After a strong rally above the bull trend line and the moving average, the bears will take profits at a new low and strong bulls will aggressively buy and try to take control of the market. The result will be a larger bear rally or possibly a reversal into a bull trend.

A similar situation occurs when there is a pullback that is large enough to make traders wonder if the trend has reversed. For example, if there is a deep, sharp pullback in a bull trend, traders will begin to look at moves below prior swing lows, but this is in the context of a pullback in a bull trend instead of as part of a bear trend. They will watch what happens as the market falls below a prior swing low. Will the market fall far enough for bears, who entered on a sell stop below that swing low, to make a profit? Did the new low find more sellers than buyers? If it did, that is a sign that the bears are strong and that the pullback will probably go further. The trend might even have reversed to down.

Another possibility on the breakout to a new low is that the market enters a trading range, which is evidence that the shorts took profits and that there was unimpressive buying by the bulls. The final alternative is that the market reverses up after the breakout to a new low. This means that there were strong bulls below that swing low just waiting for the market to test there. This is a sign that the sell-off is more likely just a big pullback in an ongoing bull trend. The shorts from higher up took profits on the breakout to the new low because they believed that the trend was still upward. The strong bulls bought aggressively because they believed that the market would not fall further and that it would rally to test the bull high.

Whenever there is any breakout below a swing low, traders will watch carefully for evidence that the bulls have returned or that the bears have taken control. They need to decide what influence is greatest at the new low, and they use the market's behavior to make that decision. If there is a strong breakout, then new selling is dominant. If the market's movement is uncertain, then profit taking by the shorts and weak buying by the bulls is taking place, and the market will likely enter a trading range. If there is a strong reversal up, then aggressive buying by the longs is the most important factor.

This part of the book describes many common trend patterns that you should look for every day. Although a trend can begin with any bar during the day, the majority of trend days begin within the first hour or so. If you see a trend pattern setting up within the first hour or two of the day, there will likely be several high-probability with-trend trades that you can then make. You need to decide many times every day if the day resembles any of the types of trends described later in this chapter, and if it does, force yourself to take the with-trend trades.

However, if none of these patterns is present, the day is a trading range day and you need to look for opportunities to fade new extremes. Also, if the market makes a run for a couple of hours and the day appears to be a trading range day, be aware that the opposite extreme might get taken out over the course of the next couple of hours, so do not be too eager to take profits on the swing portion of your reversal trade. The odds are very high that the reversal will at least test the midpoint of the day's range.

After a substantial decline in a bear market on the daily chart, people begin to become very concerned about the money that they've lost and they do not want to lose any more money. This makes them sell, regardless of the fundamentals. There was an added problem in the bear market of 2008. Baby boomers were on the verge of retiring and were shocked by what they saw as comfortable nest eggs quickly falling 40 percent in value. So what will they do? They will continue to sell every rally as they try to preserve what they have left. Also, all that money that they are taking out of the market will never return to lift prices again. They will take their money at all the "Thank you, God" points along the way. This will be just below the prior swing high, where they exit and promise God that they will never buy again in return for Him letting them recoup some of their losses. This creates a series of lower highs and lows until the last bear has sold. Once that happens, the market will then be able to rally above the prior swing highs.

The result of people selling regardless of fundamentals is that the market often falls in huge bear trend days, dropping much further than what the fundamentals warrant, and often there is a huge plunge in the final 30 minutes as funds are forced to sell because of redemption orders. There will be vicious rallies along the way as people become convinced that the bottom is in and they panic to get back long. Also, because the trend is so clearly down, there will be many who are short. They may cover aggressively on any reversal, resulting in huge bull trend bars on the daily chart, even though it is still a bear market. The end result is a collection of very large range days once the bear trend is well underway. The huge ranges offer great price action day trading opportunities but you might have to increase your stop size and therefore reduce your position size. While many people following the daily charts are selling at the low and buying at the high of each trap (every strong short covering rally), trading off emotion more than reason, a good price action trader can do very well just looking for standard price action setups.

This kind of mentality is not restricted to unsophisticated investors. In the fall of 2008, most hedge funds were down on the year and their sophisticated investors aggressively pulled their money out as the market continued to sell off. The hedge funds had to continue to liquidate on every small rally to meet redemptions and anticipated redemptions. This continued to drive the market down, independent of fundamentals, and just like with less sophisticated investors, the selling will continue until all that's left are positions that investors will hold until they fall to zero.

Also, for many hedge fund managers a big part of their income is incentive based. For example, every quarter that the fund closes at a new high, they might take 20 percent of that profit above the old equity high. If the fund instead is down 30 percent on the year, it will need to earn about 50 percent to get up to that incentive level again. Rather than working for free for several years, it might make more sense to close the fund and start over with a new fund. However, when they close the fund, they have to liquidate and since there is no incentive for them, they can liquidate at any price, no matter how low. This adds to selling that is independent of the intrinsic value of stocks. If they had a $1 billion fund, their new fund is starting from scratch and it will take a few years before they have enough equity and own as much stock as they did in the old fund, so buying by the new funds doesn't immediately lift the market.

When the volatility reaches an extremely high level, the end of the bear trend is often near as traders give up responding to the whipsaws and decide that there is nothing left that they will sell at any price. When there are no more sellers and the market is overdone on the basis of fundamentals, a good rally should follow. And just how far can a big-name stock fall in a bear market? Much farther than you might think, even for the bluest of the blue chips. Cisco (CSCO) lost 90 percent of its value in three years after the tech wreck of 2000, and Apple (AAPL) lost 95 percent of its value during the six years starting in 1991. General Motors (GM) lost 90 percent in the seven years after 2001. So don't be eager to buy just because a stock is down a Fibonacci 38 percent, 50 percent, or even 62 percent. Wait until there is a price action setup, and it must include a prior break of the bear trend line.

CHAPTER 18

Example of How to Trade a Trend

When the market is in a trend, traders should look for any reason to enter. The simple existence of a trend is reason enough to enter at least a small position at the market. Here are some other reasonable approaches that use stop entry orders:

- Buying a high 2 pullback to the moving average in a bull trend.
- Selling a low 2 pullback to the moving average in a bear trend.
- Buying a wedge bull flag pullback in a bull trend.
- Selling a wedge bear flag pullback in a bear trend.
- Buying a breakout pullback after a breakout from a bull flag in a bull trend.
- Selling a breakout pullback after a breakout from a bear flag in a bear trend.
- Buying a high 1 pullback in a strong bull spike in a bull trend, but not after a buy climax.
- Selling a low 1 pullback in a strong bear spike in a bear trend, but not after a sell climax.
- When a bull trend is very strong, buying on a stop above a prior swing high.
- When a bear trend is very strong, selling on a stop below a prior swing low.

Entering using a limit order requires more experience reading charts, because the trader is entering in a market that is going in the opposite direction to the trade. However, experienced traders can reliably use limit or market orders with these potential setups:

- Buying a bull spike in a strong bull breakout at the market, at the close of every bull trend bar in the spike, or on a limit order at or below the low of the prior bar (entering in spikes requires a wider stop and the spike happens quickly, so this combination is difficult for many traders).

- Selling a bear spike in a strong bear breakout at the market, at the close of every bear trend bar in the spike, or on a limit order at or above the high of the prior bar (entering in spikes is difficult for many traders).
- Buying the close of the first bear bar in a bull spike.
- Selling the close of the first bull bar in a bear spike.
- In a bull trend, buying at a bull trend line or at a prior swing low (a potential double bottom bull flag).
- In a bear trend, selling at a bear trend line or at a prior swing high (a potential double top bear flag).
- Buying at or below a low 1 or 2 weak signal bar on a limit order in a possible new bull trend after a strong reversal up or at the bottom of a trading range.
- Shorting at or above a high 1 or 2 weak signal bar on a limit order in a possible new bear trend after a strong reversal down or at the top of a trading range.
- Buying at or below the prior bar on a limit order in a quiet bull flag at the moving average.
- Shorting at or above the prior bar on a limit order in a quiet bear flag at the moving average.
- Buying below a bull bar that breaks above a bull flag, anticipating a breakout pullback.
- Selling above a bear bar that breaks below a bear flag, anticipating a breakout pullback.
- When trying for a swing in a bull trend, buy or buy more on a breakout test, which is an attempt to run breakeven stops from an earlier long entry.
- When trying for a swing in a bear trend, sell or sell more on a breakout test, which is an attempt to hit breakeven stops from an earlier short entry.
- Buying at a fixed number of ticks down from the high in a bull trend. For example, buying a two-, three-, or four-point pullback in a bull trend in the Emini when the average daily range has been about 12 points. Also, if the biggest pullback in the first couple of hours was 10 ticks, buying about an eight- to 12-tick pullback.
- Selling at a fixed number ticks up from the low in a bear trend. For example, selling a 50 cent bear rally in GS when the average daily range has been about $2.00. If the largest pullback in the first couple of hours was 60 cents, selling about a 50 to 70 cent pullback.
- Scaling into the direction of the trend as the market moves against you. If you scale in, plan out in advance what size each order has to be to keep your total risk the same as with a typical trade. It is easy to find yourself with too large a position and a protective stop that is too far away, so be very careful.

- In a bull trend that has not pulled back to the moving average in 20 or more bars, buy at the moving average on a limit order, and scale in lower. For example, if there is a strong bull trend in the Emini where the market has been above the moving average for 20 or more bars, buy with a limit order at one tick above the moving average. Buy more one, two, and maybe three points lower. If scaling in, consider exiting the entire position at the first entry price, but if the bull trend is strong, look to exit on a test of the high.
- In a bear trend that has not pulled back to the moving average in 20 or more bars, sell at the moving average on a limit order and scale in higher. For example, if there is a strong bear trend in the Emini where the market has been below the moving average for 20 or more bars, sell with a limit order at one tick below the moving average. Sell more one, two, and maybe three points higher. If scaling in, consider exiting the entire position at the first entry price, but if the bear trend is strong, look to exit on a test of the low.
- In a strong bull trend, buy on the close of the first bear trend bar that has a close below the moving average.
- In a strong bear trend, sell on the close of the first bull trend bar that has a close above the moving average.
- In a strong bull trend, a pullback is a small bear trend. The bulls will expect that a breakout below a prior swing low in this small bear trend will fail, and they will buy there with a limit order.
- In a strong bear trend, a pullback is a small bull trend. The bears will expect that a breakout above a prior swing high in this small bull trend will fail, and they will short there with a limit order.
- A trader can always be long, short, or flat. At any moment during a trend, only two of those choices are compatible with being a successful trader. If the market is in a bull trend, successful traders are only long or flat. If it is in a bear trend, they are either short or flat. A tiny fraction of traders have the ability to consistently make money by trading against a trend, and you should assume that you are not part of that group. Unfortunately, most traders starting out go for years believing that they are, and they consistently lose money month after month and wonder why. You now know the answer.

Every type of market does something to make trading difficult. The market is filled with very smart people who are trying as hard to take money from your account as you are trying to take money from theirs, so nothing is ever easy. This includes making profits in a strong trend. When the market is trending strongly with large trend bars, the risk is great because the stop often belongs beyond the start of the spike. Also, the spike grows quickly, and many traders are so shocked by the size and speed of the breakout that they are unable to quickly reduce their position size and increase their stop size, and instead watch the trend move rapidly as they hope for a pullback. Once the trend enters its channel phase, it always looks like it is reversing. For example, in a bull trend, there will be many reversal attempts, but almost all quickly evolve into bull flags. Most bull channels will have weak buy signal bars and the signals will force bulls to buy at the top of the weak channel. This is a low probability long trade, even though the market is continuing up. Swing traders who are comfortable taking low probability buy setups near the top of weak bull channels love this kind of price action, because they can make many times what they are risking, and this more than makes up for the relatively low probability of success. However, it is difficult for most traders to buy low probability setups near the top of a weak bull channel. Traders who only want to take high probability trades often sit back and watch the trend grind higher for many bars, because there may not be a high probability entry for 20 or more bars. The result is that they see the market going up and want to be long, but miss the entire trend. They only want a high probability trade, like a high 2 pullback to the moving average. If they do not get an acceptable pullback, they will continue to wait and miss the trend. This is acceptable because traders should always stay in their comfort one. If they are only comfortable taking high probability stop entries, then they are correct in waiting. The channel will not last forever, and they will soon find acceptable setups. Experienced traders buy on limit orders around and below the lows of prior bars, and they will sometimes take some short scalps during the bull channel. Both can be high probability trades, including the shorts, if there is a strong bear reversal bar at a resistance level, and some reason to think that a pullback is imminent.

With so many great ways to make money, why do most traders lose? It is because there are even more ways to make mistakes. One of the most common is that a trader begins with one plan and, once in the trade, manages it based on a different plan. For example, if a trader just lost on his past two long swing trades and now buys a third, he might be so afraid of losing again that he scalps out, only to watch the trade turn into a huge trend. Swing traders need these big wins to make up for the losses, since swing trading often is less than 50 percent successful. If traders do not hold on for the swing, they will not be getting the big wins that they need, and they will lose money. Something opposite to this can happen to scalpers. They might have taken a profitable scalp, but became sad when the trade turned into a huge trend and they watched from the sidelines. When they see another scalp, they take it, but once it reaches their profit target, they decide that the trade could turn into a swing trade, just like last time, and they do not exit. A few minutes later, the market comes back, hits their stop, and they take a loss. This is because most scalps are high-probability trades, and when the edge is large and obvious, the move is usually small and brief, and not the start of a big swing. The best way to make money is to have a sound strategy, and then stick to the plan. For most beginning traders, the plan should be some kind of swing trade, because the winning percentage needed to be a successful scalper is much higher than most traders can maintain for the long term.

Once traders take a position, they then have to decide how to manage it. The most important decision that they have to make is whether they are looking for a scalp or for a swing, both of which are discussed in detail in the second book, as is trade management. Only the most experienced traders should consider scalping, because the risk is sometimes greater than the potential reward. This means that they have to win about 70 percent of the time, which is impossible for anyone except an extremely good trader. You should assume that you will never be that good, because that is the reality. However, you can still be a very profitable trader. If traders are trading the Eminis at a time when the average daily range is about 10 to 15 points, they generally have to risk about two points. For example, if they are buying in a bull trend, their protective stop should be about two points below their entry price. Alternatively, their stop can be one tick below the low of the signal bar, which usually is still about two points. Some traders will risk five points or more on a swing trade if they feel confident that the trend will eventually resume. This can be a profitable approach for traders who understand the trader's equation: trade only when the chance of success times the potential reward is significantly greater than the chance of failure times the risk.

If a trader is scalping, then he is trying to make between one and three points on the trade. However, some scalpers think that two- and three-point trades are small swings, and consider a scalp to be a one-point trade. Although there are many trades every day where a trader can risk two points to make one point and have an 80 percent chance of success, there are many other setups that look similar but have only a 50 percent chance of success. The problem that most traders have is distinguishing between the two, and even a couple of mistakes a day can mean the difference between making money and losing money. Most traders simply cannot draw the distinction in real time, and end up losing money if they scalp. A trader who scalps only the two or three best setups a day and trades enough volume might be able to make a living as a scalper, but he might also find it difficult to watch the market for hours and be ready to quickly place a trade when one of the rare, brief setups unfolds.

The better way for beginning traders to make money is to swing their trades. They can enter all at once, or can press their trades by scaling in as the market continues in their direction. This means that they are adding to their positions as their earlier entries have growing profits. They can either exit all at once, or scale out as the trade goes their way. For example, if they buy early in a bull trend, their initial stop is two points, and they are confident that the trade will work, they should assume that the probability of success is at least 60 percent. Because of that, they should not take any profits until the trade has gone at least two points. The mathematics of trading are discussed in the second book. A trader should exit a trade only when the chance of success (here, 60 percent or higher) times the potential reward is significantly greater than the chance of failure (here, 40 percent or less) times the risk. Since the protective stop is two points below the entry price, the risk is two points. This means that the trader's equation begins to become favorable only when the reward is two points or more. Therefore, if traders take a smaller profit, they will lose money over time, unless they believe that their probability of success is about 80 percent, which is rarely the case. When it is, an experienced trader can scalp part out at a one-point profit and still make money while using a two-point stop. Most traders should never risk more than their reward.

So, how should traders swing their trades in that bull trend? This is addressed more in the second book. Swing trading is much more difficult than it appears when a trader looks at a chart at the end of the day. Swing setups tend to be either unclear or clear but scary. After a trader sees a reasonable setup, he has to take the trade. These setups almost always appear less certain than scalp setups, and the lower probability tends to make traders wait. A trend begins with a breakout either from a trading range or after a reversal of the current trend. When there is a potential reversal and it has a strong signal bar, it usually comes when the old trend is moving fast in a strong, final, climactic spike. Beginning traders invariably believe that the old trend is still in effect, and they probably lost on several earlier countertrend trades today and don't want to lose any more money. Their denial causes them to miss the early entry on the trend reversal. Entering as the breakout bar is forming, or after it closes, is difficult to do because the breakout spike is often large, and traders have to quickly decide to risk much more than they usually do. As a result, they often end up choosing to wait for a pullback. Even if they reduce their position size so that the dollar risk is the same as with any other trade, the thought of risking two or three times as many ticks frightens them. Entering on a pullback is difficult because every pullback begins with a minor reversal, and they are concerned that the pullback might be the start of a deep correction, their stop will be hit, and they will lose money. They end up waiting until the day is almost over. When they finally decide that the trend is clear, there is no longer any time left to place a trade. Trends do everything that they can to keep traders out, which is the only way they can keep traders chasing the market all day. When a setup is easy and clear, meaning it has a high probability of success, the move is usually a small, fast scalp. If the move is going to go a long way, it has to be unclear and difficult to take, to keep traders on the sidelines and force them to chase the trend.

Since a bull trend has trending highs and lows, then every time the market reaches a new high, traders should raise their protective stop to one tick below the most recent low. This is called trailing their stop. Also, if their profit is large enough, they should consider taking partial profits as the market goes above the most recent high. Lots of traders do this and that is why trends often pull back after reaching a new high. The pullback very often goes below the original entry price, and inexperienced swing traders will have tightened their stops to the breakeven price and will get stopped out of a great trend trade. Once the market tests the original entry price and then goes to a new high, most traders would then raise their stops to at least their entry price because they would not want the market to come back to test it a second time after reaching a new high following the first test. Others would put it below the low of the pullback that just tested their original entry.

Some traders will allow pullbacks below the signal bar as long as they believe that their premise of a bull trend is still valid. For example, assume that the average range in the Emini has been about 10 to 15 points lately, and they bought a high 2 pullback in a bull trend on the 5 minute chart. If the signal bar was two points tall, they might be willing to hold on to their position even if the market falls below the low of the signal bar, thinking that the pullback might evolve into a high 3, which is a wedge bull flag buy setup. Other traders would exit if the market falls below the signal bar and then buy again if a strong high 3 buy signal sets up. Some might even buy a position that is twice as large as their first, because they see the strong second signal as more reliable. Many of these traders would have bought just a half-size position on the high 2 buy signal if they thought that the signal did not look quite right. They were allowing for the possibility of the high 2 failing and then evolving into a wedge bull flag, which might even look stronger. If it turned out to be, they would then feel comfortable trading their usual full size.

Other traders trade half size when they see questionable signals, exit if their protective stop is hit, and then take the second signal with a full size if the signal is strong. Traders who scale in as a trade goes against them obviously do not use the signal bar extreme for their initial protective stop, and many look to scale in exactly where other traders are taking losses on their protective stops. Some simply use a wide stop. For example, when the average daily range in the Emini is less than about 15 points, a pullback in a trend is rarely more than seven points. Some traders will consider that the trend is still in effect unless the market falls more than between 50 to 75 percent of the average daily range. As long as a pullback is within their tolerance, they will hold their position and assume that their premise is correct. If they bought a pullback in a bull trend and their entry was three points below the high of the day, then they might risk five points. Since they believe that the trend is still in effect, they believe that they have a 60 percent or better chance of an equidistant move. This means that they are at least 60 percent certain that the market will go up at least five points before falling five points to their protective stop, which creates a profitable trader's equation. If their initial buy signal in the bull pullback came at five points below the high, then they might risk just three points, and they would look to exit their long on a test of the high. Since the pullback was relatively large, the trend might be a little weak, and this might make them take profits below the trend high. They would try to get at least as much as they had to risk, but they might be willing to get out just below the old high if they were concerned that the market might be transitioning into a trading range, or possibly even reversing into a bear trend.

At some point, selling pressure will be strong enough to convert the trend into a trading range, which means that a pullback might fall below the most recent low. Experienced traders have a good sense of when the market is transitioning from a trend into a trading range, and many will exit the remainder of their positions when they believe that it is about to happen. They might then trade the trading range using a trading range approach, which means looking for smaller profits. This is discussed in the second book. They might instead hold on to part of their long positions until either the close or when the market flips into always-in short. If it does, they would then either exit their longs or reverse to short. Very few traders can reverse consistently, and most prefer to exit their longs and then reassess the market, and maybe take a break before looking to go short.

Figure 18.1   EXAMPLE OF HOW TO TRADE A TREND   **297**

FIGURE 18.1   Strong Trend Day in GS

There are countless ways to trade any day, but when there is a trend like the bull trend in GS shown in Figure 18.1, traders should try to swing at least part of their trade. I had extensive discussions years back with a trader who excelled on days like this. He bought early and then determined his initial risk (how far his protective stop was from his entry price). He then took half of his position off once the market reached twice his initial risk and held the other half until there was a clear reversal. If there never was a strong reversal, he exited in the minutes before the close. After every new high, he tightened his stop to below the most recent higher low, since as long as the trend kept making higher highs and lows, it was still strong. If it stopped making higher lows, it was beginning to weaken.

There is one sure way to consistently lose money on a day like this, and all traders know it. Successful traders avoid it, but beginners are irresistibly drawn to it. They see the market as constantly overdone. The most recent bar is always at the top of the computer screen and there surely can't be enough room up there to go higher, and there clearly is a lot of room below. Also, they know trends have pull-backs, so why not short every reversal for a scalp, and then go long on the pullback? Even if the trade is a loser, the loss is not big. They don't buy the pullback when it finally comes, because the market might be reversing into a bear trend, and the buy setup does not look strong enough. Also, since they were short and the market did not quite reach their scalper's profit target, they were rooting for the market to go down just a little bit more, and therefore were not expecting, and actually not want-ing, the pullback to end just yet. They saw bars 7, 10, 18, 20, 21, and 24 as reversals that were likely to fall far enough to offer at least a scalper's profit and as potential highs of the day. However, experienced traders know that 80 percent of reversal attempts fail and become bull flags, and they held long, took some profits on their earlier longs, or bought more as the pullback progressed. The beginners don't ac-cept this premise and they take small losses all day, and by the end of the day are shocked that they have lost so much. They have been successful all their lives in other careers and are very smart. They see trading gurus on television who look more like clowns and used car salesmen than like formidable adversaries, so they are confident that they can trade at least as well as those so-called experts. They are right in their assessment of the abilities of those pundits, but wrong in their assumption that those people are successful traders. They are entertainers, and the networks hire them to create an audience that will result in advertising dollars. The networks are companies, and like all companies, their goal is to make money, not to help the viewer in any way. Beginners do not stop losing until they are able to stop themselves from looking for shorts in bull trends (or bottoms in bear trends). They can start winning only when they accept that each top is the start of a bull flag.

Some of the material that follows will be covered later in books 2 and 3, and is included here because it is important in trend trading.

Great swings usually begin with weak setups, like the two-bar reversal that be-gan at bar 3. Both bars were small dojis, and they followed a large two-bar reversal top. The setup that leads to the breakout is usually weak enough to trap traders out. Traders wait for a higher-probability setup after the breakout occurs, and miss the initial breakout. Entering either on the low-probability setup or on the higher-probability ones after the breakout are both mathematically sound approaches.

Most traders would have decided that the always-in direction was up by either bar 2 or bar 4. That means that they believed that the market was in a bull trend and they therefore would look for sensible reasons to buy, and there were many. They could have bought as bar 4 broke above bar 2, on the close of bar 4, or at one tick above its high. They could have placed a limit order to buy at or below the low of the next bar and the lows of the next several bars. They would have been filled below bar 5. Some would have placed orders to buy a small pullback to the midpoint of the prior bar, maybe 20 cents down. They also would have looked to buy a bear close because they believed that attempts to reverse should fail. The move from bar 4 to bar 5 was a tight channel, so an attempt to break to the downside was likely to fail. They could have bought below bar 5, on the close of the small bear trend bar that followed, or above it as a failed breakout below a bull micro channel. Bar 7 was a breakout pullback short but traders expected it to just lead to a pullback. The market broke below the bull micro channel on the move below bar 5, and the rally to bar 7 was a breakout pullback higher high. Traders expected the reversal to fail

Figure 18.1   EXAMPLE OF HOW TO TRADE A TREND   **299**

and some had limit orders maybe 50 cents down and in the area of the bar 6 low, expecting a double bottom bull flag. Some traders had their protective stops below bar 6 since it was a strong bull trend bar, and a strong bull trend usually would not fall below such a bar. Therefore, buying just above its low was a low-risk, high-reward trade with at least a 50 percent chance of success. They also could have bought above the bull reversal bar that followed bar 8 since it was a double bottom bull flag setup and a high 2 long (bar 6 was the high 1).

Bar 9 was another break below a bull micro channel, and traders expected it to fail. Some would have had limit orders to buy at the low of the prior bar as the micro channel was growing, and they would have been filled on bar 9. Other traders bought above the bar 9 high as a failed breakout below the bull micro channel.

Bar 11 was another high 2 buy setup, but the market had been mostly sideways for over 10 bars, and the bars were getting small. Although this was also a double bottom buy signal, the tight trading range could have continued, so many traders would have waited to see if there was a third push down and then looked to buy above the wedge bull flag, which some traders would have seen as a triangle, since it would have been sideways instead of down. These traders got long on bar 12 and above bar 12. After the breakout from this bull flag, the market went sideways for several bars and created a breakout pullback buy entry above bar 13 and again on the bar 14 outside up strong bull trend bar. This was a high 2 entry bar since bar 13 was a high 1 entry and the pullback below the next bar was a second leg down in this four-bar-long tight trading range.

Some traders bought as the market broke above bar 10, which they saw as a breakout of a trading range in a bull trend. Traders also bought the close of bar 14 and above its high. The next bar had good follow-through, which was a sign of strength, and traders therefore bought its close and above its high. There was a two-bar pause, creating a small breakout pullback bull flag, and traders bought the breakout above the bar after bar 15.

Bar 16 was a doji top but there was no prior bear strength and no significant selling pressure, and the bar was small and weak compared to the bar 14 bull spike. Traders expected the reversal attempt to fail and therefore placed limit orders to buy at and below its low. Bar 17 was a failed top buy signal, and bar 19 was a small second push down and therefore a high 2 buy setup. Traders bought as the market went above its high and above the high of the bull bar that followed it, which was a two-bar reversal buy setup.

The move up to bar 20 was another strong bull spike. Traders would have bought at and below the low of the prior bar, on the close of the bull trend bars, and on the close of the first bear trend bar, like the bar after bar 20. Since bar 20 was an especially large bull trend bar in a mature trend, it was enough of a buy climax to warrant a larger correction, one that might go sideways or down to the moving average. There was less urgency for the bulls, who were expecting a high 2 or a triangle.

Bar 21 was a one-bar final flag reversal attempt but the up momentum was strong. Traders expected another bull flag and not a reversal. Some bought below its low while others waited to see if there would be a high 2, a wedge bull flag, or a triangle. Bar 22 was another double bottom and therefore a high 2 buy setup. Traders placed stop orders to go long above its high and above the high of the inside bar that followed it. Some saw bar 23 as a high 2 buy setup with the bar after bar 20 as the signal for the high 1. Others saw it as a wedge bull flag with the first push down as the bear bar after bar 20. It was also a breakout pullback buy setup for the breakout above the bull flag that occurred on the prior bar.

Bar 24 was a very important bar. It was the third push up and third consecutive buy climax after the spike up from bar 14 (the top of the spike was the first push). The channel in a spike and channel bull often ends on a third push up and is then followed by a correction. Also, bar 24 was a particularly strong bull trend bar in a protracted bull trend. This is just the bar that strong bulls and bears were waiting for. Both saw it as a possible temporary end of the trend, and they expected it to be a brief opportunity to sell before a larger pullback developed. Both expected a correction to have at least two legs and 10 bars and to penetrate the moving average. The bulls were selling to take profits and the bears were selling to initiate shorts. Both sold at the close of bar 24, above its high, at the close of the next bar, and below its low.

The bulls thought that the market might be transitioning into a trading range, and that there was a reasonable chance that they could buy again lower. Bar 28 was a two-legged correction to the moving average and therefore a high 2 buy setup. It was also the first touch of the moving average all day, and therefore a 20 gap bar buy setup, and was likely to be followed by a test of the bull high. The bears took profits on their shorts here and the bulls bought for another leg up.

The biggest prior pullback of the day since the rally began at bar 3 was 75 cents on the pullback to bar 8. Some traders expected the largest pullback of the day to come after 11:00 a.m. or so and therefore had limit orders to go long at 75 cents below the most recent swing high. They might have scaled in at 75 cents below that and maybe risked up to a little more than twice the size of that first pullback, or about $1.60. Throughout the day, traders would have expected pullbacks to remain less than the first and they would have had limit orders to buy any pullback that was about half as big, or maybe 40 to 50 cents. The pullback to bar 11 was 40 cents, which meant that traders tried to buy a 50 cent pullback and when they did not get filled on the second attempt on the bar before bar 12, they decided to chase the market up and bought above the high of bar 12. Some traders saw the bars 9 and 11 double bottom and would have placed limit orders to buy just above its low, maybe 30 cents down from the high. Traders would then have to determine where a worst-case protective stop would be. They should pick a level where they would no longer want to be long. An obvious location would have been below the bar 8 low,

Figure 18.1   EXAMPLE OF HOW TO TRADE A TREND   **301**

since a bull trend has a series of higher highs and lows, and after each new high, the bulls expect the next pullback to stay above the most recent higher low. Since they were planning to get long at \$161.05, 30 cents down from the high, and they would need to risk to around \$160.35 or 70 cents lower, they had to determine the position size. If they normally risk \$500 or less on a trade, they could have bought 600 shares of GS. Since they were risking 70 cents and they always should have a reward that is at least as large as their risk, their profit target should have been at least 70 cents above their entry. This was clearly a strong trend day at this point and the probability of success was therefore at least 60 percent, and maybe higher.

On a strong trend day like this, it was far better to use a generous profit target. Traders should not have tried to take any profit until the market went to at least twice their risk, or \$1.40 above their entry price. They would have placed a limit order to sell half of their position at \$162.45. After the bar 12 strong bull trend bar broke above the triangle (some thought of it as a wedge bull flag), they could have tightened their protective stop to just below its low at \$161.05, reducing their risk to less than 20 cents. After the bar 14 strong bull trend bar breakout, they could have tightened their stop to just below its low, reducing their risk to a penny. Their limit order to take profits on 300 shares would have been filled on bar 20, giving them \$420. At that point, they could have tightened their protective stop to below the bar 19 start of that most recent bull spike. If the stop was hit, they would have made about 80 cents on their remaining 300 shares. At this point, they would have held their position until there was a clear reversal down or until the close. When you have a large profit, it is usually wise to exit in the final hour or so on any setup that could lead to a larger pullback and then maybe look to get long again once that two-legged pullback is complete. The bear reversal bar at bar 24 was a third push up and was followed a buy climax bar, so the market could finally have been getting ready to pull back to the moving average. If traders exited below its low, they would have made \$2.00, or \$600, on their remaining 300 shares. If they held until the close, they would have made \$375 on those shares. The market never even clearly became always-in short.

Many traders would have bought on a limit order at one tick above the moving average as bar 27 tested the moving average, since it was a 20 gap bar buy setup, and held for a test of the high. Some traders would have bought on the close of bar 27 because it was the first bear trend bar with a close below the moving average. Although it was the second bar of a two-bar bear spike and a breakout below bar 25, the bears needed follow-through before believing that the market had flipped to always-in short, and instead got a bull inside bar for the next bar. This was the bottom of a developing trading range and the test of the beginning of the channel up from the bar 22 pullback from the four-bar bull spike up to bar 20. The bull bar that followed bar 27 also closed above the moving average. Some bulls would have bought on the close of that bull bar, while others would have bought at one tick above its high. Their entry would have been three bars later. Traders would also have bought above the high of the inside bar that followed bar 28, since it was a high 2 buy signal, ending two legs down from the high of the day. It was also a small wedge bull flag where bar 25 was the first push down and bar 27 was the second.

A pullback is a minor trend in the opposite direction, and traders expect it to end soon and for the major trend to resume. When GS began its second leg down from the bar 24 high, it formed a lower high at bar 26 and the bears needed it to form a series of lower highs and lows to be able to convince the market that the trend had reversed to down. Some therefore shorted as the market broke out below the bar 25 swing low, hoping for a series of large bear trend bars. Instead, bar 25 was a small bear trend bar and there was no follow-through. In fact, the rally up showed that most traders instead bought the breakout below bar 25 because they believed that the sell-off was only a pullback and doomed to be a failed attempt at reversing the major trend into a bear trend. Since most reversal attempts fail, the first pullback in a strong bull trend that has a second leg down usually is bought aggressively as it breaks below the prior swing low, and many bulls bought this one, even though it took several bars before they could turn the market up again. This was a sign that they were not as aggressive as they could have been. This told traders that the pullback might evolve into a larger trading range, which it ultimately did.

Many traders use trend lines for entering and exiting. Some would have taken partial profits near the high of bar 7 as it moved above the trend channel line. They also would have bought as bar 9 fell below the bull trend line and above the bar 9 high, since they saw bar 9 as a failed channel breakout. Bar 12 broke above a small bear trend line, and traders bought as the bar moved above the line since they saw that as the end of the pullback and the resumption of the bull trend. Bar 24 was the third push up in the channel that followed the two-bar bull spike that began at bar 14, and some traders would take profits on their longs above that line, even on the strong bull close of bar 24. The bar was an especially large bull trend bar and the third consecutive bull climax since bar 14, and the market was likely to have a more complex correction. What better place to take profits than on a buy vacuum test of a trend channel line on the third consecutive buy climax? The move down to bar 28 broke below the bull trend line and held below it for many bars, so traders wondered if a larger correction might be starting. This made many quicker to take profits. When the move up from bar 28 could not produce any strong bull trend bars, traders thought that the market might be in a trading range and therefore took profits on the bar 29 test of the bar 26 lower high. This was a potential double top bear flag and lower high trend reversal. The next bar was a bear trend bar, which indicated that the bulls were becoming less aggressive and the bears were becoming stronger.

When a bull trend is very strong, traders can buy for any reason if they use a wide enough stop, and many traders like to buy on breakouts above prior swing

Figure 18.1 EXAMPLE OF HOW TO TRADE A TREND **303**

highs. However, buying pullbacks before the breakout generally offers more reward, smaller risk, and a higher probability of success. The breakout traders will place buy stops at one tick above the old high and will be swept into their longs as the market breaks above the old high. The most common reason for traders failing to buy a pullback is that they were hoping for a larger or better-looking pullback. Many pullbacks have bear signal bars or follow two or three bar bear spikes, making traders believe that the bull trend needs to correct more before resuming. However, it is important to get long when there is a strong bull trend, and a trader should place a buy stop above the prior swing high when the trend is very strong, in case the pullback is brief and the trend quickly resumes. Reasonable entries included the bar 4 breakout above the bar 2 high and the breakouts up to bar 10 as it moved above bar 7, the bar 14 spike as it went above bar 10, and the bar 20 spike as it moved above bar 16. These old highs are often the highs of higher time frame bars, like on the 15 or 60 minute charts, so the entry is usually a breakout above the high of a prior bull trend bar on these higher time frame charts. Since higher time frame charts have larger bars and the protective stop is initially below the signal bar, the risk is greater and traders should trade smaller size, unless they are only looking for a quick, small scalp. After the trend has gone on for a while, the pullbacks become deeper and last for more bars. Once the two-sided trading becomes apparent, the strong bulls begin to take profits above swing highs rather than buying new positions, and the strong bears begin to scale into shorts as the market goes above the old highs. For example, the bear bar after bar 20 and the bar 22 bear bar were signs of selling pressure, so most traders would have used the move above the bar 21 high to take profits rather than to buy more. At some point, most traders will see new highs as shorting opportunities and not simply as areas to take profits. Although many traders shorted below the bear bar after bar 24, most traders still believed that the trend was up and that there would be a test of the bull high after a pullback. Until there has been a strong bear move that breaks well below the bull trend line, the strong bears usually will not dominate the market.

Since this was a trend day, a trader would ideally swing part, take profits along the way, and then go back to a full position size on every pullback. However, most traders cannot continue to hold part of their trade for a swing and also repeatedly scalp the other part. Traders instead should try to put on a full position early and not take additional signals, and instead scale out of their profits as the market works higher. There are many ways to do this. For example, if they bought early on and had to risk about $1.00 (probably less), they might have taken a quarter off after a $1.00 profit and another quarter off at $2.00, and maybe a third quarter at $3.00, and held onto the final quarter until either a strong sell signal formed or until the end of the day. It was better if they instead waited until the market rallied $2.00, or twice their initial risk, before taking their initial profit, because they had to sure that they were adequately compensated for taking that initial $1.00 risk. It does not matter how they did it, but it was important to have taken some profit along the way in case the market reversed down. However, since traders subjected themselves to risk, they must resist the temptation to exit with too small a reward. As long as the trend is good, it is always best to try to resist taking profits until the market has gone at least twice as far as your initial risk. If traders are out of half of their position but then see another strong buy signal, they might put part or all of the other half back on, at least for a scalp; but most traders should simply stick to their original plan and enjoy their growing profit.

With all of these buy signals, traders could have accumulated an uncomfortably large long position if they kept adding new longs, which they should not have done. Instead, they should have simply held their position until a possible end of the trend, like at bar 24, or they could have scalped out part after each new high as soon as a bar had a weak close, like at bars 16, 21, or 24. Then they could have put the scalp portion back on when they saw another buy signal. They would have continued to hold their swing portion until the end of the trend.

When did traders see this day as a trend day? Aggressive bulls thought that the gap up and strong bull trend bar had a reasonable chance of leading to a trend from the open bull trend day, and they might have bought on the close of bar 1 or one tick above its high. Their initial protective stops were one tick below the bar 1 low, and they planned on holding part or all of the position until the close or until a clear short signal formed.

Other traders always look for double bottoms on gap up days, and they would have bought above the two-bar reversal that began at bar 3, which formed an approximate double bottom with bar 1 or with the low of doji bar that followed it.

Bar 4 was a strong bull trend bar that broke above the opening range and closed above the bar 2 high. Some traders bought at one tick above the bar 2 high, and others bought on the close of bar 4 or one tick above its high. This breakout bar was a statement by the bulls that they owned the market, and most traders at this point believed that the market was always-in long. For the time being, the best place for a protective stop was one tick below its low, but since that was almost a dollar lower, traders had to choose a small enough position size so that they were trading within their comfort zone.

Most traders saw the day as a bull trend day by bars 5 or 7, and probably as soon as bar 4 closed. Once traders believe the day is a trend day, if they are flat, they should buy a small position either at the market or on any small pullback. Traders could have placed limit orders to buy below the low of the prior bar and to buy at a certain number of cents down, like maybe 20, 30, or 50 cents. Others would have looked to buy above a high 2 on a stop or on a moving average pullback. Buying above the bar 8 two-bar reversal was a reasonable long, as was the wedge bull flag (some saw it as a triangle) that ended in a two-bar reversal at bar 12. The protective stop would still have been below the bar 4 low or maybe below its midpoint. Traders

Figure 18.1   EXAMPLE OF HOW TO TRADE A TREND   **305**

need to trade small enough so that their risk is within their normal risk tolerance. Other traders had their stops below the bars 6 and 8 double bottom, and if they got stopped out but the market then formed another buy signal and they believed that the bull trend was still intact, they would have bought again.

The most important thing that traders must force themselves to do, and it is usually difficult, is as soon as they believe that the day is in a trend, they must take at least a small position. They must decide where a worst-case protective stop would be, which is usually relatively far away, and use that as their stop. Because the stop will be large, their initial position should be small if they are entering late. Once the market moves in their direction and they can tighten their stop, they can look to add to their position, but they should never exceed their normal risk level. When everyone wants a pullback, it usually will not come for a long time. This is because everyone believes that the market will soon be higher, but they do not necessarily believe that it will be lower anytime soon. Smart traders know this and therefore they start buying in pieces. Since they have to risk to the bottom of the spike, they buy small. If their risk is three times normal, they will buy only one-third of their usual size to keep their total dollar risk within their normal range. When the strong bulls keep buying in small pieces, this is buying pressure, and it works against the formation of a pullback. The strong bears see the trend, and they too believe that the market will soon be higher. Since they think it will be higher soon, they will stop looking to short. It does not make sense for them to short if they think that they can short at a better price after a few more bars. So the strong bears are not shorting and the strong bulls are buying in small pieces, in case there is no pullback for a long time. What is the result? The market keeps working higher. Since you need to be doing what the smart traders are doing, you need to buy at least a small amount at the market or on a one- or two-tick pullback or a 10 or 20 cent pullback, and risk to the bottom of the spike (the low of bar 4 for most traders, but some would have put their stops below the low of bar 3). Even if the pullback begins on the next tick, the odds are that it won't fall far before smart bulls see it as value and buy aggressively. Remember, everyone is waiting to buy a pullback, so when it finally comes it will only be small and not last long. All of those traders who have been waiting to buy will see this as the opportunity that they wanted. The result is that your position will once again be profitable very soon. Once the market goes high enough, you can look to take partial profits or you can look to buy more on a pullback, which will probably be at a price above your original entry. The important point is that as soon as you decide that buying a pullback is a great idea, you should do exactly what the strong bulls are doing, and buy at least a small position at the market.

After the market moved above the bar 7 high, many traders trailed their protective stops below the most recent swing low, which was at bar 8. As long as the market holds above the most recent swing low, the trend is likely still very strong. If it starts to make lower lows, the market could be transitioning into a trading range or even a bear trend. In either case, traders would then trade it differently from how they would trade a one-sided market (a trend).

Bulls would continue to buy pullbacks all day long, and after the market went to another new swing high, they would move their protective stop to below the most recent swing low. For example, once the market moved above the bar 16 high, traders tightened their protective stops to below the bar 19 low. Many traders moved their stops to breakeven once there was a pullback that tested their entry price and then the market reached a new high. They did not want the market to come back down to their entry price a second time, and if it did, they would have believed that the trend was not strong.

Bar 24 was the third push up from the spike up to bar 15 (bar 21 was the second push up), so the market was likely to correct for a couple of legs sideways to down. The bar after it was a bear inside bar so the market might have reversed down at this point, especially since this would have been a failed breakout above the trend channel line. The market made a couple of attempts to pull back to the moving average earlier in the day, so it was reasonable to assume that it might succeed this time. This was a good place to take profits on the swing longs. Aggressive traders might have gone short for a scalp, but most traders would have waited to see if a 20 gap bar buy signal formed at the moving average.

Should traders try to take most of these entries? Absolutely not. However, if they are watching on the sidelines, wondering how to get in, all of these setups are reasonable. If they take just one to three of these swing entries, they are doing all that they need to do and should not worry about all of the others.

CHAPTER 19

Signs of Strength in a Trend

There are many characteristics of strong trends. The most obvious one is that they run from one corner of your chart to the diagonally opposite corner with only small pullbacks. However, in the early stages of a trend, there are signs that indicate that the move is strong and likely to last. The more of these signs that are present, the more you should focus on with-trend entries. You should start to look at countertrend setups only as great with-trend setups, with you entering on a stop exactly where those countertrend traders will be forced to exit with a loss.

One interesting phenomenon in trend days is that on many of the days, the best reversal bars and the biggest trend bars tend to be countertrend, trapping traders into the wrong direction. Also, the lack of great with-trend signal bars makes traders question their entries, forcing them to chase the market and enter late.

Finally, once you realize that the market is in a strong trend, you don't need a setup to enter. You can enter anytime all day long at the market if you wish with a relatively small stop. The only purpose of a setup is to minimize the risk.

Here are some characteristics that are commonly found in strong trends:

- There is a big gap opening on the day.
- There are trending highs and lows (swings).
- Most of the bars are trend bars in the direction of the trend.
- There is very little overlap of the bodies of consecutive bars. For example, in a bull spike, many bars have lows that are at or just one tick below the closes of the prior bar. Some bars have lows that are at and not below the close of the prior bar, so traders trying to buy on a limit order at the close of the prior bar do not get their orders filled and they have to buy higher.

- There are bars with no tails or small tails in either direction, indicating urgency. For example, in a bull trend, if a bull trend bar opens on its low tick and trends up, traders were eager to buy it as soon as the prior bar closed. If it closes on or near its high tick, traders continued their strong buying in anticipation of new buyers entering right after the bar closes. They were willing to buy going into the close because they were afraid that if they waited for the bar to close, they might have to buy a tick or two higher.
- Occasionally, there are gaps between the bodies (for example, the open of a bar might be above the close of the prior bar in a bull trend).
- A breakout gap appears in the form of a strong trend bar at the start of the trend (a trend bar is a type of gap, as discussed in book 2).
- Measuring gaps occur where the breakout test does not overlap the breakout point. For example, the pullback from a bull breakout does not drop below the high of the bar where the breakout occurred.
- Micro measuring gaps appear where there is a strong trend bar and a gap between the bar before it and the bar after it. For example, if the low of the bar after a strong bull trend bar in a bull trend is at or above the high of the bar before the trend bar, this is a gap and a breakout test and a sign of strength.
- No big climaxes appear.
- Not many large bars appear (not even large trend bars). Often, the largest trend bars are countertrend, trapping traders into looking for countertrend trades and missing with-trend trades. The countertrend setups almost always look better than the with-trend setups.
- No significant trend channel line overshoots occur, and the minor ones result in only sideways corrections.
- The corrections after trend line breaks go sideways instead of countertrend.
- Failed wedges and other failed reversals occur.
- There is a sequence of 20 moving average gap bars (20 or more consecutive bars that do not touch the moving average, discussed in book 2).
- Few if any profitable countertrend trades are found.
- There are small, infrequent, and mostly sideways pullbacks. For example, if the Emini's average range is 12 points, the pullbacks will all likely be less than three or four points, and the market will often go for five or more bars without a pullback.
- There is a sense of urgency. You find yourself waiting through countless bars for a good with-trend pullback and one never comes, yet the market slowly continues to trend.
- The pullbacks have strong setups. For example, the high 1 and high 2 pullbacks in a bull trend have strong bull reversal bars for signal bars.
- In the strongest trends, the pullbacks usually have weak signal bars, making many traders not take them, and forcing traders to chase the market. For

example, in a bear trend the signal bars for a low 2 short are often small bull bars in two or three bar bull spikes, and some of the entry bars are outside down bars. It has trending "anything": closes, highs, lows, or bodies.

- Repeated two-legged pullbacks are setting up with trend entries.
- No two consecutive trend bar closes occur on the opposite side of the moving average.
- The trend goes very far and breaks several resistance levels, like the moving average, prior swing highs, and trend lines, and each by many ticks.
- Reversal attempts in the form of spikes against the trend have no follow-through, fail, and become flags in the direction of the trend.

When a trend is in runaway mode, there will likely be no pullbacks for many bars and the bars will be good-sized trend bars with mostly small tails. Since you want to keep scalping more as the trend continues while still holding on to the swing portion of your position, you might consider looking at the 3 minute chart for additional with-trend setups. It often has more pause bars (countertrend inside bars and one-bar pullbacks) that allow for with-trend entries. The 1 minute chart also has with-trend entries but in addition it has some countertrend setups, which can be confusing when you are trying to trade only with trend. This, along with the speed of the reading required, can create too much stress during a runaway trend and can interfere with your ability to trade effectively. Since you need to be making sure that you catch every with-trend entry, it is best to trade only off the 5 minute chart in a runaway trend. Once you become experienced and successful, you might consider also looking at the 3 minute chart.

Over time, the trend weakens; more signs of two-sided trading develop and the signs of strength begin to disappear. For example, in a bull trend traders begin to take profits above the highs of the prior bars and above swing highs, and aggressive bears begin to short above the highs of bars and above swing highs and will scale in higher. The strong bulls will eventually only buy pullbacks. The initial bull spike is replaced by a bull channel, and it eventually evolves into a trading range.

Figure 19.1

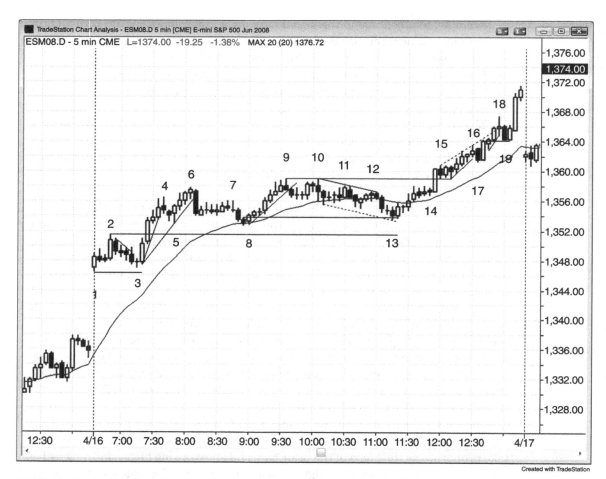

FIGURE 19.1 Big Gap Up on Bull Day

Large gaps that don't reverse early usually mark the start of a strong trend for the day and the day often closes at or near the high (or low, in a bear). As shown in Figure 19.1, the 5 minute Emini gapped up 11 points, which is huge, and the first bar was a bull trend bar. Also, the market did not test the moving average for over two hours, another sign of strength. Notice how there was not much emotional behavior (big bars, climaxes, big swings). Quiet markets with lots of small bars, many of which are dojis, often lead to the biggest trends.

On days like this, the institutions have a huge amount to buy and they want lower prices, but when the lower prices don't come, they have to fill their orders in pieces all day long, at increasingly higher prices. Even though they see the trend

Figure 19.1   SIGNS OF STRENGTH IN A TREND   **311**

day unfolding and expect that they will likely have to be buying at higher prices throughout the day, they don't dump all of their buy orders onto the market at once, because this could cause a climactic spike up and then possibly a reversal down below their average entry price. They are content filling their orders in manageable pieces all day long, understanding that they are buying higher and higher, but knowing that the market will likely go higher still. Also, strong days like this usually have higher prices over the next one to several days.

Deeper Discussion of This Chart

The market broke out above yesterday's high in Figure 19.1, but the breakout became a failed breakout when the market turned down below the bear inside bar that followed the bar 2 strong bull spike. Big gap up days often test the low of the open and form a small double bottom bull flag. When the opening range is small like this, that market is in breakout mode and traders will enter in the direction of the breakout. On a big gap up day, the odds favor an upside breakout. Aggressive bulls could enter above bar 3, based on the double bottom, but many bulls entered on a stop above the bar 2 high of the opening range. The day was a trend from the open bull trend day and a trend resumption bull day.

   The market had a small two-legged move down to bar 3. A bear trend bar and two dojis composed the first leg. The second leg was made up of a bear trend bar with a large bear tail on top (the tail was the pullback that ended the first leg down) followed by a doji. This variant of a two-legged move would certainly have two clear legs down on a smaller time frame chart, setting up an ABC buy signal. A trader could buy at one tick above bar 3. It was also a test of the gap, forming a double bottom with the low of bar 1. Since this was a possible trend day and as such could extend much further than most traders would ever suspect, smart traders would swing part or all of their positions. Note how the open of the day was very close to the low of the day, which is a sign of strength, and trend from the open days that open within a few ticks of the low of the day often close within a few ticks of the high of the day, and there is often a trend into the close.

   Bar 5 was a high 1 breakout pullback after a strong move up (four bull trend bars), and a high 1 is always a good buy in the spike phase of a strong bull trend. The bar 4 low 1 break below the trend line and reversal from the new high was not a short, even for a scalp. In fact, it is incorrect to use the term low 1 here because a low 1 sets up trades in trading ranges and bear trends, not strong bull trends. After such a strong up move, smart traders would only be looking to buy and would consider a short only if there was a second entry.

   Bar 6 was a low 2, which was a second entry short and a possible top of a trading range within a bull trend. However, in the face of the strong bull trend, shorts would only scalp this trade. They would swing it only if there was first a prior strong down move that broke a substantial trend line (maybe 20 or more bars). If they shorted, they would be quick to exit and then they would look for a long setup for a swing trade. With-trend entries in a strong trend should be mostly swung, with only a small potion taken off as a scalp. If you find that you missed a with-trend entry, stop looking for countertrend scalps and start trading only with-trend setups. During a trend day, you must try to catch every with-trend signal, because that is the source of the most consistent money.

Since the bar 6 entry bar was a strong bear trend bar, it is a breakout and therefore a spike. Spikes are usually followed by channels with at least two more pushes; but when they occur against a strong trend, they often just have one more push and become a two-legged bull flag. In any case, after a spike down, there was a good chance for at least one more leg down.

Bar 7 was an entry bar for a low 2 short into the second leg down, but after a six-bar tight trading range, any breakout in either direction would likely fail after not going very far.

Bar 8 was a two-legged pullback and the first to the moving average in a strong bull trend, which is a great buy. Whenever the market stays away from the moving average for 20 bars or more (a 20 gap bar buy setup), the trend is very strong and the odds are high that there will be buyers at the moving average.

Bar 9 was a reversal at a new swing high, but there were no bear trend bars among the prior seven bars so no short could be taken unless a second entry forms.

Bar 10 was a second entry, but in a tight trading range in a bull trend, any short is a scalp at best and it is probably best to pass on this trade. Sideways price action in a bull trend is usually a bull flag and will usually break out in the direction of the trend that was in effect before it formed. Outside bars are less reliable, but you could consider taking the short for a scalp since second entries are so reliable. Three small dojis developed at the moving average. This was a small tight trading range and therefore had a magnetic effect. The odds were high that there would be a trend bar breakout in either direction and it would fail. Traders held short and risked maybe four ticks. The bar 11 bull trend bar breakout failed, as expected, allowing traders to take a four-tick scalp profit on the next bar.

Bar 13 was a breakout test that extended one tick below the high of the signal bar that generated the strong move up from the bar 8 long. The move down from bars 9 to 13 was very weak and appeared essentially sideways. The market struggled to get down to test the breakout, meaning the bears lacked conviction. Bar 13 also set up a high 4 entry just below the moving average, and it followed the first moving average gap bar of the day (a bar with a high below the exponential moving average). This was a moving average gap bar setup in a strong trend and should be expected to test the high of the bull trend with either a lower high or a higher high. A moving average gap bar in a strong trend often leads to the final leg of the trend before a deeper, longer-lasting pullback develops, and the pullback can grow and become a trend reversal. This might have happened on the following day. Bar 13 formed a higher low (higher than bar 8)

Figure 19.1   SIGNS OF STRENGTH IN A TREND   **313**

following a higher high at bar 9, and is part of trending bull swings. It is essentially a double bottom bull flag with bar 8.

Bar 14 was a high 2 breakout signal bar, and the high 1 was the prior bar.

Bar 15 was a signal bar for a final flag short but the market never triggered the entry because it did not trade below the signal bar low. However, as a bear bar, it was a small leg down. The next bar was a bull trend bar and then there was another bear trend bar. This second bear trend bar was a small second leg down and therefore was a high 2 buy setup.

Bar 17 was the first breakout of a bull micro channel on a strong bull day, and therefore it was a setup for a buy at one tick above its high. The channel had a wedge shape and, although traders would not short here, the theoretical protective buy stop for shorts is one tick above the high of the wedge. There was a large bull trend bar that ran through those buy stops, showing a strong rejection of the bear case. The bar was so strong because there were bulls who expected the bar 17 short to fail and therefore placed buy stops above its high to get long, and there were the bears who got stopped out at one tick above the bar 16 top of the wedge.

Bar 18 broke above a bull trend channel line and gave a low 2 short signal. However, on a strong trend day, smart traders will short only if there is first a strong bear leg that broke a trend line. Otherwise, they would view all short setups as buy setups, and place orders to go long exactly where the weak shorts would have to cover (like one tick above the highs of bars 17 and 19).

Bar 19 was a one-bar trend line break that failed, and therefore a buy setup. There was a two-bar bull reversal that became the signal for the long.

FIGURE 19.2 Most Reversals Fail on Trend Days

As shown in Figure 19.2, one peculiarity of trend days is that often the best-looking reversal bars and trend bars are countertrend, trapping traders into losing trades in the wrong direction (bars 1 through 8). Notice how there was not a single great bear reversal signal bar all day, yet this was a huge bear trend. Just look at the moving average—the market could not put two consecutive closes above it until the gap bar at the top of the rally that began with bar 8. This was a bear trend, and every buy should be viewed as a short entry setup. Just place your entry order exactly where the longs would have their protective stops and let them drive the market down as they liquidate.

The weak sell signals are a key reason why the trend is so relentless. Bears keep waiting for a strong signal bar, so that they can short their full position. Trapped bulls keep waiting for strong evidence that the trend is strong and that they need to exit immediately. The signs never come, and both the bulls and the bears keep waiting. They look at the trend and see lots of bull bars and two- or three-bar bull spikes, so assume and hope that this buying pressure will soon create a larger rally. Even if they see that the market cannot get above the moving average and that all of the pullbacks are very small, they deny these signs of a strong trend and keep

Figure 19.2   SIGNS OF STRENGTH IN A TREND   **315**

hoping for the bulls to lift the market to a level where they feel more comfortable shorting. It never happens, and both the bears and the trapped longs continue to sell in pieces all day long, just in case the rally that they want never comes. Their relentless selling, along with the aggressive, relentless shorting by the strong bears who see this as the very strongest of bear trends, makes the market work lower and lower all day without any big pullback.

FIGURE 19.3   No Pullbacks Means the Trend Is Strong

When traders cannot get filled on a limit order to buy at the close of the prior bar, the trend is strong. In Figure 19.3, as soon as bar 1 closed on its high, some traders would immediately place a limit order to buy at the price where that bar closed, hoping to get filled during the opening seconds of the next bar, bar 2. But since the low of bar 2 never dipped below the close of bar 1, the limit order would likely not get filled. Instead, the buyer would keep trying to buy higher. Bars 3, 4, and 5 were also very strong, although as soon as bar 3 closed, a trader who placed a limit order to buy at the level of that close would have been filled during the first few seconds of bar 4 because the low of bar 4 dipped one tick below the close of bar 3. Usually when there is a series of strong bars like that, they create a spike and the market typically then develops a bull channel.

However, that is not always the case. The next day, bars 6 through 9 were also strong but they led to a lower high. Yesterday was a spike and channel bull trend day, so the start of the channel should get tested today. That was a downside magnet in the market, and when the market opened below yesterday's bull trend line, the lower high following the bars 6 to 9 spike led to a trend reversal down.

Stock traders would describe this bull channel up to yesterday's high as a crowded trade. Everyone who wanted to buy had already bought and there was no one left to buy. As the market started to fall, all of the buyers in the channel

Figure 19.3   SIGNS OF STRENGTH IN A TREND   **317**

were quickly holding losing positions and then everyone rushed to the exits to minimize their losses and protect some of their profits. The result was that the market fell quickly.

Deeper Discussion of This Chart

The open broke out below the bull channel of yesterday's spike and channel in Figure 19.3, and bar 6 was a bull trend bar that set up a failed breakout long. The failed breakout became a lower high and breakout pullback short with a second entry below the bull bar that followed the 7:05 a.m. PST bear spike.

CHAPTER 20

Two Legs

The market regularly tries to do something twice, and this is why all moves tend to subdivide into two smaller moves. This is true of both with-trend and countertrend moves. If it fails in its two attempts, it will usually try to do the opposite. If it succeeds, it will often then extend the trend.

Everyone is familiar with an ABC pullback in a trend that unfolds in three steps. There is a countertrend move, a small with-trend move that usually does not go beyond the trend's extreme, and then a second countertrend move that usually extends deeper than the first. Trends themselves also tend to subdivide into two smaller legs as well. Elliott Wave followers look at a trend move and see three with-trend waves. However, it is better to look at the first strong with-trend leg as the start of the momentum (the Elliott Wave 3), even if there was a prior with-trend move or wave (Elliott Wave 1). That strong with-trend move often subdivides into two smaller with-trend moves, and, after a pullback, the trend will often make two more pushes to test the extreme of the trend (these two pushes create Elliott Wave 5). This two-legged view of markets makes more sense to a trader since it offers sound logic and abundant trading opportunities, unlike Elliott Wave Theory, which is essentially useless to the vast majority of traders who are trying to make money.

A break of a trend line is the start of a new leg in the opposite direction. Any time there is a new trend or any capitulation of one side, there will usually be at least a two-legged move. This can occur in a pullback in a trend, a breakout, a major reversal, or any time that enough traders believe that the move has sufficient strength to warrant a second attempt to test whether or not a protracted trend will develop. Both the bulls and the bears will be in agreement that the momentum is strong enough that a test will be needed before they develop a strong conviction one way or the other. For example, in a two-legged rally in a bear trend, bulls will take profits above the first leg, new bears will short, and other bears who shorted the first up leg will add to their shorts as soon as the second leg up goes above the high of the first leg. If all of these shorts overwhelm the traders who bought the breakout above the first leg up, the market will go down and enter either a trading range or a new bear phase.

Some complex two-legged moves take place over dozens of bars and, if viewed on a higher time frame chart, would appear clear and simple. However, any time traders divert their attention away from their trading charts, they increase the chances that they will miss important trades. To be checking the higher time frame charts for the one signal a day that they might provide simply is not a sound financial decision.

Two legs is the ideal but there is some overlap with three-push patterns. When there is a clear double top or double bottom, the second push is the test of the prior price where the market reversed earlier, and if it fails again at that price, a reversal or pullback is likely. But when the first move is not clearly the possible end of a trend, the market will often then make a two-legged test of that extreme. Sometimes both legs are beyond the prior extreme, creating a clear three-push pattern. At other times only the second leg exceeds the prior extreme, creating a possible two-legged higher high at the end of a bull trend or a two-legged lower low at the end of a bear trend.

Sometimes one or both of the legs of a two-push move are composed of two smaller legs so that the overall move actually has three legs. This is the case in many three-push patterns where often two of the pushes really are just part of a single leg. However, if you look carefully at the leg that has the two small legs and think about what is going on, that leg with its two small legs is comparable in strength or duration or overall shape to the other leg that has just a single move. This is difficult and frustrating for traders who want perfect patterns; but when you trade, you are always in a gray fog and nothing is perfectly clear. However, whenever you are not confident about your read, do not take the trade—there will always be another trade before too long that will be much clearer to you. One of your most important goals is to avoid any confusing setups, because losses are hard to overcome. You do not want to spend the rest of the day struggling to get back to breakeven, so be patient and take only trades where you are comfortable with your read.

Figure 20.1   TWO LEGS   **321**

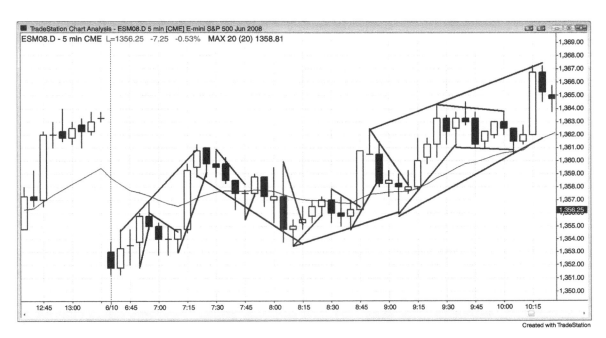

FIGURE 20.1   Every Leg Is Made of Smaller Legs

Every trend line break and every pullback is a leg, and each larger leg is made of smaller legs (see Figure 20.1). The term *leg* is very general and simply means that the direction of movement has changed, using any criterion that you choose to determine that the change exists.

PART IV

Common Trend Patterns

Trends days can be classified into specific types, and if you become familiar with the characteristics of each type, you will be prepared to spot specific trading opportunities as they are setting up. The names are meaningless because all that a trader needs to know is how to read the price action, which is the same for any pattern. On most trend days, features of more than one type of trend will be present, but don't look at that with confusion or disappointment. Instead, it is an opportunity because there will be more tradable setups once you become familiar with how each tends to develop.

With all trend patterns, the only reason to apply names to them is because they are commonly recurring patterns; if you recognize one as it is unfolding, you should be focusing on trading in the with-trend direction only and be more confident about swinging a larger part of your trade. The setups will be the same as during trading range days, but you should be trying to take every with-trend entry, no matter how weak the setup looks, and you should take countertrend entries only after a trend line break, only if there is a good reversal bar, and only if you are still able to take every with-trend signal. If you find that you are missing any with-trend entries, stop trading countertrend and focus only on with-trend setups. On the countertrend trades, you should scalp your entire position. Also, you should not find more than two or three countertrend trades in the day; if you do, you are spending too much time looking in the wrong direction and likely missing great with-trend swings. The stronger the trend, the more you need to be swinging with the trend and not scalping countertrend. In a very strong trend, all trades should be with-trend swings (scalping out part) and no trades should be countertrend scalps, as tempting as they are.

The opening range usually provides clues to how the day will unfold, and these are discussed in detail in the section on opening patterns and reversals in the third book. In general, if the opening range is small, it will be followed by a breakout. If the opening range is about half of the range of the recent days, the breakout will often lead to a measured move and a trending trading range day. If the opening range is large, there is usually a spike and the day will likely become a spike and channel trend day.

Once you are familiar with these patterns, you will find that you can see them potentially setting up in the first 30 to 60 minutes. If you do, make sure to take every with-trend trade and swing part of your position. Sometimes you will get stopped out of the swing portion a couple of times, but keep swinging a part because if the day becomes a trend day, a single swing can be as profitable as 10 scalps.

As a corollary, if you cannot see one of these patterns setting up, then assume that the day is a trading range day and look for entries in both directions. Also, a trend day can turn into a trading range day or a trend in the opposite direction at any time. When it happens, don't question it or be upset by it. Just accept it and trade it.

CHAPTER 21

Spike and Channel Trend

Primary characteristics of spike and channel trend days:

- There is a spike that is made up of one or more trend bars, and it signals that the market is breaking into a clear always-in situation. During the spike, there is a sense of urgency and traders add to their position as they press the trade. The spike is effectively a breakaway gap (discussed in book 2).
- The spike usually forms in the first hour and often within the first few bars of the day.
- The stronger the breakout, the more likely there will be follow-through in the form of a channel, and the more likely the channel will go far (see the sections on the strength of trends in Chapter 19, and the strength of breakouts in Chapter 2 of book 2).
- When the breakout is strong, it is often the basis for a measured move where the channel may end and you can ultimately take partial or complete profits.
- Immediately after the spike, there is a pullback that can be as short as a single bar or as long as a couple of dozen bars.
- The trend resumes in the form of a channel. During the channel, there is a sense of worry and uncertainty, due to the two-sided trading.
- When the market is channeling, it is better to trade it like a trending trading range (for example, in a bull channel, it is better to buy below the low of the prior bar and hold part of the trade for a swing, and if you take any shorts, sell above swing highs or the highs of prior bars and primarily scalp).
- The channel will rarely break out in the with-trend direction, but when it does, the breakout usually fails within five bars and then the market reverses.

- The channel ends at some measured move target, and often on a third push.
- If the channel breaks out against the trend, as it usually ultimately does, don't enter on the breakout and instead wait for the pullback (for example, if there is a bull spike and channel and the market breaks below the channel, look to short a lower high).
- The market usually corrects to the start of the channel, which is a test of the gap (the spike, like all spikes, is a gap).
- The market then reverses back at least 25 percent in the direction of the trend as it attempts to form a trading range. In a bull spike and channel, the pullback often forms a double bottom bull flag with the bottom of the channel, which is the bottom of the pullback that followed the spike up.
- When it is weaker, it is probably more likely a trending trading range day (discussed in the next chapter).

The spike and channel trend is the most common type of trend and is present in some form almost every day and in every trend. There are countless variations and there are often many smaller ones nested inside larger ones. Because it often is the controlling force over so much price action, it is imperative that traders understand it. It is a pattern with two components. Every trend has both a spike phase and a channel phase, and every trend is in either of those two modes at all times. First, there is a spike of one or more bars where the market is moving quickly. There is a sense of urgency and everyone believes that the market has further to go. The spike is a breakaway gap where the market quickly moves from one price level to another. Next, there is a pullback, which can be as short as a single bar or can last dozens of bars and even retrace beyond the start of the spike. For example, if there is a bull spike, occasionally the pullback will fall below the bottom of the spike, and then the channel begins. After the pullback, the trend converts into a channel, where there is less urgency and more a sense of worry and uncertainty. This is the wall of worry that you sometimes hear pundits mention on TV. Everyone sees two-sided trading taking place and the trend constantly looks like it is about to end, yet it keeps extending. Traders are quick to take profits, but as the trend continues, they keep reentering or adding to their positions because they are not certain when the trend will end and they want to make sure to participate. Rarely, there will be a second spike phase and then another channel, but usually the second spike becomes a failed breakout and is followed by a correction. For example, if there is a bull spike and then a lower-momentum bull channel, the market can break out of the top of the channel with another bull spike. Rarely, it will be followed by another bull channel, but more often the spike becomes a failed breakout and the market then corrects down.

When the market has a series of bars that cover a lot of points with little or no pulling back, this strong trend is a spike. The spike can be one trend bar, a series of trend bars with little overlap, or sometimes even a very tight channel. In fact, a spike on a given time frame is a steep, tight channel on a smaller time frame. Likewise, steep, tight channels are spikes on higher time frames. The spike ends at the first pause or pullback, but if it resumes within a bar or two, it becomes either a second spike or a spike on a larger time frame. The spike can be as small as a single moderate-sized trend bar or it can last for 10 or more bars. Spikes, climaxes, and breakouts should be thought of as being the same, and they are discussed more in the chapter on breakouts in book 2. In a spike up, everyone is in agreement that this is not an area of value for the bears and therefore the market needs to go up further to find prices where both the bulls and bears are willing to trade. The market will continue to quickly move higher until the bulls are willing to take some profits and are less willing to buy new positions, and the bears are beginning to short. This causes a pause or a pullback, and it is the first sign of significant two-sided trading. The opposite is true for a spike down.

Almost all trends begin with a spike, even if it is a single trend bar and not recognizable as the start of the trend until many bars later. Therefore, almost all trends are variations of a spike and channel trend. However, when the trend has more characteristics of one of the other types of trends discussed in this chapter, you should trade it as that other type to maximize your chances of success.

By definition, the spike ends immediately before the first pause bar or pullback because it is the pause that signifies the end of the spike. The market can then go on to do any of the obvious three things: the trend can resume, the market can enter a trading range, or the trend can reverse. The first possibility is the most common. The market pulls back for a couple of bars, or maybe a dozen bars, and then the trend resumes. This pullback is a gap test (remember, the spike is a gap) and the start of the channel. When the trend resumes, it is usually less strong as indicated by more overlapping bars, a flatter slope, some pullbacks, and some trend bars in the opposite direction. This is a channel, and the pattern then becomes a spike and channel trend.

The second possibility occurs if the pullback extends for more than 10 bars. It will then have grown into a trading range, which can break out in either direction. In general, the odds always favor the trading range breakout to be in the same direction as the original trend. If the trading range lasts for a long time, it is simply a flag on a higher time frame chart (for example, a three-day-long trading range on the 5 minute chart that follows a bull spike will usually be just a bull flag on the 60 minute chart, and the odds favor an upside breakout). This is a trend resumption situation and is discussed later in this chapter. Although the trend usually resumes before the end of the day and the day becomes a trend resumption trend day, the breakout from the trading range can sometimes fail or reverse within a few bars (final flag reversals are discussed in book 3 in the chapter on reversals). Rarely, the trading range lasts for several hours or even several days and has very small swings (this is a tight trading range and is discussed in book 2 on trading ranges). As with any trading range, the breakout can be in either direction but is slightly more likely to be in the direction of the trend.

The third possibility is that the market reverses. As long as the pullback from the spike is not strong enough to flip the always-in trade to the opposite direction, the market will likely continue the trend, and the continuation will almost always be in the form of a channel. Less often, the market will reverse and form a spike in the opposite direction. When this happens, the market will then usually enter a trading range as the bulls and bears fight for follow-through. The bulls will keep buying as they try to create a bull channel to follow their bull spike, and the bears will keep selling as they try to create a bear channel to follow their bear spike. Although the trading range can last for the rest of the day, one side usually wins and the market breaks out. At that point, either it forms a channel and the day becomes a spike and channel trend day or the breakout is soon followed by another trading range and the market forms a trending trading range day, which is discussed in the next chapter.

Besides reversing with a spike in the opposite direction, the market can also reverse if a trading range forms after the spike. For example, if there is a bull spike and then a trading range, in about a third of cases the market will break out of the bottom of the trading range instead of the top. The breakout can be by a sharp, large bear spike, but more often it is by an unremarkable bear trend bar that is followed by a bear channel.

If it forms a channel, it is better to trade it only in the direction of the trend. Sometimes there are large swings in the channel, which can provide countertrend scalping opportunities as the channel progresses. Be aware that channels can last much longer than you might imagine and they are always looking like they are reversing. There are many pullbacks along the way, trapping traders into the wrong direction. There are usually many bars with tails, many trend bars in the opposite direction, and lots of overlapping bars, but it is still a trend and it is very costly to trade countertrend prematurely.

Some days have an early strong momentum move (a spike) and then the trend continues in a less steep channel for the rest of the day. However, the channel sometimes accelerates and follows a parabolic curve instead of a linear path. At other times, it loses momentum and forms a flatter curve. Regardless, the start of the channel is usually tested later in the day or in the next day or two, and the test can then be followed by a trading range or a trend in either direction. The important thing to realize is that if the channel is fairly tight, it is tradable only in the with-trend direction because the pullbacks will not go far enough for a countertrend trade to be profitable. Much less often, the channel has broad swings and is tradable in both directions.

You should be prepared to look for entries in the countertrend direction after there is a breakout from the channel against the trend, since there is a good chance that the countertrend move will extend all the way back to test the start of the channel and attempt to form a trading range. Remember that a channel, no matter how steep, is a flag in the opposite direction. A bull channel is a bear flag and a bear channel is a bull flag. Also, even though a channel is a sloping trading range, it is also the first leg of a larger trading range, and the reversal is usually to the area around the start of the channel. For example, if there is a spike up, then a pullback, and then a bull channel, the bull channel is usually the first leg of a trading range that has yet to unfold. The market will usually correct down to the bottom of the channel, where it will try to form a double bottom bull flag with the bottom of the channel. This usually leads to a bounce, which is the third leg of the developing trading range. After the bounce, traders should begin to look for other patterns because the predictability of the spike and channel pattern at this point has ended. A spike is a breakout, which means that there will be a gap between the breakout point and the first pullback, which is the start of the channel. The test to the bottom of the channel is a test of the gap and is a breakout test.

Stock traders often describe the end of a bull channel as a crowded trade because they believe that anyone interested in the stock has gone long and there is no one left to buy. They then expect a fast sell-off down to the start of the channel as all of the channel buyers exit. As the stock quickly falls, they think of the bear leg as being caused by all of the late-entering bulls with open losses quickly exiting to minimize those losses. That rush to the exits by the crowd of bulls leads to the rapidity and depth of the sell-off. There are obviously many factors that influence every move, but this is likely an important component when there is a sharp correction down to the start of the channel.

Since the second part of the pattern is a channel, the behavior during the channel phase is like that of any other channel. Almost all spike and channel bull patterns end with a breakout through the bottom of the channel and a test to around the bottom of the channel. The easiest reversal setup to spot is a three-push pattern in a channel with a wedge shape, where the third push overshoots the trend channel line and reverses with a strong reversal bar, especially if there is a second entry. However, most of the time the reversal is not so clear and it is better to wait for a breakout pullback setup. For example, if there is a breakout below a bull channel, wait for a pullback to a higher high or lower high, and if there is a good bear setup, go short. If the sell-off reaches the bottom of the channel and sets up a buy, then look to go long for the double bottom bull flag bounce.

If there is a strong spike and any pullback, even a single bar, and then the trend resumes, the odds favor a spike and channel trend. For example, if there is a strong spike up that broke out of a trading range and then an inside bar, and then a bar that falls below the inside bar but reverses up into a bull reversal bar, traders will buy above that bar in anticipation of a bull channel. As soon as the market goes above that bull reversal bar, a channel is in effect. It can have a single push up lasting from one to several bars (a final flag reversal, which is discussed in book 3) and then reverse into a bear leg, or it can have two or more legs and then reverse. If the channel up is developing in an area where a reversal seems probable, like near the top of a trading range, it may reverse after a couple of legs up, before clear channel lines can be drawn. If it is forming in an area where a bull trend is probable, like in a reversal up from a strong bottom pattern, it will usually have at least three pushes, but it could have many more.

Just how far can a channel go? In a strong trend, it usually goes much farther than what most traders believe is likely. However, if the spike is large, one measured move target is from the open or low of the first bar of the spike to the close or high of the last bar of the spike, and then you project that same number of points up. Another measured move target is a leg 1 = leg 2 move where the spike is leg 1 and the channel is leg 2. Look to see if a reversal is setting up once the channel is at the measured move target.

You will usually see other measured move projections and trend line and trend channel line targets as well, but most of these targets will fail, especially if the trend is very strong. However, it is important to look for them because when a reversal finally does set up, it will usually be at one of these resistance areas, and that will give you more confidence to take the reversal trade. In general, it is far better to look at measured move targets as areas to take profits than as locations to take reversal trades. Traders should take a reversal trade only when the setup is strong, and reversal trading is discussed in book 3. Experienced traders will often scalp against the trend at measured move targets, sometimes scaling in if the market goes against them (scaling in is discussed in book 2), but very few traders can consistently do this profitably and most will lose money if they try.

A strong spike is a sign that the market is quickly moving to a new price level where both the bulls and bears feel that there is value in placing trades. The market usually overshoots the value area and then pulls back into what will become a trading range. Because both the bulls and the bears are satisfied with the prices in this new area, the directional probability of an equidistant move is about 50 percent in the middle of the trading range. That means that there is about an equal chance that the market will move up X ticks before it moves down X ticks. This uncertainty is the hallmark of a trading range. It does not matter why the market is trending. All that matters is that it is moving quickly. You can view the move as a breakout and a move away from some prior price or as a move toward some magnet. That magnet can be a key price level like a prior spike, a measured move, or a trend line. Or you can think of the breakout as a move toward neutrality where the directional probability is once again about 50 percent. This always occurs in a trading range, so once the directional probability has fallen to 50 percent, a trading range will become evident. A trend is simply a move from one trading range to another, and while in the new trading range, both the bulls and the bears are placing trades in an attempt to be positioned for what they believe will be the next breakout. This is discussed more in the section on the mathematics of trading in book 2.

As an example, if the market is in a bull channel, the directional probability of an equidistant move starts to fall, and at some unknown point it hits 50 percent. This will ultimately be the middle of the trading range, but no one yet knows where that is and the market usually has to overshoot to the upside and downside as it searches for neutrality. As the market is going up in the channel, traders will assume that the directional probability of higher prices is still better than 50 percent until it is clearly less than 50 percent. That clarity occurs at some magnet, and at that point everyone sees that the market has gone too far. This will be the general area of the top of the trading range, and the directional probability at the top of a trading range favors the bears. The result is that the market will trade down in search of neutrality, but it will usually overshoot it again because neutrality is never clear but excess is. Once the market gets to some magnet (discussed in book 2), traders will see that it has gone down too far and it will reverse up. Eventually, the range will become tighter as traders home in on neutrality, which is a price level where both the bulls and the bears feel there is value in placing trades. They are in balance and the market is then in breakout mode. Before long, perceived value will change and the market will have to break out again to find the new value area.

Once you recognize that a spike and channel trend is in effect, do not take countertrend trades in the hope that an ABC pullback will extend far enough for a scalper's profit. This is because invariably there will not have been any prior trend line break, and the tightness of the channel makes countertrend trading a losing strategy. The failures of these countertrend scalps are great with-trend setups. Just enter on a stop where the countertrend traders are exiting with their protective stops.

Aggressive traders will enter channels using limit orders, trading with trend until two-sided trading becomes prominent, and which point they will start trading countertrend. For example, if there is a bear spike and then a channel, bears will enter with limit orders at or above the highs of the prior bars. As the channel approaches support levels, they will watch to see if the bars are overlapping more, if there are more and stronger bull trend bars, if there are more dojis, and if there are bigger pullbacks. The more of these signs of two-sided trading that are present, the more willing the bulls will be to buy with limit orders at and below the lows of prior bars and swing lows, and the less willing bears will be to short above or below bars. Bears will scale out of their profitable trades after the trend has gone on for a while and is in the area of measured move targets or other types of support. Bulls will begin to scale into longs in the same areas. The increased buying and reduced selling ultimately lead to a breakout above the bear trend line.

Institutions and traders who have large enough accounts can scale into a countertrend position, expecting the market to test the start of the channel, but most traders should trade only with trend until there is a clear sign of a reversal. Also, it is risky to scale into a countertrend position in a channel in the second half of the day, because you will often run out of time. You will find yourself holding an ever-larger losing position and you will be forced to buy it back with a large loss by the close. When the bears are scaling in, some will look for a large bull trend bar that breaks above a prior swing high. They will see it as a possible exhaustive top of the trading range that should soon form. They will place limit orders to short the close of the bar and above its high, because they see the channel as the first leg of a trading range, and shorting bull spikes in the area of the top of a trading range is a standard trading range technique (discussed in book 2 on trading ranges). After the trading range has formed, traders will look back and see that the bull channel was the start of the range, and very experienced traders can begin to use trading range trading techniques as the channel is forming, if they believe that the market is in the area of the top of the soon-to-be trading range.

The spike that forms before the channel is a thin area on the chart (there is very little overlap of adjacent bars, and is a type of breakout or measuring gap, as discussed in the second book) where there is agreement between the bulls and the bears that the market is mispriced, and therefore the market moves through it quickly. Both are contributing to the rapid move away from the prices in the spike as they search for the equilibrium that can be inferred to exist once the channel starts to form. Yes, the market is still trending because one side is still dominant, but there is finally some two-sided trading. The channel itself usually has lots of overlapping bars and pullbacks and is essentially a steeply sloped tight trading range. Since this type of price action represents two-sided trading, it is reasonable to expect the start of the pattern to be tested before too long, despite how strong the trend has been. For example, in a spike and channel bear trend, all of those early bulls who bought at the very start of the bear channel, thinking that the spike would become a failed breakout, are finally back to breakeven on the pullback to that area, and this will make the pullback function like a double top. These bulls will exit around breakeven on those early longs and may not want to buy unless the market falls back again. This is likely an important component of the reason why there is usually at least some downward movement after the top of the channel is tested. Any channel is usually the first leg of a trading range and is most often followed by a countertrend move that tests the start of the channel and reveals the trading range. At that point, the trading range usually expands in duration and has at least a partial move in the direction of the original channel. From there, the market behaves like a trading range and is in breakout mode (traders are looking for a breakout) and the breakout into a new trend can come in either direction.

Sometimes the channel is so vertical that it accelerates and becomes parabolic. Although there is so little overlap between consecutive bars that it does not look like a typical channel, this parabolic move functions like the channel phase and is therefore a variant of a spike and channel trend. This parabolic move will often contain a large trend bar. For example, if there is a bear spike, which is one or more large bear trend bars, then a pause, and then another bear spike, then you have consecutive sell climaxes. Every large trend bar should be thought of as a spike, a breakout, a gap, and a climax. When there are consecutive climaxes (separated by a pause or a small pullback), they are usually followed by a two-legged correction that tests the pause that followed the first climax. The second climax should be thought of as the channel phase of the spike and channel pattern, even though it is another spike and not a low-momentum channel. However, since what usually follows is the same as with a conventional spike and channel pattern, consecutive climaxes form a variant of a spike and channel trend. Rarely, there will even be a third consecutive climax before a more complex correction ensues.

Why does the market tend to have a larger correction after consecutive sell climaxes? When there is a sell climax, there is panic selling. Weak bulls feel that they have to get out of their longs at any price. Also, weak bears see the strong momentum and are afraid they are missing a great move so they are shorting at the market to make sure they get in. If the market pauses and then has another large bear bar, that second sell climax again represents urgent sellers who don't want to wait for a pullback that may never come. Once these weak longs are out and the weak bears are in, there is no one left to short at these low prices and this creates an imbalance to the buy side. There aren't enough bears left to take the opposite side of the trade, so the market has to go up to find enough traders willing to short to fill the buy orders. The opposite is true with consecutive buy climaxes. They represent urgency. Traders feel compelled to buy at the market as it is rising quickly because they are afraid that there will not be a pullback that will let them sell at a better price. Once these emotional weak bears and bulls (the late bulls are weak) have bought all that they want to buy at these high prices, there is no one left to buy and the market has to come down to attract more buyers. The result is a correction that usually has two legs and lasts at least 10 bars or so.

Another type of a strong channel occurs in a spike and climax trend. Here, after the pause from the spike, the market creates another spike. All spikes are climaxes and when the market forms consecutive climaxes, it usually will form a larger correction, often to the beginning of the second spike. But this is exactly how a spike and channel behaves and it is therefore a variant, where there is a second spike instead of a channel. Sometimes the climax is a spike and the spike is more of a channel. For example, there might be a bull channel that then has a large one-bar bull spike. This can become a spike and climax reversal. Even though there was a channel and then a spike, it behaves like a traditional spike and channel pattern.

Since any strong vertical move can function as a spike, a gap opening qualifies. If you look at the Standard & Poor's (S&P) cash index on a day when the Emini has a large gap up opening, you will see that the first bar of the cash index is not a gap.

Instead, it is a large bull trend bar with its open around the close of yesterday and its close around the close of the first bar of the Emini. If there is then a pause or pullback and then a channel, this is a gap spike and channel trend.

When the channel is very steep, the spike and channel often together form just a spike on a higher time frame chart, and that spike will usually be followed by a channel on that higher time frame. At other times there will be a spike that lasts several bars but there is no channel. Usually the final bars of the spike have some overlap and there actually is a channel on a smaller time frame chart.

There will sometimes be a large bull trend bar, which is a spike up, and then a large bear trend bar, which is a spike down. When this happens in a bull trend that has gone on for a while, the market usually enters a trading range, with the bulls trying to generate a bull channel and the bears trying for a bear channel. Eventually one side wins and either the trend resumes or the market forms a spike and channel bear trend. The opposite happens in bear trends, where there is then a large bear trend bar. If there is a bull spike bar soon afterward, the market usually goes sideways as the two sides fight over the direction of the channel. If the bears win, the bear trend will resume, and if the bulls win, there will be a reversal. Sometimes one side appears to win in the form of a second spike, but it fails within a bar or two and leads to a channel in the opposite direction.

A spike and channel pattern is composed of two parts, and they are best traded differently. A spike is a breakout and is traded like all breakouts, which are discussed in book 2. In general, if the breakout appears to be very strong and in the context where it is likely to be successful, you can enter at the market or on small pullbacks as the spike is forming. Since a spike is also a climax, there will be a pullback at some point and this provides other opportunities to enter with the trend. Finally, the channel is no different from any other channel. If it is a tight bull channel, you can enter in the direction of the trend on pullbacks, such as those to the trend line or the moving average, or on a limit order below the low of the prior bar, or every 10 cents lower in Intel (INTC) when it is trading at $20. If the channel has broader swings, it has stronger two-sided trading and you can take trades in both directions. Since a channel is a flag in the opposite direction, once it starts to reverse you can take the reversal trade. It usually corrects to around the beginning of the channel where you can enter on a test of the start of the channel, which will be a double bottom bull flag in a spike and channel bull pullback, and a double top bear flag in a spike and channel bear pullback.

If the channel has lots of overlap between adjacent bars and many trend bars in the opposite direction and several pullbacks that last several bars, it is a weak channel. The weaker the channel, the more aggressive the institutional counter trend traders will be. For example, if there is a weak bear channel after a bear spike, strong bulls will scale in as the market moves lower. There will be firms buying with every conceivable reason, like buying below the low of every bar or every prior swing low, or buying every $1.00 lower in Google (GOOG) when it is trading at $500, or on every test of the trend channel line, or on every reversal bar on a small time frame chart, or on every $1.00 bounce up off the low in GOOG, in case the reversal up has begun. If, instead of breaking out of the top of the channel, the market breaks strongly out of the bottom and creates a strong bear spike that lasts several bars, these bulls will have to cover by exiting their longs. As they sell out of their longs, they add to the strength of the bear breakout, and they might even reverse to short for a momentum trade down. However, in most cases the downside breakout will not go very far, and once the last desperate bulls have sold out of their positions, there is no one left who is willing to short at these low prices. The market will usually rally for at least two legs and at least 10 bars as it searches for a higher price where bears might be willing to short once again.

When the market is trending strongly and then develops a spike in the opposite direction, the spike will usually lead to just a pullback (a flag) and then the trend will resume. However, it is a statement that the traders who believe that the market might reverse are now willing to begin taking positions. If the market begins to form one or two more spikes over the next 10 to 20 bars, the countertrend force of those spikes is cumulative and the market is transitioning to more two-sided trading. This can develop into a trading range, a deeper correction, or even a trend reversal. For example, if there is a very strong bull trend of any type, not simply a spike and channel bull, and the market has been above the moving average for 20 or more bars and it is at its high, then the bull trend is very strong. If there is suddenly a moderately sized bear trend bar that opens near its high and closes near its low, this is a bear spike. The bar can be a bear reversal bar, an entry bar below a bear reversal bar, or even an inside bar, and it does not matter. This first spike down will almost always just lead to a bull flag. After the bull trend resumes, watch for another bear spike. Eventually one will be followed by a pullback to the moving average. This first pullback to the moving average will usually be followed by a test of the high of the bull trend. The test can be in the form of a higher high, a double top, or a lower high. However, the pullback to the moving average is usually enough to break at least some bull trend line and then the rally that follows might be the final rally before a significant pullback or even a reversal takes place.

If there is a third and larger bear spike at the new high, the odds of at least a two-legged correction increase, and the move down after the spike down will usually be in some type of channel. Is the market ignoring those prior two bear spikes? The market never ignores anything. Although this latest bear spike might be the one everyone considers to be the seminal event, there is a cumulative effect from the other bear spikes as well. In fact, if the second bear spike was particularly strong and then the market rallied to a new high, and the next bear spike was modest but it led to a correction, you have to consider a different interpretation of what just took place. It is possible that the second bear spike was actually the more important one, and was the actual start of the down move, and that the rally to the new high after the spike was simply a pullback from that spike. It is important to understand that any breakout pullback can test the old extreme with either a lower high, a double top, or a higher high, and that test can often be the start of the bear channel. Although it may appear that the small spike down began the bear trend and that the channel that followed it was the first bear channel, sometimes the earlier spike is more influential. Its channel can begin at the high of the bull trend, and it can begin with that smaller spike down from the high. The channel that follows that small bear spike is then inside the larger channel that began at the bull high, just before that small bear spike formed.

When the market is in a trading range, it often has both a bull spike and a bear spike. The bulls and bears then fight to create a channel. Eventually one side will dominate and will be able to form a trend channel. It often begins with a breakout, which is then a second spike. Both spikes contribute to the formation of the channel.

A bull channel is a bear flag and a bear channel is a bull flag, and like all flags they are continuation patterns that usually break out in the direction of the trend. However, sometimes they break out in the opposite direction, leading to a trend reversal. The breakout is a spike, so instead of a spike and channel trend, the market forms a channel and spike trend that is unrelated to a spike and channel pattern. But usually the spike is followed by a channel. For example, if there is a bear trend and it has a pullback, the pullback is a rising channel and therefore a bear flag. Sometimes the channel will break out to the upside. A breakout is a bull trend bar and a spike, and if the breakout is successful, the follow-through will be a channel. The bull trend began with the spike, and that spike and the channel that follows form a spike and channel bull trend. The original channel was the final flag of the bear trend and it broke to the upside, but it is not related to the spike and channel bull trend that followed. The spike changed the market and it is the start of the new perspective for traders, who will then ignore the bear flag that preceded it.

A similar situation happens when a wedge reversal fails. For example, a wedge top is a rising bull channel, and therefore a bear flag, and it usually breaks to the downside. If instead it breaks to the upside, the breakout is a spike and it may be followed by a channel and a measured move up. The breakout always resets the mind-set and should be thought of as the start of a new trend. In this case, the trend is still a bull trend, like the trend before the wedge, but now it is an even stronger bull trend. Usually, upside breakouts do not go more than five to 10 bars before reversing into either a protracted, two-legged pullback or a trend in the opposite direction. They represent exceptionally climactic and therefore overdone buying. This is at the tails of the bell curve of behavior, and institutions will have all sorts of indicators telling them that the bull trend is overdone and should correct. Each institution will rely on its own measure of excess, but enough institutions usually will see the rally as excessive and their bets that the market will fall will soon overwhelm the bulls, and the reversal will ensue.

Spike and channel behavior is one of the most common and therefore most important things that you will see on every chart. There are countless variations and many interpretations of every pattern. Sometimes the spike will be one bar, but then, after a pause, there will be an even better-looking spike. The channel can be so vertical that it functions as part of the spike, and the spike and channel might be simply a spike on a higher time frame. That channel can be very small or very large relative to the spike. When there is a strong trend, there will usually be several spikes within the channel, and the channel can subdivide into smaller spike and channel patterns. Be open to all possibilities because they all have the potential to offer profitable trading opportunities.

FIGURE 21.1 Three Pushes in a Spike and Channel

Sometimes a bull spike and channel can end with three pushes up, a trend channel line overshoot, and a strong bear reversal bar, but most reversals are not so straightforward. In Figure 21.1, bar 6 was part of a two-bar spike up but the move up from the bar 5 low was so steep that you can also consider bar 5 as the start of the spike. It does not matter because any strong reversal up on the open is likely to have follow-through buying, and there will be buy programs based on each. Here, it was in the form of a channel that had three pushes up and a wedge shape. Channels often pull back after a third push up. Bar 10 overshot the trend channel line and reversed down into a bear reversal bar, which set up a short trade. A bull wedge usually corrects in two legs down to around the bottom of the wedge, and a channel in a spike and channel bull usually corrects down in two legs to the start of the channel, which is also the bar 7 low.

Spikes can be cumulative. The bar before bar 7 was a bear spike but it simply led to a test of the moving average. Bar 9 was a second bear spike. These two spikes indicate that the bears were trying to seize control over the market and that the market was becoming two-sided. Bar 10 was the first bar of a two-bar bear spike, and bar 11 was followed by another bear spike. Just because that final spike broke below the wedge and clearly led to the bear leg does not mean that it turned the market all by itself. Those earlier spikes were also part of the transition and should

Figure 21.1   SPIKE AND CHANNEL TREND   **339**

not be overlooked. As they were forming, you should understand that the market was telling you that it was in transition and you should begin to look for trades in both directions and not just buy setups.

Bar 16 was a one-bar spike but the spike up also can be considered to have begun with bar 15. There was a pullback to bar 17 and then three small pushes up to bar 21, where the market reversed.

The bar after 15 is a one-bar spike, and the four bars that followed formed a small channel, ending at bar 16; the entire move up to 16 was also a spike.

Bar 22 was a spike down and it corrected sideways to bar 25, where a channel began down to bar 27, which was the third push down after the spike (bars 23 and 26 were the first two), and bar 27 overshot the trend channel line and closed in its middle. That was not a strong signal bar and neither was the bear inside bar that followed, but the market reversed up into the close.

Deeper Discussion of This Chart

In Figure 21.1, the market broke below the moving average and the trading range at the close of yesterday. Since there were many bear trend bars in that trading range and the first bar of today had a strong bear body, it is reasonable not to buy the failed breakout long that was set up by the second bar of today and instead to wait for a second signal before going long. Even though the second bar was a strong bull reversal bar, there was nothing to reverse since it totally overlapped the prior bar. This was a small trading range, not a good reversal. All down gaps are bear spikes and can be followed by bear channels. Bar 2 trapped bulls and became a breakout pullback short setup for a bear spike and channel trend to bar 3. Bar 3 was a breakout below a one-bar final flag and became the first bar of a strong two-bar reversal that became the low of the day. Arguably, this bull reversal can be described as a failed breakout but it more accurately is a reversal up at the end of a bear channel.

The bull trend bar before bar 6 is when traders gave up on the possibility that the rally from bar 3 was just a bear flag. That bar was a breakout from the notion that the market was in a bear trend to the idea that it had flipped into a bull trend. This idea was confirmed on bar 6, when most traders finally believed that the market became always-in long. Many believed that the market had reversed to up by the close of the bar before bar 6, and that bull trend bar was also a spike, a breakout bar, and a gap. The low of the bar that followed it (bar 6, in this case) formed the bottom of the gap, and the high of the breakout point formed the top of the gap. Here it was both bar 5 and the small bear inside bar that followed it. Since the bar before bar 6 was a gap, that gap was a magnet and had a good chance of being tested over the next 10 bars or so. Bar 7 was the test, and it became the bottom of the channel that followed the spike up. Some saw the spike beginning on the trend bar before bar 6, and others saw it as beginning at bar 5 or the bull bar after bar 3. Bar 12 was the correction down from the channel high, and, as expected in a spike and channel pattern, the pullback again tested the gap and tried to form a double bottom with the bar 7 bottom of the channel up to bar 10. In this case, it failed.

Bar 12 was the test of the bar 7 bottom of the bull channel that ended at bar 10, but the move down to bar 12 was in a tight channel so it was likely just the first of two legs down. Because of this, a double bottom bull flag long never triggered above the bull inside bar after bar 12. Instead, bar 13 was a large bear trend bar. Since it was occurring at the end of a relatively long bear leg, it was more likely to be an exhaustive climax that should lead to at least a 10-bar, two-legged sideways to up correction. I use the phrase "10-bar, two-legged" often, and my intention is to say that the correction will last longer and be more complex than a small pullback. That usually requires at least 10 bars and two legs.

The move up to bar 14 was the first leg, and then it pulled back to a lower low at bar 15, and this was followed by a second leg up to bar 21. Bar 15 might have been the second leg down from the bar 10 high but it turns out that the correction became more complex and the second leg ended at bar 27, which formed a double bottom bull flag with bar 5 and again with bar 15. It does not matter which you consider, because the implication is the same. There will be some programs that use one and other programs will use the other, but both types of programs will be buying for a measured move up. They were looking for a second leg up from the bar 3 low in the form of leg 1 = leg 2 where leg 1 was bar 3 to bar 10, and leg 2 was the bar 27 low up to the bar 31 high. On a higher time frame chart, bar 27 was a simple high 2 buy setup, since it was two legs down from the rally to bar 10. It was a two-legged higher low after a strong move up, and became the pullback that led to the measured move up to bar 31. The rally to bar 31 overshot the measured move by a few ticks but it was close enough to satisfy the bulls who took profits there. The market then sold off to the bar 32 low.

The move down to bar 15 was a wedge bull flag where the first two pushes ended at bars 7 and 13. It does not matter that bar 10 was a higher high test of bar 6 instead of a lower high because this is common in wedge flags.

Bar 21 was a wedge bear flag, which is common when the breakout above a double top fails. Bars 16 and 18 formed a double top but instead of breaking out to the downside, the market broke out above. The market had two small legs up to bar 21, where the market reversed and the breakout failed. Bars 16, 18, and 21 are the three pushes up in the wedge bear flag.

Figure 21.2   SPIKE AND CHANNEL TREND   **341**

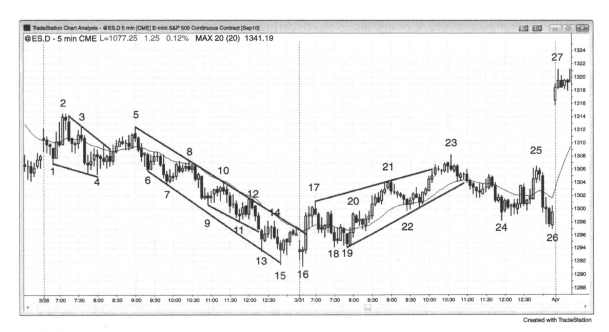

FIGURE 21.2 Spike and Channels Occur Every Day

Some form of a spike and channel trend is present every day. In Figure 21.2, the first day, March 28, was a bear spike and channel day that began with a spike up but reversed into a three-bar spike down from bar 2 and then again from bar 3. There, it attempted to form a double bottom with the swing low at the end of the prior day. Either of the two large bear trend bars between bars 2 and 4 could also be considered the initial spike of the bear trend. Bar 8 formed a double top with the top of the small bear flag that followed bar 6, and then the market drifted down in a tight channel all day, with several good short entries near the moving average.

The market broke above the channel on the next day with the spike up to bar 17. Since the start of the channel usually gets tested, traders could now start to look for long setups for a test of the bar 5 area. The bar 5 start of the bear channel was tested by bar 23 and exceeded by the bar 27 gap up on the following day.

The channel down to bar 15 became slightly parabolic (it broke below the bear trend channel line from bar 9 to bar 11, indicating that the slope of the decline increased), which is climactic behavior and therefore not sustainable long-term. Traders could have also created the trend channel line by taking a parallel of the bar 5 to bar 8 trend line, and then anchoring it to the bar 6 or 7 low. Bars 13 and 15 would have overshot that line as well.

During the sell-off, the bears scale into shorts and scalp for every conceivable reason. For example, they might sell on every two-point bounce or above the high of the previous bar, like above bar 9 and above the high of each of the five bars that followed bar 9 and had a high above the high of the prior bar. They would short at the moving average and at the trend line, like at bar 10. They would short on every tiny break above the trend line, like at bar 11. They would also short below the low of every pullback bar, like below the low of bar 10. Other bears will short on a fixed amount below every test of the top of the channel, like one or two points down after the test, betting that the downward momentum will have follow-through. Since this bear trend will be evident on every other small time frame and every other type of chart, traders will be shorting based on those charts as well, and on higher time frame charts.

Aggressive bulls would be buying in that same bear channel. Some will be buying for scalps, like maybe at every test of the trend channel line, like at the bar 13 and bar 15 lows. Others will be scaling in, believing that the market should test the bar 8 or bar 10 top of the channel either today or tomorrow. They might buy every test of the trend channel line and every new swing low. For example, they might have limit orders to buy as the market fell below the bar 11 low during the spike down to bar 13. They might buy at the low, a few ticks lower, or a couple of points lower. Others will buy at the first sign that the sell climax down to bar 13 is stalling. They would see the smaller bear body and the large tail as a sign of exhaustion and therefore likely to be followed by a tradable rally. Some traders will scale in with larger positions, like two to three times the size of the prior position. Some will buy on a stop two points above the low, seeing a bounce of that size as a sign that the reversal in underway. Others will be trading off smaller and larger time frame charts or charts based on ticks or volume. The sell-off might be a pullback to the 60 minute or daily moving average, or to a strong bull trend line on a higher time frame chart. There are traders both buying and selling for every conceivable reason and scaling in and out using every imaginable approach. They can all make money if they know what they are doing. For most traders, however, it is risky to scale into longs in a bear channel in the final couple of hours of the day. They will too often find themselves holding a large losing position that they will be forced to exit before the close with a loss. Traders are more likely to make a profit in a bear channel if they look for short setups rather than trying to scale into longs, especially in the final couple of hours of the day.

The spike up to bar 17 was followed by a wedge-shaped channel up to bar 23, and then a pullback, and then a large gap up on the next day. That gap up move might still be part of the channel up. Any gap is also a spike, and it can then be followed by another channel.

The move down from bar 8 to bar 9 was also a spike, and the bear channel from bar 10 to bar 15 was retraced by the rally to bar 21. The move down from the double top bear flag created by bars 10 and 21 ended at bar 22, which was also a test of the moving average. A strong bear move should not be expected since there has been a

Figure 21.2   SPIKE AND CHANNEL TREND   **343**

trend reversal into a bull trend and the move up to bar 21 was strong. Seven of the prior eight bars had bull bodies and trending highs, lows, and closes.

Deeper Discussion of This Chart

Bar 4 in Figure 21.2 was a wedge bull flag buy setup and the rally ended in a double top bear flag (bars 3 and 5).

The bear channel tested the bear trend line five times, yet was never able to accelerate to the downside very far. Whenever the market repeatedly tests a line and does not fall far from it, the market usually breaks above it.

The bottom was formed by the three pushes down at bars 13, 15, and 16. Even though the pattern did not have a wedge shape, the implication is identical.

The spike up to bar 17 broke above the bear trend line. Bar 17 was a moving average gap bar, which often begins the final leg of the trend before a larger reversal takes place.

The sell-off from the moving average gap bar tested the bear low in the form of a higher low at bar 18, which formed a double bottom bull flag with bar 19, and a double bottom pullback with the bar 15 and 16 double bottom. A double bottom bull flag is just a higher low that has two tests down.

Channels often pull back after the third push up, and since the rally to bar 23 was below the top of yesterday's bear trend, many traders saw it as a bear rally and were looking to short it. The wedge bear flag and the bar 23 bear reversal bar formed a good sell setup for at least a two-legged move down. Traders expected it to last about 10 or more bars and maybe test the bar 22 or bar 19 lows. The move down to bar 24 had two legs but was steep enough to make traders wonder if it was actually just a complex first leg. This resulted in the sell-off to bar 26 at the close. Bar 26 tested near the bottom of the bull channel, where it formed a double bottom bull flag with bar 18 (or 19).

The bar 17 gap up opening was almost a measured move up above the wedge, which is common when the market breaks above the top of a wedge.

There was a small wedge bear flag from bar 24 to bar 25.

The rally from bar 4 to bar 5 was also a wedge bear flag.

There was a large wedge bull flag using bars 22, 24, and 26, even though the rally to bar 25 eliminated the wedge shape. Most three-push patterns function exactly like wedges and they should all be considered to be variants.

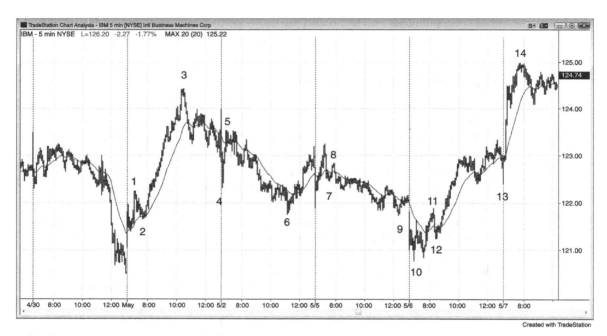

FIGURE 21.3   Spike and Channel Trends Are Common

IBM had several spike and channel days on the 5 minute chart in Figure 21.3, and some were nested, with larger ones subdividing into smaller ones, which is common. Since the start of the channel often gets tested within a day or two, make sure to consider countertrend setups even on the next day. Each of the channel beginnings (bars 2, 5, and 8) was tested except the last one (bar 12). Bar 13 tried to begin the sell-off to test bar 12, but it instead it quickly failed and reversed up strongly.

The spike up to bar 1 was followed by a nearly vertical and slightly parabolic move up to bar 3 instead of a typical channel. This is a variant of a spike and channel trend. This also happened with the spike up to bar 11 and the channel up from bar 12. When channels are this steep, they usually are spikes on higher time frame charts.

The rally to bar 3, from either bar 2 or the low of the chart, was so steep that it was a large spike. In fact, it formed a four-bar bull spike on the 60 minute chart, and was followed by a large, two-legged pullback that ended at bar 10 (bar 6 was the end of the first leg). The market rallied for the next two weeks to almost an exact measured move up (at $128.83, which was equal to about the height of the low of the chart to the top of bar 3, added to the high of bar 3).

Figure 21.3   SPIKE AND CHANNEL TREND   **345**

Although the spike down to bar 7 appears to be the obvious choice for the start of the bear leg, there was another interpretation and both probably influenced the market. Notice the large spike down on the open of May 5. Although the market rallied to a nominal higher high, this bear spike was very important and can be considered the spike that led to the channel down. The higher high might have been simply a higher high pullback from the bear spike and can be viewed as the start of the bear channel.

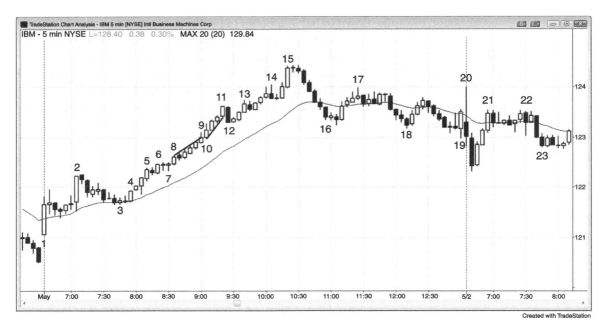

FIGURE 21.4   Steep, Parabolic Micro Channel

Figure 21.4 is a close-up of the prior chart that illustrates the parabolic nature of the channel. The move from bars 8 to 9 was in a steep micro channel but the market broke above the channel and formed an even steeper bull channel from bars 10 to 11. This increase in the slope creates a parabolic shape, which is unsustainable and therefore a type of climax. However, a climax can last longer than you can sustain your account, so never look to short such a strong bull trend, even though you know it cannot last indefinitely.

Although it did not seem likely, the market tested below the low of the beginning of the channel at bar 3 on the following day.

Whenever a market starts to develop about 10 or more strongly trending bars with little overlap and small tails, it is in a very strong trend and traders are buying it at the market. Why are they not waiting for a pullback? Because they are so certain that prices will be higher very soon and they are not certain that there will a pullback soon, so they don't wait for a pullback that might not come. Even if there is a pullback, they are confident that it will be shallow and last only a few bars before there is a new high.

The move from bar 1 to bar 2 is a spike and climax trend. Bar 1 is the spike, but instead of a channel, the market created a second spike at bar 2. Consecutive climaxes are usually followed by a deeper pullback, often to the bottom of the

Figure 21.4   SPIKE AND CHANNEL TREND   **347**

second climax, as it did here. Since this is exactly what spike and channels do, a spike and climax should be thought of as another type of spike and channel trend.

Although the move from bar 7 to bar 11 was a micro channel, it was tight enough so that traders expected it to be a spike on a higher time frame chart. The entire move from bar 3 to bar 15 was tight enough to be a spike as well. In fact, the market pulled back to near the bottom of the spike over the next three days. This was followed by a seven-day bull channel that reached a measured move up, based on the height of the spike.

The move up from bar 12 to bar 14 was in a channel, and it was followed by a spike breakout consisting of two bull trend bars to the bar 15 high. Here, there is a spike following a channel, which is sometimes the case in a spike and climax variant of a spike and channel pattern. The spike is the channel up to bar 14 and the channel is the spike up to bar 15, and the combination behaves like a traditional spike and channel pattern.

As strong as the three-bar bull spike up to bar 21 was, on a small enough time frame—for example, a 10 tick chart—it was almost certainly a tight channel, as are most spikes.

Deeper Discussion of This Chart

In Figure 21.4, bar 1 was a strong bull breakout bar that broke above the bear channel of yesterday's close and above the moving average. It opened almost on its low tick and was a bull spike that was likely to be followed by a bull channel. There was a second bull spike at bar 2, and these back-to-back buy climaxes were followed by an eight-bar pullback to the moving average, where bar 3 tested the low of the pullback after bar 1 and set up a double bottom bull flag long.

The four bull trend bars ending at bar 9 were fairly uniform in size, not too large so not climactic, and contained in a micro channel. This kind of strength would almost certainly be followed by higher prices and traders could have traded it like a bull spike, which it probably was on a higher time frame chart. They could simply buy on the close of any of the bars and put a protective stop below the bottom of the spike, which was the bull bar that formed two bars after bar 8. Whenever the market is trending strongly and has not yet had a climax, experienced traders are buying small positions all of the way up. Since their protective stop is relatively far away, their risk is greater so their position size is smaller, but they keep adding to their position as the market rises. Bar 12 was the first attempt to reverse the channel and was likely to fail, but the bulls started taking profits on the bear bars that followed, like the bar after bar 13 and again on bar 14. They took their remaining profits on the two-bar buy climax up to bar 15, on the small bear inside bars that followed, and on the strong bear trend bar after that, which was probably going to lead to at least a two-legged correction after the buy climax.

Bar 15 was a large bull trend bar at the end of a protracted trend. Although it might have been a breakout and the start of another leg up, it was more likely a buy vacuum. The strong bulls and bears were waiting for a bar like this to sell around its close. It always forms just below one or more resistance levels, and as the market approaches the area, the bears and many bulls step aside. The bulls who like to buy strongly rising markets were unopposed and quickly pushed it up to the target. The strong bulls took profits and the strong bears shorted. Both expected the buy climax to be followed by a deeper, more complex correction, where they would then both buy. The bears would take profits on their shorts and the bulls would reestablish their longs.

Figure 21.5   SPIKE AND CHANNEL TREND   **349**

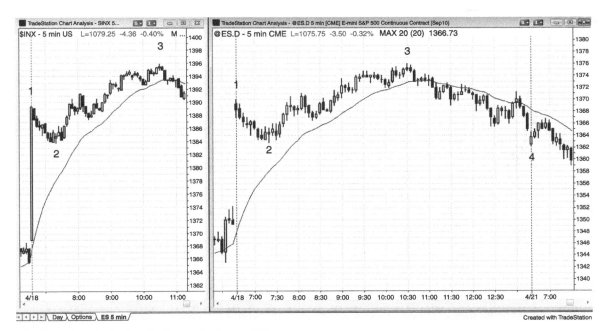

FIGURE 21.5   A Gap Spike and Channel Day

Sometimes a gap can be the spike, forming a gap spike and channel day (see Figure 21.5). The chart on the left is the S&P cash index, and you can see that the gap up on the Emini chart on the right was just a large bull trend bar and therefore a spike up on the cash index. Therefore, it makes sense to consider a gap on the Emini as just a large trend bar.

The bar 2 start of the channel was tested on the next day (bar 4). The channel up to bar 3 was losing momentum and began to curve downward as it rounded over at the top.

Deeper Discussion of This Chart

The bull flag from bars 1 to 2 that led to the channel in Figure 21.5 also functioned like a final flag, but the breakout before the reversal down from bar 3 was protracted. It might have been a final flag on a higher time frame.

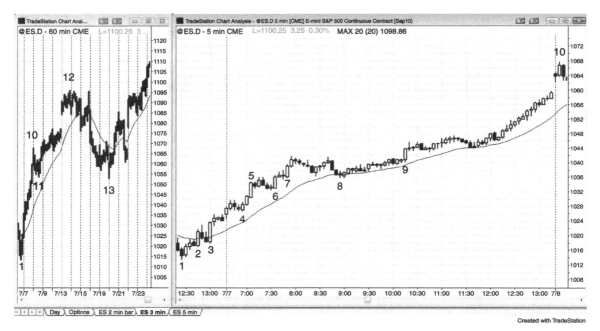

Created with TradeStation

FIGURE 21.6   Steep Channels Are Spikes

Sometimes the market just keeps forming a series of spikes, and the channels are so steep that they become spikes on a higher time frame chart (see Figure 21.6). The 5 minute Emini chart on the right had many spikes up, and the channel from bars 8 to 10 was so steep that there was no pullback that tested the beginning of the channel. Instead, the entire spike and channel pattern up to bar 10 was just a spike on the 60 minute chart on the left. Bar 10 on the 60 minute chart corresponds to bar 10 on the 5 minute chart. The 60 minute chart then formed a channel up to bar 12 and the market corrected back to the bottom of the 60 minute channel by bar 13.

Although the three-bar spike from bar 4 to bar 5 formed the clearest spike of the day on the 5 minute chart, there were several other spikes, like bars 2, 3, 6, 7, and 9, and all had the possibility of being followed by a channel up. The three-bar move down to bar 8 was a spike down, and it could have led to a channel down to test the start of either of the channels up from bars 4 or 6, but the bull trend was so strong that it was simply a 20 gap bar buy signal leading to a protracted channel up.

Deeper Discussion of This Chart

Yesterday closed in a small bull trend in Figure 21.6, and today's open broke above a two-bar bull flag from yesterday's close. Bar 4 was a breakout pullback long entry in this trend from the open bull trend day.

Figure 21.7   SPIKE AND CHANNEL TREND   **351**

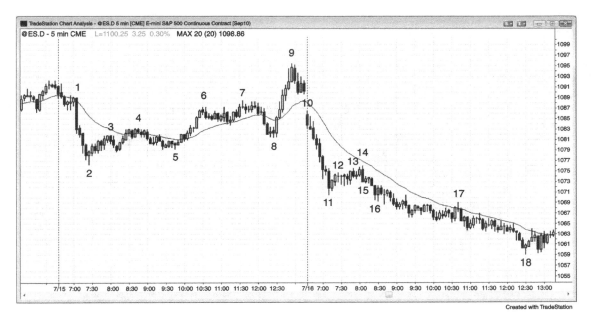

FIGURE 21.7 A Channel Can Follow Long after the Spike

As shown in Figure 21.7, strong spikes don't always *appear* to lead to channels, like the spike down to bar 2 or the spike up to bar 9. However, trends almost always begin with some spike, even though it might be easy to overlook. Sometimes, spikes and channels look very different on higher and lower time frame charts, but you do not need to look at them if you can infer what they show from what you can see on the 5 minute chart. What at first glance appears to be a big spike might in fact, on a smaller time frame, be a spike and channel that is so steep that it is easy to miss the channel. Conversely, what appears to be a steep spike and channel might be simply a spike on a higher time frame chart.

The move down from bar 1 to bar 2 looks like a spike but the market instead saw bar 1 as a spike and the next four bars down to bar 2 as a channel, which was probably much easier to see on a smaller time frame chart. The entire move down to bar 2 can also be viewed as a spike down that was followed by a pullback to a higher high at bar 9, and then the channel down began. Sometimes the pullback from the spike goes beyond the start of the spike before the channel begins.

The first part of that channel down was a spike from bar 9 to bar 11, which was followed by a channel down from bar 14 to bar 18. Also, the gap before bar 10 together with bar 10 itself formed a spike down, and then the move down to bar 11 was a channel.

Once you understand how to see the subtleties of spike and channel patterns, you will adjust your assessment of probabilities of your potential trades, and you will also find many more trading opportunities.

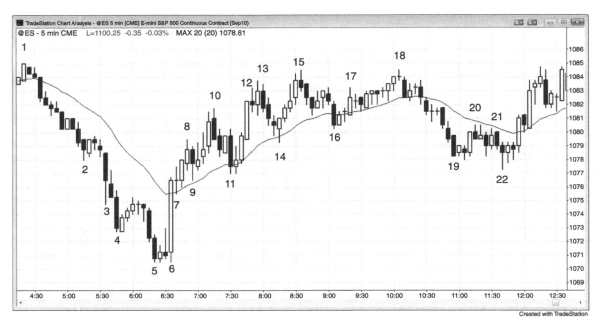

FIGURE 21.8 Consecutive Climaxes

Consecutive climaxes create a variant of a spike and channel trend pattern. Every large trend bar should be thought of as a breakout, a spike, and a climax. In Figure 21.8, bar 3 was a large bear trend bar in a bear trend, and it was a sell climax. However, a climax does not mean that the market will reverse. It simply means that it went too far, too fast, and it might pause for one or more bars. The trend can then resume, or the market could go sideways or even reverse.

This climax was corrected by a one-bar pause, which was a bear inside bar, and was then followed by bar 4, another sell climax. Bar 4 was followed by a three-bar correction and then a third consecutive sell climax that marked the low of the bear trend. This final sell climax was the two-bar move down to the bar 5 low. It does not matter that the bars are strong bear bars with large bodies, small tails, and little overlap. A climax usually leads to a correction. These traders were desperate to sell and could not take the chance of waiting for a bounce that would allow them to sell at a better price. Once these weak traders have sold, there is no one left who wants to sell and this leaves the buyers in control, lifting the market. There was a one-bar correction after the bar 3 climax, a three-bar correction after the bar 4 climax, and a major reversal after the bar 5 climax. Usually when there are two consecutive climaxes, there is at least a two-legged correction. When there are three, the reversal is generally even larger, as it was here.

Figure 21.8   SPIKE AND CHANNEL TREND   **353**

Since consecutive climaxes are a variant of spike and channel trends, you can think of bar 3 as a spike and bar 4 as a channel, even though there is no series of small overlapping bars with tails as you would see in a typical channel. Then bar 4 became a spike for the channel down to bar 5.

Bar 6 was a bull spike that ended with the bar 8 channel. The move up to bar 8 was so steep that bars 6 to 8 could have been considered a spike, and they probably formed a spike on a higher time frame chart. Bars 7 to 10 formed a channel after the bar 6 spike. At this point, the breakout gap created by the bar 6 spike had two breakout points, the top of the small rally after bar 4 and the high of the bar before bar 6. Different traders have put more emphasis on one over the other, but both were important. Bar 11 was a test of the bottom of the channel and therefore a test of the gap. This made bar 11 a breakout test, and as usual it formed a double bottom bull flag with the bar 7 or bar 9 start of the bull channel. Once the market started moving up again, the bulls would not have wanted it to test back down. If it did, they would have seen that as a sign of weakness and the chance of a strong move up would have been greatly reduced.

Bar 10 was at the end of a four-bar parabolic move up. If you connect the highs of the consecutive bars from bar 9 through bar 10, the line created would have a parabolic shape. Its slope increased two bars after bar 9 and decreased between the final two bars. The channel from bar 7 to bar 10 was so steep that the move from bar 6 to bar 10 was probably a spike on a higher time frame chart.

Bar 12 ended a two-bar spike and bar 15 ended a parabolic channel.

Bars 7 through 15 created a larger channel with three pushes.

Bar 17 was a three-bar spike, and it was followed by a parabolic channel up to bar 18.

The three-bar spike down to bar 19 was followed by a small channel down to bar 22. Bars 21 and 22 formed a small spike and a second sell climax (the move to bar 19 was the first) and were therefore likely to lead to a correction up.

Deeper Discussion of This Chart

When beginning traders looked at the chart in Figure 21.8 at the end of the day, they immediately would see a trading range that began around bars 7, 9, or 11. As the bull channel from bar 7 to bar 15 was forming, they were probably not aware that a bull channel in a spike and channel day is usually the start of a trading range. However, experienced traders knew this, and they began to short above every prior swing high, and many scaled in higher. They exited their shorts around the bar 22 double bottom test of the bar 9 or bar 11 bottom of the bull channel. Bar 22 also appeared to be a possible final flag reversal, as well as a second entry long setup at the bottom of the developing trading range. Finally, it was a lower low pullback from the bar 20 breakout above the bear micro channel down to bar 19.

The wedge up to bar 15 was also a shrinking stairs bull channel since the second peak was eight ticks above the first and the third was only three ticks above the second. This indicates waning momentum.

A wedge usually has a two-legged correction, but when the wedge is large, the legs often subdivide. The move down to bar 16 was contained in a fairly tight bear channel and therefore was likely to be just the first leg down, even though it subdivided into two legs. It had too few bars to adequately correct a wedge of this size. The low-momentum move to bar 18 was the pullback that led to the second leg down, which ended at bar 22. Bar 18 was an exact double top with the bar 15 top of the wedge, and when the market reverses down at a double top test of a wedge high, traders become more confident that the top is in for the near term. The sell-off is usually strong and has at least two legs. Bar 22 tested the bars 9 and 11 bottom of the channel and formed a double bottom bull flag with them. Since bar 20 broke above the micro channel down to bar 19, bar 22 was a two-legged lower low pullback from that channel breakout. The two-bar reversal that began with bar 22 was therefore a reasonable buy setup for at least a small swing up.

The move from bar 6 to bar 15 was so strong that the trading range to bar 22 that followed would likely have an upside breakout and maybe lead to a leg 1 = leg 2 measured move up (leg 1 was from bars 6 to 15 and leg 2 began at bar 22 and its end had not yet formed).

Most breakouts of trading ranges fail, so traders were expecting the move down to bar 19 to have little follow-through, since it was near the bottom of the trading range. If they shorted the low 2 at bar 21, they were expecting a final flag (bars 19 through 21) and a reversal up from the bottom of the trading range.

Since bar 6 was a large bull spike, traders should look to take profits at possible measured move targets based on the spike. You should look at the open or low and measure to the close or high of the bar. In this case, the top of the spike was the bar 7 doji, which is not an obvious choice to consider, but it is best to look at every possibility. The bar 15 high of the wedge was a measured move to the tick from the low of bar 6 to the high of bar 7, projecting that number of points up from the bar 7 high.

Figure 21.9   SPIKE AND CHANNEL TREND   **355**

FIGURE 21.9   A Gap Up and Double Bottom

A large gap up on the open often has a two-legged sideways or down move before the trend up begins. Whenever the opening range (the first five to 10 bars or so) is under 30 percent of an average daily range, the day is in breakout mode and traders will buy a breakout above and short a breakout below. If this small range occurs when there is a large gap up, the odds of a trend day up or down are high.

In Figure 21.9, the rally from bar 5 to the bar before bar 6 was a strong bull spike. The market corrected sideways to bar 9 and then had a buy climax rally up to bar 10, completing the spike and climax type of spike and channel bull trend.

Bar 6 was the first bear spike in a strong bull trend, and it led to a bull flag (an iii pattern) as expected.

Once traders saw the strong bar 11 bear spike, they wondered if there might be a trend reversal because it was a reversal down from a higher high after the final bull flag to bar 9 broke the steep bull trend line. It followed a strong spike up after bar 9. When the market has two strong spikes in opposite directions within a few bars of each other, it then usually goes sideways as the two sides fight over the creation of the channel. The bulls want the channel to go up and the bears want it to go down. The market went sideways here but ultimately the bear spike won.

As the market went sideways, it formed a lower high in the form of a small double top at bar 12 and then a pullback to bar 13. Bar 13 was a bull trend bar that trapped bulls into a long position, and was the first bar of a two-bar reversal that led to a large sell-off.

There will often be a spike down and a spike up within a trading range, and this usually puts the market in breakout mode. The bulls are hoping for follow-through in the form of a bull channel, whereas the bears want a bear channel. Bar 9 led to a two-bar bull spike, and the pullback that could lead to a bull channel began with the bar 11 bear spike. At this point, the bears were looking for a bear channel. The market entered a tight trading range and the bulls attempted to begin their channel with the bar 13 bull trend bar, but the bears overwhelmed them and were able to turn the market down into a bear channel.

Deeper Discussion of This Chart

The market gapped up strongly in Figure 21.9, breaking out above yesterday's high, but the first bar was a bear reversal bar and it set up a failed breakout short. The market went sideways and formed a double bottom at the bar 4 outside up bar. Some traders would have reversed to long as bar 4 went above the high of the prior bar, because many large gap up days have small double bottoms and then huge bull trends. Other traders bought above the bar 5 breakout pullback setup (an inside bar is a pause and, therefore, a type of pullback), and still others waited to buy until there was a breakout above the opening range, above bar 2.

Bar 5 was a breakout pullback buy setup for the breakout above the bars 3 and 4 double bottom or high 2. Bars 3, 4, and 5 also formed a triangle after a large gap up. The large gap up was a spike and the triangle was likely to be a bull flag, since most trading ranges in bull trends break out to the upside.

Bars 6, 8, and 9 created a triangle (it could also be called a wedge bull flag), and any trading range in a bull trend is a bull flag. Bar 9 was also a one-bar pullback from the breakout on the bar before it from the bars 6 and 8 double bottom.

Although the bars 6, 8, and 9 triangle became a large final flag, the four bars down from bar 12 and the double bottom bull flag created by bar 11 and the third bar after bar 12 were also a final bull flag. The bull breakout to the bar 13 high was brief and could not even go above the bar 12 lower high, but it was still a final flag. It was a bull flag and the final attempt by the bulls to resume the trend, but it immediately reversed down after just a one-bar bull breakout.

Figure 21.10   SPIKE AND CHANNEL TREND   **357**

FIGURE 21.10   Spike and Climax

A spike and climax variant of a spike and channel pattern often has the spike and channel reversed. In Figure 21.10, there was a channel from bar 2 to bar 3, and it was followed by a large bull trend bar. The channel functions as the spike up and that one-bar spike functions like the channel.

Deeper Discussion of This Chart

The reversal down from the bar 5 high of the day in Figure 21.10 was also a final flag reversal where bar 4 was a one-bar final flag. After a climax, especially after a final flag reversal, the market usually has a two-legged correction, which means that a high 1 and maybe a high 2 would fail. If you shorted below bar 5, you then have to expect pullbacks and keep your protective stop above the bar 5 high until after the market has begun its second leg.

Once the market broke to the downside on the move down to bar 11, traders believed that there was going to be more selling, which meant that the breakout turned the market into always-in short. The breakout bar was therefore likely to lead to a measured move down and there could be a measuring gap. The gap between the bar 8 breakout point and the bar 11 pullback became that gap.

Since the spike up was sharp and therefore climactic, the high 1 above bar 6 was likely to fail. Aggressive traders would place limit orders to short at or above the bar 6 high 1 signal bar high and above the bar 7 high 2 signal bar high.

Bar 8 was a wedge bull flag (a high 3) and a reasonable scalp, but only if you were emotionally prepared to reverse to short as you took profits on your long, since a second leg down was likely. Since the move down to bar 8 was a channel, it was probably just the first leg.

The opening range was about half of the size of an average daily range, and therefore the day could become a trending trading range day, which it did. The upper range was from the bar 2 low to the high of the day, and the lower range was from around bar 12 to bar 22. The market then broke again to the downside and formed a channel from the bar 24 tight trading range, final flag area to the bar 26 low of the day, although there was very little two-sided trading and the market quickly reversed back into the middle range by the close.

It also became a spike and channel bear trend day where the move from bar 5 to bar 12 was the spike and the three pushes down to bars 12, 18, and 26 created a parabolic, climactic channel.

Once the market reversed up from the breakout below the channel at the bar 26 low, the next objective was a poke above the top of the channel, which it accomplished on the close.

CHAPTER 22

Trending Trading Range Days

Primary characteristics of trending trading range days:

- The opening range is about a third to half the size of the range of recent days.
- There is a breakout after an hour or two and then the market forms another trading range.
- Because there are trading ranges, there are usually opportunities to take trades in both directions.
- There sometimes are multiple breakouts and trading ranges, but when this happens, it is usually better to consider the day as a stronger type of trend day and trade only with trend.
- After the second trading range begins to form, there is usually a pullback that tests the earlier trading range.
- The test often breaks back into the earlier range. When it comes close to but does not penetrate the prior range, the trend is a little stronger.
- Sometimes the market goes all the way through the earlier range and the day becomes a reversal day.
- Most reversal days begin as trending trading range days.
- When the breakout is very strong, the day is more likely to become a weak spike and channel trend.

Since every trend has pullbacks and they are small trading ranges, some form of a trending trading range day is present during every trend day, and the trending trading ranges are the dominant features at least a couple of times each week. If the opening range is about a third to half of the size of the recent average daily range, then look for a breakout and an approximate doubling of the range of the day. These trend days are made of a series of usually two, or occasionally more, trading ranges separated by brief breakouts, and the formations are sometimes not readily seen as trading ranges. However, on the daily chart, the day is clearly a trend day, opening near one end of the bar and closing near the other. Whenever the market is creating trending swings but the day does not look like a clear trend day, it is probably a trending trading range day. Also, if the day's range in the first hour or two is only about a third to half of the average range of recent days, watch for a breakout and an approximate measured move, and then a second trading range forming over the rest of the day. This type of trend is present in some form several days each week but is often better classified as another type of trend or even a large trading range.

Many days can be classified as either spike and channel trend days or trending trading range days, depending on their strength. The stronger the trend, the more the day will behave like a spike and channel trend day. The reason to try to distinguish between them is that they should be traded differently. When a day is more of a spike and channel trend day, it is a strong trend, and traders should focus on with-trend trades and swing trades. They should avoid countertrend trades unless there is a clear transition into a trading range or an opposite trend. When the day is more of a trending trading range day, traders can usually take trades in both directions and look for more scalps. As a day is forming, there are clues that tell traders if the breakout is more likely to lead to a strong trend day, like a spike and channel trend day (or even a small pullback trend day), or to a trending trading range day. Trading ranges are more common than strong trends, and trending trading range days, in particular, are about twice as common as spike and channel trend days, although every day has at least one spike and channel swing. The spike in a spike and channel trend day is most likely to begin early in the day, often from the first bar or with a large gap up or down. Also, it usually either breaks well beyond bars from yesterday or strongly reverses from a breakout, like a sharp rally from the first bar on a large gap down day. The spike in a trending trading range day is a breakout from a trading range, but it is usually still within the range of the prior day.

The opening trading range often lasts one to three hours and can be about half of the size of an average day's range. This lack of urgency is a sign that the day is less likely to become a strong trend day. Also, the initial trading range has a magnetic pull, as does any trading range, and that works against the breakout going too far before pulling back and forming another trading range. The breakout on a spike and channel trend day is often large and fast. The spike can have three or more large bull trend bars with small tails and very little overlap. On a trending trading range day, the spike is usually just one to three bars, and they tend to be smaller and have larger tails and more overlap. If the pullback is just a single bar and the breakout from the pullback is another spike, even if it is smaller and only a single bar, the day is more likely to be a spike and channel trend day. If the pullback goes sideways for five to 10 bars, or if the breakout from the pullback is a weak channel with overlapping bars and trend bars in the opposite direction, the day is more likely to be a trending trading range day. If the pullback after the spike is strong enough to make traders uncertain of the always-in direction, a trading range is more likely than a trend channel, so look for scalps instead of swings.

Entering on the breakout of any trading range is a low-probability trade, except in special circumstances, which are discussed in book 2 on trading ranges. It is usually much better to enter on a breakout pullback or on some earlier reversal from the opposite side of the range, but if a trader is confident that the day might be evolving into a trending trading range day and the breakout is strong, the trader can consider entering as the breakout bar is forming, or around the close of the breakout bar or on the close of the next bar, if it is also strong. The breakout spike is usually followed by a channel, but it will often stop around the measured move area, and then the market will begin to form a trading range. The market breaks out of one range and then forms another. Rarely, three or four small trading ranges will develop in a day, but when that happens, the day should probably be thought of and traded as a stronger type of trend day, like a spike and channel or a small pullback trend day. Traders should focus much more if not exclusively on with-trend setups. If the market later pulls back into a prior range, it will often retrace all the way to the other side of that range. The implication is that the market consolidates in a range after the breakout. This means that there will be two-sided trading that tests both the top and bottom of the new range and possibly breaks out in either direction at some point. Once the market reaches the measured move area, it is likely to transition into a second trading range. Traders should then transition with it from trend style trading to trading range trading. For example, if the day is a bull trending trading range day, traders should take profits in the area that is approximately a measured move up, if the trend is weakening, based on the height of the lower trading range. This is because the market will then usually test down into the breakout area and then form a trading range.

Traders should not trail their protective stops below a swing low once they think that the market is in a trending trading range, because those stops will usually get hit. It makes more sense to look to exit on strength when the market is forming an upper range, than to exit on weakness. Remember, in a trading range, traders should buy low, sell high. Aggressive traders will fade big trend bars in the area of the measured move target. For example, in a bull trending trading range day, once the market gets close to the measured move target, bears will look for a large bull trend bar. If one forms, they will often short its close or just above its high, and then scale into more shorts if the market goes higher. They expect that the large bull trend bar is an exhaustive buy climax, and that it will be followed by an eventual test down into the gap (the two or three bull trend bars forming a breakout from the lower trading range), and possibly to the top of the lower range. Since they are expecting an upper trading range to develop, shorting at the top of a bull spike in the area where the market is likely to form the top of the upper trading range gives them an excellent entry price. This is discussed more in the second book in the section on trading range trading. Even if the market goes higher, the odds are very strong that the market will come back below their entry price. If they scaled in higher, they could exit their first entry at breakeven, and then move the stop on their higher entry to breakeven, and hold for a test into the gap.

Since there is two-sided trading throughout the day, it is common for the day to reverse through at least one of the trading ranges in the final hour or two of the day. Since each trading range has two-sided trading, it is a comfort zone for bulls and bears, who both see the area as value. This creates a magnetic pull and tends to draw breakouts back into the range.

The importance of recognizing this type of trend day is that this reversal is a reliable countertrend trade, since the market will usually form a breakout test. Because of this, once the breakout reaches the approximate measured move target where trend traders will take profits, traders will watch for a trade in the opposite direction, looking to exit on the breakout test. Experienced traders will fade strong trend bars around the measured move area, looking for the pullback to test the breakout gap. For example, when the average daily range in the Emini is about 10 points, if there is a trading range for a couple of hours and then an upside breakout, strong bears will begin to scale into shorts at about four to six points above the lower range. They are looking for a pullback into the breakout area and maybe all the way back to the top of the lower trading range. If the market reverses back into the prior range, it will likely test the countertrend signal bars in the prior range. For example, if a bear trend reverses up, it will attempt to reach the high of prior failed bull signal bars. If the rally extends to the top or above the upper trading range and the day closes up there, the day will be a reversal day on the daily chart. The day sold off and then reversed up and closed near its high. Most reversal days begin as trending trading range days (the section on reversal days in the third book has examples), so whenever traders recognize that the day is a trending trading range day, they should always be prepared for a possible late reversal swing trade, which might become a large intraday trend trade that can cover the entire day's range.

Trending trading range days often give a subtle clue that a breakout should be expected. If you see a trading range day forming, but each swing high is a little higher than the prior one and each swing low is higher than the prior one, the market may already be trending even though it is still in a trading range. Once enough participants recognize this, the market breaks out and quickly moves to a higher level, where it once again will become two-sided and form another trading range.

When the initial breakout occurs, do not assume that a measured move is assured as the market tries to grow to an average daily range. In about a third of cases, the market will break out of one side and extend the range a little, and then reverse and break out of the opposite side and extend the range a little more, resulting in a quiet trading range day.

Sometimes there is a trading range with a height that is about half of the recent average daily range and the range stays small until the final hour. For example, if the day's range in the Emini has been just five points as the market enters the final hour and the average recent range has been 12 points, and only two days in the past 12 months ended up with a range of five points or less, be prepared for a breakout at the end of the day. Every day has a range of five points at some point, if only for the first minute. Most trending trading range days with an initial range of only five points have a breakout within the first two or three hours, but several times a year the day will stay small until the final hour or two. When that happens, most of the time there will be a breakout that will increase the range, but usually not all the way up to the recent daily average. Don't give up on the day and assume that it will end up as only a five-point range day, because in 90 percent of the cases the range will increase before the close and you can often profitably trade the brief breakout. Because the breakout occurs so late, there is often not enough time left to form much of a trading range, but because the day appeared likely all day long to be a trending trading range day, it is appropriate to discuss it here.

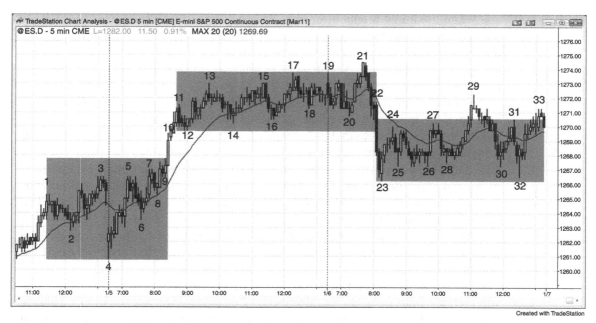

FIGURE 22.1 Trending Trading Range Days

Trending trading range days often have a single large trend bar in between the ranges. In Figure 22.1, the market was in a trading range for the final couple of hours of yesterday from bar 1 to bar 3, and the trading range continued through the first couple of hours of today. Bar 10 was a large bull trend bar that broke out of the trading range and above the wedge top formed by bars 5, 7, and 9. The next bar was a bull trend bar, and it confirmed the breakout (it significantly increased the chance of higher prices and some kind of measured move up). The market immediately entered a small trading range for the rest of the day.

That range continued into the third day. Any trading range has a magnetic pull on the market, and this makes most breakout attempts fail. The trading range from bar 11 to bar 19 was the final bull flag in the rally, and the breakout to bar 21 failed. The market then broke below this upper trading range with the large bar 22 bear trend bar. The sell-off tested the top of the range from the prior day and formed another trading range. Bar 29 was a failed breakout of the top of the lower range and a third push up, and the pull of the lower range was greater than that of the upper range. The market traded back through the lower range, tested the bottom at bar 32, and then closed near the top of the lower trading range.

The bull spike from bar 8 to bar 13 was large but the follow-through channel from bar 12 to bar 17 was disproportionally small. The breakout gap in between the

Figure 22.1   TRENDING TRADING RANGE DAYS   **365**

bar 9 top of the lower trading range and the bar 12 bottom of the upper trading range was large compared to the height of the upper range. This increased the chances that the market would come back into the gap to test its strength. The trading range from bar 23 to bar 33 was mostly within that breakout gap between bar 9 and bar 12, which often happens.

The initial range from bar 4 to bar 9 was about half the size of an average day. So traders expected the range to approximately double. When there is a trading range that is about half of the size of an average daily range, the most common way that the range increases is by a breakout and the formation of a trending trading range day.

The third day's opening range from bar 19 to bar 21 was about a third of the size of an average day, and traders expected a breakout. Since they also expected a test into the gap of the prior day, a downside breakout was likely, and it followed the failed attempt to break out of the top of the range. The spike down to bar 23 was strong and it was possible that the day could have become a spike and channel bear trend day, but bar 23 tested the support provided by yesterday's trading range (the highs of bars 3, 5, and 7). It was about a measured move down, and it also tested a three-day trend line (not shown). This means that the sell-off might have simply been a sell vacuum created by strong bulls and bears stepping aside until the market fell down to the support zone, at which point they bought aggressively. The bull spikes up from bars 23, 25, and 26; the double bottom bull flag created by the spikes in between bars 25 and 26; and the double bottom pullback at bar 28 all represented increasing buying pressure, and the market even flipped to always-in up on the spike up to bar 29. This is not what typically happens in the pullback after a spike in a spike and channel bear trend day, and this made a trending trading range more likely. If this was to become a spike and channel bear trend day, the pullback from the bar 23 spike would not typically have much buying pressure compared to the strength of the bear spike. The uncertainty created by the buying pressure increased the chances of a trading range instead of a brief pullback and then a protracted bear channel. Uncertainty is the hallmark of trading ranges and not of bear flags (a pullback leading to a bear channel).

The distinction between a spike and channel trend day and a trending trading range day is not always clear and sometimes not important. Although the trading range that began at bar 12 made the day a trending trading range day, it also had higher lows and highs and therefore was a weak bull channel. Remember, a channel is just a sloped trading range and both are areas of two-sided trading. The less sloped it is, the more it behaves like a trading range and the more safely traders can trade in both directions.

FIGURE 22.2   Initial Trading Range Is About Half of the Average Daily Range

As shown in Figure 22.2, for the first couple of hours of both days, the range was about half that of the recent days. This alerted traders to a possible breakout in either direction. When the breakout starts later in the day like this, without a clear direction in the opening range, and the initial range is about half that of an average day, the breakout usually does not result in a strong, relentless trend, like a spike and channel trend. Instead, it usually has a pullback and then the market forms a lower trading range. The lower range may or may not break back into the upper range, and may sometimes break out again to the downside and form a third or fourth trading range. Since a lower trading range is more likely than a strong bear trend, the trading should be two-sided and the market usually works its way back to the breakout area. Once the breakout extends below the breakout point for about a third of an average range, traders will start looking to buy for a swing up to the bottom of the upper range. They would have bought the second attempt to reverse up above bar 11 and above bar 28. They also would have bought the double bottom at bar 5 and the higher low at bar 29.

Once the market breaks back into the upper range and holds up there, it often tests up near the top of the upper range, as it did on the second day. If the day closes near the top or above the upper range, the day becomes a reversal day. Aggressive bulls would have bought the close of the large bear trend bar before

Figure 22.2   TRENDING TRADING RANGE DAYS   **367**

bar 27, expecting it to be an exhaustive sell climax that would lead to a test up to the bottom of the upper trading range. Some would have bought on limit orders at a measured move down from the height of the upper trading range. They would have counted the number of points between the top of bar 22 down to the bottom of bars 21 or 25, and then subtracted that number from the low of bars 21 or 25. They would have then begun to scale in around that price level, maybe starting a point or two above to a few points below. Others would have bought at the first sign of two-sided trading, like the close of bar 27, or as bar 27 was reversing off its low. Assuming that the average daily range was about 10 points, some bulls would have scaled in at four to six points below the bar 25 bottom of the upper range, looking to make three to six points on the pullback into the breakout gap (the bear trend bars below bar 25).

Although the sell-off from bar 19 to bar 21 was sharp, so was the rally up to bar 22. This led to enough uncertainty about the direction in the opening range to reduce the chances of a spike and channel trend day and increase the chances of a trending trading range day.

FIGURE 22.3   Trending Trading Ranges Create a Trend

Sometimes a day can spend most of its time in trading ranges but still be a trend day. As shown in Figure 22.3, today may not look like a trend day, but it is, as can be seen in the thumbnail of the daily chart (today is bar 1), and it is made up of a series of trending small trading ranges. These days frequently reverse in the final couple of hours and retrace at least the final trading range.

Deeper Discussion of This Chart

Some days do not have reliable setups for an hour or more. In Figure 22.3, today opened at a flat moving average within the range of the final bar of yesterday, which had been in a small trading range, and that range continued for the first two bars of today's open. The first two bars of today were large compared to the height of the trading range, and this makes them risky signal bars. Although shorting below the second bar was acceptable since it was a two-bar reversal short setup and a wedge bear flag below the moving average, the entry would be near the low of the trading range. It was safer to wait for the breakout and then short a breakout pullback, if there was one. One developed a few bars later but it was in a small, tight trading range and the bars had big tails, making

Figure 22.3   TRENDING TRADING RANGE DAYS   **369**

it a less reliable trade. A better entry was below the 8:00 a.m. PST two-bar reversal and pullback to the moving average, which was a low 2 short.

There was a moving average gap bar short at 11:45 and the test of the bear low was in the form of a higher low. It is also appropriate to call it a double bottom bull flag.

This was a trending trading range day, so once it started to base around the $185 level, traders could have bought in that area for a test of the bottom of the upper range just above $186. The market made a two-legged sell-off down to the $185 level and the second leg was an approximate measured move. The middle of the morning trading range was about $2.00 below the high of the day and the large two-bar reversal at 10:15 a.m. was about $2.00 lower, so traders would start buying. The bears were buying back some of their shorts and the bulls were buying for a test of the bottom of the upper trading range. The market entered a tight trading range and there were three small pushes down that ended with a large bear trend bar at 11:05. This was followed by a higher low at 11:30, and the signal bar had a bull body. This higher low was also a high 2 since the bar before it and the bar two bars before that had bear bodies. This is microscopic analysis and most traders would not trust this in real time, but experienced traders are always looking for signs that the market might turn, and these subtle hints would help give them confidence to take the long. If they bought above the 11:30 low, they could risk about 50 cents to below that low with the goal of making about a dollar on the test of the upper trading range.

Although you never know the directional probability of an equidistant move with certainty, whenever you feel that there is an imbalance, you should assume that it is at least 60 percent. Here, it was reasonable to assume that if you bought around $185, there was at least a 60 percent chance that the test of $186 would happen before your protective stop was hit if you placed that stop equidistantly below your entry (there is a 60 percent chance that you would make a dollar before you lost a dollar). You could have taken a partial profit on the doji inside bar after the bull spike up at 11:40 and exited the rest at breakeven as the breakout failed. Once the market double bottomed at 12:25, you could try the same long again and you would have succeeded. There was a chance of a measured move up to a $2.00 profit from the double bottom, but with so little time left in the day, this was unlikely.

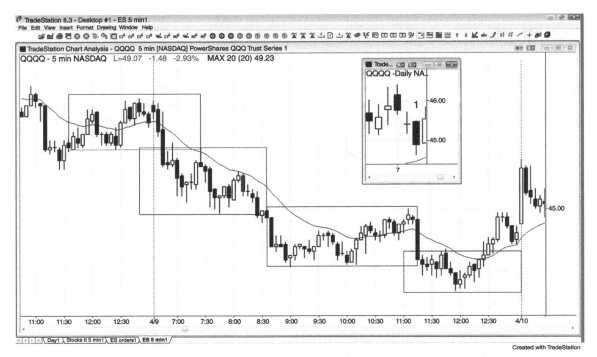

FIGURE 22.4 The First Trading Range Can Form Yesterday

As shown in Figure 22.4, this was another trending trading range day with the first trading range beginning yesterday. The thumbnail of the daily chart shows it was a bear trend day (bar 1).

The final trading range reversed up and the market tested near the top of the higher trading range just before it. This often happens, since the two-sided trading means that the trending forces are not as strong as they are during other trend days. When a day is less strong, it is less likely to close on its low. Traders know this and look for a reversal trade going into the close.

Deeper Discussion of This Chart

In Figure 22.4, today again opened essentially unchanged and near a flat moving average. However, the three-bar bear spike made a bear trend day likely. The spike broke below the trading range that formed in the final hour of yesterday. That trading range was also a two-legged rally and therefore a bear flag, so the breakout can be thought of as a breakout below the bull trend line along the bottom of the bear flag. Traders could short below the first pullback and then again below the moving average test, which was also a two-legged sideways correction to the moving average and an approximate double top bear flag setup.

Figure 22.5   TRENDING TRADING RANGE DAYS   **371**

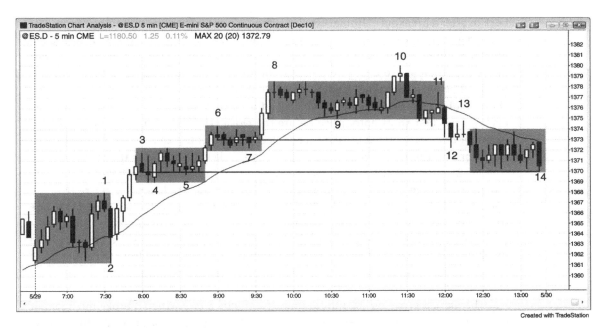

FIGURE 22.5 Trading Ranges Separated by Breakouts

As shown in Figure 22.5, the first hour was contained in a seven-point range but the average range lately had been about 20 points, so traders expected the range to approximately double. Whenever a trend begins after an hour into the day, the day often becomes a trending trading range day, in part because by definition that first hour obviously was a trading range. The day often reverses back into and sometimes through one or more of the lower trading ranges late in the day, as it did here.

Deeper Discussion of This Chart

When the day is forming multiple trending trading ranges as in Figure 22.5, traders should concentrate on taking with-trend trades. Traders should have looked to buy only from the two-bar reversal at bar 2 to the 20 gap bar high 2 at bar 9. They should have considered shorting only at the bar 10 final flag reversal setup.

Many bulls would have taken profits on their longs, and aggressive bears would have shorted on the close and above the high of the bull trend bar before bar 10. The market had a spike up to bar 3 and then a channel or a series of small trading ranges, but the one that began at bar 8 was relatively tight and horizontal. This was an area of strong two-sided trading, and therefore a magnet that would tend to draw the market back in after a breakout. The market also often retraces into the prior trading range later in the day, and since 11:30 a.m. PST is a common time for reversals, the odds of a failed breakout and final flag reversal were high. The pullback could have tested the bar 4 start of the bull channel, so bears were happy shorting at the high of a large bull trend bar breakout above a swing high and potential final flag. Many would have scaled into more shorts higher, believing that the market had a 70 percent chance or better of at least testing their first short entry price before the close. This would have enabled them to exit their original shorts at breakeven and decide whether to exit their shorts from above with a profit or to move the protective stops to breakeven and swing the trade down.

Bar 2 was the first bar of a two-bar reversal up from a possible failed low 2 from a double or triple bottom, and the start of a bull trend. Traders were aware that the market could break out and run. Once the market broke out, it formed a higher range from bars 4 to 6, and that range contained two small tight trading ranges. The high 2 long above bar 5 was a reasonable breakout pullback entry, despite the barbwire. The breakout was both from the small bull flag from bar 3 to bar 4, and from the entire bar 3 to bar 5 trading range, which was a two-legged sideways pullback from the breakout above bar 1.

The market broke out to a third range, from bars 8 to 9. When it broke out again, it failed at bar 10 (a final flag reversal) and retraced through the bottom of the third range and ultimately to the bottom of the second range. There was a breakout pullback short below bar 11 after the bear spike, but the barbwire made it more risky. After the two bear bars forming a spike that ended at bar 12, there was a second breakout pullback short below bar 13.

The implication in the word *range* is that the market will test the low of the range at some point, although it could continue trading up. When a market retraces a strong move, the first target is always the earlier countertrend entry points. Here, the closest bear entry point after the market broke out of the top range was the low of the closest bear signal bar, bar 6. The market broke out of the top range, and then broke into the next lower range and took out that bear signal bar low on bar 13.

By the close, the market had tested the low of the bar 3 lowest bear signal bar in the second range.

Figure 22.6

TRENDING TRADING RANGE DAYS   **373**

FIGURE 22.6 Two-Sided Trading in a Trend Day

Although today (see Figure 22.6) opened on its high and closed on its low, and was a trend from the open bear trend day, there was too much sideways action during the first two hours for this to trade like one. A trend from the open trend day usually doesn't have many significant tradable countertrend swings, but a trending trading range does, and is a weaker, less predictable type of trend day. The initial trading range broke down into a lower range on bar 4, creating a trending trading range day.

Until bar 3, the day's range was only about half that of recent days, so traders were aware of the possibility of a lower trading range forming.

Bar 6 was a breakout pullback to the moving average and a breakout test of the bar 2 bottom of the upper range, offering a reasonable short entry.

Bar 9 was a breakout test of the upper range and failed breakout of the top of this lower range, setting up another short.

Bar 12 broke down into a third range, but there was not enough time left in the day for a test up to the bar 13 top of the range.

Deeper Discussion of This Chart

In Figure 22.6, yesterday closed below the moving average and today's open was a bull breakout above the close and moving average. The first bar of the day was a doji and therefore not a reliable short signal bar. The bar 1 strong bear trend bar was a reasonable signal bar for a short one tick below its low for a test of the moving average and maybe the close of yesterday. Since large gap openings often lead to trends and this bear bar was a sign of urgency on the part of the bears, today could become a bear trend day and traders should short early and swing part until there is a strong bull reversal or until the close of the day.

After the two-bar bear spike, traders were expecting a bear channel and began to short pullbacks. The first pullback short was the low 2 that was triggered by the outside down bar just after 7:00 a.m. PST, and the next short was below the bar 3 bear reversal bar. It was a dueling lines short setup, forming both a double top with the earlier pullback and a wedge bear flag (the first push up was two bars before bar 2).

Bar 14 was a bull reversal bar, but it overlapped the prior two bars too much for it to be reliable. Also, it was within a relatively tight channel after the bar 12 bear spike, so it would be better to wait for a breakout pullback higher low before going long in a bear trend. Since it was a weak buy setup in a bull trend, its failure would likely be a good short setup. Bar 15 was failed high 2, and a low 2 with a bear reversal bar near the moving average in a bear trend is a very high-probability short setup because the bulls who bought the high 1 and the high 2 trend reversal attempts usually exit on a low 2. The market just made two attempts to reverse the new low of the day, and this second one failed on the bar after the bar 15 long. When the market fails twice at trying to do something, it usually then goes in the opposite direction.

Figure 22.7   TRENDING TRADING RANGE DAYS   **375**

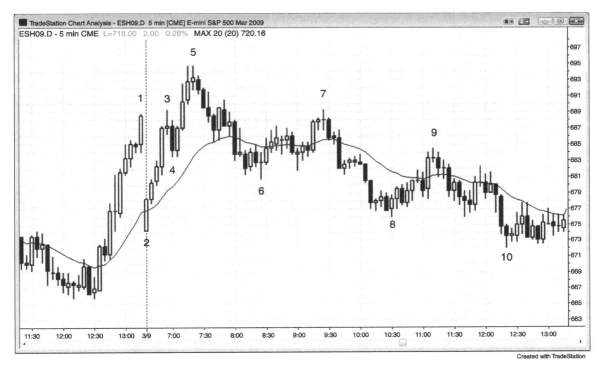

FIGURE 22.7 A Trend Starting after the First Hour Is Often Weak

Whenever a market begins a trend after the first hour, assume that it will lead to a trending trading range day or that it will behave like one, and look for scalps in both directions. Although there was a bull trend from the open in Figure 22.7, it ended with a spike and climax at bar 5 and then reversed down into a trending trading range bear trend. It also can be viewed as a spike and channel bear trend, with the move from bar 5 to bar 6 being the bear spike, and the moves down from bar 7 to bar 8 and then the three-bar breakout to bar 10 as additional spikes. The channel down was broad enough and the pullbacks after the two breakouts overlapped the prior swing lows so that it was also a bear stair pattern.

Deeper Discussion of This Chart

The market gapped down to a higher low and formed a possible bull trend from the open in Figure 22.7. It was a test of the moving average after a strong spike into the close and a failed breakout below that strong bull channel.

A two-legged move up ended in a final flag short at bar 5. This was followed by a four-bar bear spike, which became part of a larger spike that ended at bar 6. This move broke below the bull trend line of the rally from the open, so a lower high could lead to a trend reversal down.

A two-legged lower high ended at bar 7, alerting traders to a possible continued move down. Bar 7 was a dueling lines pattern. It formed a double top with the top of the wedge bear channel down to bar 6 (the channel began with the small lower high that formed after the four-bar bear spike below bar 5), and it was a wedge bear flag (the first push up ended with the bar before bar 6, and bar 7 was the third push up).

The market behaved like a trending trading range bear for the rest of the day. The strong bull momentum up to bar 1 and again up to bar 5 were spikes up and could be followed by a bull channel at some point over the next day or two. Bars 6, 8, and 10 created a large wedge bull flag, and a test of the bar 5 high was possible. Bar 4 can also be considered part of that bear channel. The next day (not shown) in fact gapped up near the high of bar 7 and became a strong bull trend from the open day.

Figure 22.8   TRENDING TRADING RANGE DAYS   **377**

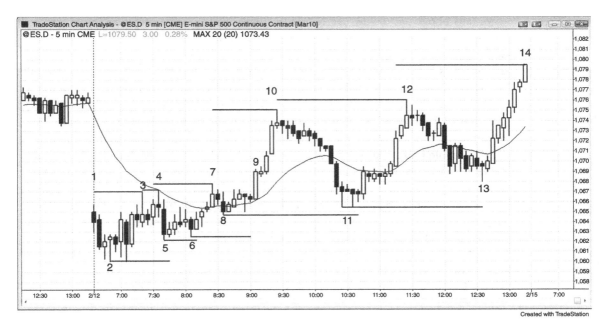

FIGURE 22.8 Initial Trading Range Often Presages Another Trading Range

In Figure 22.8, the range for the first couple of hours was about half of an average daily range and this alerted traders to a possible breakout and the formation of a higher or lower trading range and the creation of a trending trading range day. The bull trend was already apparent before the bar 9 breakout. Notice how the bar 5 swing low was above the bar 2 low, the bar 6 low was above the bar 5 low, and the bar 8 low was above the bar 6 low. The same thing was happening with the swing highs at bars 3, 4, and 7. Even though the market was in a trading range for the first two and a half hours, both the swing highs and the swing lows were trending upward, indicating that there was already a bull trend going on within the trading range. This alerted traders to watch for a breakout, which occurred at bar 9. This higher trading range lasted until the breakout that followed the reversal up at bar 13. Both bars 11 and 13 were breakout tests. The double bottom at bar 11 dropped into the lower trading range, but the bar 13 low tested the bar 7 top of the lower trading range to the tick. When a pullback cannot drop below the breakout point, it is a sign of strength by the bulls.

Deeper Discussion of This Chart

The market broke out below yesterday's close in Figure 22.8, and the first bar had a bear body, so the day could become a trend from the open bear trend day. However, there were tails above and below bar 1, and this increased the chances of an initial trading range. Traders should wait. Bar 2 was a micro double bottom, but both bars were dojis so this was not a setup for a strong trend. Even the bar 4 wedge bear flag at the moving average was a weak setup because it was part of a six-bar tight trading range and all of the bars had tails. This means that there is uncertainty, and that is the hallmark of a trading range. Traders could have bought above the bull inside bar that followed bar 5, but after that bar 4 wedge bear flag the market should have a second test down. This occurred at bar 6 and formed a double bottom with bar 5 and a double bottom pullback for the double bottom at the low of the day (bar 2 and the bar three bars later). It would be safer to wait to buy until after more evidence of bull strength, like the four-bar bull spike up to bar 7, but there were a couple of strong bull trend bars just after bar 2, and this is a good enough sign of strength to start taking long trades on pullbacks. Those large bull trend bars are a sign of buying pressure, which is cumulative. Once there is a critical mass of buying, the bulls take control and the market goes up.

After that bull spike to bar 7, there was a breakout pullback buy setup above the bull inside bar that followed bar 8, and that was also a failed low 2 buy signal. There was a high 2 long setup four bars later that led to the bar 9 strong bull breakout.

Figure 22.9   TRENDING TRADING RANGE DAYS   **379**

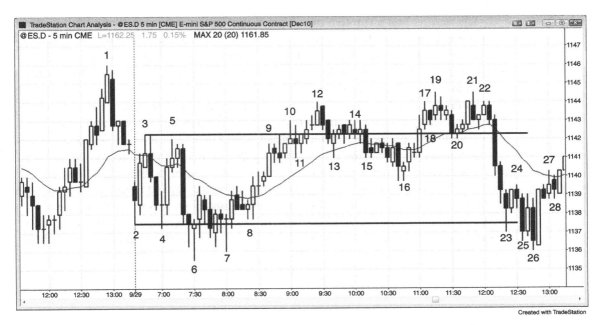

FIGURE 22.9   An Initial Trading Range Can Be Followed by a Trading Range Day

Just because the range of the first couple of hours is about half that of an average day does not mean there will be a breakout into a trending trading range day. In about a third of cases, the range increases by a breakout of both the high and low of the day, as it did in Figure 22.9. The market reversed up from new lows of the day at bars 4 and 6, and down from new highs of the day at bars 3, 10, 12, 19, and 21. The opening range probably ended with the reversal down from bar 5, and at that point the range of the day was about half that of recent days. This alerted traders to the possibility of a breakout either up or down and then a measured move that would approximately double the day's range. However, simply entering on the breakout of a trading range is a losing strategy since the market always has inertia and most attempts to change from a trading range to a trend, or from a trend to a trading range, fail. No good short developed after the bar 6 breakout to a new low of the day, and in fact the bar 7 higher low after the three pushes down (bars 2, 4, and 6) and the bar 8 breakout pullback were reasonable buy signals for a test of the high of the day.

Bar 10 reversed down after breaking to a new high of the day, but the market was in a tight bull channel and therefore this was not a good short setup. The momentum up was not particularly strong so buying the bar 11 breakout pullback was a scalp trade at best. The market turned down again with a two-bar reversal at bar 12. Second-entry reversals on trading range days are usually reliable for at least a scalp.

The market had a run to a new high of the day after the bar 16 wedge bull flag and the market again failed at bars 19 and 21. Once it was clear that the upside breakout would not succeed, the market once again tried for a breakout of the opposite end of the day. As is often the case on trading range days, the market closed in the middle of the range.

When there are several possibilities for the top and bottom of the opening range, it usually does not matter which you choose because there is no agreement. When looking for a measured move target where you can take profits, initially use the smallest possibility for the opening range, like bar 2 to bar 3. If the market does not pause in that area, then look at the next larger possibility, like bar 3 to bar 4, or bar 3 to bar 6. Since today ended as a trading range day and not a trending trading range day, the obvious measured move targets were not reached. However, every reversal is due to computer algorithms based on some measurement, and there is almost always some type of measured move in the equation, even if it is not obvious.

Figure 22.10   TRENDING TRADING RANGE DAYS   **381**

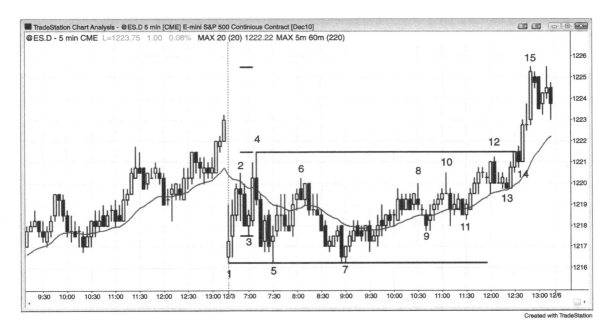

FIGURE 22.10 Late Breakout

Sometimes the initial trading range is about half of the size of an average daily range and the breakout does not come until the final hour. In Figure 22.10, although there was not enough time left to form much of an upper range, the day was a setup for a breakout into a trending trading range day all day long. The range prior to the breakout was only 5.25 points and there were only two days in the past 11 months that ended with a range of 5.25 points or less. This meant that other days this year that may have had a 5.25 range for most of the day had a bigger range by the close, and that made it likely for today to have a late breakout up or down as well. Since the market had been trending up since the bar 7 triple bottom and triangle, and the number of bars between bars 9 and 12 with bull bodies was high, buying pressure was present and an upside breakout was likely. Traders would have bought on the bar 14 breakout above the bar 4 high of the day and on the close of the strong bar 14 breakout bar and again above its high.

The initial bear spike from bar 3 to bar 4 generated a measured move to the high of the day. Traders never know which of the possible measured move targets will be the level where the bulls will take profits, but it is good to be aware of the possibilities so you, too, can take profits as the market is racing up rather than a couple of points lower on the sell-off. The market might have also topped out at a measured move based on the bar 1 low to the bar 2 high or from the bar 5 low to the bar 4, 6, 10, or 12 high.

CHAPTER 23

Trend from the Open and Small Pullback Trends

P rimary characteristics of trend from the open days:

- The low of a bull trend day or the high of a bear trend day is formed within the first few bars of the day.
- If the opening range of the day is less than 25 percent of the average daily range of recent days, there may be a double bottom on a bull trend day or a double top on a bear trend day (if the opening range is about 50 percent of the average daily range, a breakout is more likely to lead to a trending trading range day).
- The day may begin with a strong spike lasting many bars or it may have a small opening range.
- If the market trends from the first bar or so and the initial spike lasts three or more bars, entering on the first pullback is usually good for at least a scalp.
- If there is a strong spike on the open that lasts many bars and covers many points, the day will usually become a spike and channel trend day.
- A large gap opening often leads to a trend from the open day, and the trend can go in either direction. When there is a large gap up and a trend from the open day forms, the day will be a bull trend day about 60 percent of the time and a bear trend day 40 percent of the time. The opposite is true for gap down openings. The larger the gap, the more likely the day will be a trend day and the more likely the trend will be in the direction of the gap.
- Trend from the open days have urgency and conviction from the outset and are usually the strongest trends and have the smallest pullbacks.
- Twenty gap bar and moving average gap bar setups come late in the trend.

- The strongest type of a trend from the open day and the strongest type of trend is one where the opening range is small, and then the day trends relentlessly with small pullbacks all day long. This is a small pullback trend day. For example, the pullbacks in the Emini might be just 10 to 12 ticks (10 to 30 percent of the average daily range). When that is the case, there is usually a pullback in the final couple of hours that is about 150 to 200 percent of the size of the earlier pullbacks, followed by a resumption of the trend into the close.
- To an experienced trader, the swing setups are 70 percent or more likely to work, even though to they never look that certain to a beginner. Many of the signal bars look bad, as is the case for all strong trends. Most setups *appear* to have 50 percent or less probability of success. This makes traders not take the trades and forces them to chase the market, or miss the trend completely.
- There are often many trend bars in the opposite direction, which is a sign of countertrend pressure, and it keeps beginning traders looking for reversals instead of with-trend trades. For example, in a bull trend, there will be many bear trend bars and many two-bar and three-bar bear spikes. Beginners repeatedly short them and lose. The spikes evolve into bull flags that look weak, which discourages beginners from buying them. They just got out of a losing short and are not ready emotionally to risk losing again, especially on a setup that does not look strong. Each bad-looking bull flag is successful, and is followed by another good-looking short setup that fails.
- The trend is often in a relatively tight channel, and pullbacks often come back and hit breakeven stops, trapping traders out. Traders need to trail their stops below swing lows in a bull trend or above swing highs in a bear trend. If they are too eager to move their stops to breakeven, they will get trapped out.

Since almost all small pullback days are trend from the open days, they should be considered to be a strong variant. A trend from the open day is usually the strongest form of trend pattern, but it develops in only about 20 percent of days. That means that buying above the first bar or shorting below it, expecting it to be the start of a strong trend, is a low-probability trade. Reversals are far more common in the first hour, as is discussed in book 3. The chance of the first bar being the high or low of the day on a day when there is a large gap opening can be 50 percent or more, if the bar is a strong trend bar in either direction. The high or low of the day forms within the first five bars or so in about 50 percent of days. However, it forms within the opening range, which can last a couple of hours, in about 90 percent of days. Any type of trend day can trend from the open. In a trend from the open day, the market forms one extreme in the first bar or first few bars and then trends all day, and often closes at or near the opposite extreme. There may be a small trading range for the first 30 minutes or so and then a breakout, but the open of the day will usually be very close to one extreme of the day (the low in a bull trend or the high in a bear trend). These days often open with large gaps and then the market continues as a trend in either direction. In other words, a large gap down can lead to either a bull or a bear trend from the open day. The setup is more reliable if it forms at a strong magnet like a trend channel line (for example, forming a wedge reversal setup) or if it is part of a reversal pattern, like a reversal from a final flag at yesterday's close.

This type of trend can be so strong that there can be follow-through in the first hour or two of the next day, so traders should be looking to enter with trend on pullbacks after the open of the next day. The pullback often is strong enough to make traders wonder if the market is reversing, but it is usually just a higher time frame, two-legged correction, like a pullback to the 15 minute moving average. However, most traders would find it easier to simply read only one chart when trading and there is always a 5 minute setup at the end of the pullback.

As a trend from the open day is evolving, the pullbacks are often very small all day long. When this happens, this is a small pullback trend day. This is the strongest type of trend day and it forms only once or twice a month. About two-thirds of these days have a larger pullback after 11:00 a.m. PST. That pullback is often about twice the size of the biggest pullback since the trend began in the first hour. It is often heralded by a relatively large, strong trend bar or two in the direction of the trend, but representing climactic exhaustion. Take the example of a small pullback bull trend day when the biggest pullback has been nine ticks and the market has been channeling up all day. If sometime between 11:00 a.m. PST and noon the market has two relatively large consecutive bull trend bars breaking out to a new high, the move is more likely an exhaustive buy climax than the start of a new leg. Climaxes are discussed more in the third book, but when a trend has gone on for a long time and then has unusual further strength, it usually signals the end of the move for the time being and the start of a two-legged pullback that will last about 10 bars or so. Experienced traders are expecting a three- to five-point pullback and they will exit their longs. Some will even short the close of that second bull trend bar, or maybe a tick or two above its high, expecting the pullback. They might wait for the next bar to close, and if it has a close around the middle, they might short the close. If it is a bear reversal bar, they might short below its low. If they entered below a bear reversal bar, their protective stop would be above its high, but if they entered at the market at the close of the bull spike, they might use a three- or four-point stop and scale in a point or two higher. Even if they are wrong and the market does not sell off for a few points, it will likely enter a trading range and they should be able to get out with a small profit within the final hour.

There might have been a slightly larger pullback in the first hour just before the trend began, but only the pullbacks after the trend began are important. Look at their size and if they are all very small and each subsequent one stays around the same size or smaller than the first, the day is a strong trend day. For example, in a bull trend in the Emini where the average daily range has been about 12 points, the pullbacks might all be just two or three points. The bulls want a bigger pullback where they can get long, hoping for less risk. After waiting and not getting what they want, they start taking small positions at the market and on small pullbacks. This small buying all day long keeps lifting the market. The bears never see a great short and they decide instead to short smaller positions and weaker setups. There is no follow-through and they are forced to cover, and this buying adds to the slow rise in the market. Momentum traders see the trend and they, too, buy all day long. The trend usually continues all day with only small pullbacks, but because the bulls have been buying small positions all day long, they never have to chase the market up in a panic. Also, because the bears are never heavily short, there is not strong short covering. The result is that even though the day is a trend day, it often does not cover too many points and the bulls do not make a windfall profit, even though they were on the right side of a strong trend.

A report at 7:00 a.m. PST can often lead to a reversal bar, a breakout bar, or a large outside bar that becomes the start of a strong trend, which can last all day. However, computers have a huge edge on reports. They receive the data instantly in a format that they can process to make decisions that lead to orders. All of this happens within a second, and it gives them a significant advantage over traders. When the computers have a big edge, traders are at a disadvantage and therefore should rarely enter at the moment a report is released. The computers will usually show what the always-in trade is within a bar or two, or they will set up a strong reversal. Traders will then have probability on their side, and can look to enter in the appropriate direction. The strong bar that leads to the start of the trend does not always come on a report and can form several bars before or after the report. It happens on the report often enough for traders to be ready for it and then to enter as soon as the always-in position becomes clear.

Sometimes, after about 30 minutes of a small range, there is a test of the open that occurs around 7:00 a.m. PST, usually coinciding with a report. Although this results in a small trading range, the trend that breaks out is much stronger than that seen on a trending trading range day; it is identical to a trend from the open day and should be considered a variant.

Even the best patterns still fail to do what you expect about 40 percent of the time. If the market does not pause by the third or fourth bar, it might have gone too far too fast, and this increases the chances that the market will reverse instead of trend.

Every day begins as a trend from the open day within the first few bars of the day. As soon as a bar moves above the high of the prior bar, the day is a trend from the open bull trend day, at least for that moment. If instead it trades below the low of the first bar, it is a trend from the open bear trend day. On most days, the move does not have much follow-through and there is a reversal, and the day evolves into some other type of day. However, when the breakout of the prior bar grows into a larger spike, the odds of a strong trend from the open trend day increase considerably, and traders should begin to trade the day as a strong trend day.

If the market trends for four or more bars without a pullback, or even two large trend bars, the move should be considered to be a strong spike. The spike is an area where both bulls and bears agree that very little trading should take place, and the market therefore needs to quickly move to another price level. When the spike begins during the first few bars, the day is a trend from the open day. It may remain so for the rest of the day, but sometimes the market soon reverses and breaks out in the other direction. This can result in a trend in the opposite direction, like a spike and channel trend or a trending trading range day, or simply a trading range day. As with any strong spike, the bulls who bought early on will take partial profits at some point, creating a small pullback (as discussed earlier in the section on trends). Other bulls who missed the move will aggressively buy the pullback, as will bulls who want a larger position. The bulls will buy with limit orders at and below the low of the prior bar, hoping that the current bar will fall below the prior bar and allow them to buy a little lower. Other bulls will buy with stop orders above the high of the pullback bar (a high 1 buy signal).

A spike is usually followed by one of three things. First, the market might have gone too far too fast and be experiencing exhaustive climactic behavior. For example, if there is then a pause or pullback like an inside bar or a small wedge flag, this could become a final flag and lead to a reversal after a small breakout, and the reversal could last for several hours. Alternatively, the market might go sideways in a tight trading range for several hours, followed by the trend resuming into the close, resulting in a trend resumption day. This small, sideways movement is very common following a relentless five- to 10-bar spike. The third and most common outcome, when the spike is not so large as to be exhaustive, is the formation of a trend channel, and the day then becomes a spike and channel trend day.

Entering on the first pullback after a strong first leg is simply capitalizing on the propensity for strong moves to test the extreme. Most strong moves have at least two legs, so entering on the first pullback has a very good chance of leading to a profitable trade. This entry is especially important on trend from the open days if you missed the original entry. In strong trends, what constitutes the first pullback is not always clear because trends frequently have two or three sideways bars that don't break a meaningful trend line and therefore really aren't significant enough to constitute a pull "back." However, even if there is no retracement and no real pulling back in price, a pause is a sideways correction and is a variant of a pullback.

The single most difficult part of trading these very strong trend days is that the trends do not look particularly strong as they are forming. There are usually no impressive spikes or easy, high-probability pullbacks to the moving average. Instead, the market has pullbacks after every few bars and lots of trend bars in the opposite direction. It often is in a weak-looking channel. What beginners fail to see is that the pullbacks are all small, the market never seems to get back to the moving average, and the price keeps moving slowly away from the open. Experienced traders see all of these things as signs that the bull trend is very strong, and this gives them the confidence to take swing trades. They correctly know that, although the bars look like they are part of a weak channel and therefore should create low-probability setups, when they occur in a small pullback bull trend day, they form high-probability swing setups. All pullbacks in trend from the open days are great with trend entries, even though they almost always look weak. A trader can continue to have confidence entering with trend even after a pullback finally breaks a meaningful trend line. In a strong bull trend, look to buy at the low of the prior bar, or one or two ticks below its low, or on a stop at one tick above high 1 and high 2 setups. Look at the size of the pullbacks since the trend began. For example, in a small pullback bull trend, if the largest pullback in the past couple of hours has been only eight ticks, buy with a limit order at five to seven ticks below the high of the day. In strong bear trends, traders will do the opposite and short at the high of the prior bar or one or two ticks above it, on a stop at one tick below low 1 and low 2 signal bars, and on any bounce that is about the size of an average bar.

The market has inertia and the first attempt to end the trend usually fails. Once a trend line has been broken and there has been a significant pullback, then the first leg of the trend has likely ended. Even then, the first break of the trend line has high odds of setting up a with-trend entry that will lead to a second trend leg and a new extreme in the trend.

The pullbacks often have weak signal bars, and there are many countertrend trend bars. For example, in a strong bull trend, most of the buy signal bars might be small bear trend bars or doji bars, and several of the entry bars might be outside up bars with small bodies. They often follow two or three consecutive bear trend bars or bear micro channels. This constant selling pressure makes many traders look for sell signals, trapping them out of the bull trend. The sell signals never look quite strong enough, but the traders sell anyway because they look better than the buy signals, and they want to trade. They see that there was a pullback after just about every buy signal that comes back and hits a breakeven stop and think that this is a sign of a weak bull trend. They see that it is a bull trend and want to get long, but can't figure out how to do so, because they think every buy signal looks bad. The pullbacks are too small and the setups are too weak. Also, since these days happen only a couple of times a month, they are conditioned to the other days, when selling pressure usually leads to a tradable short, so they continue to short sell setups that don't quite look right. They don't look right because they are the start of bull flags, not reversals. However, when experienced traders see a bull trend with small pullbacks and an inability to fall below the moving average, along with many bear trend bars and weak buy signals, they understand what is going on. They see traders being trapped out of longs and being fooled into constantly looking for tops, and know that this bull trend is especially strong. The experienced trader knows that too many traders will be doing the opposite of what they should be doing, and will be forced to exit their losing shorts and chase the market up. This creates a relentless tension on the upside where many traders want to buy but don't, and experienced traders buy relentlessly and have a very profitable day.

These days are usually in relatively tight channels, and if traders are looking to swing their trades, they should not be overly eager to move their stops to breakeven. When a trend is in a tight channel, it will usually come back to the entry price before reaching a new trend extreme, and inexperienced, fearful traders will mistakenly let themselves get trapped out of a strong trend. For example, if there is a strong bull trend, the market will often come back to the entry price at the signal bar high in five to 10 bars, and will often dip a tick or two below it. This can make beginning traders nervous. They had enough profit for a scalp, but since the day was a trend day, they wanted to swing the trade for a larger profit. Now, after an hour, the market is back to the entry price. They worried for an hour because the market was not going much above the entry price, and they are now afraid that their winner will turn into a loser. They cannot take the pain anymore and exit with a small profit or loss. A few bars later, they are upset because the market is now at a new high and they are on the sidelines, trapped out of a great trade, waiting to buy the next pullback. They should trail their protective stops below the most recent swing low only after the market pulls back to the area of the signal bar high and then rallies to a new high. Trends tend to have trending highs and lows, so once a bull trend makes a new high, traders will raise their protective stops to just below the most recent swing low. Since they expect trending lows, they want the next pullback to stay above the last. If the market begins to enter a trading range, pullbacks will fall below prior higher lows, and they will then adjust to a trading range style of trading (discussed in book 2).

If there is a gap open that is more than just a few ticks and the first bar is a strong trend bar (small tail, good-sized bar), trading its breakout in either direction is usually a good trade. The first bar of every day is a signal bar for a trend from the open bull day and a trend from the open bear day, depending on the direction of the breakout of the bar. If you enter and your protective stop is hit on the next bar, consider reversing for a swing trade because the market will usually move more than the number of ticks that you lost on the first entry, and there is always the possibility that it could develop into a trend from the open day.

Even if there is not a gap open, a trend bar for the first bar is a good setup for a trade; but the chance for success is higher if there is a gap, since the market is more overdone and any move will tend to be stronger.

FIGURE 23.1 Buy the First Pullback in Strong Trend

The market formed a bull trend from the open in Figure 23.1, and the bar 2 break below the trend line was the first pullback. Traders bought on a stop at one tick above its high, even though it was a weak signal bar (bear close, but at least the close was above the midpoint). Aggressive bulls bought on a limit order at the low of the bar before bar 2, anticipating a failed micro channel breakout and higher prices.

It was reasonable but aggressive to short below the first bar of the day because it was a bear trend bar and there was a gap up, and there was room to the moving

Figure 23.1   TREND FROM THE OPEN AND SMALL PULLBACK TRENDS   **391**

average and to yesterday's close. However, yesterday ended with several strong bull trend bars in the final hour, which is a sign of buying pressure. When there is any doubt, especially on the open, it is better to wait for more information or until one side is trapped. The problem with this initial short is that most traders would not have been able to change their mind-set quickly enough to reverse to long above bar 2. They would have been trapped out; most would have waited to buy above the first pullback, and that later entry would have cost them several points of profit.

FIGURE 23.2 Small Pullback Bull Trend Day

A trend from the open day is the strongest type of trend day, and a small pullback day is the strongest type of trend from the open day. Trend from the open days occur about once or twice a week, but small pullback days (seen in Figure 23.2) form only once or twice a month. The average daily range in the Eminis had been about 12 points, and by bar 9 the biggest pullback of the day was only nine ticks. The pullback to bar 11 was only 11 ticks. Smart bulls saw this and therefore placed limit orders to buy maybe from six to 10 ticks down from the most recent high. Their initial stops might have been a couple of points. The market tried to create a larger pullback in the move down to bar 17 but could not drive the market down more than 14 ticks. Bulls saw the large bull trend bar before bar 14 as a possible buy climax, and many exited longs. A sudden surge that was likely to be followed by a pullback is a great opportunity to exit at a very good price that was likely to be brief. Other experienced traders shorted the close of the bar and the close of bar 14 and the next bar, since they had tails on the top, which is a sign of selling pressure. These traders expected a two-legged pullback lasting about 10 bars, and almost certainly a test of the moving average, since the market already tested it at bars 9 and 11. On a small pullback trend day, the market usually has a pullback sometime after 11:00 a.m. PST that is about twice the size of the largest pullback of the day.

Figure 23.2   TREND FROM THE OPEN AND SMALL PULLBACK TRENDS   **393**

There was a 20 gap bar long above bar 9 and the bulls bought the moving average tests at bars 8, 9, 11, 13, 17, and 19. There was not a strong sell signal all day, but aggressive bears could have scalped below the inside bar after bar 14. However, most traders instead would have looked to buy pullbacks instead of shorting new highs since this was such a strong bull trend day.

The market had a strong bull spike up from bar 2 and then the rest of the day was a bull channel. Traders became always-in long on bar 2 or on the strong bull trend bar that followed. Most of the channel was a slightly upward-sloping tight trading range with very little price gain, which is often the case on small pullback days. The high of the day was only four points above the bar 5 high at 8:25 a.m.

As is the case with all strong trends, most of the buy signal bars looked bad. This kept bulls from buying, trapping them out, and they ended up having to chase the market higher. It also kept shorts from exiting, and they were trapped into larger and larger losses. There were also many bear trend bars and bear spikes. This selling pressure made beginning traders look for reversal setups and not take buy signals. Experienced, unemotional traders understand that bad buy signal bars and bear trend bars in a trend day with very small pullbacks are signs of a very strong bull trend. They made sure to buy despite the weak setups. They bought on bar 2 as it broke above the doji high 1 signal bar. They bought again as bar 4 reversed up into an outside bar after forming a double bottom with the bull reversal bar from seven bars earlier. They bought the high 2 above bar 8 and above the bull bar that followed it, which created a two-bar reversal.

Bar 9 was a triangle (bars 6 and 8 were the first two pushes down) in a bull trend day and therefore a bull flag buy setup. They bought above the bar 11 bear trend bar that closed below the moving average, because it was a failed one-tick breakout below the bars 8 and 9 double bottom. It was also a pullback from the breakout to bar 10 of the triangle. At this point, the market was in a trading range, so most bulls would not have exited on a breakout below. They know that most breakout attempts fail and that most trading ranges in bull trends are bull flags and will ultimately break out of the top of the range. Most bulls either would have exited their longs below the bear bars after bar 10 or would have used the bottom of the most recent bull spike for their protective stops. For example, they might have had their stops at one tick below bar 4 or below the outside up bar that formed three bars later.

Usually, when there is a bear micro channel, like the one from bar 10 to bar 11, it is better to buy a pullback from the breakout, but there is a sense of urgency when the trend is strong, and smart traders are unwilling to wait for perfection because they don't want to risk missing the move. They also bought above the bear bar after bar 13, even though it had a bear body. It was a high 2 buy setup (the high 1 was the bull bar after bar 12) and a second-entry breakout pullback buy setup from the breakout above the bear micro channel down from bar 10 (the high 1 was the first setup). They bought again as bar 17 became an outside up bar, even though it followed a small doji bar and a big bear trend bar. The moving average was continuing to contain all sell-offs. They bought above the bar 17 bull doji, and above the bull bar that followed it. They bought above the bear bar after bar 19 because it was another small high 2 at the moving average. It was a bear bar, and the first leg down was made of the two bear bars after bar 18. Others bought on a stop above bar 19 because it was a bull bar in a pullback to the moving average in a strong bull trend.

The market spent most the day trying to reverse down, running stops on the bulls and trapping beginners into losing shorts, but relentlessly forming higher highs and lows, opening near the low of the day and closing near the high of the day. The buy setups all looked like they were low probability, and this trapped inexperienced bulls out. However, experienced traders knew what was going on and bought every sharp sell-off all day. They realized that, as bad as the long setups looked, the trend was so strong that the probability of success was much higher than it appeared.

Figure 23.3   TREND FROM THE OPEN AND SMALL PULLBACK TRENDS   **395**

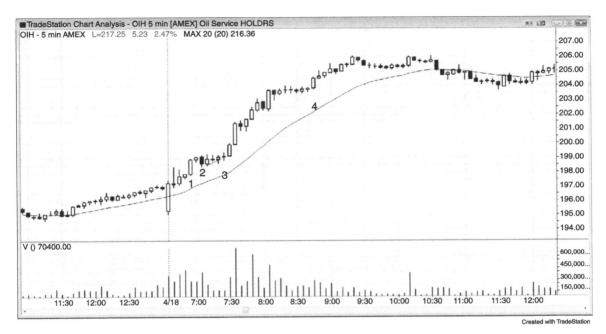

FIGURE 23.3   A Small Pullback Day Is the Strongest Type of Trend

When there is a trend from the open and all of the pullbacks are less than 20 to 30 percent of the recent average daily range, the day is a small pullback day, which is the strongest type of trend day. There is usually a pullback later in the day that is about 150 to 200 percent larger than the size of the earlier pullbacks, and that was the case here in the OIH (see Figure 23.3). Any sideways movement was a pause and a type of pullback and was a buy setup. The ii breakout at bar 1 was a good entry, and the bar 3 breakout of the two-legged sideways correction was another. Finally, there was the tight trading range breakout at bar 4. All of these entries should be considered to be part of the first up leg and not a first pullback, which comes after the first leg and sets up the second leg. Rarely, days just don't seem to pull back and traders are forced to enter on breakouts from even brief sideways pauses. The reality is that on strong days like this you can just buy at the market at any point, trusting that even if there is a reversal, the odds are overwhelming that the market will make another high before the pullback retraces very far. Many traders buy the closes of bull and bear trend bars and at or below the low of the prior bar.

Figure 23.4

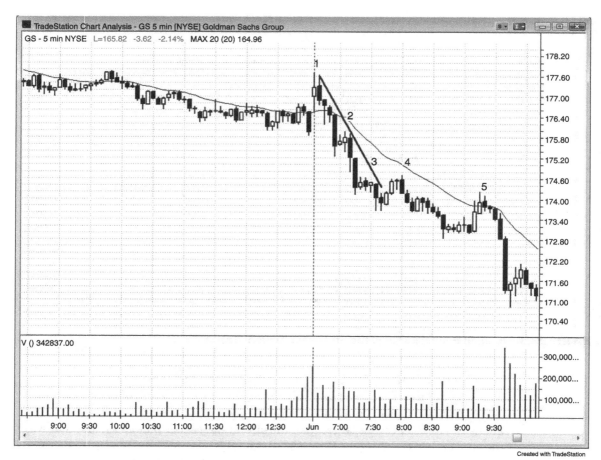

FIGURE 23.4   The First Trend Line Break Usually Fails

In a strong trend, determining which pullback is the first significant pullback is often difficult to do. When that is the case, the odds are very high that your trade will be profitable because an unclear pullback means the countertrend traders are very weak. In Figure 23.4, bars 2 and 3 were tiny pullbacks that did not break a meaningful trend line. The first pullback to break a trend line was bar 4. The first trend line break has a very good chance of being followed by another trend leg and is therefore a great entry (like shorting below the bar 4 bear trend bar). Today was a small pullback type of trend from the open bear trend day.

Figure 23.5   TREND FROM THE OPEN AND SMALL PULLBACK TRENDS   **397**

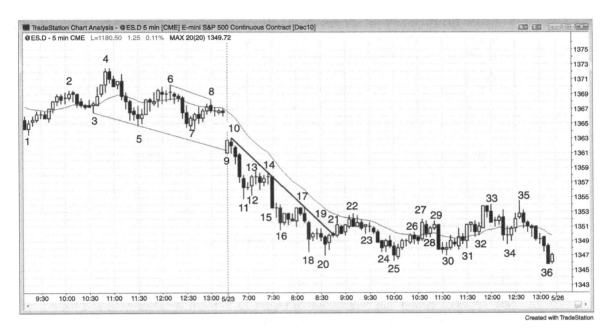

FIGURE 23.5   Strong First Bar Can Trap Traders in the Wrong Direction

Sometimes the first bar of the day can trap traders into entering in the wrong direction, and the day can then become a strong trend day in the opposite direction. In Figure 23.5, the market gapped below yesterday's low and broke out of a large trading range formed over the second half of yesterday (a head and shoulders top bear flag). The first bar today, bar 9, was a bull trend bar, which usually would lead to a partial gap closure or even a bull trend. Many went long on a stop at one tick above its high. However, the market trapped those longs two bars later when it traded below its low. That bull trend bar trapped bulls in and bears out because traders assumed that its strength was a sign that the market was going to try to close the gap and maybe become a bull trend day. It tried to reverse up from the breakout below yesterday's trading range and from breaking below the trend channel line. You have to be very flexible on the open and assume that the exact opposite of what you believed a minute ago can happen. You want to be able to see what is happening as early as it is happening so that you can enter as early as possible. The market tried to reverse back up above the trend channel line and failed, and this two-bar breakout pullback could lead to some kind of measured move down. If the day becomes a trend day and you miss the earliest entry, there will be chances to enter all day long.

Bar 10 provided a great opportunity to go short at one tick below the low of the bar 9 bull trend bar because this is where most of those trapped longs would get out, driving the market down. Also, any potential buyers would be waiting for more price action, so there were only sellers in the market, making for a high-probability short. Shorts added on at the bear flags along that way that trapped other early longs into believing that the market was bottoming.

Traders became confident that the market was always-in short by the close of bar 11, which confirmed the downside breakout. Many traders were confident of the always-in trade at the close of the bear breakout bar, just before bar 11.

Despite all of the reversal attempts, the market closed on its low. This is a good example of why it is important to try to swing at least part of your trade when you see a strong trend from the open day. If you do take long trades, you have to force yourself to get back on the short side as you exit your longs because you don't want to miss out on a huge short just to catch a small long.

Deeper Discussion of This Chart

Bar 12 was a strong bull reversal bar in Figure 23.5, but it largely overlapped the prior two bars and therefore it was part of a small trading range and was not functioning as a reversal bar, despite its appearance. Reversal bars always have to be judged in context, and when they overlap the prior bars by too much they are part of a small trading range, and buying above a trading range in a bear trend is a losing strategy. Smart traders are doing just the opposite. They have limit orders to go short at and above the high of the prior bar, even if the bar has a strong bull body.

Bar 13 was a low 2 short setup but the signal bar was a small doji. A doji is a weak signal bar, and weak setups often mean that the market is not yet ready to break out. However, in a strong bear trend like this, you can short for any reason and just use a wider stop. You could also go short below the bar 12 or bar 11 lows. In a strong bear trend, you can sell below the lows of bars and below swing lows and expect to make a profit.

Bar 14 was an attempt to reverse up after the failed low 2 and was therefore the third push up. The doji after bar 11 was the first push and bar 12 was the second. A third push up in a bear flag creates a wedge bear flag, so it is reasonable to short below its low.

This bar 14 failed low 2 buy setup illustrates one of the worst things that a trader can do, which is buying above a weak bar in a bear flag in search of a scalper's profit. You will not only lose on the scalp, but your mind-set will be that of a buyer. You will not be mentally prepared to short the breakout of the bear flag, which has a much higher chance of success and is more likely to result in a swing trade and not just a scalp.

The bar 15 breakout bar was a strong bear trend bar and a statement that the bears controlled the market. When there is a strong bear breakout like this, there will usually

Figure 23.5   TREND FROM THE OPEN AND SMALL PULLBACK TRENDS   **399**

be at least two more legs down in the form of a bear channel, and those two additional legs often create a wedge bear flag. This usually leads to a two-legged correction, as it did here in the rally to the moving average at bar 22.

Bar 22 was a bear reversal bar at the moving average and a low 2 short. It was also a 20 gap bar short and a wedge bear flag where the push up to bar 19 was the first leg up in the wedge.

The market sold off to a new bear low at the two-bar reversal at bar 25. It was also a reversal up from a one-bar final flag and a high 2 buy signal at the bottom of a developing trading range.

Bar 27 was a strong bull trend bar and an attempt to form an upside breakout, but it formed a double top bear flag with bar 22.

The bar 28 ii pattern became a final flag as the market reversed down from the small bar 29 lower high and moving average gap bar short setup.

Bar 30 was a two-legged higher low test of the bear low.

The bear rally ended with a wedge bear flag at bar 35, where bars 27 and 33 were the first two pushes up. The higher highs trapped bulls in and bears out, but alert traders were prepared for the bear day to resume, and they noticed how bar 35 missed the breakeven stops on the shorts below bar 11. This means that the strongest bears were reasserting themselves. They took over the market on the strong bar 15 bear spike; they were sitting on the sidelines, waiting for a test, and then they appeared out of nowhere and drove the market down into the close.

FIGURE 23.6   Gaps Can Lead to Trends Up or Down

Here, in Figure 23.6, are three consecutive gap openings but with different results, even though the first bar on each day was a bear trend bar. Bars 1 and 9 were also gap openings on the daily chart.

Bar 1 had no tail at the top and a small tail on the bottom and was a large bear trend bar, which is a good short setup on a day with a large gap up open. It was followed by a strong bear entry bar. If the first bar of the day is a strong trend bar (see thumbnail), there will usually be follow-through, and when the first two bars are strong, an attempted reversal up usually becomes a lower high, as it did here. A large gap up with strong selling usually becomes a trend from the open bear trend day. There was a sharp rally to bar 3 that tested the open, but this failed opening reversal resulted in a lower high or a double top, and then a lengthy down move.

Bar 2 was an attempt to form a breakout pullback from the breakout above yesterday's high, but the bears were too strong and the rally failed at bar 3.

Two bars after bar 6 was a strong bull reversal bar, and an opening reversal after a bear trend bar on the open broke below the bull channel of the final two hours of the day before. A bull channel is a bear flag, and the bull reversal bar that formed two bars after bar 6 was an attempt to have the breakout of the bear flag fail. Shorting below the first bar of the day was risky here, even though it was a bear trend bar, because the bar was at the level of a trading range at the end of yesterday and shorting at the bottom of a trading range is usually a losing strategy, especially in a market where there is no clear direction (a trading range).

The sharp rally up to bar 7 tested the close of the prior day and formed a lower high or a double top. The bear signal bar made this a good short. Pullbacks happen when bulls take profits. Why do traders ever take profits when a trend is strong? Because no matter how strong a trend is, it can have a deep pullback that would allow traders to enter again at a much better price, and sometimes the trend can reverse. If they did not take at least partial profits, they would then watch their big profit disappear and even turn into a loss.

Bar 9 gapped below the low of the prior day and formed a bear trend bar, but it had big tails, indicating that traders bought into the close of the bar. The second bar was a bear trend bar with a close on its low, indicating that the bears were strong, but it was followed by a strong bull trend bar, forming a reversal. Although the long did not trigger, this was again evidence that the bears lacked urgency. When the gap is this large, everyone knows that the behavior is extreme and if there is no immediate follow-through, the market will reverse quickly to undo this extreme situation.

Bar 10 was a large bear trend bar and therefore a sell climax. The next bar was an inside bar and this created a breakout mode situation. If there was no immediate follow-through selling, the bears would aggressively begin to buy back their shorts and look to sell higher, and bulls would buy, hoping for a low of the day. The market had been in a large bear channel for a couple of days and it was at the bottom of the channel, so there was a good chance that it would reverse up and a smaller chance that it would break through the bottom of the bear channel and form an even steeper bear trend. The channel lines are not shown, but the bear trend line is above the bar 1 and bar 7 highs and the bear trend channel line is a best fit line that could be drawn along the bar 4 and bar 8 lows. Bulls also bought above bull trend bars, like above the bull trend bar before bar 10 and the bull trend bar that formed two bars after bar 10. They would also buy above the small inside bar after bar 12, since that would be a failed low 2. Since this is a possible reversal up from the low of the day and the bottom of a two-day bull flag (a bear channel is a bull flag), it is a good buy setup.

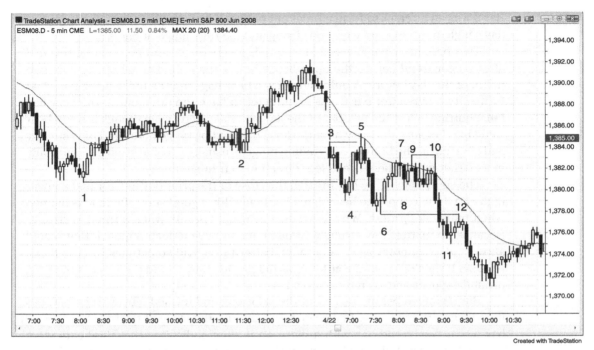

FIGURE 23.7   First Bar on Gap Day Often Points to Trend's Direction

The market in Figure 23.7 opened with a moderate gap down, which can be near the high or low of the day. Bar 3 was the first bar and it was a bear trend bar and a possible start of a bear trend from the open. The market failed to reverse the bar 2 swing low from yesterday so it would likely test the next level of support from yesterday, which was its low at bar 1. A trader would place an order to go short at one tick below the low of bar 3. Once the market fell below yesterday's low, it was likely to try to reverse up again, at least briefly, so a trader would place an order to go long on a stop at one tick above the first good signal bar. Although some traders would buy above bar 4, it was a bear trend bar with a close below its middle. It would be safer to wait until the next bar closed to see if a better setup would develop. The bar had a good-sized bull body and it formed a two-bar reversal with bar 4. The entry is above its high. In general, it is always better to buy above bull trend bars, especially when trading countertrend.

If the buy order wasn't filled and the next bar had a lower low, traders would try to buy above its high since they would be looking for a failed breakout below yesterday's low to form an opening reversal. However, if the market fell much further without a good buy setup, traders should only trade shorts until after a rally breaks a trend line.

Figure 23.7   TREND FROM THE OPEN AND SMALL PULLBACK TRENDS   **403**

The market made a small two-legged rally to the moving average and above the high of the day, where it set up a double top bear flag at the moving average. The large bull trend bar that broke above the bar 4 reversal was followed by a bear bar, which is bad follow-through and a signal that the market might be forming a trading range instead of a bull trend. The market continued in a trading range until midday. Up to that point, the range was about half the size of an average daily range. This alerted traders to the possibility of a breakout, an approximate doubling of the range, and the formation of a trending trading range day. The breakout began with the strong spike down from bar 10. Although not shown, the day ended with a strong reversal, as is often the case on trending trading range days, and it closed back in the tight trading range that began at bar 7. Tight trading ranges are magnets and tend to pull breakouts back into them.

FIGURE 23.8 Open on High Tick of the Day

Sometimes, a trend from the open day opens on the highest tick of the day. In Figure 23.8, bar 12 was the first bar of the day and it opened on its high tick and broke out below the wedge from yesterday's close. Most traders would not be nimble enough to sell below the inside bar at the end of yesterday, but it would be reasonable to sell a small position on the close of the first bar. If you missed the first entry, you could look at a 1 minute chart for a small pullback (there were many) to short or simply wait for a 5 minute setup. When there is a trend from the open, selling the first pullback is a high-probability trade, even though it is hard to take since you are selling near the low of a big move down in this case. Bar 15 was the signal bar for that first pullback short, and it was also a pullback that reversed down just below the moving average. The shorts were so eager to get in that they were selling below the moving average without waiting for the market to actually touch the moving average. Some traders would be afraid to short after five bars with bull bodies, but the bodies were small and this was the first pullback after a strong bear spike and therefore a reliable low 1 short setup. It was also a moving average test and a double top bear flag with the bar 13 high.

The day became a spike and channel bear with the bear channel beginning at bar 15 and also at bar 17 and ending at bar 19. The market rallied into the close and did not close on the low.

Figure 23.8   TREND FROM THE OPEN AND SMALL PULLBACK TRENDS   **405**

Deeper Discussion of This Chart

There was other spike and channel behavior in Figure 23.8, as is the case on most days. Bar 12 and the bar after it formed a spike, as did bar 13 and the bar before bar 14, and the entire move down to bar 14 was a spike. The two bars after bar 15 formed another spike, which was followed by the channel that began with the bar 17 low 2 and ended at bar 19.

Bar 16 was also a breakout pullback from the breakout below bar 14 and bar 1. It was also close enough to a breakout below yesterday's low to behave like a pullback from an actual breakout (close is close enough). The eagerness of the bears to short prevented that first pullback from reaching the moving average. They were afraid that it might not get there and therefore shorted so heavily on the approach that it never reached the moving average target. When the pullback turns back down just below the moving average, the bears are very aggressive and have a sense of urgency. They are very eager to short, even at relatively low prices, so lower prices are likely to follow.

Bar 19 was a spike up, and a channel up began with the bar 20 higher low. The bar after bar 20 was also a spike that ended with a three-bar channel at bar 21, the final bar on the chart.

Yesterday also had spike and channel activity, such as the spike up to bar 2 and the channel that began with either bar 3 or bar 5. The move from bar 5 to bar 6 was another spike, as was the bar before bar 7. The channel for both began with the bar 8 low. The entire move up from bar 5 to bar 7 was probably a spike on a higher time frame chart.

Yesterday's bull channel into the close poked above the trend channel line, which was drawn as a parallel of the bull trend line from bar 5 to bar 9. Once the market reversed back into the channel on the bar 12 first bar of the day, it was likely to poke through the bottom of the channel at a minimum. The next target is a measured move down using the vertical height of the channel, and the target after that is the bottom of the channel from yesterday, which was the bar 8 low. Since the move up to bar 11 had a wedge shape and the market tested below the start of the wedge, the next downside target is a measured move down. Use the height of the wedge (the bar 11 high minus the bar 8 low) and subtract that from the bar 8 bottom of the wedge. This target was exceeded during the sell-off below bar 17.

Bar 19 was a reversal up from a second break below a bear trend channel line (drawn parallel to the bar 15 to bar 17 trend line), so two legs up were likely. Bar 18 tried to reverse up from a tiny poke below the trend channel line, but the market never went above the high of the two-bar reversal so there was no long entry.

It is important to realize that although yesterday ended with a wedge top, there was still a strong bull trend into the close. This made beginning traders look for an additional rally on today's open, and deny the unfolding reversal. Always be ready for the opposite of what might appear likely, because it will happen in about 40 percent of the time.

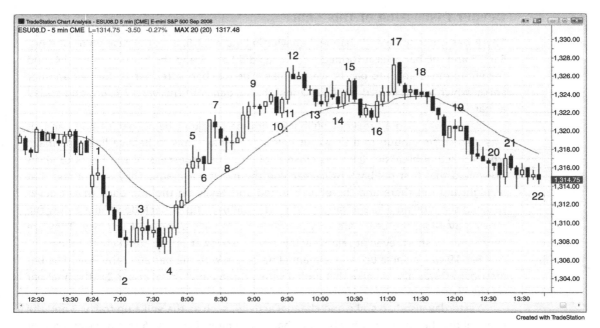

FIGURE 23.9 Reversal after Trend from the Open

Not all days that begin as trend from the open days result in strong trend days in the direction of the initial trend. In Figure 23.9, the day started as a bear trend from the open. It gapped below yesterday's low but then pulled back and almost closed the gap, and bar 1 became a breakout pullback short setup. The market sold off for five bars and set up a first pullback short below bar 3, but it then entered a tight trading range instead of immediately triggering a short. Although a scalp was possible, the market reversed up in a higher low at bar 4.

Deeper Discussion of This Chart

In Figure 23.9, bar 1 was a breakout pullback short following the breakout below yesterday's closing trading range. The initial sell-off down to bar 2 was around 12 points, which was about the average daily range recently. Once the market reversed back above the high of the open and broke to the upside, a measured move up was likely. Sometimes the market will make a measured move up equal to the open of the day to the low of the day and then close back down near the open, creating a doji day on the daily chart. Other times the measured move up is equal to about the height of the entire initial leg down. The bar 17 high of the day was three ticks below that measured move target. That reversal up above the opening range created a large bottom tail on the daily chart. When

Figure 23.9   TREND FROM THE OPEN AND SMALL PULLBACK TRENDS   **407**

the market turns down from about a measured move up from a large opening range, it often comes back down and the day closes somewhere in the middle of the range, as it did here.

The spike up from bar 4 to bar 5 was also a good basis for a measured move, but it did not happen here. Instead, the market went one tick higher than a leg 1 = leg 2 move where leg 1 was from bar 4 to bar 5 and leg 2 was from the bar 6 low to the bar 17 high of the day. The sell-off into the close was also a test of the bar 6 bottom of the bull channel that followed the spike up.

The two-bar spike down from bar 15 was followed by a pullback to a higher high at bar 17, which was the start of the bear channel. Sometimes the pullback after the spike down can be a higher high, but when it is, there is usually another spike down after the pullback. Here, the large bear inside bar after bar 17 was a spike down, and the move down from bar 18 formed another spike down, with the large bear trend bars being the most influential. The three-bar move down to bar 13 was also a bear spike and therefore probably had some influence on the sell-off that eventually followed. When the market starts to form many bear trend bars, it is accumulating selling pressure, and it often is able to overwhelm the bulls eventually, as it did here.

FIGURE 23.10   Strong Trends Have Weak Setups

Figure 23.10 shows a trend from the open bull trend day, but why are the best trends so difficult to trade? Because most of the with-trend entries look weak and there are many small pullbacks that trap traders out of the market. None of these pullbacks would have hit a two-point money stop, which is usually the best stop to use in a strong trend. With so many small, sideways bars, price-action stops below the lows of prior bars get hit too often and it makes more sense to rely on the original two-point stop. When the trend is strong, you need to do whatever you can do to stay long. Strong, relentless trends are often made of small bars with tails and lots of overlap but very small pullbacks that are mostly sideways pauses.

With a large gap up on the open, the odds favored a trend day up or down, and a larger gap like this makes a bull trend more likely. Because there was no significant selling in the first several bars, there was a possibility of a bull trend from the open, so traders had to be looking long. The market moved up quietly all day because institutions had buy orders to fill, and they filled them in pieces during the day because they were afraid that a pullback might not come and they needed to buy. Their constant buying prevented a significant pullback from forming. They don't buy all at once because they might create an exhaustive buy climax and a significant reversal to well below their purchase price. Also, as the market is going up, they are receiving additional buy orders throughout the day as investors become more confident.

Figure 23.10   TREND FROM THE OPEN AND SMALL PULLBACK TRENDS   **409**

Deeper Discussion of This Chart

In a strong trend such as that shown in Figure 23.10, you can buy for any reason and at any time. Buying above pullback bars is reliable, but you can also place limit orders to buy at or below the low of the prior bar. Shorting below bars is a loser's strategy. If you were to look for shorts, you should short only above the highs of bars or at the close of strong bull trend bars. When a day is this strong, most traders should not short, because shorting would probably be a distraction and result in missing buy setups, which are swing trades in a strong trend and therefore more profitable than scalps.

Bar 3 was the first bar of a two-bar spike up, and the market corrected sideways in a tight trading range before the channel up began. The very strongest trends tend to create reversal patterns all day long, but they somehow don't look just right. However, they constantly trap early bears into shorting, thinking that the small bars mean small risk, but after four or five small losses, they are so far behind that they will never catch up. You cannot take a trade simply because the risk is small. You need to consider the probability of success and the size of the profit target as well.

Bears saw bars 5, 7, and 9 as a three-push pattern and therefore a wedge variant, and they then saw bars 7, 9, and 10 as another wedge. When the correction from a wedge is sideways instead of down, you should conclude that the trend is very strong; stop looking for reversals and only trade with trend.

Bar 14 coincided with a Federal Open Market Committee (FOMC) report, and the market sold off sharply but immediately reversed up after missing the bar 5 high by one tick.

Going into the close, there were several two-bar bull spikes (bars 16, 17, and 21 were the first of the two bars in each spike).

A strong trend like this sets up reversals all day long, but the setups are never quite right and they almost always fail. The wedge that ended at bar 9 was in a tight bull channel composed almost entirely of bull trend bars. The market had not hit the moving average in over two hours. The odds were high that there would be buyers there, so there was little to be gained by shorting. Bar 10 broke above the trend channel line but it had a bull body. Again, the channel was very tight with no prior bear strength. You could only short a second signal and only if there was some prior bear strength, like a five- to 10-bar pullback to the moving average. In the absence of that, any short is a bet that the market would do something that it had not done all day. The biggest pullback all day was only nine ticks. If you short below a bar, your entry is about five ticks down and you need the market to go another five ticks down for you to make a one-point scalp. Since the market has tried to pull back repeatedly and could not fall more than nine ticks, betting that your short would now succeed is a very low-probability trade. You can scalp for one point and risk six or seven ticks only if the probability of success is 60 percent or higher, so you cannot short this market. You could argue that the move to bar 12 broke the bull trend line and therefore it was acceptable to short the bar 13 higher high, but the market still had not yet pulled back to the moving average, which is just six ticks below, and there would certainly be buyers there. Also, bar 13 was the fifth consecutive bull body and that represents too much strength to be shorting.

On most strong trend days, there is usually a sharp, brief reversal between 11:00 a.m. and noon PST that shakes out weak longs and traps overly eager bears who are hoping to recoup their earlier losses. It is always attributed to some news event, but that is irrelevant. What is important is that it usually sets up a buying opportunity for those who do not get frightened by the spike down.

Today, there was an FOMC report at 11:15 a.m. When the report came out, bar 14 was briefly a bear trend bar with a large bear body. If you shorted before the bar closed, believing that the market was going to sell off hard on the report, you were ignoring a very important rule: you should wait for the bar to close, because what appears as a large bear trend bar at four minutes into the bar can become a doji bar or even a bull reversal bar by the time the bar closes.

Bar 16 was a higher low after the rally from the bottom of bar 14 to the top of bar 15, and it was followed by the bar 17 breakout pullback long entry. All spikes should be thought of as spikes, climaxes, and breakouts, so the two-bar spike that began with bar 16 was a breakout and bar 17 was the entry from the pullback.

Bar 19 was a double top bear flag, but there was no prior strong spike down so the market was more likely just going sideways after the bar 17 spike up.

Bar 20 was a bull reversal bar and a high 2 long, and bar 21, the bar after the entry bar, traded below the entry bar and trapped longs out. However, since the move up from bar 20 had gone only one tick, the protective stop was below the bar 20 signal bar and you should not tighten it too soon. Strong trend days constantly trick traders into exiting longs early and into taking shorts. The bears have to buy back their shorts, which adds to the buying pressure and removes the bears from additionally shorting for at least a bar or two. They just lost and will need to recover before they look to short again. Also, the bulls who were just trapped out will chase the market as it goes up, adding to the buying.

Figure 23.11 TREND FROM THE OPEN AND SMALL PULLBACK TRENDS **411**

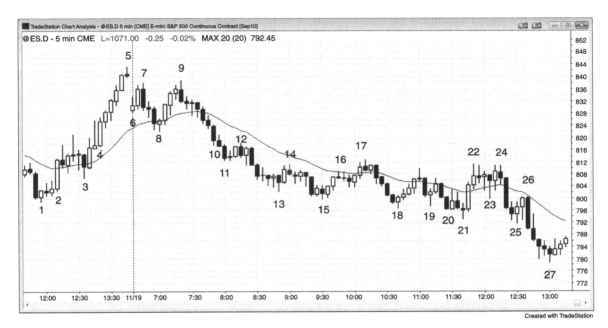

FIGURE 23.11 Double Top in a Strong Bear Day

A trend from the open can have a double top or bottom before the strong trend begins. In Figure 23.11, bar 7 tried to set up a bear trend from the open but the high was tested on a 7:00 a.m. report, which commonly happens. Even though the market formed a small trading range up to bar 9, you always have to consider the possibility that the market was just waiting for the report before it unleashed its strength.

The opening range was less than a third of the size of the range of recent days, and this put the market in breakout mode. Once there was a spike down and a spike up after the first bar (a reversal down and then a reversal up), some traders would enter on a breakout, expecting the range to increase severalfold. After the market fell below the bar 7 two-bar reversal, the bar 7 reversal down became a swing high. After the market moved above bar 8, bar 8 became a swing low and a reversal up. These traders placed a buy stop at one tick above the bar 7 spike top and a sell stop at one tick below the bar 8 spike bottom. Once the buy order got filled as bar 9 moved above the high of bar 7, they doubled the size of the sell stop below bar 8. As that second order got filled, as it did in the move below bar 8, they got stopped out of their longs and they reversed into shorts. This is the traditional approach to this setup, but it is generally better to be more aggressive. A better approach would have been for traders to short below the bar 7 two-bar reversal and scalp out part, and then tighten their protective stops. Next, they could reverse to long on the bar 8 high 2 at the moving average. They could scalp out part and tighten their stops. They could reverse to short below the bar 9 outside down bear bar, since there were trapped bull breakout traders and the market was forming a double top bear flag with bar 7. They could scalp out part, tighten their stops, and swing the balance until there was a clear buy signal; if there was none, they could hold short into the close. If they did buy at maybe the bar 15, 18, or 21 lows, they had to reverse to short as they took profits. If they were unable to do that, they should either continue to hold short or exit on those minor buy signals and look to short rallies.

Even though the day began with a small trading range and some traders might call this a trending trading range day or a bear trend resumption day, when the pullbacks are this small, you are dealing with a very strong bear trend. When that is the case, it is better to make sure that you are short for most or all of the day. Thinking of this as a trending trading range day will make you take longs and often miss shorts. The pullback that began at bar 15 was about twice the size of the earlier pullbacks since the trend began at bar 9. The day was not a classic small pullback trend day because those days usually don't have a larger pullback until later in the day, like after 11:00 a.m. PST, but today was still a strong bear trend day.

Deeper Discussion of This Chart

Bars 11, 13, and 15 formed a wedge in Figure 23.11, but since the market had not touched the moving average in about 20 bars and the bear channel was tight, this would likely lead to a test of the moving average where bears would short aggressively. The bulls were able to generate two legs up to bar 17, which was a moving average gap bar. The first moving average gap bar in a bear trend often leads to the final leg down before there is a larger correction up.

Since the leg up to the moving average gap bar almost always breaks a significant bear trend line, the higher low or lower low test of the bear low usually leads to a protracted correction up or even a reversal. The market tried to reverse up at bar 18 and again at the small wedge that ended at bar 21. The market created a strong two-bar bull spike up to bar 22, trapping bulls in and bears out, but experienced traders know that the market often has a strong countertrend move after 11 a.m. PST on a trend day and they would be ready to short the failure, like the small double top at bar 24. There was a bear inside bar for the signal bar and the bar 22 and 24 double top formed a larger double top bear flag with bar 17. The spike down to bar 25 was followed by a couple of strong bull trend bars, which set up the bar 26 breakout pullback short for the sell-off into the close. That reversal attempt at bar 25 was the signal bar for an expanding triangle bottom, where bars 18, 21, and 25 were the three lows. Instead, the

Figure 23.11   TREND FROM THE OPEN AND SMALL PULLBACK TRENDS   **413**

bottom failed and bar 26 became the breakout pullback short entry bar. A failed wedge often leads to a measured move down, and the sell-off into the close came close to the target.

This turned the day into a trend resumption bear, where there was an initial bear trend down to bar 13, then a trading range that lasted a couple of hours to bar 24, and then another bear leg into the close.

CHAPTER 24

Reversal Day

Primary characteristics of reversal days:

- The day trends in one direction and then it trends in the opposite direction into the close.
- Most start as trending trading range days.
- If the reversal starts in the last couple of hours and is strong, it will usually have follow-through on the next day and often the next several days.

Some of the strongest trends begin in the middle or end of the day. Sometimes they originate as trading range breakouts or climactic trend reversals, usually attributed to some news item, but this is unimportant. In either case, the market can enter a runaway trend mode where it trends relentlessly with only minor pullbacks. There are large trend bars with little overlap and mostly small tails. This is a breakout and a clear always-in flip. You must enter quickly, even if the new trend looks climactic and overdone (and it is, but it will likely continue to get much more so!), and swing most of your position. You should trade these breakout spikes aggressively and make sure that you have at least a small position because the move can go very far. Trading strong spikes is described in detail in the section on breakouts in book 2, and reversals are discussed in detail in book 3.

At other times, the market is trending and then begins a pullback, but the pullback just grows endlessly and becomes a trend channel in the opposite direction. There is almost always at least one countertrend spike before the channel begins, so whenever you see a pullback that has a strong countertrend spike, be aware that the trend might be reversing. For example, if the market has a strong sell-off for the first hour or two and you think there might be a two-legged rally to the moving average, but that pullback begins with a fairly strong bull trend bar, make sure to consider the possibility that the bar could be a bull spike that could be followed by a relentless bull channel instead of a small bear flag. By the end of the day, the pullback can grow larger than the bear trend that preceded it, and the day could become a bull reversal bar on the daily chart. If you recognize this behavior early, you should restrict your trading to buying only, because you will lose money on shorts as you desperately hope that the bear trend from the first hour resumes. Many of these days can be classified as other types of trend days, and they are commonly trending trading range days. In fact, most reversal days begin as trending trading range days. The opposite is true for bear trends on the open that reverse into relentless bear channels.

Figure 24.1   REVERSAL DAY   **417**

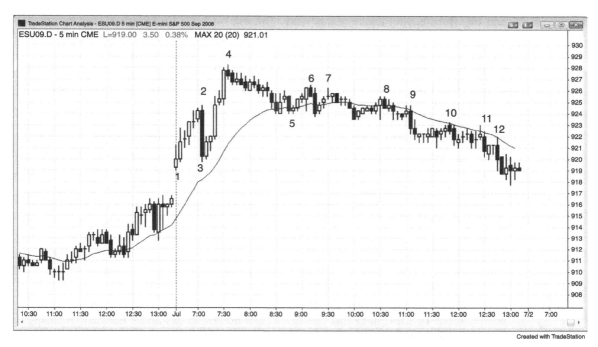

FIGURE 24.1   Strong Trend Can Fail

A strong trend can start at any time during the day, even if the day initially had a strong trend in the opposite direction. As shown in Figure 24.1, there was a sharp two-legged move up in the first hour, followed by a tight channel pullback to test the moving average. The market then went sideways for over two hours and finally broke down at bar 9 into a lower range. The last profitable long entry was at 8:50 a.m. PST at bar 5. If you continued to take long scalps, you would eventually realize that you were losing on every trade, which is a sure sign that the market is trending in the wrong direction and either you didn't see it or you didn't believe it.

Pullbacks happen when bulls take profits. Why do traders ever take profits when a trend is strong? Because no matter how strong a trend is, it can have a deep pullback that would allow traders to enter again at a much better price, and sometimes the trend can reverse. If they did not take at least partial profits, they would then watch their big profit disappear and even turn into a loss.

Deeper Discussion of This Chart

The market in Figure 24.1 broke out above the trading range of the final hour of yesterday. The large tail on top of the first bar indicates that sellers were reasonably strong and therefore buying above it was risky. The market rallied for six bars and reversed down hard during bar 2, presumably on a 7:00 a.m. report. After the bull momentum leading up to the report and no sign of a top or a buy climax, it was not good to short below the top bar of this rally. This was the first pullback in a trend from the open bull trend and is a buy setup. However, the strength of the bar 2 bear spike was unusual if the day was to become a bull trend day.

The bar 3 low (the bottom of bar 2) formed a possible double bottom with the bar 1 low. It is common for a gap up day to have a pullback that tests the low of the open and then to become a bull trend day. Since the opening range was greater than about 30 percent of the average range of recent days, the opening range was not a good breakout mode setup. The likelihood of a strong, relentless trend after a bull breakout was less. If the market was to become a bull trend day, it would more likely be a weaker version, perhaps like a trending trading range day. The bull ii setup after bar 3 was a good signal for a long, but since a strong bull trend was unlikely, bulls should take at least half off after about two to four points' profit. It is also possible that the bar 3 strong bear spike could be followed by a bear channel after a pullback. Here, the pullback was to a higher high at bar 4, which followed buy climax bars on the bar before and two bars before that. Consecutive buy climaxes usually lead to at least a two-legged correction lasting about 10 bars. Since this was not a clear bull trend day and it had strong selling at bar 3, this bear reversal bar was an acceptable low 2 short setup.

The pullback to bar 5 broke the bull trend line, and the bar 6 lower high set the stage for a bear trend day into the close. Bar 6 was the first bar of a two-bar bear spike, which alerted traders to the possibility that a channel down might follow. The bar before bar 5 was a bear spike, as was the very large bar 3 bear trend bar. There were other bear spikes as the bear channel progressed, and the market could not close above the moving average after the bar before bar 8.

As with most strong trend channels, you would make more by swinging than by scalping because there are frequent pullbacks that would run stops on even the with-trend scalps (like the shorts from bars 8 and 10), resulting in losses. It is better to trail your stop above the prior swing high.

The bar 9 spike down that broke below the upper trading range was followed by a perfect measured move into the close. Bar 9 was a breakaway gap, the gap being between the bottom of the upper range and the bar 10 breakout pullback. The middle of that gap was the middle of the move down from bar 4 to the low just before the close of the day.

On the daily chart, this would be a doji bar with a small body and a large tail at the top, and if it is in the area on the chart where a bear reversal is likely, it can be a good signal bar for a short trade on the daily chart.

Notice that the market was forming lower highs and lows between bars 5 and 9, hinting that a bear trend might be underway.

Figure 24.2   REVERSAL DAY   **419**

FIGURE 24.2   Most Reversals Begin as Trending Trading Range Days

Most reversal days begin as trending trading range days as shown in Figure 24.2, and this day was also a spike and channel bear trend day and a trend from the open bear day. It reversed up after three pushes down (bars 8, 15, and 17) into a bull reversal day that trended up into the close. This is a common occurrence in trending trading range days.

Deeper Discussion of This Chart

A large gap opening often is followed by a trend in either direction, and since the first bar of the day in Figure 24.2 was a strong bear trend bar, the odds of a bear trend were greater. This is a failed breakout setup, and traders would short below its low for a possible trend from the open bear day.

Bars 4 and 5 were large bear trend bars and therefore bear spikes and sell climaxes. A pair of consecutive climaxes is usually followed by at least a several-bar pause or pull-back, as happened here (a pullback to the bar 7 high). Bar 7 was then a third sell climax, and a third consecutive sell climax is usually followed by an even larger correction. The move down to bar 8 was a spike and climax type of bear trend, and it was followed by a rally to bar 10 that tested the bar 7 start of the channel down to bar 8. This formed a double top bear flag, and ultimately an approximate measured move down to the low of the day. The entire move down to bar 8 was in a tight channel and was therefore a larger spike.

After a large wedge bottom, the market usually has at least a two-legged rally that tests the top of the wedge (here, the bar 10 high), and the number of bars in the correction is usually at least a third or so of the number of bars in the wedge. This large wedge was also the bear channel that followed the bear spike from bar 4 to bar 8, and that was also a reason for the test of the bar 10 high (the beginning of a channel usually gets tested). The test may break above that high but more often forms a double top bear flag, as it did here.

When there is a wedge reversal, it is usually safer to buy after a higher low like at bar 19 or above the bar 22 failed low 2. You can see the large bull spike entry bar there, and it was a sign that traders believed that the rally was no longer just a bear flag and the market could have a measured move up and trade into the upper trading range. This was a complex day, and the wedge reversal could also be thought of as the bottom of a lower trading range on a trending trading range day. If enough traders believed that was the case, buying the first entry above the inside bar after bar 17 was reasonable, with the expectation of a test of the bottom of the upper trading range.

Bars 11, 13, and 14 formed a wedge bull flag, but the market broke to the downside instead of reversing up. When that happens, the market usually falls to about a measured move down from the top to the bottom of the wedge. Bar 10 was the top of the wedge, and the move down to bar 15 exceeded the measured move objective. When that happens, there is usually another leg down after a pullback, as was the case here.

Although the move up to bar 18 had two legs, this rally had too few bars to adequately correct that large wedge bottom. Also, it was in a tight channel and was therefore likely just the first of two or more legs up. There was a second leg up to bar 20, but the problem was the same. The move from bar 17 up to bar 20 had too few bars to correct such a large wedge and it was still in a relatively tight channel. This creates uncertainty and increases the odds that the market will need a larger second leg up to convince traders that the wedge was adequately corrected.

The move from bar 21 to bar 25 might be good enough to satisfy traders that an adequate two-legged correction was complete, but the market then broke out to the upside in a three-bar bull spike up to bar 27. Since the bears could not generate much of a downside breakout in the channel from bar 17 to bar 25, no clear two-legged move ever developed. This absence of any clear pullback after a first leg up was a sign of strength by the bulls.

Figure 24.3   REVERSAL DAY   **421**

FIGURE 24.3 Strong Trend Entries on Smaller Time Frames

In a runaway bull trend, there are more chances to buy on the 3 minute chart than on the 5 minute chart (see Figure 24.3). Bars 1 and 2 were small countertrend inside bars on the 3 minute chart on the left, setting up high 1 longs, but they were not clear signals on the 5 minute chart. The bar 3 long was present on both charts (on the 5 minute chart, it was a high 1 long in a strong bull spike, even though it had a bear body).

CHAPTER 25

Trend
Resumption Day

Primary characteristics of trend resumption days:

- The day has a strong trend in the first hour or so and then enters a trading range.
- The trading range lasts for hours and often lulls traders into thinking that the day will be quiet into the close.
- The trend resumes in the final hour or two.
- The second leg often is about the same size as the first leg.
- The protracted trading range is often a very tight trading range.
- There is often a breakout from the trading range late in the day that tries to reverse the trend, but it is usually a trap. The market then reverses and breaks out in the opposite direction into the close. A trap is more likely when the trading range is unusually tight.
- There is often a breakout pullback entry for traders who did not enter earlier or on the breakout.

Sometimes there will be a strong trend for the first hour or so and then the market goes sideways for several hours. Whenever this happens and especially if the sideways action is in a very tight trading range, the day is likely becoming a trend resumption day. Don't give up on the boring midday trading range, because there might be a strong trend in the final hour or so. The breakout is usually in the direction of the earlier trend, but sometimes it can be in the opposite direction and turn the day into a reversal day. For example, if the trend from the open was a bear trend, there is usually a late downside breakout from the trading range, and the day often opens near its high and closes near its low. There is frequently a brief one- or two-bar strong reversal breakout that fails between 11 a.m. and noon PST, trapping traders into the wrong (long) direction, and it is usually followed by a breakout in the other direction. This happens quickly, but if you are expecting it, you have a chance of catching a big bear move into the close. Less often, the reversal breakout succeeds and the trend in the final hour, if there is one, can retrace all or part of the opening bear trend.

The midday sideways action does not have to be a tight trading range, and it often has tradable legs in both directions. Sometimes there are three countertrend lazy pushes, creating a wedge flag. At other times the third leg fails to surpass the second, and this forms a head and shoulders flag (most head and shoulders reversal patterns fail and become continuation patterns). Because the pattern often has three pushes instead of two, it traps traders out of their positions from the open, thinking that this countertrend action might in fact be a new, opposite trend. However, don't let yourself get trapped out, and be ready to enter when you see a good setup that will get you into the market in the same direction as the morning trend. Traders are scaling into positions in both directions and, at some point, many reach their maximum size. Once there is a breakout, the losing side cannot scale in anymore, and their only choices are hope and getting stopped out. For example, if there is a strong morning bear trend and then the market goes sideways, both the bulls and the bears will continue to add to their positions during the trading range over the next several hours, and many will reach the maximum size that they are willing to hold. Once the market begins to break to the downside, the bulls can no longer continue to buy. With a lot of bulls no longer able to buy, the bears are unopposed. As the market falls, it will often accelerate as more and more bulls give up and sell out of their losing longs, adding to the collapse into the close. The difficult part of this type of day is that the quiet midday sideways movement often leads traders to give up on the day when in fact they should view this as an opportunity. Just be ready to enter. The best forms of this pattern occur only a couple of times a month.

Instead of a midday trading range, the market will sometimes form a weakly trending countertrend move for a couple of hours, leaving traders wondering if the day is a reversal day instead of a trend resumption day. What might be developing is a weak trend resumption day, one that feels more like a trading range day but ends up opening on one extreme and closing on the other. Watch for the trend of the open to resume in the final hour, and be prepared to enter. For example, if there was a strong sell-off on the open, and then a lower-momentum rally with three pushes up that retraces some or even all of the initial sell-off, be prepared for a break below that bull channel and a resumption of the bear trend into the close. If there is a breakout of the top of the bull channel that reverses back down, this can be a good swing short entry for the trend into the close. Instead, there might be a setup that looks like a good low-risk short on the breakout below the channel. Otherwise, you can wait for the bear trend to resume and then look to enter on a breakout pullback or a pullback near the moving average. Even though the 5 minute chart might look like a trading range, maybe like an ABC on a higher time frame chart, if the market closes near the low, the day will create a bear trend bar on the daily chart.

Trend resumption patterns often take place over two or more days. Although the 5 minute chart might look like it has huge swings during those days, they may create a simple ABC on the 60 minute chart. For example, if yesterday had a strong bull spike for a couple of hours and then entered a trading range and that trading range continued for a couple of hours today, yesterday's trend might resume at any point. If you are aware of this, you will be more likely to be willing to swing a larger part of your position for what could be a big move.

FIGURE 25.1   Gap Test after a Gap Up

On big gap days, the market often tests the open before the trend begins. In Figure 25.1, the market opened with a large gap up and then had a double bottom test of the low followed by a big rally up to bar 3. From there, it traded in a tight range for more than three hours, lulling traders into thinking that the good trading was done. Bar 6 reversed up from a poke below a bear trend channel line and it also dipped one tick below the bar 4 signal bar high. This trapped some bears into a short and many bulls out of their longs. The signal bar for the rally into the close was the first moving average gap bar of the day.

There were several other chances to get long, like the reversal up from the failed breakouts below micro trend lines at bars 7, 9, and 10.

Deeper Discussion of This Chart

In Figure 25.1, bar 7 was a high 2 entry and a reversal up from a one-tick break of a small bull trend line. Bar 1 was the high 1 entry.

Bar 8 was a high 2 variant (bear-bull-bear bars: the bar after bar 7 had a bear body and therefore the first push down, the next bar had a bull body and therefore traded up, and then the following bar had a bear body again, for a second push down).

Figure 25.2   TREND RESUMPTION DAY   **427**

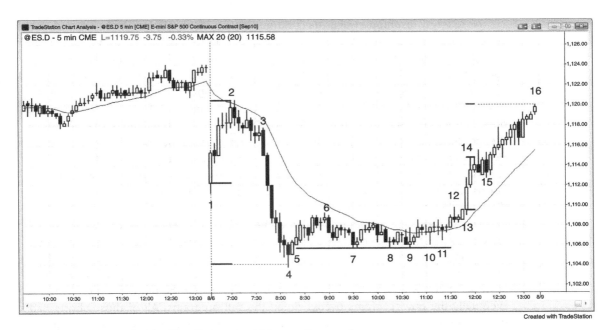

FIGURE 25.2 Tight Trading Range and Then a Reversal

Sometimes a tight trading range that follows a strong trend can lead to a reversal instead of trend resumption. In Figure 25.2, today had a strong sell-off from bar 3 and then entered a tight trading range for a few hours. This often leads to a bear trend resumption into the close with the final sell-off often being as large as the initial one. There is frequently a failed breakout of the top of the range before the final bear leg begins. Bar 12 was a perfect setup for a swing short because it was a bear reversal bar that broke out of the top of the tight trading range late in the day. However, instead of the next bar being an entry bar for a large bear move, it was a small bull inside bar, and therefore a breakout pullback long setup. Bar 12 broke out and this inside bar was a pause, which is a type of pullback.

Deeper Discussion of This Chart

In Figure 25.2, the day opened with a large gap down and a strong bull reversal bar, setting up a failed breakout long and a possible trend from the open bull day.

Bars 13 and 14 were large bull trend bars that formed a two-bar breakout. Any breakout often is followed by a measured move based on the spike. It is usually based on the height from the open or low of the first bar of the spike to the close or high of the final bar. The closing high of the day was at a measured move from the open of bar 13 to the high of bar 14.

Most trend resumption bear days do not have a large rally on the open, and that large rally is an indication that the bulls were willing to buy aggressively today. Even though the middle of the day was setting up perfectly for a big sell-off into the close, you can never be certain and there is always about a 40 percent chance that the exact opposite can happen. Another clue that the market might rally to test the open of the day was that the low of the day was almost a perfect measured move down from the open of the day to the top of the initial rally. That means that the open of the day was in the middle of the day's range. If the market could get back up there, the day could be close to a doji day, which is fairly common. Notice how the market repeatedly tested the support line at the bar 7 low to the tick and continued to find buyers. There were double bottom pullback long setups at the inside bar after bar 8, the inside bar after bar 9, and the higher lows at bars 9 and 11.

The support line was one tick below the initial bar 5 entry bar for the expected pullback from the sell climax. Bar 5 was the entry bar above the two-bar reversal setup at the low of the day. The market ran the stops below that entry bar by one tick, but, despite many attempts, it could not go any further down. This is a sign of strong bulls at work. Both buy and sell programs continued throughout the tight trading range, but eventually the buy programs overwhelmed the sell programs. All of those shorts had to be bought back, and this added to the buying pressure. Also, many sell programs reversed to buy programs, adding to the buying. The bars 14 and 15 spike up was followed by a channel into the close.

Figure 25.3　　　　　　　　　　　　　　　　　　　TREND RESUMPTION DAY　**429**

FIGURE 25.3 Trend Resumption

Even though the initial rally may only have a couple of strong trend bars and appear to be leading to a trading range day, the trend resumption can still be strong. In Figure 25.3, the market started as a trend from the open bull trend when it rallied from an expanding triangle bottom and a failed breakout of yesterday's low. It then ran for two bars, but it stalled in the middle of yesterday's trading range. A rally from any three-push pattern usually results in at least two legs up, which ultimately developed here. Bar 2 was a breakout pullback that led to another small rally, but then the market lost momentum. It continued to weakly trend above the moving average until bar 3. At this point, it was clear that something was not right. A trend from the open bull trend is one of the strongest forms of trends but this was clearly not trending strongly. That meant that traders would soon decide that the day was not what they thought and they would exit and wait. They would then be looking for a trading range day and a possible new low for the day. It was possible for the bar 2 low to be followed by a double bottom bull flag, but, in the absence of strong early bulls, bears would aggressively push for a new low of the day and the bar 2 low would likely fail. Bar 4 was a second small push below bar 2 and it was followed by a trend into the close, creating a trend resumption bull day, albeit a weak one, and giving the expected second leg up from the expanding triangle bottom. Bar 4 was an exact breakout test of the trend from the open signal bar high.

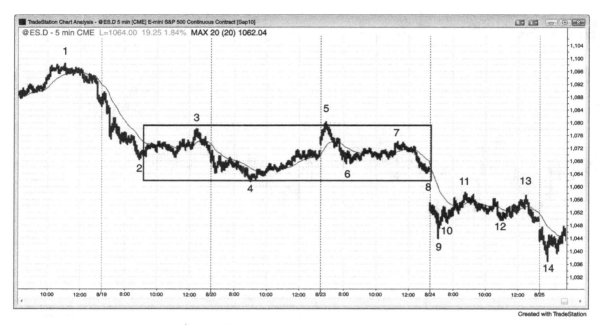

FIGURE 25.4 Trend Resumption after Several Days

Trend resumption can take place over the course of several days. In Figure 25.4, the market had a strong move down to bar 2 and then entered a trading range that lasted two and a half days. Trading ranges can last a long time, but usually break out in the direction of the trend. The bear trend resumed and had a second leg down from bar 5 to bar 14, five days after the first move down.

The bear leg down from bar 5 to bar 6 was followed by a trading range, and the second leg down ended on the open of the next day at bar 9.

The sell-off from bar 7 to bar 9 was followed by a trading range to bar 13, and the bear trend resumption occurred with the move down to bar 14. This was a three-day trend resumption pattern.

CHAPTER 26

Stairs: Broad Channel Trend

Primary characteristics of stairs days:

- A stairs day is a variant of a trending trading range day where there are at least three trading ranges.
- The day has broad swings, but trending highs and lows.
- Because the swings are large, traders can usually place trades in both directions, but they should try to swing part or all of their with-trend trades.
- Almost every breakout is followed by a pullback (a breakout test) beyond the breakout point, so that there is some overlap between consecutive swings. For example, in a broad bear channel, every breakout to a new low is followed by a rally that goes back above the breakout point but stays below the most recent swing high. However, there is sometimes a swing or two that will extend above the prior swing high by a little. This will make some traders wonder if the market is reversing, but the trend will usually soon resume.
- If each breakout gets a little smaller than the prior one, then this is a shrinking stairs pattern and a sign of waning momentum, which can lead to a larger correction.

When a market has a series of three or more trending swings that resemble a mildly sloping trading range or channel, both the bulls and the bears are active but one side is exerting somewhat more control. Each pullback retraces beyond its breakout point, creating overlap between each breakout spike and the following pullback. Two-way trading is taking place within the broad channel, so traders can look for entries in both directions. If the breakouts get smaller and smaller, then this is a shrinking stairs pattern and indicates waning momentum. It often leads to a two-legged reversal and a trend line break. Many three-push reversals qualify as stairs or shrinking stairs trends that failed and reversed. Stairs are often just pullbacks or flags in higher time frame trends, and it is common to see stairs over the final hour or two of the day and then a breakout of the flag on the open of the next day. For example, a broad bull channel today might just be a large bear flag, and the bear trend could break out tomorrow.

Alternatively, one stair might suddenly accelerate and break out of the trend channel in the with-trend direction. If it then reverses, this overshoot and reversal will likely result in at least a two-legged move. If it does not, the breakout will probably continue for at least two more legs or at least the approximate height of the channel in an imprecise measured move (the distance beyond the channel should be about the same as the distance within the channel).

Traders pay attention to how many ticks breakouts run past the most recent swing point, and then use that number to fade subsequent breakouts, expecting a breakout test. For example, if the last swing low fell 14 ticks below the swing low before it, traders will look to scale into longs beginning around 10 ticks below the most recent swing low, which will usually be around the trend channel line. If the pullback from the most recent breakout was about 15 ticks, they will look to take profits around 10 to 15 ticks up from the low, which will usually be around the trend line (the top of the bear channel).

Figure 26.1   STAIRS: BROAD CHANNEL TREND   **433**

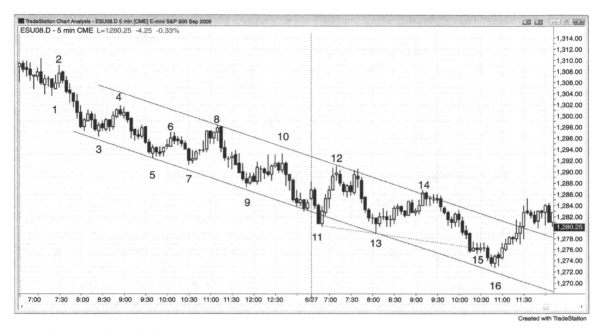

FIGURE 26.1   Bear Stairs

A bear stairs pattern is a downwardly sloping channel where each breakout to a new low is followed by a pullback that goes back above the breakout point. For example, in Figure 26.1 the breakout leg below bar 6 down to bar 9 was followed by a pullback that went back above the bar 7 low, and the rally after the leg that broke below bar 9 down to bar 13 was followed by a pullback that went above the bar 9 breakout point, overlapping the prior range.

Some traders buy near the trend channel line and short near the trend line. Other traders pay attention to how far a breakout goes before there is a pullback. For example, the low of bar 5 was about four points below the low of bar 3. Aggressive bulls placed limit orders to buy at about three to four points below the low of bar 5. They were not filled on the sell-off to bar 7. However, as the market fell below bar 7, they again placed limit orders to buy three to four points lower, and were filled on the move down to bar 9, which had a low that was four points below the low of bar 7. Since prior rallies were about four points, they took profits at around three points above their entries. They did the same on the sell-offs to bars 11 and 16. They tried on the sell-off to bar 13, but the market did not fall far enough for their orders to get filled. Bears did the opposite. They saw that past rallies were about four to six points, so they scaled into shorts around three to five points above the most recent swing low, which was in the area of the bear trend line. This style of trading is only for experienced traders. Beginners should restrict themselves to stop entries, so that the market is already going their way (this is discussed in the second book).

Bar 7 was the third push down and a shrinking stair (it extended less below bar 5 than bar 5 extended below bar 3). The channel lines are drawn as best fit lines to highlight that the market is trending down and in a channel. There is clearly two-sided trading and traders should be buying the lows and selling the highs when they see appropriate setups.

Deeper Discussion of This Chart

The market opened near the bottom of the bear channel that started yesterday in Figure 26.1 and broke out below the channel. The breakout failed with a two-bar reversal that led to a four-bar bull spike. After a double top that tested the bear trend line (drawn as a parallel of the best fit trend channel line), the market had a spike down to bar 13. With both bull and bear spikes, the two sides were fighting over the direction of the expected channel. The bulls started a channel but it failed at the trend line and reversed down in a bear channel. The market reversed up from a test of the trend channel line where the bar 16 low could not reach the line. This is a sign of aggressive buying. The bar 16 two-bar reversal was also a final flag long setup from the bar 15 four-bar final flag.

Three pushes down does not guarantee a trend reversal. The move down to bar 7 had very little buying pressure. There were no large bull trend bars and no strong climactic reversals. The move up from bar 7 was also not particularly strong. This was not how strong reversals typically look, and because of that, it did not attract enough strong bulls to reverse the market. Instead, the market formed a wedge bear flag (bar 6 and then the two small pushes up from bar 7 were the three pushes) and a lower high (although the rally was above bar 6 and therefore a sign of some strength, it was still below bar 4), and the bear trend resumed.

Figure 26.2   STAIRS: BROAD CHANNEL TREND   **435**

FIGURE 26.2   Stairs Accelerating into a Strong Trend

A stairs pattern can accelerate into a stronger trend (see Figure 26.2). By bar 7, the EUR/USD forex chart had three higher highs and lows in a channel and therefore formed a stair type of bull trend.

Bar 8 was a bull trend bar that broke out of the top of the channel, and it was followed by a bear reversal bar that never triggered a short. The breakout should extend to about a measured move up to a parallel line that is about the same distance from the middle line as the middle line is from the bottom line (an Andrew's Pitchfork move), which it did. The acceleration upward is typical when a wedge top fails. There were three pushes up that ended at bar 6, but you could also view the small swing high just before bar 8 as the third push up if you restarted your count with the strong bull spike up to bar 4. The failed wedge was followed by about a measured move up equal to about the height of the wedge (the bar 6 high to the bar 3 or maybe bar 1 low).

FIGURE 26.3 Shrinking Stairs

When each breakout is smaller than the previous one, the trend's momentum is waning and a deeper pullback or a reversal might soon follow. Figure 26.3 shows a bull trend stairs pattern with three or more trending higher highs and lows contained in a roughly drawn channel. Bars 4, 6, and 8 formed shrinking stairs, representing loss of bullish momentum and presaging the reversal. The channel functioned like a large bear flag and the bear breakout occurred at bar 9.

After the bar 9 breakout, there was a lower high breakout pullback to bar 10 that resulted in a stairs bear trend. Bar 10 was a rough double top bear flag with the high of the first pullback in the move down to bar 9.

Bar 11 overshot the bear channel to the downside and led to a small two-legged reversal up and the expected penetration of the top of the channel.

Once the market begins to form stairs down, you can usually fade the close of every strong trend bar breakout for a scalp. Buy every bear trend bar that closes below a prior bear stair for a scalp. Likewise, in bull stairs, you can scalp a short on the close of any trend bar that exceeds the high of the prior stair. In general, though, it is safer to enter on a stop as the market reverses (for example, if the market reverses up from the bottom of the channel, enter on a stop above the prior bar).

About the Author

Al Brooks is a technical analysis contributor to *Futures* magazine and an independent day trader. Called the trader's trader, he has a devoted following, and provides live market commentary and daily chart analysis updates on his website at www.brookspriceaction.com. After changing careers from ophthalmology to trading 25 years ago, he discovered consistent trading success once he developed his unique approach to reading price charts bar by bar. He graduated from the University of Chicago Pritzker School of Medicine and received his BS in mathematics from Trinity College.

About the Website

This book includes a companion website, which can be found at:

www.wiley.com/go/tradingtrends

All of the charts provided in the book are included on the website for your convenience. The password to enter this site is: Brooks1.

Index